Marx, Lenin, and the Revolutionary Experience

To C. J.
with warm
revolutionary regards,

3/31/2012

PERMISSION ACKNOWLEDGMENTS

Every effort has been made to contact copyright holders for their permission to reprint selections in this book. The publishers would be grateful to hear from any copyright holder who is not here acknowledged and will undertake to rectify any errors or omissions in future editions or printings of this book.

"Lenin," from *The Collected Poems of Langston Hughes* by Langston Hughes, copyright (c) 1994 by The Estate of Langston Hughes. Used by permission of Alfred A. Knopf, a division of Random House, Inc.

"Tomorrow's Seed," from *The Collected Poems of Langston Hughes* by Langston Hughes, copyright (c) 1994 by The Estate of Langston Hughes. Used by permission of Alfred A. Knopf, a division of Random House, Inc.

"Rough times," by Marge Piercy. Copyright (c) 1973, 1976 by Marge Piercy and Middlemarsh, Inc.

From *Living Out in the Open*, Alfred A. Knopf, Inc., New York, NY. First published in *Rough Times*, Vol. 3, #4, Feb./Mar., 1973. Used by permission of the Wallace Literary Agency, Inc.

"The consumer," by Marge Piercy. Copyright (c) 1976, 1981 by Marge Piercy and Middlemarsh, Inc.

From *Living Out in the Open*, Alfred A. Knopf, New York, NY. First published in *Monthly Review*, Vol. 33, #5, October 1981. Used by permission of the Wallace Literary Agency, Inc.

"Moscow," by Claude McKay: Courtesy of the Literary Representative for the Works of Claude McKay, Schomburg Center for Research in Black Culture, The New York Public Library, Astor, Lenox and Tilden Foundations.

Excerpts from "The Cradle Will Rock" reprinted courtesy of Stephen E. Davis and The Estate of Marc Blitzstein.

"Lines to Lenin," by Pablo Neruda, is reprinted from *Lenin in Profile, World Writers and Artists on Lenin*, Moscow: Progress Publishers, 1975.

Marx, Lenin, and the Revolutionary Experience

Studies of Communism and Radicalism
in the Age of Globalization

Paul Le Blanc

with a foreword by Dennis Brutus

Routledge
Taylor & Francis Group
New York   London

Routledge is an imprint of the
Taylor & Francis Group, an informa business

Routledge
Taylor & Francis Group
270 Madison Avenue
New York, NY 10016

Routledge
Taylor & Francis Group
2 Park Square
Milton Park, Abingdon
Oxon OX14 4RN

Printed in the United States of America on acid-free paper
10 9 8 7 6 5 4 3 2 1

International Standard Book Number-10: 0-415-97973-0 (Softcover) 0-415-97974-9 (Hardcover)
International Standard Book Number-13: 978-0-415-97973-3 (Softcover) 978-0-415-97974-0 (Hardcover)

Library of Congress Cataloging-in-Publication Data

Le Blanc, Paul, 1947-
    Marx, Lenin, and the revolutionary experience : studies of communism and radicalism in the age of globalization / by Paul Le Blanc.
        p. cm.
    Includes bibliographical references and index.
    ISBN 0-415-97974-9 (hb) -- ISBN 0-415-97973-0 (pb)
        1. Marx, Karl, 1818-1883. 2. Lenin, Vladimir Il'ich, 1870-1924. 3. Communism. 4. Revolutions. 5. Globalization. I. Title.

HX73.L413 2006
335.4--dc22   2006003774

Visit the Taylor & Francis Web site at
http://www.taylorandfrancis.com

and the Routledge Web site at
http://www.routledge-ny.com

To Jonah Yan McAllister-Erickson (born in 1979)
and to others of his generation seeking paths to a better future
but also
to the memory of
Adrian Leon Le Blanc (1918–2003)
and to the many others who preceded us in that quest
and
To Gabriel Seth Le Blanc and Rima Agemy Le Blanc
bravely taking risks and crossing boundaries
in this scary and wondrous adventure of life
and
to their bright-eyed daughter
Sophia Noelle
who entered the world with a cry of fear
and of hopeful expectation

Contents

Foreword

It is an honor to write a foreword to these revolutionary studies by Paul Le Blanc. The book is a contribution to a rich dialogue not only of scholars but — most importantly — of activists who are seeking to assess the revolutionary social-ist tradition and explore its relevance for our time.

People all over the world find themselves engaged in struggles to protect their living conditions and working conditions, their communities and their cultures, and these are often interpreted in local terms. But this also adds up to a struggle that is being waged internationally, globally.

When we talk about local elections, local politics, when we talk about job-lessness, when we talk about homelessness, the creation of a prison industrial complex, increasing police brutality, the number of people who die now in the hands of the police in detention, we talk of a whole scale of injustices, but we have to put them together. And we not only have to put them together and ask what does it all add up to, but we have to understand that if we think it's bad in this country, it's happening all over the world, and it's happening particularly in countries of what is generally called the Third World.

That is why, at the massive global justice demonstration that took place in Seattle at the close of the 20th century, there were people from Nicaragua, from Ecuador, from Kenya, from Ghana, from across the world, people who came all the way up from Chiapas to say we are not going to tolerate what is being done to us by the World Trade Organization, the World Bank, the Inter-national Monetary Fund. They said that it is time that, if they are globalizing oppression, then we must globalize resistance, and this is what is happening in our time. Their slogans were: "We Say No to the WTO" and "No New Round, Turn Around."

It is true that over the past 200 years we have seen exploitation and oppres-sion all over the world. We've seen the processes of colonization, of re-colo-nization, neo-colonialism, we've seen genocidal wars in different parts of the world; we've seen all of that. But when people say that this new globalizing is nothing new, I think there's a serious danger of underestimating the nature of this new globalizing process. It is different. It's different in scale, and it's different in design, and perhaps most importantly, it is different in declar-ing what it is about. The WTO, under its first director, Renato Ruggiero, said that it was writing a constitution for the world. This is a whole new kind of approach to the conquest and control of the entire world.

Of course, the World Bank and IMF were formed in 1945, so they've been around a long time. Bretton Woods was where they were created, up in New

Hampshire, but for many years they were unable to implement their agenda of global control because there was a power struggle. There was the Cold War. There were two superpowers confronting each other, East and West, rival ideologies, rival military forces, and that is no longer true. There is only one superpower. There is only one power now that writes the global agenda, and there is no power to impede it in this process. That is why we must understand that, sure, imperialism has been around a long time, colonialism has been around a long time, but we make a mistake if we say this is just the same old system all over again.

The WTO and its sister institutions are committed to affirming this dangerous agenda and extending it. It is an agenda that is going to destroy the forests of the world. It is an agenda that is going to legitimize gas emissions that kill people and cause cancer. It is an agenda that puts corporate profits before life. And now, in the wake of the terrible calamity of September 11, 2001, the U.S. government under George W. Bush — in the name of "fighting terrorism" — is seeking a dominant role in the entire process, threatening a dramatic and devastating escalation of violence. And using that tragedy as a pretext for imposing a repressive regime that was already "in the works" prior to September 11.

All of it adds up to a systematic determination to concentrate power and wealth in the hands of a minority and to reduce the rest of us to beggars and even superfluous people because they no longer need us; their robotics, their automation, their use of prison labor do the job cheaply, outside industry, outside the factory. That's why you have privatization, that's why you have outsourcing, that's why you have downsizing, that's why you have rightsizing; the whole process has to be seen as a series of elements that must be put together, and when you put them together you then understand the global agenda. And when you understand the global agenda, that is the time you can begin to challenge the global agenda.

When the people of South Africa and the people of Africa make their statement of rejection to this globalizing process of oppression (as they did at the time of the World Summit on Sustainable Development in Sandton, Johannesburg), they are not alone. They have with them people from other parts of the world — the jobless, the homeless, the neglected, the oppressed, the racially dominated — all of us can unite with them to say, "We challenge you, we reject you, and we now go on building the solidarity that creates a global movement. Increasing numbers of people throughout Africa, Asia, and Latin America reject this globalizing process. We reject the exploitation of people and the division of the world into the rich and the poor, into billionaires and beggars." And this is a commitment that finds an increasing number of partisans from Eastern Europe through Western Europe through North America and beyond. Our answer to global oppression must be global resistance.

Things are lively these days, and I continue in my cautious optimism. There has been the worldwide opposition — swelling even in the American heartland — to the war in Iraq. Much of this opposition grew organically out of a global justice movement that involved increasing numbers of activists, especially young activists, making their voices heard in Seattle, Quebec City, Durban, Prague, Genoa, Johannesburg, Porto Alegre, Mumbai, and many other places.

We may need some kind of global peoples' resistance organization to counter the World Trade Organization and World Economic Forum. A better world is possible, but it can be brought into existence only through an intensification of our efforts and a systematic evolution from protest to resistance, and from resistance to radical social changes that will give masses of people the possibility of a decent life and control over their own situations. In order to struggle in the present for a better future, we need to comprehend the efforts and the lessons of the past. Here is where Paul Le Blanc's book comes in.

This book is especially useful because it connects ideas from the rich socialist past ("echoes" Le Blanc calls them) with contemporary ideas on the struggle for a just social order. And it does that in a highly readable, accessible form. This usefulness is especially evident in the efforts to make sense of contemporary activism by putting it in a larger framework. Thus, we see thoughts of the giants of the past — whether a Karl Marx or a Rosa Luxemburg or an Antonio Gramsci — connected with present writers like Naomi Klein, activists like Kevin Danaher, and actions of Seattle, Prague, Washington, and Genoa, pointing to possible futures perhaps foreshadowed by the World Social Forum and its meetings.

Of the many useful elements in the book, I single out particularly the notion of convergence (a term young activists have made their own) and the challenging "From Lenin to Stalin" — and the sub-chapter that explores "The Two Lenins." Many young people are skeptical, if not deeply distrustful of old-time socialists, let alone "red-diaper" babies, but the book makes a persuasive argument for going back to read the left classics of the past. Particularly pleasing to me, given the current upsurge in activism, was the section entitled "The Global Justice Movement" in the final chapter.

There will, of course, be disagreements, but the author does not hesitate to state his views clearly (with all kinds of historical tidbits that are thrown in, just in passing), and he is clearly open to engaging in challenging dialogue. This book does not claim to provide all the answers, but I would hope that thoughtful activists coming from various ideological orientations, by critically engaging with it, will be helped to find answers of their own on how we are to create a better world. Le Blanc's earlier valuable book, *From Marx to Gramsci*, I thought, "should make a useful contribution in our struggle for human freedom." I am hopeful that the same will be true of this volume, which is up to the author's usual high standards, and should be of interest and value to many.

Dennis Brutus

Acknowledgments

Institutions that contributed to my work include: the Center for Changes (Detroit), Espaces Marx (Paris), the International Institute for Research and Education (Amsterdam), La Roche College (Pittsburgh), the now-defunct Lovell-Giunta Fund, and the Rosa Luxemburg Foundation (Johannesburg and Berlin).

I would like to thank the following for reading one or another version or portion of the manuscript for this book and offering encouragement, criticism, and suggestions: Gloria Albrecht, Kevin Anderson, Anthony Arnove, Joshua Bellin, Regina Birchem, Sister Michele Bisbey, Ed Bortz, Edward Brett, Dennis Brutus, Paul Buhle, Geoffroy de Laforcade, Brad Duncan, Nancy Ferrari, David Finkel, Joshua Forrest, Joel Kovel, Adrian Nicole Le Blanc, Willie Mantaris, Laurie Matheson, Sister Mary Christine Morkovsky, Immanuel Ness, Ann O'Hear, Bryan Palmer, Peter Solenberger, Alan Wald, Michael Yates, Sergei Zhuk. Also invaluable was critical interaction with a late draft of the text — through a special course entitled "Historians Writing History" — from Stephanie Adair, John Clendaniel, Amanda Leight, Joseph Marks, Devin McClain-Kennedy, Katie McCurdy, Hana Qorri, Audra Snow, and Elizabeth Williams. Those at Routledge (especially my editors, Kimberly Guinta, Sylvia Wood, Daniel Webb, and Brendan O'Neill) deserve truly heartfelt thanks as well.

I should mention at least a few of the people I have known who, before they died, taught me, verbally or through example, important things about matters discussed in this book: Ashton Allen, Sanjulo Ber, Philip Berrigan, Lou Bortz, Dorothea Breitman, George Breitman, George Brodsky, Harry Brodsky, Rose Brodsky, Robert Colodny, David Dellinger, Philip S. Foner, Fred Halstead, Asher Harer, Ali Hebshi, Richard N. Hunt, Adrian Le Blanc, Gaston Le Blanc, Shirley Le Blanc, Morris Lewit, Frank Lovell, Sarah Lovell, Reverend Willie Ludlow, Harry Magdoff, Livio Maitan, Ernest Mandel, Ruth Querio, James Quinn, Monsignor Charles Owen Rice, Steve Sapolsky, Paul Siegle, Morris Slavin, and Paul Sweezy. There are many people, incredibly important to me, who (so far as I know) have neither died nor read earlier drafts of this book, and who — except for several of those to whom this book is dedicated — shall remain nameless, at least for now.

Whatever ties such people have had with me or with this book, I am confident that none of them would agree entirely with what I have written, the flaws of which are entirely my own responsibility.

Introduction

More than one person has asked me what this book is about, and often I have felt at a loss to explain it. In this paragraph I will offer a short answer, and in the remainder of the Introduction I will offer elements of a longer answer. In light of today's "globalized" realities, this book explores the heritage of Communism — finding what is "good" (but also "the evil within the good") in the experiences associated with it. Touching on such diverse matters as the Russian Revolution, the Spanish Civil War, struggles against Stalinist tyranny, and the legacy of American Communism, it draws from multiple streams — anarchist, conservative, Christian, liberal, and socialist — with special attention being given to 1930s and 1960s insurgencies in the United States. A critical and spiritual sensibility is employed to study tragedies of the past in order to yield hope for the future.

When two passenger planes were flown into the World Trade Center and another was flown into the Pentagon, and yet another was brought down in a western Pennsylvania field not far from where I live — with the horrifying death of innocents, which has now (with U.S. military action in Afghanistan and Iraq) brought about many more deaths, and which will quite likely be generating the future destruction of even more innocent people — my own world tilted more sharply than ever toward a belief in the necessity for radical change. That is one of the reasons for these revolutionary studies, with their echoes of tragedy and hope.

Here is a book that is full of odd combinations. Many people are jostling together in its pages: secular political theorists as well as Christian theologians; maverick conservatives and radical mavericks; such "fallen" leftists gone rightward as Max Eastman, Bertram D. Wolfe, and David Horowitz — all blended into a dialogue with the likes of Karl Marx, Rosa Luxemburg, and Vladimir Ilyich Lenin. And a diverse lot of others chime in — literary critics and civil rights activists, poets and economists, novelists and trade unionists, heads of state and uncompromising rebels, socialists of many varieties, and many types of Communist (authoritarian, libertarian, dissident, ex- and anti-). Leon Trotsky has his say, but so does someone who may have plotted his death, Vittorio Vidali. Not to mention a bunch of truly marvelous and divergently opinionated anarchists.

How can I explain what I have done? Once upon a time, when my parents were young, they — like many millions of workers and students and peasants and others around the world — were inspired by the dream of a better world, and they related to powerful traditions and social movements that were infused by that dream and informed by the ideas of Karl Marx. These two fine people, who were both active in the labor movement, met each other, and not long afterward I was born — just as the conditions that had brought the dream into being seemed to be passing out of existence forever.

Both the golden age of classical Marxism and the heroic years of revolutionary Communism, with massive workers' movements characterized by significant levels of class-consciousness, are "gone with the snows of yesteryear," leaving behind a warm nostalgic glow and a bitterly authoritarian aftertaste. A radical resurgence that swept many of us up beginning in the 1960s has also faded into the past. We live in the wake of Communism's collapse, in the age of globalization, in the shadow of September 11th, at the violent dawn of a new world order inaugurated under the counterposed leadership of Osama bin Laden and George W. Bush.

The revolutionary studies in this volume challenge the conventional wisdom that seems to permeate the very air we breathe. It goes something like this: Communism was an evil ideology and system comparable to Nazism. Its collapse obviously demonstrates that it could not endure, that Communism was and remains a road to nowhere. This is also true for its less malevolent sibling, socialism. The market economy and a more or less democratic republic, American-style, is the best we can hope for. This is the Verdict of History.

To insist that such conventional wisdom distorts the actual history that has unfolded on our planet over the past two centuries, and that it also closes off a possible and desirable future, is to be seen simply as denying reality. Worse — to deny that Communism was the moral equivalent of Nazism, to claim that there was even something good in it, is seen by some as similar to the contortions of those Holocaust deniers who insist that Hitler was a heroic German patriot, that the genocide at Auschwitz and other death camps is merely the fabrication of an anti-German, pro-Jewish conspiracy. For right-wing pundits, it also adds up to nothing less than treason.[1]

Echoes of Orwell

Among the formative intellectual influences on many of us who grew up in the 1950s and early '60s were the writings of George Orwell. I read and re-read the horrifying polemical novel *1984*, the marvelous fable *Animal Farm*, and many of Orwell's lucid essays. "Every line of serious work that I have written since 1936 has been written, directly or indirectly, *against* totalitarianism and *for* democratic socialism," he explained in 1947 (the year of my birth). In the early 1960s I wondered fearfully if what this tough-minded partisan of freedom predicted for 1984 would come to pass: global tyranny symbolized by "a boot stamping on a human face — forever." For some, this was simply a warning against Communism — but it went far beyond that. As World War II was moving toward its conclusion, Orwell had commented that "totalitarianism, leader worship, etc., are really on the upgrade," noting: "Hitler, no doubt, will soon disappear, but only at the expense of strengthening (a) Stalin, (b) the Anglo-American millionaires, and (c) all sorts of petty führers of the type of de Gaulle." Nonetheless, he supported the Allied coalition against Nazism and Japanese imperialism — seeing British imperialism and Stalin's dictatorship as lesser evils. His comment on this latter evil is worth recalling: "I would support the U.S.S.R. against Germany because I think the U.S.S.R. cannot altogether escape its past and retains enough of the original ideas of the Revolution to make it a more hopeful phenomenon than Nazi Germany."[2]

Orwell's comments make no sense from the standpoint of the conventional wisdom (and right-wing pundits might sum up his heretical views with the word *crimethink*) — but to the extent that we can determine the historical truths to which they are related, I believe, precisely to that extent can we find pathways to a better future. And I think we are very much in need of such pathways. "The idea of an earthly paradise in which people should live together in a state of brotherhood, without laws and without brute labor, had haunted the human imagination for thousands of years," he wrote, but "the earthly paradise had been discredited at exactly the moment when it became realizable." This possibility of a better world existed because "as early as the beginning of the twentieth century, human equality had become technically possible." There was no question in Orwell's mind that "if the machine were used deliberately for that end, hunger, overwork, dirt, illiteracy, and disease could be eliminated within a few generations." The problem with this, from the standpoint of those who enjoyed positions of privilege and power, was that "an all-around increase in wealth threatened the destruction ... of a hierarchical society. ... For if leisure and security were enjoyed by all alike, the great mass of human beings who are normally stupefied by poverty would become literate and would learn to think for themselves; and when once they had done this, they would sooner or later realize that the privileged minority had no function, and they would sweep it away."[3]

Instead, both in capitalist and "post-capitalist" nations, in Orwell's view, global development seemed "to be in the direction of centralized economies which can be made to 'work' in an economic sense but which are not democratically organized and which tend to establish a caste system." Accompanying this, he predicted, would be an "emotional nationalism and a tendency to disbelieve in the existence of objective truth because all the facts have to fit in with the words and prophecies of some infallible führer." At the close of World War II, he believed, there would be "a peace of exhaustion, with only minor and unofficial wars raging all over the place, and perhaps this so-called peace may last for decades. But after that, by the way the world is actually shaping, it may well be that war will *become permanent*."[4]

The so-called "peace" of the Cold War did, in fact, last from 1947 until 1991 — yet, ten years after the capitalist alliance led by the United States triumphed over the Communist Bloc, there commenced what some tell us is a permanent war on "terrorism." As Orwell put it in *1984*: "War is a way of shattering to pieces ... materials which might otherwise be used to make the masses too comfortable, and hence, in the long run, too intelligent. ... At the same time the consciousness of being at war, and therefore in danger, makes the handing-over of all power to a small caste seem the natural, unavoidable condition of survival."[5]

Of course, political realities in modern-day America seem qualitatively different from the super-totalitarian grotesque of *1984*'s "Big Brother," and yet the diversity of ideology and policy perspectives within the ruling circles of the U.S. — whether liberal or conservative, Democrat or Republican — is narrower and flatter than many are inclined to recognize. More than one perceptive commentator has noted that the ideology of 19th-century democratic-liberalism that became predominant in the early American republic tended, on the one hand, to overlap with and, at the same time, ward off the influence of more radical socialist ideologies that played such an important role among the lower classes in aristocracy-bound Europe. The furthest left that a majority-based political ideology has stretched in this country is the liberal welfare-state capitalism of Franklin D. Roosevelt's New Deal. At the same time, a study of speeches by Ronald Reagan or George W. Bush reveals how much modern-day U.S. conservatism is also permeated by classical liberal ideology.

Tracing liberalism's roots in the philosophical perspectives of Adam Smith, David Hume, John Locke, and others, distinguished scholar Neil Smith has pointed out that "liberalism is not the antithesis of contemporary conservatism but its political backbone." He observes that "Republicans and Democrats throughout the twentieth century have shared the same imperial agenda while differing at times on how it might be achieved." Such a dynamic is certainly not unique to the United States. "The wealthy nations tend to develop a grand strategy, or a fundamental approach to the world — a conflict-ridden process fueled by competition among elites," Walden Bello has recently pointed out. "Contending elites mobilize mass constituencies to provide them with a decisive edge in imposing their policies."[6]

Thus, the hotly contested 2004 U.S. presidential elections pitted a wealthy elite-liberal against a wealthy elite-conservative, both of whom favored — despite secondary differences — an escalating U.S. intervention in Iraq as an essential element in securing U.S. leadership of the "globalization" process that is transforming our planet. Within two years, however, brutal realities caused a growing number of Americans to question the wisdom of an intervention in Iraq that seemed to have done much to undermine their security and well-being and that of many others throughout the world. It seemed obvious to many that lies had been told to initiate that war, and it was clear that the Bush administration had led the way with an amazing display of what the late Senator J. William Fulbright once described as "the arrogance of power."[7] But to place exclusive blame on the Bush administration would involve throwing important facts down "the memory hole" that Orwell describes in *1984* — where censors obliterated inconvenient facts and documents the better to rewrite history.

Empire

Even before the September 11th tragedy, a growing chorus of both conservative and liberal analysts and policy advisors were singing melodies of empire. In explaining this orientation, a number of analysts have pointed — not without reason — to foreign-policy perspectives fashioned by Theodore Roosevelt and Woodrow Wilson in the early 20th century. At the beginning of 2001, William Pfaff was reporting in the influential journal *Foreign Affairs* on an "implicit alliance [that] has emerged in Washington since the Cold War's end: internationalist liberals, anxious to extend American influence and to federate the world's democracies, and unilateralist neoconservatives who believe in aggressive American leadership for the world's own good." In the same journal in the summer of 1996, William Kristol and Robert Kagan advocated what they called "a neo-Reaganite foreign policy of military supremacy and moral confidence," in which Americans (or, more precisely, American leaders) would exercise "their responsibility to lead the world," because "peace and American security depend on American power and the will to use it." In the wake of September 11, Sebastian Mallaby argued — also in the pages of *Foreign Affairs* — that "the logic of neoimperialism is too compelling for the Bush administration to resist," and that "a new imperial moment has arrived, and by virtue of its power America is bound to play the leading role." The title of Mallaby's article was far less provocative than it might have been in earlier times: "The Reluctant Imperialist: Terrorism, Failed States, and the Case for American Empire."[8]

One of the most penetrating analyses was offered, less than three months before the U.S. invasion of Iraq, by the director of Harvard University's Carr Center for the Kennedy School of Government, Michael Ignatieff, in the *New York Times Magazine*. The title the magazine editors splashed across the front page was: "The American Empire: Get Used to It." Ignatieff himself gave his ambivalent article a more ambivalent title, "The Burden." His reflections merit extensive examination. Commenting on the much-denounced "unilateralism" of the Bush administration, Ignatieff noted that "multilateral solutions to the world's problems are all very well, but they have no teeth unless America bares its fangs." He mused:

> Being an imperial power, however, is more than being the most powerful nation or just the most hated one. It means enforcing such order as there is on the world and doing so in the American interest. It means laying down the rules America wants (on everything from markets to weapons of mass destruction) while exempting itself from other rules

(the Kyoto Protocol on climate change and the International Criminal Court) that go against its interest. It also means carrying out imperial functions in places America has inherited from the failed empires of the 20th century — Ottoman, British and Soviet. In the 21st century, America rules alone, struggling to manage the insurgent zones — Palestine and the northwest frontier of Pakistan, to name but two — that have proved to be the nemeses of empires past.[9]

According to Ignatieff, as the Bush administration was preparing to knock over the regime of Saddam Hussein, "the impending operation in Iraq is ... the defining moment in America's long debate with itself about whether its overseas role as an empire threatens or strengthens its existence as a republic," with a growing proportion of the U.S. population wondering whether Bush's "proclamation of a war without end against terrorists and tyrants may only increase its vulnerability while endangering its liberties and its economic health at home...." Ignatieff added that "regime change is an imperial task par excellence, since it assumes that the empire's interest has a right to trump the sovereignty of a state," although many Iraqi exiles "fear that a mere change of regime, a coup in which one Baathist thug replaces another, would suit America's interests just as well. Provided the thug complied with the interests of the Pentagon and American oil companies." Ignatieff didn't shy away from an elaboration on this theme:

> Whenever it has exerted power overseas, America has never been sure whether it values stability — which means not only political stability but also the steady, profitable flow of goods and raw materials — more than it values its own rhetoric about democracy. Where the two values have collided, American power has come down heavily on the side of stability, for example, toppling democratically elected leaders from Mossadegh in Iran to Allende in Chile. Iraq is yet another test of this choice. Next door in Iran, from the 1950s to the 1970s, America backed stability over democracy, propping up the autocratic rule of the shah, only to reap the whirlwind of an Islamic fundamentalist revolution in 1979 that delivered neither stability nor real democracy. Does the same fate await an American operation in Iraq?[10]

Ignatieff seems to believe, on the one hand, that there is a compelling logic to the drive toward global empire ("into the ... vacuum of chaos and massacre a new imperialism has reluctantly stepped"), but — on the other hand — that the goal may be beyond "our" reach: "The question ... is not whether America is too powerful but whether it is powerful enough. Does it have what it takes to be grandmaster of what Colin Powell has called the chessboard of the world's most inflammable region?" Trying to square the circle, he writes: "Bringing order is the paradigmatic imperial task, but it is essential, for reasons of both economy and principle, to do so without denying local peoples their rights to some degree of self-determination." And to the anti-imperialists he says: "Those who want America to remain a republic rather than become an empire imagine rightly, but they have not factored in what tyranny and chaos can do to vital American interests."[11]

This logic of empire has been manifest among "mainstream" liberals and conservatives alike in both of the major political parties of the United States. There are differences in matters of detail and nuance, particularly regarding whether U.S. global policies should be advanced with a unilateral or multilateral tilt. But either variant seems inconsistent with democratic and humanist values — not to mention the injunction: "Do unto others as you would have them do unto you."

War Is Peace

"The concept of Empire is presented as a global concert under the direction of a single conductor, a unitary power that maintains the social peace and produces its ethical truths," commented Michael Hardt and Antonio Negri in their surprise best-seller *Empire*, read with rapt attention by both partisans and opponents of U.S. dominance. "And in order to achieve these ends, the single power is given the necessary force to conduct, when necessary, 'just wars' at the borders against the barbarians and internally against rebellion." The two analysts note that, "Empire presents its order as permanent, eternal, and necessary," that it "is formed not on the basis of force itself but on the basis of the capacity to present force as being in the service of right and peace" — or, to phrase it somewhat differently, "although the practice of Empire is continually bathed in blood, the concept of Empire is always dedicated to peace — a perpetual and universal peace outside of history."[12]

The necessity of bathing the Empire in blood to advance "perpetual and universal peace" is acknowledged by its most sophisticated partisans. This includes Michael Ignatieff, who emphasizes: "To defeat evil, we may have to traffic in evils: indefinite detention of suspects, coercive interrogations, targeted assassinations, even pre-emptive war." Indeed, if "we" are committed to the imperial role of the United States in the world, Ignatieff writes, "we need to change the way we think, to step outside the confines of our cozy conservative and liberal boxes."[13]

Policies of "pre-emptive" conquest, intervention, exploitation often generate terrorist backlash. "Terrorists represent causes and grievances and claim to speak in the name of millions," he notes, observing that there exist liberation, anti-occupation, and separatist types of terrorism directed against "the attempt to rule others without their consent."[14]

Ignatieff writes that "much of the war against terror has to be fought in secret, and the killing, interrogating and bribing are done in the shadows." He characterizes this as "democracy's dark secret," although from a careful reading of his own analysis it is actually something else: the dark secret of an allegedly "democratic" nation-state that assumes an imperial role. In any event, as he concludes, "only dirty hands can get the job done." He waxes poetic:

> The siren song in any war on terror is "let slip the dogs of war." Let them hunt. Let them kill. Already we have dogs salivating at the prospect. A liberal society cannot be defended by herbivores. We need carnivores to save us, but we better make sure the meat-eaters hunt only on our orders.[15]

Committed to humanistic and liberal values, Ignatieff wants to avoid the worst of this. An advocate of "regulating a war on terror with ethical rules and democratic oversight," he shares the anxious thought that "a war on terror, declared against a global enemy, with no clear end in sight, raises the prospect of an out of control presidency," with the prospect — if things go badly (particularly with renewed terrorist attacks in the United States) — of "living in a national-security state on continuous alert, with sealed borders, constant identity checks and permanent detention camps for dissidents and aliens. Our constitutional rights might disappear from our courts while torture might reappear in our interrogation cells."[16]

Another World Is Possible

If there is to be any hope of finding our way to another world than one that corresponds too closely to Orwell's despairing vision, we need to critically examine the revolutionary and socialist traditions with which he himself critically identified.

This book opens with an examination of the relevance of the *Communist Manifesto* after Communism's collapse. It then considers the "moral disaster" of Communism in light of the "moral disaster" of Christianity — and the saving grace of each. Touching on the seemingly bright promise of Lenin's 1917 revolution, and brooding over his relation to Stalinism and the double-edged question of "what's wrong with Lenin" (and why we need him), it pauses to reflect on America's notorious "Red Decade." For balance, it considers the challenge of anarchism, before touching on how the recent past blends into the near future. Saturated with scholarly footnotes, it ends with a militant dream.

Setting aside a rhetorical flourish here and an overly optimistic (or pessimistic) error there, the basic Marxist critique of capitalism — economically, socially, culturally, politically — still holds up all too well, even though the socialist vision of an alternative to it has been (we are told over and over and over and over again) discredited. For many, it was discredited long before its collapse — by 1984 Michael Ignatieff was able to observe that "by a perverse irony, the actually existing abundance of Western capitalist society has become the utopia for many inhabitants of actually existing socialism," referring to the dismal dictatorships of the Communist countries.[17] Yet the passage of time can do cruel things to more than the socialist ideal, and this shining "capitalist abundance," never universally enjoyed, has dimmed and contracted significantly since 1984.

Even though there has been a general decline in living standards for a majority of people in Western capitalist societies such as the United States, the gap has widened between these and the less fortunate, less developed, countries that enjoy more abundant populations, more abundant resources, and more abundant exploitation by multinational corporations. The insight expressed by the conservative ex-Communist Whittaker Chambers in 1959 remains more relevant than ever: "One of the beneficent side-effects of the crisis of the twentieth century as a whole, is a dawning realization, not so much that the mass of mankind is degradingly poor, as that there will be no peace for the islands of relative plenty until the continents of proliferating poverty have been lifted to something like the general material level of the islanders." Chambers added, with uncharacteristic optimism, that "it is this perfectly practical challenge, abetted by a sound self-interest, which must engross the energies of mankind, and more and more, perhaps, inspire it as a perfectly realizable vision."[18]

While it was a perfectly realizable vision, it was not sufficiently profitable for the private companies and public institutions of our global market economy to ensure that the vision would in fact be realized. Indeed, the failure to rise to this challenge contributed mightily to the terrorist disaster 42 years later on September 11.

One might say that the Marxist analysis of capitalism remains powerful, while the perspective of revolutionary working-class struggle for socialism is in shambles. But as Bertolt Brecht once said, "because things are as they are, they will not stay as they are." Although we live in terrible and incredibly dangerous times, many people seem unable to abandon certain deeply held ideals and hopes for a better future. In many parts of the world, women and men (peasants and indigenous peoples, workers and intellectuals, people from oppressed racial or ethnic groups, artists and scientists, and many others) have joined together and forged alliances for the preservation of human life with dignity and freedom, against powerful market forces and the relentless "progress" imposed by ruling elites.

They often identify with the movement for global justice associated with massive international protests in Seattle, Prague, Washington, Genoa, and elsewhere. Some of them find representation in such developments as the World Social Forum that began in Porto Alegre, Brazil, designed to provide an internationalist space in which a diverse array of activists, organizations, and social movements could connect, learn from each other, grow stronger. One of the most interesting people writing about this phenomenon, Naomi Klein, ended her book *No Logo* with this observation:

When this resistance began taking place in the mid-nineties, it seemed to be a collection of protectionists getting together out of necessity to fight everything and anything global. But as connections have formed across national lines, a different agenda has taken hold, one that embraces globalization but seeks to wrest it from the grasp of the multinationals. Ethical shareholders, culture jammers, street reclaimers, McUnion organizers, human-rights hacktivists, school-logo fighters and Internet corporate watchdogs are at the early stages of demanding a citizen-centered alternative to the international rule of the brands. That demand, still sometimes in some areas of the world whispered for a fear of a jinx, is to build a resistance — both high-tech and grassroots, both focused and fragmented — that is as global, and as capable of coordinated action, as the multinational corporations it seeks to subvert.[19]

That is an appropriate goal, but a tall order. Accomplishing it can come only from much collective discussion and experience. The contents of this book are informed by hopeful convictions about our ability to do that. With some intellectual audacity, blending immense respect for those we are studying with some sense of how things have turned out, perhaps we can reach into the complexities of the past and gain new insights into the history that has brought us to the present moment. Perhaps some of these insights will be useful for those wishing to understand some of the future's possibilities.

My own contribution to this effort is shaped by multiple identities:

- I grew up in a household immersed in the American labor movement and became a "new left" activist in the 1960s, involved in Students for a Democratic Society and other groups, a conscientious objector to war working for (and becoming entangled in spirituality and radical pacifism within) the American Friends Service Committee, a Trotskyist deeply committed to and expelled from the Socialist Workers Party, a secular half-Jew becoming involved with the radical-Catholic Thomas Merton Center, an aging radical going out of his way to connect with a variety of left-wing organizations and social struggles.

- I am an internationalist whose most profound experiences have included joining with radical activists from different countries at Amsterdam's International Institute for Research and Education, going to Nicaragua just as an inspiring revolution was about to succumb to its own contradictions and to the pressures of U.S. imperialism, participating in an international conference in Paris to critically evaluate the 1917 Russian Revolution 80 years after the fact, discussing the relevance of Rosa Luxemburg at a conference of militant activists in Johannesburg, and again at an international conference on Luxemburg at China's Wuhan University, and participating in the World Social Forum in the Brazilian city of Porto Alegre and the Indian city of Mumbai with tens of thousands of activists from all continents.

• I am a scholar and writer reaching to understand and give creative expression to the rich history of struggles for a better world that have shaped me (along with so many others), and that provide insights and clues that may help us to move beyond the limitations of the past and of our own time. In this effort to comprehend the vast living current of history, I receive invaluable aid from innumerable others — those who have studied deeply and written eloquently, those who have shared knowledge of what they know from their own lives, those whose critical minds engage with me in the classroom and press for a coherent understanding of what is so.

What I have to say will not fit in neatly with majority opinions — including majority opinion within the Left. A central theme of what I have written is that traditional ways of understanding Marxist perspectives have limited relevance to the realities of our time — with the collapse of Communism, the disaster of September 11, and the acceleration of globalization — but that the actual perspectives of Marx and others close to him continue to be invaluable as we seek to understand where we are and where we might go.

What I have to say will also grate against the rising fashion of left-bashing in some quarters. John Earl Haynes and Harvey Klehr, in their recent book *In Denial*, insist that anti-Red repression in the United States was "a rational and understandable response to a real danger to American democracy" in the face of the U.S. Communist Party's connection to the USSR and espionage.[20] It is difficult to share their blandly uncritical assumptions about the actualities of *democracy* in our corporation-dominated country, as well as their flat, one-note conception of American Communism, and of Communism in general (whose horrific totalitarian degeneration must be explained, not assumed).

Their book follows in the wake of the sensational *Black Book on Communism*, composed by a cluster of ex-Maoist and ex-Trotskyist scholars in France, which argues that Communism (with an alleged death toll of 100 million to its credit) was at least as disastrous for humanity as fascism and Nazism.[21] This is hardly a new argument (it was predominant in the Cold War culture of the United States), and we have noted that it is the accepted wisdom in many quarters today. Without question, there *are* genuine crimes against humanity that these authors document. But their book is flawed in more ways than one. Most serious is their one-sided account of the furies of terror and violence in the 20th century — a similarly mind-numbing chronicle of violence and suffering and death tolls can certainly be constructed from an examination of capitalism, colonialism, and imperialism in the 19th and 20th centuries.

One could also construct a book of "crimes, terror, repression" of anti-Communism to rival this one, and then — perhaps more fruitfully — explore the interactive dynamic of inhumanity that seems so horrifying a component of the march of civilization. (Certainly the book's attribution of one million Vietnamese deaths to "Communism" while ignoring the one million deaths attributable to the U.S. war in Vietnam suggests a methodological flaw.) Some of the *Black Book's* sweeping conclusions might be deflated, too, by considering serious comparative analyses, for example, of estimated fatalities in the French Revolution (7.7 percent of the population) and America's Civil War (1.63 percent) with those of the Russian Civil War (0.7 percent).[22] Another problem is the pretense of "stunning revelations" (as some of the *Black Book's* partisans and publicists put it) of crimes committed under the banner of Communism. These were being documented and denounced from the left end of the spectrum — not only by George Orwell, but by various anarchists, socialists, dissident Communists, and disillusioned ex-Communists — before the authors of the *Black Book* were born, and we draw on some of this vast literature in the present volume.

But our history, our present, and our possible futures cannot be understood through the wholesale rejection of the Communist tradition represented by the *Black Book* and similar works. A theme of the present volume is that the political perspectives of the Russian revolutionary Lenin — whom it is so fashionable to denigrate — are poorly understood and contain elements without which a better world will not be possible, and that (along with Marx) he represents what Hal Draper has shown to be a radically democratic "socialism from below."[23] At the same time, I hold to certain views that may provoke a dismissive response among some would-be Leninists: the need to approach the great revolutionary critically, the need to recognize that his organizational perspectives cannot be simplistically superimposed on our complex and fluid reality, which is so different from his, and the need to respect and learn from diverse currents of thought and experience.

I have discovered something startling while trying to make sense of things: an erosion of boundaries, for me, between secular and religious sensibilities. More than half a century ago, Daniel Bell wrote in his thoughtful and despairing 1952 study *Marxian Socialism in the United States* that the revolutionary movement "was trapped by the unhappy problem of living '*in* but not *of* the world,' so it could only act, and then inadequately, as the moral, but not political, man in immoral society." This is based on the assumption that (in the words of Max Weber) "he who seeks the salvation of souls, his own as well as others, should not seek it along the avenue of politics."[24] That assumption does not seem valid to me. If there is a conception of God that makes sense (see Chapters 2 and 7), and if the Golden Rule that reflects this understanding of God — "do unto others as you would have them do unto you" — has spiritual, practical, personal, and social relevance, then it is reasonable (contrary to Bell and Weber) to embrace the injunction of the Lord's Prayer: God's kingdom should come and God's will should be done *on earth*. Only by acting on this can there be hope of saving all that we value most (including our souls).

More than one friend has identified a problematical aspect of this study. While animated throughout by the perspective of the author, it seeks to draw together a diversity of voices. I shy away from simply offering my own summaries and assertions. I want those to whom I refer to speak for themselves, risking an overabundance of quotation in order to allow patterns of thought and eddies of conclusion to emerge from a broader and sometimes dissonant chorus. I *have* sought to prune the wild proliferation of others' voices, and I apologize to those who find that I have done so too sparingly. Part of the problem is that I don't see this as "my" book — it is a collaborative effort between myself and many others wrestling with difficult questions. My hope is that, at least for some readers, this basic problem of the text will also constitute a strength, enabling them to connect more directly with a multifaceted body of experience and reflection. Such readers are encouraged to follow additional debate and dialogue to be found in many of the footnotes — in some cases, perhaps shuttling back and forth between the main text and footnotes at the end of this volume.

Another problematical aspect of this study is its limited geographical focus. Grappling with the meaning of Communism and radicalism as they pertain to Russia and Eastern Europe on the one hand and the United States on the other (with a fleeting look at Spain during the 1930s and at Palestine in the time of Jesus) leaves out most of our planet's revolutionary experience. What is offered here may have relevance beyond the regions on which it concentrates, however, and I hope to deal with a broader range of this experience in the future, including in a multi-volume encyclopedia of protest movements and revolutions throughout the world that a number of colleagues and I will be producing in the near future.

The incredibly dynamic developments of our time, opening up a range of horrifying and also inspiring possibilities, are generating new waves of radical activism, and youthful activists must learn through their own experiences — hard work, promising successes, inevitably foolish and sometimes terrible blunders, hopefully inspiring victories as well. I am also convinced that their efforts will be more fruitful as they are able to connect with and learn from the experiences and efforts and thinking of generations of activists — activists in many ways much like themselves — who came before. This contribution toward an understanding of the revolutionary tradition is composed especially for them.

Hope, superior to fear, is neither passive like the latter, nor locked into nothingness. The emotion of hope goes out of itself, makes people broad instead of confining them, cannot know nearly enough of what it is that makes them inwardly aimed, of what may be allied to them outwardly. The work of this emotion requires people who throw themselves actively into what is becoming, to which they themselves belong. ...

The rigid divisions between future and past thus themselves collapse, unbecome future becomes visible in the past, avenged and inherited, mediated and fulfilled past in the future. ... True action in the present itself occurs solely in the totality of this process which is unclosed backwards and forwards ...

— **Ernst Bloch,** *The Principle of Hope*

I pondered all these things and how men fight and lose the battle, and the thing they fought for comes about in spite of their defeat, and when it comes about it turns out not to be what they meant, and other men have to fight for what they meant under another name.

— **William Morris,** *A Dream of John Ball*

It will be seen that this establishment [the utopian socialist Neshoba community] is founded on the principle of community of property and labor; presenting every advantage to those desirous not of accumulating money but of enjoying life and rendering services to their fellow creatures.... Labor is wealth; its reward should be enjoyment.... Deeds are better than words. After all that has been said, let something be at least attempted. An experiment that has such an end in view is surely worth the trial.... Let us dare to express our feelings and to act in accordance with them....

— **Frances Wright,** "Statement on Nashoba"

1
Marx's Manifesto after Communism's Collapse

In discussions of Marxism occasioned by the 1998 anniversary of *The Communist Manifesto* that Karl Marx and Frederick Engels wrote 150 years before, many thoughtful adherents to the Marxist tradition critically noted serious limitations in the ambitious pamphlet of these youthful authors. There were criticisms on the failure of Marx and Engels to give sufficient attention to the centrality — in the minds of most people — of such nonclass identities as race, ethnicity, nationality, gender (especially from the standpoint of women's oppression), sexual orientation, and so on. There were also criticisms of the absence in the *Manifesto* of any serious discussion of the lethal impact of the Industrial Revolution on the increasingly vulnerable ecosystem of our planet.

Some of the most interesting comments were offered by shrewd non-Marxists in such publications as the *New York Times*, the *Los Angeles Times*, the *New Yorker*, the London *Times Literary Supplement*, and the *London Review of Books*.[1] The point they make is that, of course, the vision of a working-class revolution that would usher in a shining communist future has proved to be a colossal illusion, but that to understand the workings of the capitalist economy, Marx's analysis continues to be remarkably relevant.

This widely articulated judgment among knowledgeable commentators in the U.S. and British intellectual establishment generated extreme consternation among such right-wing ideologues as the ex-leftist David Horowitz, who complained bitterly that "leading intellectuals, including many who would not allow themselves to be called marxists ... have rushed to celebrate the only text that most of the millions who served in Marxist vanguards ever bothered to read" — shamelessly and shamefully "proclaiming the indispensability of Marx's malevolent tract for understanding the failings of American capitalism." Horowitz himself would have none of this, insisting: "The Manifesto is, as the historical record attests, an incitement to totalitarian ambitions whose results were even bloodier than those inspired by [Hitler's] *Mein Kampf.*" He found the nice things scholars have to say about Marx disgustingly typical of "an intellectual class whose own record in this bloodiest of centuries is a sorry and sordid one of apology and support for the totalitarian enemies of America both abroad and within."[2]

A less strident and far more judicious evaluation of Marx was provided some years earlier by Isaiah Berlin, who Horowitz lists in his pantheon of antitotalitarian heroes (along with Ludwig von Mises, Friedrich von Hayek, Raymond Aron, Karl Popper, Leo Strauss, and others). Berlin's insightful comments — close in spirit to those Horowitz denounces — are worth considering. Insisting that, for the rise of 20th-century totalitarianism, "the works of Karl Marx are certainly no more responsible than the other tendencies of our time," Berlin noted that Marx's works "poured much light (and some darkness) on many vexed problems, and led to much fruitful (and sterile) revaluation and reinterpretation" of issues that have long concerned central figures of what might be called "the Western tradition." Nor can there be any question, despite Horowitz's sectarian indignation, that much of the *Communist Manifesto*'s analysis is remarkably relevant to our own time.[3]

It is worth brooding over both sides of this non-Horowitz consensus — the alleged relevance of the Marxist diagnosis and the alleged irrelevance of the Marxist cure.

Enduring Relevance

There are many of us who have experienced what A. Philip Randolph — the leading African-American labor leader of the 20th century — once described as his own "exciting discovery" of Marx, which, as he put it, "was like finally running into an idea which gives you your outlook on life."[4] This includes:

- The insight that economic development is the foundation of human development
- The insight that there are illuminating interconnections between this economic reality and our social, political, and ideological realities
- The insight that there have been a succession of different economic systems that help us define the evolution of humanity, through the rise and decline of ancient slave and tributary civilizations, and the evolution of feudalism and its eventually explosive transition into capitalism
- The insight that the development of human societies since the rise of civilization has been shaped by both technological innovation and by the constant, fluctuating tensions and conflicts between socioeconomic classes (and most fundamentally between the powerful minority of "haves" who exploit the laboring majority of "have-nots")

All of these insights have been absorbed in various ways into the discipline of history and those of the social sciences. They are essential tools that help us understand much of our past, our present, and our future possibilities, and they are utilized by many who nonetheless reject other aspects of Marxism that were important to socialist-minded people like Randolph.

But it is not merely this "common wisdom" aspect of Marx's thought that has excited the jaundiced reviewers in the *New Yorker* and the *London Review of Books.* Rather, it is the more specific analysis of capitalism's incredible dynamism. Of course, for many years, the most common criticism of Marxism was that it was based on an obsolete analysis of capitalism — and it is certainly the case that there have been profound, incredible changes as the global economy has developed from the Victorian era of Marx and Engels to our own era of "postmodernity." Ours is an economic system that is in constant decomposition and recomposition. But this is, of course, precisely what was predicted in the *Communist Manifesto*:

> The bourgeoisie [that is, the capitalists, the upper-class of big businessmen] cannot exist without constantly revolutionizing the instruments of production, and thereby the relations of production, and with them the whole relations of society.... Constant revolutionizing of production, uninterrupted disturbance of all social conditions, everlasting uncertainty and agitation distinguish the bourgeois epoch from all earlier ones. All fixed, fast-frozen relations, with their train of ancient and venerable prejudices and opinions, are swept away, all new-formed ones become antiquated before they can ossify. All that is solid melts into air, all that is holy is profaned, and [people are] at last compelled to face, with sober senses, [their] real conditions of life and [their] relations with [their] kind.[5]

In a richly articulated critique of the *Manifesto*, intellectual historian Jerry Z. Muller tells us that "Marx and Engels interpreted what was in fact the agony of a declining preindustrial order as the birthpangs of a postcapitalist future."[6] But this insight is only half right, because the capitalism they described has continued to transform the cultures and societies of our planet. This eloquent description of destructive creativity resonates with my own experience as I consider how the world around me has changed, and changed again and yet again over the course of my own life. The god-like (or demonic) power of the market economy has generated what is now often tagged "global restructuring," but this too was prophetically described in the *Manifesto*:

> The need of a constantly expanding market for its products chases the bourgeoisie over the whole surface of the globe. It must nestle everywhere, settle everywhere, establish conditions everywhere.
> The bourgeoisie has, through its exploitation of the world market, given a cosmopolitan character to production and consumption in every country. To the great chagrin of Reactionists, it has drawn from under the feet of industry the national ground in which it stood. All old-established national industries have been destroyed and are daily being destroyed. They are dislodged by new industries, whose introduction becomes a life-and-death question for all civilized nations, by industries that no longer work up indigenous raw material, but raw material drawn

from the remotest zones; industries whose products are consumed not only at home, but in every quarter of the globe. In place of the old wants, satisfied by the productions of the country, we find new wants, requiring for their satisfaction the products of distant lands and climes. In place of the old local and national seclusion and self-sufficiency, we have intercourse in every direction, universal interdependence of nations.[7]

As we survey the operations of the multinational corporations that dominate the global economy — from ALCOA to AT&T, from Disney to DuPont, from General Electric to General Motors, from McDonalds to Microsoft, from Texas Instruments to Toyota — we know that the truth of this description is greater now than when Marx and Engels published it over 150 years ago.[8] For that matter, these two young Communists even provided a hint of the circumstances under which the seemingly impenetrable dictatorships of the Iron Curtain would ultimately be overwhelmed by capitalist civilization. They put it this way:

The bourgeoisie, by the rapid improvement of all instruments of production, by the immensely facilitated means of communication, draws all, even the most barbarian, nations into civilization. The cheap prices of its commodities are the heavy artillery with which it batters down all Chinese walls, with which it forces the barbarians' intensely obstinate hatred of foreigners to capitulate. It compels all nations, on pain of extinction, to adopt the bourgeois mode of production; it compels them to introduce what it calls civilization into their midst, i.e., to become bourgeois themselves. In one word, it creates a world after its own image.[9]

More and more over the final decade of the 20th century and into the 21st, the global trend has been what Marx and Engels described as "free competition, accompanied by a social and political constitution adapted to it and by the economic and political sway of the bourgeois class."[10]

And yet, there are potentially disastrous instabilities that are inherent in this dynamic global economy. We have seen most recently in the rapidly industrializing sectors of Asia what Marx and Engels called "an epidemic" in which "society suddenly finds itself put back into a state of momentary barbarism; it appears as if a famine, a universal war of devastation, had cut off the supply of every means of subsistence; industry and commerce seem to be destroyed" as many of yesterday's successful local entrepreneurs go bankrupt and in some cases end up on the street trying to sell their previously acquired luxury items, while their former employees face circumstances that are even more bleak, to put things much too mildly.[11] Such realities have, in different ways, also been felt in Latin America and in Eastern Europe, and there have been fears that at some point this kind of "epidemic" could spread to market economies in Japan, Western Europe, and the United States.

Ways of dealing with such problems, the *Manifesto* tells us, include the attempt to secure "the conquest of new markets and ... the more thorough exploitation of the old ones," but they warn that this could eventually mean "paving the way for more extensive and more destructive crises and ... diminishing the means whereby crises are prevented."[12] We have also seen in recent decades efforts to increase various countries' "competitiveness" in the global economy by increasing the exploitation of the working classes — cutting incomes, cutting benefits (including the junking of various social welfare policies), while forcing the pace of work and prolonging the amount of time one must work. The danger in pushing down the living standards of the working-class majority, however, is that the consequent increase in profits may ultimately be offset by the declining buying power of the working-class consumers. Such things can set the economic dominos tumbling — falling sales, falling profits, business failures, and mass unemployment.

Another aspect of the *Manifesto*'s analysis of capitalism has largely been vindicated in our time — what is sometimes called the "proletarianization" of the labor force throughout the capitalist world. In various countries, "the lower strata of the middle class — the small trades people, shopkeepers, and retired tradesmen generally, the handicraftsmen and peasants — all these gradually sink into the proletariat," which Marx and Engels define as "the modern working class." Some commentators (including would-be Marxists) have described this working class simply as manual laborers or factory workers, but Marx and Engels themselves put forward a broader definition. In 1848 they wrote of "a class of laborers who live only so long as they find work and who find work only so long as their labor increases capital. These laborers, who must sell themselves piecemeal, are a commodity, like every other article of commerce, and are consequently exposed to all the vicissitudes of competition, to all fluctuations of the market." In an 1888 footnote, Engels repeats that the proletariat is "the class of modern wage-laborers who, having no means of production of their own, are reduced to selling their labor-power in order to live."[13]

Certainly in the U.S. today, this defines the great bulk of the labor force, blue-collar and white-collar workers, service and production workers, as well as many so-called "professional" employees. (Also included in this broadly defined working class, I would suggest, are all family members who are dependent on the breadwinner's paycheck, as well as retired workers and unemployed workers.) As Marx and Engels put it, the working class becomes "the immense majority" of the population. In all proletarianized occupations, especially with the development of technological innovations, employers have greater and greater control over the labor process (and over the individual workers), and work tends to become increasingly monotonous and repulsive. They add that "in proportion as the use of machinery and division of labor increases, in the same proportion the burden of toil also increases, whether by prolongation of the working hours, by increase of the work exacted in a given time, or by increased speed of the machinery, etc." Certainly such trends can be documented in the U.S. economy.[14]

Another aspect of the Marxist analysis is that the capitalist minority secures not only increasing power over the working-class majority, but also secures an increasing proportion of the wealth produced. This has certainly been the trend in the U.S. As the *Philadelphia Inquirer*'s Pulitzer Prize-winning journalists Donald Bartlett and James Steele summed it up in 1992:

> The already richer are richer than ever; there has been an explosion in overnight new rich; life for the working class is deteriorating, and those on the bottom are trapped. While in 1959 the country's richest 4 percent had the same income ($31 billion) as the bottom 35 percent, and in 1970 the richest 4 percent had the same income as the bottom 38 percent, by 1989 the income of the wealthy 4 percent (now $452 billion) was equivalent to that of the bottom 51 percent.

Several years into the new century, even economic "good news" in *USA Today* contained the bitter note that while the rich get richer still, "prosperity hasn't been spread evenly. The poverty rate has risen. Wage gains are among the slowest on record. Many corporate pension plans are in a death spiral. Health care costs are rising. The personal savings rate has fallen." Real wages for U.S. production workers (80 percent of the private sector workforce) rose 2.9 percent between 2004 and 2005 but was outpaced by a rise in consumer inflation of 4.3 percent.[15]

On a global level, the same trend is quite dramatically evident. In 1970, the richest 20 percent of the world's people received 30 times more income than the poorest 20 percent. By 1989, the richest 20 percent received 60 times more income than the poorest 20 percent of the world's people. Just as the richest 20 percent of the global population receives more than 80 percent of the global income, so the richest 20 percent of families in the U.S. control 80 percent of the wealth in our own country. The last two decades of the 20th century worldwide have generated greater inequality between "developing" and "advanced" regions just as inequality is greater in the early 21st century than it was in the 19th century.[16]

The solution to such problems seemed clear to Marx and Engels. They believed that the proletarianization process would generate an increasingly radicalized and militant working-class consciousness that would generate increasingly vital and aggressive working-class organizations. Workers would form tough, democratic, socially conscious trade unions in their workplaces. They would join together in their communities to struggle for social reforms. They would struggle for the inclusion of the entire working class in the political process, they would build their own labor party to run in the elections, and with this "self-conscious, independent movement of the immense majority, in the interests of the immense majority," they would eventually "win the battle of democracy" and take political power in their own hands. Once the proletariat replaced the bourgeoisie as the ruling class, they would begin the socialist reconstruction of the economy. The social ownership and democratic control of society's economic resources would result in a new society of freedom, creativity, and abundance in which "the free development of each is the condition for the free development of all."[17]

It is important to note not only what is in the *Manifesto*, but also what is missing.

It is entirely appropriate for a sweeping vision of humanity's struggle for a better world that Marx and Engels should deal with such central issues as gender and family life. After all, the utopian socialist Charles Fourier — whose views on such matters both men viewed favorably — had argued some years before that "the change in a historical epoch can always be determined by the progress of women towards freedom, because in the relation of woman to man, of the weak to the strong, the victory of human nature over brutality is most evident." Flora Tristan, an outstanding socialist-feminist of the early 1840s, had written penetrating critiques of the devastating impact of poverty on family life, and also of restrictive social mores that so frequently consigned women to what often amounted to a stultifying domestic oppression. The conditions of capitalist society guaranteed that "there are few workers' homes that are happy. The husband is head by law and also by reason of the money he brings in. He believes himself superior to his wife, who only earns a fraction of his wage and is his very humble servant." The fact that often "taverns are the temples of working-class men" often led to domestic conflict: "She rails at him. He swears at her and hits her." This on top of "constant child-bearing, illness and unemployment," not to mention "the yells and romping of four to five children eddying round her in one small cramped room, and one would have to be an angel not to be brutalized by it all." Tristan's conviction was similar to that of the American transcendentalist and socialist Margaret Fuller, who argued that women needed a certain independence of men, "not that I do not think the sexes mutually needed one another, but because in Woman this fact has led to an excessive devotion which has cooled love, degraded marriage, and prevented either sex from being what it should be to itself." Tristan believed that the workers' movement must, in its resistance to capitalist oppression, create an extensive counter-culture that would build "workers' palaces" to serve as centers for education and organizing in every town that would provide "education, moral intellectual and technical," for working-class women. One also can envision a call for communal meals and "housework," creating kindergartens and other social forms of child care, etc. — all of which can be found in the thinking and practical efforts of reformers and socialists of the 1840s and which were to flourish in left-wing thought and activity of the late 19th and early 20th centuries.[18]

Yet such things did not find their way into the *Manifesto*. Marx and Engels defend Communists from those who claim that they wish men not only to own all property in common but also to own all women in common (while at the same time taking a swipe at a capitalist "morality" that generates adultery and prostitution), and they point out that industrial capitalism has had a destructive impact on working-class families — and that is all. Their meager comments are abstract, as Sheila Rowbotham has noted, ignoring "the ideas and participation of women themselves," which amounts to "the exclusion of all reference to women's part in [their] own emancipation," and adds up to a vision of women "as all weakness and working men as all strength."[19]

A strength of the *Manifesto* is that this missing dimension so naturally suggests itself and can be integrated into — or, more precisely, serves to complete, deepen, enrich — the fundamental perspective laid out by the two young authors. (Particularly in recent decades, much vital work has been done along these lines.)[20] A weakness of the *Manifesto* is that this *is* a missing dimension, and this contributed to serious limitations in much of the subsequent Marxist tradition. There are additional (and perhaps related) limitations that are no less serious, despite the *Manifesto*'s enduring relevance.

Failure and Transcendence

Of course, those who adhere to the *Manifesto*'s vision have a responsibility to help make it become reality. "The communists fight for the attainment of the immediate aims … of the working class," according to Marx and Engels, "but in the movement of the present, they also represent the future of the movement," helping more and more workers to understand "the line of march, the conditions, and the ultimate results of the proletarian movement." As Rev. A. J. Muste — a remarkable American radical who blended Marxism with Christianity — put it in the 1930s, "a group which devotes itself to theory in the Marxian sense does not do it for the sake of agreeable mental exercise, as an alternative perhaps to working cross-word puzzles. It is concerned with theory because it needs to know how to act and will not act on a merely opportunistic basis. Elaboration of theory leads, therefore, to practical work in the labor scene." [21]

But here is precisely where the whole thing falls apart. One problem — a very human problem, made especially understandable given the complexities of reality — is that there have been huge differences among those influenced by Marx on what "practical work" should look like to transition from capitalism to socialism. Most socialists believed in an indestructible link between socialism and democracy (which is why most socialists, including Lenin, once called themselves "Social-Democrats"), but some were inclined to believe that capitalism could be democratically and gradually reformed out of existence (and were sometimes called "reformists") while others, though still favoring reform efforts, argued that the democratic process was or would be fatally undermined under capitalism, which they believed could only be overcome — ultimately — through a revolution. Even those inclined toward revolutionary socialism found that they had significant differences — so much so that by 1918 Lenin and his co-thinkers made use of the once-synonymous term "Communist" to distinguish themselves from all the others. Many other differences even further fragmented the ranks of those inspired by the *Communist Manifesto*.

The problem runs even deeper than such disunity. As Muste confessed a dozen years after his more hopeful comments: "Socialists and Communists of an earlier day were constantly proclaiming that the new order was just around the corner. They never, most of them, really believed it. As soon as socialism seemed imminent Social Democrats ran away from it as fast as possible; when Communists got political power, they set about building — totalitarianism!" [22] Many Communists from the 1920s and 1930s onward argued that a harsh political dictatorship was necessary to eventually usher in the vibrant new society called for by Marx and Engels. Instead, it ushered in a bureaucratic, corrupt, inefficient, and demoralized reality that was incapable of preventing its own sorry collapse.

It can be argued quite effectively that this was not the socialism or communism that Marx and Engels called for. But we are left with the difficult question: why did the working-class political movements inspired by the ideas of the *Communist Manifesto* fail so miserably? There seems to be nothing in the *Manifesto* itself that would lead us to anticipate this possibility — and this certainly points up a limitation in that document. On the other hand, if the analysis of capitalism developed by Marx and Engels continues to be more or less accurate, can we afford simply to shrug off the apparent inadequacy of their proposed alternative?

It may be that it is necessary, rather than simply abandoning the *Communist Manifesto* at the point where it poses the alternative of Communist revolution, instead to wrestle with it in order to achieve a transcendence of its limitations. Because we have been considering the assessments of Rev. Muste, let's follow him a bit further to see what he has to say. He says: "Men cannot live a democratic life in a world that is autocratically organized, nor a peaceful life in a world organized for war." Marx would have agreed, arguing that it was necessary to change the conditions that shape people, and referring to what he called "the categorical imperative to overthrow all conditions in which man is a degraded, enslaved, neglected, contemptible being."[23] Muste raised a further challenge, however, writing:

> But it is equally, and perhaps in a sense even more fundamentally, true that the character of the social order cannot be abstracted from the quality of the persons who compose it. People who are autocrats and

lovers of power in their own hearts, or whose egos are possessive, defensive and hence stricken with fear, are not going to build a democratic world. They do not want freedom; they want to dictate or be dictated to. People who know no peace in their own spirits do not really want peace in the outward order and their fitful and distracted efforts to achieve it will be constantly thwarted.[24]

This poses a question. How can people who are damaged by oppression under capitalism create a non-oppressive society? As Nicolas Berdyaev has pointed out, this contradiction is actually highlighted in Marxism — or, as he puts it, "there was a demoniacal element in Marx's teaching, which gave it its invincible dynamism. He believed that good can be produced by evil, that light can be obtained through darkness, that freedom would result from dire necessity. That is how he understood the dialectics of the social process."[25] But such an approach risks underestimating the ways in which the brutalization inherent in social oppression can fatally mark the process of liberation. Indeed, how can a mass of degraded individuals become a cohesive force?

There are other complications. Even if the laboring majority of individuals are somehow capable of organizing themselves as a cohesive force, it is hardly a simple thing for this majority to take power. The popular writer, adventurer, and socialist of early 20th-century America, Jack London, has one of his capitalist oligarchs in *The Iron Heel* (1907) tell the socialist hero: "We are in power. Nobody will deny it. By virtue of that power we shall remain in power." The socialist responds, "By the power of our ballots on election day we will take your government away from you —" at which point the oligarch interrupts: "What if you do get a majority, a sweeping majority on election day? Suppose we refuse to turn the government over to you after you have captured it at the ballot box?" He intones:

> We have no words to waste on you. When you reach out your vaunted strong hands for our palaces and purpled ease, we will show you what strength is. In roar of shell and shrapnel and in whine of machine-guns will our answer be couched. We will grind you revolutionists down under our heel, and we shall walk upon your faces. The world is ours, we are its lords, and ours it shall remain. As for the host of labor, it has been in the dirt since history began, and I read history aright. And in the dirt it shall remain so long as I and mine and those that come after us have the power.[26]

The socialist hero predicts this will result in a socialist revolution. But instead of the working-class revolution, London envisions fierce repression and intensified exploitation, throwing the majority of people into an abyss of oppression, degradation, brutalization. Since "the people of the abyss had nothing to lose but the misery and pain of living," they became "mad with drink and wrong," at moments exploding with murderous rage — "men, women, and children, in rags and tatters, dim ferocious intelligences with all the godlike blotted from their features and all the fiendlike stamped in ... wan faces from which vampire society had sucked the juice of life ... blasted by the ravages of disease and all the horrors of chronic innutrition — the refuse and the scum of life, a raging, screaming, screeching demoniacal horde."[27]

Out of the despair and desperation, London envisioned, there would arise "many terrorist organizations" whose members "were careless about their own lives and hopeless about the future" — including "a new religious sect ... called the Wrath of God." The terrorists "placed no value whatsoever on their own lives" and proved capable of killing many thousands of people. They were systematically stamped out. The revolutionary socialists following London's hero had nothing to do with such terrorist activities, but remained "hard at work reorganizing the forces of the Revolution." While working-class revolutions had triumphed in several countries and gave aid to the U.S. revolutionaries, however, the order of the capitalist oligarchs had sufficient power not only to crush London's socialist heroes and heroines after two decades of struggle, but also succeeded in overturning the existing socialist regimes and replacing them with capitalist oligarchies. "For three centuries they were able to hold back the mighty tide of human progress," until finally — somehow — working-class revolutions proved capable of ushering in a new, humane socialist commonwealth on a global scale.[28]

But the happy ending of this nightmare vision seems implausible. How can people who are so oppressed and brutalized — and whose struggles would have to be intensely brutal (in London's universe) in order to triumph — usher in a humane order of the free and the equal? Of course, London's vivid speculative fiction does not describe what actually happened — and yet, there are ways and places and moments in the history of the past hundred years where aspects of his vision do seem to have come to life. Even in our own capitalist reality, how can one expect that a glowing communist future could be possible if its elements must arise within this exploitative, corrupting, and violent reality? One is struck by the reasonableness of Michael Harrington's comment that "the *Manifesto* is a schizophrenic statement" in which one finds "an overestimation of both capitalism and Communism."[29]

In the *Manifesto* itself one finds elements of an answer to Harrington's challenge. "Now and then the workers are victorious, but only for a time," Marx and Engels tell us. "The real fruit of their battles lies, not in the immediate result, but in the ever-expanding union of the workers." A perceptive commentator on their political thought and practice, August Nimtz, has stressed: "In the real world, then, the working class engages the bourgeoisie in battle regardless of whether it can actually win or sustain victories .... Through such battles — defeats as well as victories — the proletariat learns for itself." This revolutionary pragmatism interconnects with the insight of certain social and historical analysts that (in the words of Nimtz) "the 'self-organization of the working-class' in the second half of the nineteenth century was responsible for the democratic breakthrough, that is, the institution of 'universal suffrage,' the 'responsibility of the state apparatus to the elected parliament,' and the acquisition of civil liberties — a finding about which Marx and Engels could have justifiably said, 'We told you so!'" Nimtz goes further, asserting that it was the success of Marx and Engels, during their decades of political activism, "in advancing the fight for socialism [within the working-class movement] that advanced the democratic struggle."[30]

This suggests that people who are damaged by oppression under capitalism transform themselves and society through their own struggles, and that such transformations can facilitate more effective struggles for a nonoppressive society. Only such transcendence, it would seem, can give life to the *Manifesto*'s hopeful vision of a better future.

Muste believed that this might be possible — he devoted his entire life to it — but also that it was a far more difficult proposition than one might imagine by simply reading the *Communist Manifesto*. He pointed to a letter written by the great revolutionary Marxist Rosa Luxemburg from a prison cell during World War I, where she said: "Everything would be much easier if I only didn't forget the basic commandment I have set myself for life: the main thing is to be good. Simply and plainly to be good, that is what binds and unbinds all things, it is better than cleverness and self-righteousness... . I decided to be good, again, simply good at any price: that is better than being right and booking every injury." Muste's commentary is interesting:

> She too, it would seem, confronted by an impersonal economic system which man had created and which had become his master and by the elemental forces which produced the class struggle and were unloosed by it, felt suddenly the need of another kind, another order, of power, of a moral science to set over against political science, and so turned to conscience, being good, simply, plainly and at any price, for deliverance for herself and the exploited peoples![31]

In a way, this links up with the critique of Marxism offered by another Christian theologian, Paul Tillich, who quite sincerely praised Marx as "the most successful of all theologians since the Reformation." But Tillich stressed a profound difference between secular thought (which he described as following "a horizontal line") and the transcendent ethical-spiritual element of religious thought (which he described as following "a vertical line"). Believing in the need for both, Tillich embraced the abundant passion for justice in Marx's secular critique of capitalism, but deplored the fact, in his view, that "Marx lacked a vertical criticism against himself."[32] This contributed, in his opinion, to the later failure of the Communist movement after Marx's death. It is worth considering Tillich's argument:

The tragic thing is that the revolutionary movements in Europe, Asia, and Africa originally came from a prophetic message, but when they became victorious, they did not apply their own criticism against themselves. They could not do it because they had nothing above themselves.... The lack of the transcendent line is the reason for the tragic situation that the revolutionary movement that set out to liberate a whole social class has resulted in a new slavery, the totalitarian slavery we have today in the Communist systems .... The Marxist movement was not able to judge itself because of its whole structure, and so it could become the social group which we now identify as Stalinism. In this form everything for which the original groups were struggling became suppressed and distorted.[33]

Critical questions can be raised about this criticism. Perhaps the most serious is this: Christianity itself — whose early founders were, unlike Marx, immersed in the "transcendent vertical line" — proved equally capable of degenerating into murderous authoritarianism. We will explore this and related matters in Chapter 2.

In any event, the *Manifesto*, with its vision of a working-class majority sweeping away capitalism to create a glowing Communist future, is certainly challenged by much (but hardly all) of what happened over the next 150 years. It is worth giving attention here to the three essential categories of the *Manifesto* — Communism, capitalism, and working class.

Communism: Here we must begin to do what we will do more extensively in Chapters 4 and 5 — look into the face and heart and soul of what became the human disaster of the "actually existing Communism" of the 20th century.

Capitalism: This is our present-day "actuality" — and if it is good enough, despite inevitable imperfections, to allow for humanity to continue a reasonable existence, then the *Manifesto*'s injunction to overthrow it is clearly wrong. Again, we must look more closely into its face and heart and soul.

Working Class: In considering this last category, which in some sense includes most of us, we are dealing with what Marx saw as the elemental source of creative activity, of community, of freedom. Many critics term this conception of the working class as "religious" — and we will conclude by exploring this as a possible source of strength. Marx and Engels placed such immense hope in us — in the collective ability of laboring humanity to overcome the destructive dynamics of the modern world, and to "overthrow all relations in which man is a debased, enslaved, forsaken, despicable being."[34] The question remains: Can we really do that?

Communist Disaster

In *1984*, George Orwell says that throughout human history society has been divided into groups he terms Upper, Middle, and Lower. The Upper (once landed aristocracy, now capitalists) dominates society, the Middle (once capitalists, now managers, professionals, and the upper levels of the working class) aids in running the society, and the Lower consists of the vast majority of laborers. The aim of the High is to maintain their own power and privilege, which they can do unless "they lose either their belief in themselves or their capacity to govern efficiently, or both." The aim of the Low, "when they have an aim — for it is an abiding characteristic of the Low that they are too much crushed by drudgery to be more than intermittently conscious of anything outside their daily lives — is to abolish all distinctions and create a society in which all men shall be equal." The aim of the Middle, he writes, is to "change places with the High," which they are able to do by enlisting the Low on their side "by pretending to them that they are fighting for liberty and justice." When the victory is won, "the Middle thrust the Low back into their old position of servitude, and themselves become High." He concludes that "it would be an exaggeration to say that throughout history there has been no progress of a material kind," but he insists that "no advance in wealth, no softening of manners, no reform or revolution has ever brought human equality a millimeter nearer. From the point of view of the Low, no historic change has ever meant much more than a change in the name of their masters." One of the characters in the novel asserts that the Russian Communists "never had the courage to recognize their own motives. They pretended, perhaps they even believed, that they had seized power unwillingly and for a limited period of time, and that just around the corner there lay a paradise where human beings would be free and equal." But from the movement of "universal human brotherhood, red flags, barricades, Karl Marx, and the Paris Commune," they quickly became "a tightly knit organization and a well-defined body of doctrine" with which — after taking power in Russia — they dominated the workers and peasants and all others.[35]

In the name of socialism, the leadership of the Communist Party of the Soviet Union staffed and administered "a political bureaucracy [that] uses, enjoys, and disposes of nationalized property," Milovan Djilas (a dissident who was once part of Yugoslavia's Communist elite) observed in the 1950s, resulting in "discrepancies between the pay of workers and party functionaries [that] are extreme." Ernest Mandel has documented that "the apparatus of full-time functionaries in the Communist Party soared from barely 700 in 1919 to 15,300 in 1922 and more than 100,000 some years later," adding that the functionaries owed "allegiance, and their own job security, to the party Secretariat and its general secretary, J.V. Stalin." A knowledgeable analyst, David J. Dallin, estimated that, in the USSR of 1940, government employees, constituting at least 14 percent of the labor force, consumed as much as 35 percent of the wealth; that the working class, constituting about 20 percent of the labor force, received no more than 33 percent of the wealth, that peasants, 53 percent of the labor force, received 29 percent of the wealth, and that forced laborers, estimated at a minimum of 8 percent of the labor force, received 3 percent of the wealth. Over the next several decades, an increase in industrialization and social wealth altered the situation and the forced labor camps were finally eliminated, but the inequalities increased dramatically. The bureaucracy's material privileges "grew and became institutionalized in a monstrous way — bloated incomes, special shops, weekend houses (dachas), private rooms in hospitals, special education ..., reserved access to foreign travel, and so on," as Mandel points out. Boris Yeltsin, who had reached the lower rungs of the *nomenklatura* (the bureaucratic elite of party and state) notes that he had a luxurious marble-lined house "with a domestic staff consisting of three cooks, three waitresses, a housemaid, and a gardener with his own team of under-gardeners."[36]

The Stalinist variant of "Communism" justified itself by brutally imposing a rapid "modernization" that not only converted the USSR into a major world power (utterly beyond the reach of the pre-revolutionary social order) but also brought education, health services, and gradually rising living standards and cultural opportunities to the laboring millions. The price for this, in addition to a horrific number of deaths, was the domination of society by an authoritarian bureaucracy that amassed substantial material privileges for itself while denying free expression and self-determination among those same laboring millions.

This same system was extended, largely thanks to the role of the Soviet Red Army pushing westward as it drove back Hitler's armies in the final year of the World War II, into Poland, Hungary, Romania, Bulgaria, Czechoslovakia, and East Germany. Stalin's regime established Communist Party dictatorships in those countries as part of what became known as "the Soviet Bloc." (Yugoslavia also went Communist in this period, but was a special case because this happened through a popular revolution, and this independence soon caused that country to break from the Bloc when Stalin sought to assert his domination over it.)[37]

Many saw this as a triumphant extension of socialism, because it extended a "socially owned, planned economy" over a substantially expanded portion of the world. But there was a problem with this. "In the writings of Marx and Engels two conditions are held to be essential as the basis for socialist society: public ownership of land and productive capital *and* political democracy," protested Freda Utley, one of many Communists transformed into anti-Communists (and finally despairing of the possibility of socialism). "In Marx's and Engels' view, and in Lenin's theory, socialism was to be an extension of democracy; it was to make possible real democracy for the first time in history. ... For them, *communal* ownership would be socialism; communal ownership was impossible without political democracy."[38]

In fact, the imposition of Stalinist norms dramatically sparked a 1953 rebellion in East Berlin (where Socialist and Communist roots ran deep among the working class) against this Communist regime of the German Democratic Republic. "While our workers' Government made its mistakes, as they themselves have confessed, one mistake after the other, we said nothing, we took it, we waited. Waited long enough," as one rebellious worker put it. "We're sick and tired of being ordered about by people who are no better than we are. Working class rule — we're the working class, where are we ruling? Dictatorship of the proletariat — we're the proletariat, and we're not even permitted to dictate our own wages and our own norms." A general strike and mass demonstrations against the government paralyzed the country. This was quickly repressed by Soviet military forces. Of course, "murkier elements" from the recent Nazi period, and some connected with Western intelligence agencies, had also become involved, but the bulk of the workers — while determined to protest the increasing workload imposed from above — were indignant over an alleged "workers' state" that forced them to work harder for less compensation. "The whole thing had primarily been to guarantee the right of the workers to co-manage in the factories, so that orders sent down from the ministries could only be enforced with the agreement of the factory committees and the shop stewards," writes Oskar Hippe, who was in an East German prison at the time because of Trotskyist activities, and was therefore able to talk extensively with the newly arrested shop stewards. "Only later had it been a case of improving the conditions of the working population."[39] After the suppression of the uprising, the great Communist playwright Bertolt Brecht wrote bitterly but privately:

> After the rising of the seventeenth of June
> The secretary of the Writers' Union
> Had leaflets distributed on Stalinallee
> In which one could read that
> The people had forfeited the confidence of the government
> And could only win it back by doing twice as much work.
> Would it not be easier to
> Dissolve the people and
> Elect another?[40]

In a brilliant composite portrait of a once-idealistic top Communist functionary in a Soviet Bloc country, Isaac Deutscher wrote in 1950 of this "Polrugarian" Communist leader that "his Stalinist orthodoxy has never been questioned, his devotion to the party has never flagged, and his virtues as leader and statesman are held to be unsurpassed," but that inwardly he "is almost constantly tormented by his Communist conscience, a prey to scruple and fear, to illusion and disillusion." At first he had been elated — after years in struggle and persecution (including even an arrest, with time in a labor camp in the land of Stalin) — to find himself placed in a Communist government that broke up semi-feudal estates to give land to poor peasants, established public ownership of large-scale industry, developed far-reaching plans for economic development and modernization, and "sponsored a great deal of progressive social legislation and an ambitious educational reform." But although this was done by what claimed to be a working-class regime, "there is no way the working class can rule without governing" (as Mandel has put it). Or as Deutscher says of the "Polrugarian" Communist, the majority of workers and peasants in his country "resented the revolution that was being carried out over their heads by people whom they had not chosen and who did not often bother to consult them and who looked like stooges of a foreign power." He reflects that "a revolution without genuine popular enthusiasm behind it is half defeated" and "is inclined to distrust the people whom it should serve." At the same time, he had initially believed that at least "Polrugaria would be spared the experience of purges and concentration camps, of abject subservience and fear" that had afflicted the land of Stalin. Indeed, there were even some who were committed to establishing their own "national road" to socialist development, with greater autonomy, cultural freedom, and perhaps even an approximation of democratic practices.[41]

By the late 1940s and early 1950s, however, such things were brutally repressed throughout the Soviet Bloc as Stalin's regime sought — through the more subservient elements in the various Communist regimes it had established — to tighten its control. One of those who sought to "go too far" down the democratic path — expelled from the Communist Party and imprisoned (but unlike many, not executed) — was the Hungarian Imre Nagy, who wrote:

> The degeneration of power is seriously endangering the fate of socialism and the democratic basis of our social system. Power is increasingly being torn away from the people and turned sharply against them. The People's Democracy as a type of dictatorship of the proletariat, in which the power is exercised by the working class and depends on the partnership of the two large working groups — the workers and the peasantry — is obviously being replaced by a Party dictatorship which does not rely on Party membership, but relies on a personal dictatorship and attempts to make the Party apparatus, and through it the Party membership, a mere tool of this dictatorship.[42]

Nagy also made the point that "there are those who, corrupted by their favorable material status and abandoning principled moral conduct, will do anything as servants of degenerate Bonapartist power and personal dictatorship," and "that raw power and reprisal are used more and more not only against hostile, reactionary, antipopular forces [opposing the positive reforms] but also against the broad masses of the working people," as the "Bonapartist spirit, personal dictatorship, regimentation, and slavish subordination are supplanting party democracy, democratic centralism, and Leninist theories of party life." He predicted that "no enemy propaganda ... will destroy more completely the people's faith in socialism and in a better, happier, and more human future" than such developments as these. And in 1956 he was at the head of an uprising — with dissident Communists and a variety of non-Communists — mobilizing workers, intellectuals, students and others for genuine democracy and independence from the Soviet Bloc. It was brutally crushed by a military onslaught from the USSR, and Nagy was executed. A similar if less bloody development unfolded in Czechoslovakia as dissident Communists struggled for "socialism with a human face" in 1968.[43]

By the late 1980s, however, the story played out differently — but with results not anticipated by many participants. The aspirations of the masses of people who helped to bring down Communism in country after country in Eastern Europe involved transferring power to themselves — the masses of the people — and to compel the economy to truly function according to the cardinal precepts of communism: that the free development of each individual would be the basis for the free development of all society.

In the 1960s, Polish dissidents Jacek Kuron and Karol Modzelewski had argued that under the Stalinist system the workers were exploited (that is, "the surplus product is taken from the working class by force ... while the unproductive sectors serve to maintain and strengthen the rule of a bureaucracy"), and that "to abolish exploitation means ... to create a system in which the organized working class will be master of its own labor and the resulting product; in which it will set the goals of social production, decide on the sharing and use of the national income, hence the size and purpose of investments, the size and disbursement of expenditures for social benefits, health services, education, science, and culture ... in brief, a system in which the working class will exercise economic, social and political power in the state."[44]

This was echoed a decade and a half later in the massive working-class insurgency of the independent trade unions gathered around *Solidarnosc*. "We cannot accept the scorn which those who are what they are solely thanks to the labor of the worker and the efforts of the whole of society often show towards the workers," commented one strike newspaper. At the Lenin Shipyard in Gdansk, the Independent Self-Managed Trade Union declared: "In accord with the basic principles of our state, we are the co-owners of our places of work, and the trade union formed by us will guarantee the realization of this right. As co-owners we have the moral right and duty to concern ourselves with the well-being of our enterprise and its products." Other activists proclaimed: "In Poland a struggle is being waged for a self-managing society. ... The necessary economic and institutional reforms ... must concretize our visions of a self-managing society. We must not allow a situation in which, yet again, laws (dealing with trade unions, censorship, self-government, the workplaces) are handed down 'from above' by a committee of experts. We cannot entrust the perspectives for the development of the country to anyone but working people as a whole."[45]

Similar stirrings — while not assuming quite the scale as in Poland — were manifest in the USSR itself. In the early 1970s, Marxist dissident Roy Medvedev was insisting:

> Socialist democracy is simultaneously a goal and a means. Democracy is essential as a value in itself. To be able to express one's thoughts and convictions freely without fear of persecution or repression is a vital aspect of a free socialist way of life. Without freedom to receive and impart information, without freedom of movement and residence, without many other democratic freedoms, a true socialist society is impossible. Democracy — with all government activity open to public scrutiny as its most important element — is also necessary as a means of ridding our society of bureaucracy and corruption.[46]

A decade before the crisis, Ernest Mandel gave confident expression to the viewpoint, held by many revolutionary Marxists, that it would be "impossible" for there to be a "gradual restoration of capitalism" in the USSR and other "bureaucratically deformed workers' states" either through a "cold" process carried out by the bureaucracy or through a "palace revolution" initiated by a section of the bureaucracy. This reversion to capitalism could occur only "through violent social and political upheavals" involving "disastrous defeats for the Soviet and international proletariat" — perhaps along the lines of a successful version of Hitler's invasion during World War II. And when it was clear, in 1989, that the days of the bureaucratic dictatorship were numbered in the USSR, Mandel asserted in a highly informative study entitled *Beyond Perestroika* that what was "more realistic and more probable" than other scenarios would be a political revolution based on the insurgency of the USSR's working class reestablishing full-scale Soviet democracy, matched with a socialist-oriented control of the economy by the working-class majority — the consequences of which would involve the flourishing of cultural freedom within the USSR and a foreign policy guided, in the spirit of Lenin and Trotsky, by revolutionary internationalism.[47] Yet, the "more probable" outcome never materialized, and instead the "impossible" scenario came to pass.

Seeking to save the increasingly stultifying Communist system through far-reaching modernization efforts involving the openness (*glasnost*) of increasing democratic freedoms and economic restructuring (*perestroika*) that would somehow blend capitalist market forces with some sort of "socialism," the new reforming Communist leader of the USSR, Mikhail Gorbachev, excited growing expectations. But these could not be met while maintaining (as he sought to do) the old structures of Communist Party power. There was a three-way split in the Communist elite: many old-line bureaucrats sought to overthrow Gorbachev in order to reestablish the old order; an impotent minority held to Gorbachev's middle path; an audacious grouping of pro-capitalist "democrats" rallied mass support around Boris Yeltsin — denouncing the "socialist experiment" as a bureaucratic tyranny that should be left behind. It was Yeltsin's forces who carried the day. There was no intervention by the socialist-minded working class projected by Mandel.

In fact, Mandel himself had some understanding of the reason. "The Soviet working class has been profoundly disappointed by the way the October Revolution turned, through the Stalinist degeneration, towards a model of social leadership which does not meet the workers' needs," he noted. "The workers have not been attracted to the capitalist model either. But they see no alternative in the world today, no third model." Mandel's next comment identified the key point: "There are no cadres within the Soviet working class able to propose a different model of management."[48]

Coming out of a tradition quite different from Mandel's Trotskyism, Prabhat Patnaik — a leading intellectual in the Communist Party of India (Marxist) — similarly observed that "the omnipotence of the party made it into a leviathan increasingly accommodating careerists and opportunists, even as bureaucratism resulted in a depoliticization of the working class." One survivor of the forced labor camps, Vladimir Glebov, characterized the USSR's Communist "leaders" from the 1960s to 1990s, people who had been elevated into positions vacated by idealists swept away during Stalin's purges of the 1930s, as "grave worms — those who gorged on the corpse of the murdered country, who did not care whether it was socialism or capitalism, only whether their armchairs were soft."[49]

This phenomenon was also described by the ex-Marxist dissident Leszek Kolakowski regarding the pervasive ideological cynicism that triumphed throughout the Communist Bloc after the 1960s, even at the highest levels: "Instead of people who, even if they had taken part in the atrocities of Stalinism, were in their way loyal Communists and had been attached to Communist ideals, the reins of power were now held by cynical, disillusioned careerists who were perfectly aware of the emptiness of the Communist slogans they made use of."[50]

Obviously, there were repercussions from the half-century domination of the USSR's political life by this stultifying bureaucratic layer. Canadian historian David Mandel, spending years in close contact with Soviet and Russian workers, commented that "they needed time to overcome the legacy of totalitarian rule: fear, cynicism, atomization, subservience to and complicity with arbitrary authority, and, not least, a weak sense of rights and dignity," adding that "the capacity for self-organization and solidarity develop through struggle." Such a process had taken decades in the 19th and early 20th centuries — but the window of opportunity under Gorbachev existed for about three years.[51]

The inability of Soviet workers to crystallize as a self-conscious and independent force by 1990 also had profound repercussions. It has been estimated, at the dawn of the 21st century, that 20 percent of the Russian population receives 50 percent of the wealth, while one-third of all Russians live in poverty. "Western-style stores and cafés are full of these 'New Russians' wantonly spending several times a typical citizen's monthly salary on a single purchase," wrote U.S. historian and observer Stephen Cohen. Boris Kagarlitsky details the impact on the mass of Russians:

> Diseases once thought to have been conquered, diphtheria and in some places cholera, again made an appearance. The numbers of people infected with scabies and lice increased sharply. Typhoid fever began spreading once again. A shift to compulsory medical insurance ushered in the collapse of the entire health care system. Ambulance services, hospitals and regional polyclinics were left completely without funds. Consumption of meat fell by 23 percent, of fish by a quarter, and of milk by 28 percent. In the pre-reform years, the average Russian family has spent a third of its income on food. By 1993 it was necessary to pay 70 percent of earnings for a significantly worse diet .... For the first time since the end of the Second World War the majority of Russian citizens were chronically malnourished.[52]

"As a result of the Yeltsin era, all the fundamental sectors of our state, economic, cultural, and moral life have been destroyed or looted," wrote the old dissident Alexander Solzhenitsyn in 2000. "We heard that great reforms were being carried out in our country. They were false reforms because they left more than half of our country's people in poverty .... God forbid these reforms should continue," intoned the bitterly anti-Communist literary giant.[53]

"Only in the famine years of 1932–33 and the Stalin terror of 1937–38 did the Russian people suffer such losses during peacetime," according to Roy Medvedev. "Freedom and social justice — not market reform — were the slogans that attracted rank-and-file participation in the 'democratic' movement," he noted. Most ordinary people had believed that the market economy would bring "the onset of American-style affluence, combined with European-style social welfare," Stephen Kotkin comments, but instead, they "got an economic involution and mass impoverishment combined with a headlong expansion of precisely what had helped bring down the Soviet Union — the squalid appropriation of state functions and state property by Soviet-era elites."[54]

Indeed, of Yeltsin's pro-capitalist administration, 75 percent had been part of the old Communist Party elite; of Russia's newly home-grown businessmen, 85 percent were former Communist Party members. Together, these elites created corruption and inequality "even more ruinous," according to Kotkin, than the bureaucratic inefficiency of the old Communist order: "unfettered state officials whose larceny helped cashier the Soviet system, and whose bloated ranks swelled with many grasping newcomers." David Mandel comments: "When criminal elements do not directly control enterprises (according to the government, the mafia controls 50 percent of the non-state and 60 percent of the state sectors), management is paying tribute to them or to corrupt state officials, or stealing on its own. It is usually a combination of all these things."[55]

Many people in the USSR, concluding that the hard years since 1917 had been a detour leading only to failure and collapse, joked by the early 1990s: "What is socialism? The longest road from capitalism to capitalism." By the late 1990s, the joke went the other way: "What has the market economy been able to accomplish in six years that the Communists couldn't bring about in seven decades? Making Communism look good."

This was reflected by opinion polls ten years after the collapse of the USSR. While no more than 3.9 percent of Russians polled considered Yeltsin's decade of rule a "necessary stage" for Russia's development, the Stalin era got a relatively high approval rating: 44 percent saw it as containing equal portions of good and bad, 19 percent saw it as more good than bad, and 3 percent saw it as "absolutely good" — 66 percent altogether. An even larger majority rejected the neo-liberal glorification of private enterprise, with 79 percent supporting strengthened state control over the economy. While 89 percent supported guarantees of democratic rights and freedoms for each person, only 47.8 percent were inclined to think that democracy is "the best form of rule despite certain problems" (only 9.1 percent gave unqualified support to that notion). This may be related to the fact that 60 percent believed that their votes were not capable of changing anything, that only 14 percent believed that Russia was a democratic state, and that Yeltsin-era "reformers" had utilized effusive democratic rhetoric to push through policies resulting in "a crushed, looted, and humiliated country," in the words of Russian social scientist and legal expert Alexander Dourin, adding up to "an unprecedented social catastrophe ... which the UN Development Program calls 'a human crisis of monumental proportions.'"[56]

In Poland, reactions were similar. Lech Walesa, one of the leaders of the workers' Solidarity movement, which helped to bring down the Communist regime, later rose to become the somewhat bloated leader of the country and was confronted by one of his former co-workers with the accusation: "You said that you would leave the Communists standing in nothing but their socks, but in fact you left us without even our socks on." Anna Walentynowicz, the militant crane driver who had helped to spark the 1980 workers rebellion, was ranting in 1999: "The people were cheated and, contrary to appearances, Solidarity was used to destroy the nation, to plunge it into poverty, to create conditions that are even worse than under Communism." Interviewing workers he had known during the glory days of the struggle, Timothy Garton Ash found them bitterly complaining that they "were still at the bottom of the pile," paying "a heavy price for the transformation from a planned to a market economy. Yes, they had freedom: but what good was that if you had no money to buy the shiny goods in the shops? ... There was more stress and less security." The story told by Orwell in *1984* — "the Middle thrust the Low back into their old position of servitude" — had been repeated in Poland of the 1990s. "Workers started the great changes, yet they have paid the highest price," Ash observed. "Solidarity was originally a trades union, yet the result of its triumph is that Gdansk workers are employed by their former workmates, now turned capitalist, in private firms with no trades unions at all."[57]

The failure of Communism hardly meant that capitalism was less exploitative, less oppressive, less apt to violate the labor and living conditions of the working class — the abuses Marx and Engels had denounced in the *Manifesto*. As the late Pope John Paul II explained, "The exploitation produced by inhuman capitalism was a real evil, and that's the kernel of truth in Marxism .... These seeds of truth [in Marxism] shouldn't be destroyed, shouldn't be blown away by the wind." He argued that "the supporters of capitalism in its extreme forms tend to overlook the good things achieved by Communism: its effort to overcome unemployment, its concern for the poor."[58]

Capitalism in Our Time

Capitalism is the most dynamic economic system that has ever existed. Privately owned and controlled by a minority of the population, the economy is utilized for the purpose of maximizing profits for the owners — the profit motive is the sparkplug that makes this mighty system go. Meeting human needs is at best a secondary consideration. It is a system of generalized commodity production — that is, a voraciously expansive market economy that draws more and more and more aspects of life and reality into the vortex of buying and selling. And it has always demonstrated a powerful global reach in its quest for markets, raw materials, and investment opportunities.[59]

Some analysts argue that, at least since the 1980s, the world capitalist system has been undergoing a process of transformation that they refer to as "globalization." By this they mean that developments in technology, communications, and transportation have caused economic expansion to transcend national frameworks more dramatically than ever before. This has enabled multinational corporations (that is, large-scale business corporations with holdings and operations in a number of different countries) to rise above restraints or impositions that national governments or labor movements or the populations of any country may wish to establish.

In 1980, radical-populist reformer Ralph Nader — hardly a Marxist — described various aspects of our economy that were no less relevant twenty years later, but that also could have been written as an update to the manifesto of Marx and Engels:

The mercantile values of the modern giant corporations shape more than market forces in their image. They pervade government, politics, law, taxation, environment, education, communications, foundations, athletics, and even institutions formerly believed to be outside their influence, such as the family or organized religion. The calculated penetration of children's minds by exploitive advertisements on children's television illustrates how the mercantile thrust can undermine parental authority, as well as a proper diet. Indeed, both in space and time, the large corporation is expanding its impact, as multinational activity and chemical and other technological burdens on future generations increase. Many multinational corporations' general revenues today dwarf the GNPs of dozens of foreign nations.[60]

That was in 1980. Of the 100 largest economies in the world today, 49 are those of nations, while 51 are those of multinational corporations, and the sales figures of the largest corporations in the United States exceed the gross domestic product of countries such as Denmark, Thailand, Turkey, South Africa, Portugal, Israel, and Ireland. The richest 20 percent of the world's population receives 82.7 percent of the total world income, the second 20 percent receives 11.7 percent of the income, and the bottom 60 percent of the world's people are left with 5.6 percent of the world's income.

This translates into half the global population of 6 billion living on less than $2 per day — with 1.3 billion getting by on less than $1 per day. The world's 225 richest people now have a combined income of $1 trillion — which is equal to the combined annual income of the world's 2.5 billion poorest people. It has been estimated that a tax of 4 percent levied on these 225 richest people would pay for basic and adequate health care, food, clear water, and safe sewers for every person on earth.[61]

This enormous concentration of economic power in a few hands translates into political power. Of course, by owning the great majority of jobs and workplaces throughout the U.S., the corporate elite exercises a dictatorship (sometimes benevolent, often oppressive) over the working lives, 40 hours a week, more or less, of the great majority of those who make up the U.S. labor force — and indirectly over their families as well. But this power is also felt off the job. The ownership and control of the mass media, of the major institutions of "high culture" and popular culture, over key educational and research centers, "think tanks" and philanthropic foundations, etc., give this wealthy elite an incredibly powerful impact on the shaping of popular sensibilities and public opinion.[62]

In 1980, the average corporate Chief Executive Officer (CEO) was paid as much as 42 factory workers, while in 1998, the average CEO was paid as much as 419 workers. "In this climate," political analyst Kevin Phillips observed, "top executives lost compunctions about terminating blue-collar and white-collar jobs in order to make their companies 'competitive.' They moved production to Taiwan and Mexico, liquidated company pension plans and reduced other employee benefits."[63]

The 200 largest multinational corporations — concentrated especially in growing sectors of the world economy (electronics, chemicals, automobiles, drugs, and machinery) — control fully half of the global trade in goods, with gross revenues equal to a quarter of the world gross product. Taken together, multinational corporations control 70 percent of world trade and 75 percent of direct foreign investment.[64]

By the end of the 20th century, a profound shift in the nature of multinational investments had taken place thanks to the fall of trade barriers, allowing a much freer flow of goods and capital across national boundaries. As Robert Went, economist from the University of Amsterdam and the Netherlands Court of Audit, has summarized the data: "More and more companies are taking advantage of new technologies and drastically reduced transport and telecommunication costs to produce their goods and services, at least in part, through production processes spread around the world.... A growing number of people and companies find it easier and easier to meet, travel, send goods, receive images, cooperate and compete across frontiers .... Products from cigarettes to cars are assembled today with parts brought together from every corner of the world."[65]

Economist Prabhat Patnaik has argued that "there is a tremendous globalization of capital," and "this fluidity of finance represents globalization in a double sense: not only in the sense that finance flows everywhere, but also in the sense that it is sucked out of everywhere," and that "national economies become the plaything of speculative forces with nation-states being reduced to the role of helpless spectators." The global expansion of capital has also meant the global expansion of paid labor (working class occupations doubling between 1975 and 1995 to 2.5 billion), with developing technologies and job mobility — according to sociologist Ronaldo Munck — impacting negatively on "the industrial workers of the old smokestack industries." He adds that "any gains from increased economic integration will go to capital and not to labor, especially the traditional working class outside of the high-tech sectors."[66]

In a 1995 study, Eric Toussaint and Denise Comanne described one impact of this on the world's richest countries: "In the countries making up the Organization for Economic Cooperation and Development (OECD), there are officially 35 million unemployed people: three times as many as in the early 1970s, out of a population that has experienced zero growth." This naturally gives corporations much greater leverage in dealing with workers in these and in other countries. "If the company thinks it profitable, it can close or move its operations," observes Went. "More often it can threaten to do so in order to extract concessions from trade unions."[67]

Things are worse elsewhere. The average income in Africa fell steadily in the last three decades of the 20th century to barely 7 percent of that in the industrialized nations. The average income in Latin America was one-third of that in the industrialized North at the end of the 1970s, but only one-fourth by the end of the century. "Only a handful of East Asian countries seemed at the time to have succeeded in narrowing the gap or even joined the North," Went reports. "But since the outbreak of the Asian crisis in 1997 it is these very prodigies that have been demoted to total losses."[68]

The effects of poverty in these "less developed" — but increasingly "developing" (and increasingly exploited) — areas can be devastating. A billion people or more suffer from hunger in the world, and many die from hunger-related causes, including from diseases resulting from low resistance due to malnutrition. Children account for the majority of these deaths, dying at a rate of 40,000 each day. Very serious health problems are generated due to the serious vitamin and mineral deficiencies that afflict about 2 billion of the world's people.[69]

Given time, one might hope that eventually — by means that Marx and Engels called for (not bureaucratic tyranny, but the free association of the producers) — the "everyday" violence that is being done to so many of the world's people can be overcome. Jack London, remember, had speculated that there would be abortive socialist revolutions in the early 20th century — and then three centuries would pass before the workers of the world finally were able to unite and struggle to final victory.

But it is not certain that we have that much time, given the ongoing violence being done to the environment that sustains human life. In 1970, the planetary ecology appeared to be sufficiently threatened to generate a substantial education and reform effort to preserve and enhance the environment, which included the first Earth Day observances. Despite three decades of educational and reform effort, however, by the opening of the 21st century, the extent of environmental problems was deepening and accelerating: 40 percent of the Earth's wetlands had been filled or drained, half of the forests had disappeared, species were vanishing at a rate that has not occurred in 65 million years, human carbon emissions had increased from 3.9 million metric tons to 6.4 million tons annually, and global warming had shifted from being an alarming prediction to a widely-acknowledged fact.[70]

Paul Kennedy — a respected historian and social scientist whose book *Preparing for the Twenty-First Century* has remained all too relevant since it was published in 1993 — surveyed the global spread and impact of the neverending Industrial Revolution at the close of the 20th century. He saw "new factories, assembly plants, road systems, airports, and housing complexes" whose impact on the environment "not only reduce the amount of natural land but contribute to the demand for more energy (especially electricity) and more automobiles and trucks, infrastructure, foodstuffs, paper and packaging, cement, steel ores, and so on. All this increases the ecological damage: more polluted rivers and dead lakes, smog-covered cities, industrial waste, soil erosion, and devastated forests litter the earth." More "human economic activities are creating a dangerous 'greenhouse effect' of global warming, with consequences for the earth's entire ecosystem and for the way of life of rich and poor societies alike." It has been difficult to reverse this destruction because what guides human economic activities in our time has been the competitive drive between firms and between countries to maximize profits, and governments refuse to challenge that. The resulting "piecemeal agreements" are unlikely to safeguard "the future of the earth's thin film of life."[71]

"Suppose that the age of the earth (five billion years) were represented by a year," wrote Marxist social critic Carl Marzani back in 1972. "The oceans have been born four months ago, life would have appeared three and a half months ago. Man appeared on earth an hour and a half ago, Egyptian civilization 30 seconds ago, Julius Caesar 10 seconds ago, and the United States became a nation one second ago!" Marzani concluded: "It's in that last second, since the Industrial Revolution, that man has become a menace to his own species." And he explained: "Water, air, and thermal pollution, squandering of resources, the degradation of the environment, whether on farm land or in urban ghetto … all are inextricably intertwined in one fundamental problem — man's relationship to his environment, to the planet Earth in all its aspects."[72]

Joel Kovel points out, however, that "industrialization is not an independent force … but the hammer with which nature is smashed for the sake of capital." What Marx described in *Capital* as "the accumulation process" is a key: Capital in the form of money is invested in *capital* in the form of raw materials and tools and labor-power, which is transformed — by the squeezing of actual labor out of the labor-power of the workers — into *capital* in the form of the commodities thereby produced, whose increased value is realized through the sale of the commodities for more money than was originally invested, which is the *increased capital* out of which the capitalist extracts his profits, only to be driven to invest more capital for the purpose of achieving ever greater *capital accumulation*. The economic necessity of ever-expanding accumulation to maximize profits drives the entire economic machine forward. The need for increasing productivity to boost profits generates the growth of capital goods industries, according to James O'Connor — and consequently "the more rapid is economic growth, the higher will be the rates of depletion and exhaustion of resources, as well as of the production of unwanted by-products (pollution)."[73]

John Bellamy Foster is one of many Marxists who has advanced the notion that "the free association of producers" that Marx and Engels call for in the *Manifesto* is the key to the solution of the crisis. "Only through the democratically organized social governance of both production and nature on a global scale is there any meaningful hope … that the world will be cared for in common and in the interest of generations still to come," he writes.

Practical solutions have long been suggested. "Experts have estimated that underdeveloped countries can be industrialized to European levels at a cost of 35 billion dollars a year for 10 years," Carl Marzani asserted in the early 1970s, adding that creating a pollution-free environment in the world would cost another 65 billion dollars a year for ten years. Referring to the incredibly expensive arms race between the U.S. and the USSR at that time, he commented that "the world has already wasted 2,000 billion dollars in armaments in the last 20 years, an average of 100 billion a year." He concluded: "In other words, the world has thrown away three times the amount of money sufficient to have the world industrialized and pollution-free on a European standard of living!"[74]

With the passage of decades since Marzani's ignored proposal, the environment was further compromised. *The Washington Post* would report 34 years later, for example, that "new data … from satellite imagery … give fresh urgency to worries about the role of human activity in global warming." Data on melting glaciers in Greenland "are mirrored by findings from Bolivia to the Himalayas, scientists said, noting that rising sea levels threaten widespread flooding and severe storm damage in low-lying areas worldwide," with consequences such as the 2005 devastation wrought in Louisiana by Hurricane Katrina. Global warming results from dramatic increases in carbon dioxide and several other gases trapping the sun's heat and raising the Earth's atmospheric temperatures (the "greenhouse effect"). "Most climate scientists believe a major cause for Earth's warming climate is increasing emissions of greenhouse gases as a result of burning fossil fuels, largely in the United States and other wealthy, industrialized nations such as those of western Europe but increasingly in rapidly developing nations such as China and India." This hardly invalidates the thrust of Marzani's proposal — rather, it suggests a greater urgency, and a need for even deeper changes. These have proved to be inconsistent with natural trends generated by a dynamically profit-driven economy.

There are ecological activists who sharply challenge the notion, however, that the elimination of capitalism will automatically solve the problem. Some warn that Marx's ecological perspectives were, at best, undeveloped — that there is a tendency to see nature as "passive and inert," something to be acted upon by humanity, rather than as a living and vibrant web of ecosystems of which humanity is a component. Many in the Marxist and socialist traditions (William Morris and Rosa Luxemburg being salient exceptions) were inclined to project a future in which humanity would *dominate* nature, rather than seeing itself with more humility as an interactive and vibrant part of nature. It was certainly the case that the Stalinist regime in the USSR and regimes shaped under its influence contributed substantially to the ecological crisis. "Global warming, loss of biodiversity and ozone, acid rain, ocean pollution, deforestation, exhaustion of energy and metal ore reserves, soil loss, and other major ecological changes are all the result of two or more centuries of rapid growth in the industrial capitalist (and ex-state socialist) economies," in the words of James O'Connor — and it has been widely noted that the environmental sensibilities of Communist "industrializers" tended to be similar to those of the capitalist robber barons of the late 19th century.[75]

Such "state socialism," as we have seen, had little in common with the vision of socialism in the *Manifesto*. The free association of producers (that is, communism) was seen by Marx in his 1844 *Economic and Philosophical Manuscripts* as allowing for "the genuine resolution of the conflict between man and nature, between man and man, the free resolution between freedom and necessity, between individual and species." Overcoming the fragmentation of humanity and nature generated by the capitalist dictatorship over the economy, and also by the accumulation process as the driving force of industry, libertarian-communism at one and the same time eliminates the "universal prostitution of the worker" and the "universal pollution" that had been generated by the dominance of "dead matter" (whether it takes the form of money or bureaucracy or out-of-control industrialization) over life. This would be superseded by "the true resurrection of nature, the realized naturalism of man and the realized humanism of nature."[76]

Workers and the Transforming Spirit

Even if this socialist/communist future is necessary, *is it possible*? The persistent failure of the working class to secure political power has raised a fundamental question about whether there are forces capable of creating a socialist future. A bitter ex-Marxist named Bertram D. Wolfe once asked: "What if History fails to force the working class to accept the goal that Marx's science has assigned to it? What if enslavement and degradation, or corruption, or willfulness, or caprice, should be such as to unfit it for, or cause it to reject, the mission of redeeming all mankind? What if the proletariat stubbornly continues to choose other goals or other methods than this 'science' prescribes?"[77]

Almost as if in response to this, the theologian Paul Tillich insisted:

In Marx there is no glorification of the proletariat. The revolutionary movements made the proletariat the messiah, the savior, so to speak, not because the proletarians are such wonderful people — Marx never believed that; he knew them — but because they stood at a particular point in history which involved them in a class struggle, and through this struggle a new reality might come into existence.[78]

The defense of Marx by a Protestant theologian suggests a religious quality to the vision presented in the *Manifesto*. No one has more aptly emphasized this than the ex-Marxist and radical dissident of the Russian Orthodox Church, Nicolas Berdyaev. He capped a remarkable religious summary of the *Manifesto*'s meaning with the twin assertions that there is "a great deal of social truth in Communism," but that the Godless aspect of Marx's approach is fatal. Berdyaev called for an "integral Christianity ... working out its eternal truth towards consistent life, consistent culture, consistent social justice," that would "leave off supporting capitalism and social injustice," and that would "accept all that is true in Communism and reject all that is false." He added: "The future belongs, whatever happens, to the working classes, to the workers; it is inevitable, and it is just."[79]

None of this conjures away the skeptical question posed by Bertram Wolfe. When we look at the incredibly diverse working-class majority of our own country, we certainly do *not* see a class-conscious mass of socially idealistic saints. There are, of course, all the human frailties, personal limitations, and psychological wounds one should expect to find in any large group of people in our society. Among other things, we see that nonclass identities (race, ethnicity, gender, education, occupational status, religious orientation, sexual orientation, cultural tastes, etc.) often have a more vibrant meaning for individuals who are technically part of the working class but who don't see that as a primary identification for themselves. In fact, many don't even see themselves as working class, but instead as middle class, because they are neither rich nor poor but instead are somewhere in between.

But it is this multifaceted working-class majority that has the *potential* — if it can ever create sufficient unity among its various elements — to establish democratic control over our economy in such a way as to draw humanity back from the catastrophes that may soon engulf us. As the *Communist Manifesto* suggests, the dilemmas of global capitalism may be resolved either "in a revolutionary reconstitution of society at large or in the common ruin of the contending classes."[80]

Capitalism has gone through multiple traumas and transformations of industrialization, imperialist expansion, a world war, economic depression, a grand procession of murderous dictatorships, a second world war, the collision of revolution and counter-revolution, the Cold War, and most recently an accelerating restructuring of the global economy. This has generated at various moments the radicalization, de-radicalization, decomposition, and recomposition of the working classes of various countries. As the noted left-wing labor analyst Kim Moody has observed, the U.S. working class has been experiencing a process of being "pulled apart and pushed together."[81] The increasingly difficult realities that many of us have been facing may make possible an interweaving of a renewed working-class consciousness with the radicalized consciousness connected with social movements seeking to overcome oppression related to race and gender. A missed opportunity from the past — involving the labor and civil rights movements — may help clarify what I mean.

In 1966, A. Philip Randolph and others in the labor movement advanced — with the support of a broad array of liberal and progressive forces — an ambitious ten-year plan called *The Freedom Budget for All Americans* that projected the mobilization of economic resources to accomplish a number of goals: "abolition of poverty; guaranteed full employment; full production and high economic growth; adequate minimum wages; farm income equity; guaranteed incomes for all unable to work; a decent home for every American family; modern health services for all; full educational opportunity for all; updated social security and welfare programs; equitable tax and money policies." Many top labor leaders of the AFL-CIO signed on to the "Freedom Budget." Civil rights leaders such as Martin Luther King also embraced this program, moving in the direction of supporting an interracial "poor people's movement" and progressive trade union struggles. "The emergence of social initiatives by a revitalized labor movement would be taking place as Negroes are placing economic issues on the highest agenda," King commented. "The coalition of an energized section of labor, Negroes, unemployed and welfare recipients may be the source of power that reshapes economic relationships and ushers in a breakthrough to a new level of social reform."[82]

Such a far-reaching social program was beyond the scope of either the Republican or Democratic parties, which were not inclined to challenge the more conservative and narrowly profit-minded priorities established by the big corporations that controlled the country's economic resources. Because labor did not have a political party of its own, the door was closed on such proposals as the "Freedom Budget." Randolph acidly noted that the persistence of poverty and racism were rooted in "fundamentally economic problems which are caused by the nature of the system in which we live." He added, "This system is a market economy in which investment and production are determined more by the anticipation of profits than by the desire to achieve social justice."[83]

It is worth recalling a concept popularized by Leon Trotsky during the 1930s — the notion of a *transitional program* that connects with the consciousness, the aspirations, and the struggles of masses of people while at the same time colliding with the workings of the capitalist economy. Practical mass struggles could generate a revolutionary overturn.[84]

What if a majority of the American people — which means a majority of our richly diverse working class — became convinced of the need for such a "Freedom Budget" to begin solving the problems that we face? What if a coalition of trade unions, African-American and Hispanic and women's organizations, religious groups, youth activists, and others began to mobilize around such a program? Victory might require not only massive education and well-organized protest actions, but also independent political action designed to draw together the working-class majority to struggle for political power and economic transformation. The "Freedom Budget" would have revolutionary impact.

Two points need to be made in conclusion.

One point is that even organizations dedicated to meaningful social change can be clogged and corroded by arrogant top-down elitism, shallow routinism, and deadening bureaucracy. We know that from history and, in some cases, from our own personal experiences. The unions and other progressive organizations of today will be incapable of leading the political transformation we need unless masses of people are inspired by the transcendent spirituality to which Paul Tillich alluded, which is capable of helping people grow beyond their limitations and draw from the best that is in them.

The words of Leonardo Boff get at it when he expresses his own commitments through his continual engagement with Christianity: "Jesus Christ did not merely teach some truths. He journeyed on a path in which he assumed the whole of life, both its positive and negative features, as a life lived, endured, and assumed vis-à-vis God and always with God as the starting point." Boff asserts: "God leaves the inaccessible light and comes down in order to liberate the oppressed. Things are not all the same to God; God takes sides against the pharaoh and against all the oppressors of history; God takes the side of those who suffer and cry out for life." To follow the path of Jesus, says Boff, your life must be animated by this spirit.[85]

To put it differently, we have need — among a growing number of activists — of the idealistic integrity, the valuing of all people, the moral passion and revolutionary creativity that, as A. J. Muste emphasized, illuminated the life of Rosa Luxemburg. From a more secular standpoint, Joel Kovel speaks of spirit as an elemental and dynamic life force, not opposed to matter or flesh but instead "revealed, indeed created, in the freeing of matter and flesh" as a "lived process." While "spirituality is inherent to human beings, and arises wherever there is human existence," he observes that "the conditions of modern society are such that spirituality must always contend with the pressure of despiritualization." Kovel adds that, "It is capitalism which has created modernity in such a way that traditional spirituality has eroded," and warns: "A world order that commits planetary suicide in the search for profit while driving the majority of human beings into despair and poverty is a killing/producing machine without spiritual center." The hope for the future can be found when "spirit breaks loose from [existing] reality and … transforms society."[86]

Marx and Engels were convinced that such transformation would — as we have seen Tillich explain — be generated within the majority sectors of the population (the working class) through their own idealistically animated struggle for liberation from material oppression, the class struggle, "and through this struggle a new reality might come into existence." Elemental qualities — the need for community, the passion for creative labor, the capacity for freedom — can come to the fore among masses of people engaged in struggle, transforming them in ways that make them capable of bringing about meaningful and immensely positive social transformation.

The final point is that the development of such a movement to transform society with something like the "Freedom Budget" would put the question of working-class political power — what the *Manifesto* terms "winning the battle of democracy" — on the agenda. Establishing a working-class democracy that will utilize our economic resources to ensure the well-being, dignity, and free development of all people, as Marx and Engels urged, may turn out to be the only real solution to the problems that these two young revolutionaries so insightfully identified more than a century and a half ago.[87]

One of the most pressing questions for citizens of the United States certainly involves the question of what policies will truly protect and advance our *national interest*. But to answer this question, it is crucial that we be able to define precisely what is meant by this "national interest." As we seek to answer it, we would do well to remind ourselves that 1 percent of the families in our country control 40 percent of our country's wealth, that the next 19 percent own another 40 percent of the wealth, and that those of us in the "bottom" 80 percent of our nation's families are left with only 20 percent of the wealth. We should be clear that those who shape U.S. foreign policy and domestic policies are those from the wealthiest 20 percent of the population — and what is in their interest is not necessarily what is in our interest.

Paul Tillich was hardly the only alert and serious Christian to express concern over such realities. Pope John Paul II — by no means a representative of Christianity's left wing — denounced capitalism "when it is organized so as to ensure maximum returns and profits with no concern whether the worker, through his own labor, grows or diminishes as a person through increased sharing in a genuinely supportive community or through increased isolation in a maze of relationships marked by destructive competitiveness and estrangement, in which he is considered only a means and not an end." The only variant of capitalism he would consider positively was one tamed through regulation by a democratic government, by socialist-influenced welfare-state programs, and by strong trade unions. In his words: "The needs of the poor take priority over the desires of the rich; the rights of workers over the maximization of profits; the preservation of the environment over uncontrolled industrial expansion; production to meet social needs over production for military purposes."[88]

More than three decades ago, Rev. Martin Luther King, Jr. posed questions that continue to haunt us. Noting in 1968 that 40 million Americans were living in poverty (there are more today), he commented:

> And one day we must ask the question, "Why are there forty million poor people in America?" And when you ask that question, you begin to question the capitalist economy. And I'm simply saying that more and more, we've got to begin to ask questions about the whole society. ...
>
> What I'm saying to you this morning is that communism forgets that life is individual. Capitalism forgets that life is social, and the kingdom of brotherhood is found neither in the thesis of communism nor the antithesis of capitalism but in a higher synthesis. It is found in a higher synthesis that combines the truths of both. Now, when I say question the whole society, it means ultimately coming to see that the problem of

racism, the problem of economic exploitation, and the problem of war are all tied together. These are the triple evils that are interrelated. ...

A nation that will keep people in slavery for 244 years will "thingify" them — make them things. Therefore they will exploit them, and poor people generally, economically. And a nation that will exploit economically will have to have foreign investments and everything else, and will have to use its military might to protect them. All of these problems are tied together. ...

King realized that such interrelated problems could not be overcome easily, but he insisted that "there is a creative force in the universe, working to pull down the gigantic mountains of evil, a power that is able to make a way out of no way and transform dark yesterdays into bright tomorrows." Whether this creative force is to be found in God or in humanity (or in both), it lends plausibility to the point that King made over and over again: "The arc of the moral universe is long, but it bends toward justice."[89]

A transformative mix of spirit and practical action, expressed so eloquently in King's words, is essential if the hoped-for future projected by the *Communist Manifesto* is to make any sense at all. To comprehend this, perhaps we should follow this great religious and political leader into a consideration of the Kingdom of God.

2
The Kingdom of God

Communism has often been characterized as being a form of religion, with a passionate commitment to bringing about "heaven on earth." Those turning away from it in disillusionment have sometimes referred to Communism as "the God that failed."[1] Affinities between Marxism and religion may be worth probing, particularly considering Marxism's undeniable cultural roots in the Judeo-Christian tradition. In seeking some perspective on the moral disaster of Communism, we might be well served by considering what some see as the moral disaster of Christianity.

Challenging Religion

The alleged disaster of Christianity is not unrelated to a far-reaching critique that can be extended to religion as such. The young Frederick Engels, drawing on the thinkers of the Enlightenment, on the most radical disciples of philosopher G. W. F. Hegel, and especially on the analysis of Ludwig Feuerbach, wrote that "religion is essentially the emptying of man and nature of all content, the transferring of this content to the phantom of a distant God who then in his turn graciously allows something from his abundance to come to human beings and to nature."[2] Basing himself on this and on Sigmund Freud's classic *The Future of an Illusion*, Marxist literary critic Paul Siegel — in a comparative critique of world religions — elaborated:

> Prostrating themselves before the God of their own creation, human beings are alienated from themselves and their fellows. The protection they gain from this God is at the cost of the integrity of the self. Just as with a child submitting to a domineering and capricious father, submission to God only increases insecurity by creating dependence on an arbitrary force and fosters a repressed rebelliousness against Big Daddy that adds to fears of retaliation. It is only when humanity has finally freed itself from this dependence that it can be free.[3]

But there is a paradox. The meekness that such religion inculcates among believers (in regard to their God) has combined with an explosive militancy — capable of incredible violence and cruelty — toward nonbelievers. Nowhere is this more true than within Christianity. Bertrand Russell, one of Christianity's most lucid critics, has succinctly identified a Christian as someone who believes in God, life after death, and in the divinity and moral superiority of Jesus. Russell identifies these elements as morally lethal, and his blunt comment sums up the historical record with admirable clarity:

> You find this curious fact, that the more intense has been the religion of any period and the more profound has been the dogmatic belief, the greater has been the cruelty and the worse has been the state of affairs. In the so-called ages of faith, when men really did believe the Christian religion in all its completeness, there was the Inquisition, with its tortures; there were millions of unfortunate women burned as witches; and there was every kind of cruelty practiced upon all sorts of people in the name of religion.[4]

Russell's explanation — which he linked to the determination to maintain ideological orthodoxy (and the privileged positions of the official interpreters of such orthodoxy) — caused him to note similarities between Christianity and the Communism represented by Stalin's tyranny. "The most dangerous features of Communism are reminiscent of the medieval church," he commented. "They consist of fanatical acceptance of doctrines embodied in a sacred book, and savage persecution of those who reject them."[5]

In a similar vein, Simone Weil — shortly before her death as she was drawing close to, but resistant to embracing, the Catholic Church — commented: "After the fall of the Roman Empire, which had been totalitarian, it was the Church that was the first to establish a rough form of totalitarianism in Europe in the thirteenth century, after the war with the Albigenses. This tree bore much fruit." This will be an issue to which we will need to return later in this chapter — simply noting here that some of the most intensive repressions and waves of mass murder down through the centuries were carried out in the name of God and Christ.[6]

Religion's Two "Souls"

Of course, there is more than one way of understanding religion. The great 20th-century physicist Albert Einstein once made a sharp distinction between "a religion of fear" and "cosmic religious feeling."[7]

Essential to the religion of fear, according to Einstein, is the concept of God as "a being from whose care one hopes to benefit and whose punishment one fears." He noted that "during the youthful period of mankind's spiritual evolution human fantasy created gods in man's own image, who by operations of their will were supposed to determine, or at any rate to influence, the phenomenal world. ... Man sought after the disposition of these gods in his own favor by means of magic and prayer." Such a religion of fear "is in an important degree stabilized by the formation of a special priestly caste that sets itself up as a mediator between the people and the beings they fear, and erects a hegemony on this basis. In many cases a leader or ruler or a privileged class whose position rests on other factors combines priestly functions with its secular authority in order to make the latter more secure; or the political rulers and the priestly caste make common cause in their own interests."[8]

Einstein explained that such religion is incompatible with science. The scientific-minded person "is imbued with the ordered regularity of all events" and recognizes that "there is no room left by the side of this ordered regularity for causes of a different nature. For him neither the rule of human nor the rule of divine will exists as an independent cause of natural events." At the same time, Einstein acknowledged that "the doctrine of a personal God interfering with natural events could never be refuted, in the real sense, by science, for this doctrine can always take refuge in those domains in which scientific knowledge has not yet been able to set foot." But he argued that "a doctrine which is able to maintain itself not in clear light but only in the dark will of necessity lose its effect on mankind," and that religion can survive in the long run only if its teachers "have the stature to give up that source of fear and hope which in the past placed such power in the hands of priests." Instead, "a man's ethical behavior should be based on sympathy, education, and social ties and needs," and he concluded: "Man would indeed be in a poor way if he had to be restrained by fear of punishment and hope of reward after death." [9]

Against this religion of fear, Einstein counterposed what he called "cosmic religious feeling," elements of which he believed could also be found in the early religious development of humanity. In modern times, however, it could best be awakened and kept alive by art and science. The scientist, for example, "is possessed by the sense of universal causation. The future, to him, is every whit as necessary and determined as the past. There is nothing divine [i.e., supernatural] about morality; it is a purely human affair. His religious feeling takes the form of a rapturous amazement at the harmony of natural law," and in the face of this "the individual feels the futility of human desires and aims, and the sublimity and marvelous order which reveal themselves both in nature and in the world of thought. Individual existence impresses him as a sort of prison and he wants to experience the universe as a single significant whole." This outlook is also inconsistent with "the shackles of selfish desire" and the "bondage of egocentric cravings." The "profound reverence for the rationality made manifest in existence" leads the individual toward "a far-reaching emancipation from the shackles of personal hopes and desires, and thereby ... [to] that humble attitude of mind to the grandeur of reason incarnate in existence, and which in its profoundest depths is inaccessible to man."[10]

In celebrating this nonmystical "true religion," Einstein asserts that "a person who is religiously enlightened appears to be one who has, to the best of his ability, liberated himself from the fetters of his selfish desires and is preoccupied with thoughts, feelings, and aspirations to which he clings because of their superpersonal value." He argues that "the religious geniuses of all ages have been distinguished by this kind of religious feeling, which knows no dogma and no God conceived in man's image; so that there can be no church whose central teachings are based on it. Hence it is precisely among the heretics of every age that we find men who were filled with this highest kind of religious feeling and who were in many cases regarded by their contemporaries as atheists, sometimes also as saints."[11]

Erich Fromm also identified the two different approaches to religion, which he related to conflicting political realities. "Early Christianity was a religion of the poor and downtrodden" in opposition to "authoritarian political pressure," he wrote, and Judaism also had "a strong anti-authoritarian tradition," both of which "developed the humanistic aspect of religion to a remarkable degree." On the other hand, whenever "religion allied itself with secular power, the religion had by necessity to become authoritarian." Nor was the anti-authoritarian and humanist variant of religion the monopoly of the Judeo-Christian tradition. "The human reality, for instance, underlying the teachings of Buddha, Isaiah, Christ, Socrates, or Spinoza is essentially the same," according to Fromm. "It is determined by the striving for love, truth, and justice."[12]

The Religious Challenge

Flowing naturally from the insights expressed by Fromm and Einstein is the verity that there is more than one way of comprehending God. "Someone has to be the boss," was how Dorothee Soelle summed up one conception, expressed by a man she knew. "Power, authority, command — those are the most important attributes of his God." For many people, she lamented, "their relationship to God remains childish; they do not want to be friends of God but want to remain subordinates and dependents."[13]

One remarkable "friend of God" authored one of the most devastating critiques of organized religion, *The Age of Reason* (1794–95). This was the great hero of the American Revolution and defender of the French Revolution, Tom Paine. Denounced by the likes of Empire-builder Theodore Roosevelt as a "filthy little atheist" because of his scathing demolition of the Bible, Paine was actually motivated by belief in a God with whom the Bible (written by men, not by God) did not measure up: "When we contemplate the immensity of that being who directs and governs the incomprehensible WHOLE, of which the utmost ken of human sight can discover but a part, we ought to feel shame at calling such paltry stories the word of God." The amazing vastness of reality, according to Paine, is made up of creatures (such as ourselves) and other wondrous creations that did not bring themselves into being. "There is a power superior to all those things, and that power is God," he insisted. "The only idea man can affix to the name of God is that of a *first cause*, the cause of all things." Therefore: "THE WORD OF GOD IS THE CREATION WE BEHOLD: and it is in *this word*, which no human invention can counterfeit or alter, that God speaketh universally to man."[14]

From this conception of God, Paine derived very specific ways of coming to know God, to be one with God, and to honor God. "That which is now called natural philosophy, embracing the whole circle of science, of which astronomy occupies the chief place, is the study of the world of God in his works, and is the true theology," he asserted. "It is from the study of the true theology that all our knowledge of science is derived, and it is from that knowledge that all the arts have originated." Defining religion as "the belief of a God and the practice of moral truth," he concluded that "the practice of moral truth, or, in other words, a practical imitation of the moral goodness of God, is no other than our acting toward each other as he acts benignly toward all," and that "the only idea we can have of serving God is that of contributing to the happiness of the living creation that God has made."[15]

Paine's understanding of God seems consistent with the more recent reflections of Joel Kovel, who challenges the "spiritual pride" that results in an all-too-common "conception of God which directly extends human propensities and characteristics into the heavens." Kovel sees God as Ultimate Being and (with implications fully consistent with Paine's notion of "the true theology" from which "all our knowledge of science is derived") asserts that "the purely formal relations of mathematics have been recognized as expressing a kind of homology with the spirit" — that "by expressing a harmony with the eternal and universal, mathematics transcends the contingent and narrow boundaries of the self." Yet Kovel insists that this Ultimate Being is at the same time "a living god" whose immanence is reflected in a spirituality — a life force — that permeates our existence. Consistent with Paine's line of thought, Kovel says that "it is the evolution of spirit itself which can bring love into historical being." He observes that increasingly in modern society there has been a dominance of oppressive and "de-spirtualizing" forces, yet he sees a natural and necessary struggle within humanity toward "radical transcendence of domination." He concludes: "A world in which human beings are equal and live in loving respect for nature — in other words, a world beyond domination — is along the asymptotic curve toward Ultimate Being."[16]

Kovel makes a distinction between spirituality and *religion* (structures of thought and practice sustaining spirit within human communities) — although, he acknowledges, "religion is the principal manifestation taken by spirit." As we have noted, there are different kinds of religion. Soelle makes a key distinction: "The main virtue in authoritarian religion is obedience, its cardinal sin rebellion, in contrast to humanitarian religion, which moves self-actualization and lapses of the self into center stage." She calls for people "finally to get rid of the old white man in heaven" in order to connect with God's actuality: "Life itself is so permeated with this quality that we call God that we cannot avoid feeding on it and hungering after it." Solle celebrates "the faith and hope that binds people to the poor man from Nazareth," concluding: "I believe in God, in the creative energy that 'calls into existence the things that do not exist' (Romans 4:17), that is good and wants the good for us, which means being whole and flourishing in our ability to reflect God."[17]

The question of where Jews fit into such a Christian perspective is suggested by the Marxist-turned-Jewish theologian Will Herberg, who commented: "Judaism and Christianity represent one religious reality, Judaism facing inward to the Jews and Christianity facing outward to the gentiles, who through it are brought to God and under the covenant of Israel, and therefore cease to be gentiles." His explanation is worth considering: "The covenant of Israel is understood by the prophets, and perhaps much earlier, as the covenant of a redeemed and redeeming community; the purpose it defines is a universal purpose, and the people it brings into being are an instrument of God for the redemption of mankind. All are to be gathered into the covenant and, within the covenant, restored to a right relation with God." He emphasized: "It is hard to avoid the conviction that Christianity emerges, in God's plan of redemption, to open the covenant of Israel to the 'nations of the world.'" He adds: "In Jesus — not merely Jesus the moral teacher, or Jesus the prophetic voice, but also the Jesus whom Christians confess the Christ — Jew and Christian find their unity ... and their difference."[18]

Objections have been raised in regard to the very conception of a unified "Judeo-Christian tradition." Simone Weil's rejection of Judaism, against which she counterposed a "superior" Christianity, is at odds with perspectives emphasized in these pages, and finds a sharp critique in Hans Meyerhoff, who (commenting that Weil "leaped into faith on the wings of the absurd") puts forward the view of many that "Jesus came to fulfill, not to abolish, the old law of Moses." Yet Weil receives backhanded support from Jacob Taubes, another defender of Judaism, who offers this interesting comment: "The controversy between the Jewish and Christian religions points to the perennial conflict between the principle of law and the principle of love. The 'yoke of the Law' is challenged by the enthusiasm of love. But the 'justice of the Law' may, in the end, be the only challenge to the arbitrariness of love."[19]

This dichotomy of the passion for justice and the passion of love is open to question, and in the counterposition of Jesus to Judaism, a key is how one understands the Hebrew prophets. "Prophecy among the Israelites was a characteristic form of divination of the nature of both an exalted profession and a religious frenzy," comments Homer W. Smith. The prophets varied "from worldly individuals who participated in the life of the community to austere mountain recluses; their notions ranged from the most primitive magic to the most unselfish conceptions of society. Most of their revelations were characterized by orgiastic attacks in which they poured out intense patriotism combined with zealous devotion to the current doctrines of Yahweh's will, the voice of the people's conscience and the arbiters of national politics." Abraham J. Heschel says the prophets' language "is luminous and explosive, firm and contingent, harsh and compassionate, a fusion of contradictions," adding: "He whose thinking is guided by the prophets would say: God's presence is my first thought; His unity and transcendence my second; His concern and involvement (justice and compassion), my third. Upon deeper reflection, however, he will realize that all three thoughts are one." Megan McKenna persuasively terms "the crucified and risen one" as an essential link in a continuity stretching "through the history of those called the chosen people of God, through those called to the Kingdom of God, as the brothers and sisters of the prophet Jesus up through our own day — and on into our as yet unknown futures."[20]

From other quarters, Muslim scholar Seyyed Hossein Nasr has described "the flame of love for Christ that is inculcated in the hearts of Muslims in general," who (in terms similar to those of some Jewish theologians) are inclined to "view Christ as the greatest prophet before the prophet of Islam, but not as an incarnation of God, which Islam rejects, since it bases its understanding of God on the absolute itself rather than on its manifestation." And yet Buddhist monk Thich Nhat Hanh has written:

> When we look into and touch deeply the life and teaching of Jesus, we can penetrate the reality of God. Love, understanding, courage, and acceptance are expressions of the life of Jesus. God made himself known to us through Jesus Christ. With the Holy Spirit and the Kingdom of God within Him, Jesus touched the people of his time … and had the courage to do whatever was needed to heal His society. … The fact that Jesus is both the Son of Man and the Son of God is not difficult for a Buddhist to accept. … For me, the life of Jesus is His most basic teaching, more important than even faith in the resurrection or faith in eternity. … If you do not really look at His life, you cannot see the way. If you satisfy yourself with praising a name, even the *name* of Jesus, it is not practicing the life of Jesus. … *When we understand and practice deeply the life and teachings of Buddha or the life and teachings of Jesus, we penetrate the door and enter the abode of the living Buddha and the living Christ, and life eternal presents itself to us.*[21]

Nor have we exhausted the question of how Christianity connects with other religious traditions. Religious historian Eduardo Hoornaert takes up the broad category "paganism" and its relationship to early Christianity. "Earliest Christianity by no means represented a condemnation of paganism," he notes. "On the contrary, it sprang up in the Roman Empire as a new interpretation of paganism." Leaders of the early church "were tireless in their insistence that Christianity was consonant with paganism's deepest aspirations." More than this, "paganism raises the great problems of humanity — health, life, justice, land, peace, happiness. Paganism is as necessary to Christianity as is the soil of a garden to the growing things that strike root in it." The new values of early Christianity — accepting all people as the children of God — provided them "with the dynamic capacity to open themselves up to the paganism around them," absorbing vital elements of it into Christianity while at the same time facilitating a Christianization of varieties of paganism with which it came into contact. By the 16th and 17th centuries, however, "Christianity had been transformed into a Christendom allied with colonial powers that were embarking on a project of economic and political expansion in America, Africa, and even Asia," and this prevented the fruitful and creative interaction of Christianity with the paganism of those areas.[22]

This implies that Christianity has much to learn from and to offer non-Christian belief systems. Hoornaert is not the only Christian who believes that the self-concept of the church must not be a "perfect society," but rather a community that is "reformed and to be reformed" as a continual process — "a church ever in need of reform."[23]

Many among Christian, Jewish, and Islamic believers share a common conception of God at odds with that of religious authoritarians. In discussing the views of Paul Tillich, the atheist philosopher Sidney Hook summarized it aptly and sympathetically, even as he stubbornly rejected it:

> For if God is not an entity or a being but being-itself, no religion truly oriented to Him or It could be persecutory. All religions would be equal in their sense of stuttering inadequacy as they sought to articulate that which was beyond articulation. Full of humility and awe before the Power of Being, they would revise or reinterpret their religious symbols in order to express the highest moral reaches of human experience. They would seek more explicitly than in the past to devise symbols which would integrate rather than disintegrate human personality. They would turn to the findings of modern psychology, sociology, and moral theory for leads and material rather than go adventuring on an impossible quest for being. They would provide aesthetic and emotional supports for the various types of humanisms and ethical culture whose rituals are so often dreary and funereal. Religion would forever cease its warfare against science and remove its "no trespass" signs from the roads of intellectual inquiry into the mysteries of mind and spirit.[24]

If this is God, then those attributing to God authoritarian, sadistic, and murderous qualities that justified heresy hunts, terror, inquisitions, and lethal crusades down through the years have, in fact, been guilty of blasphemy and idolatry.[25] But pointing to the vision of God shared by the likes of Soelle and Tillich hardly gets Christianity off the hook.

The Soul of Christ

In the last four decades of the 20th century, radical Catholic theologian Leonardo Boff emphasized, "Christ did not begin by preaching himself but the kingdom of God," a new tomorrow "when all human alienation and all evil, be it physical or moral, would be overcome. ... The kingdom of God is not to be another world but is the old world transformed into a new one."[26] And it is a vision of the kingdom of God to which Pope John XXIII gave the most eloquent expression in the 1963 encyclical *Pacem in Terris*:

Man has the right to live. He has the right to bodily integrity and to the means necessary for the proper development of life, particularly food, clothing, shelter, medical care, rest, and finally, the necessary social services. ...

Moreover, man has a natural right to be respected. He has a right to his good name. He has a right to freedom in investigating the truth, and — within the limits of the moral order and the common good — to freedom of speech and publication, and to freedom to pursue whatever profession he may choose. He has the right, also, to be accurately informed about public events.

In the economic sphere, it is evident that a man has the inherent right not only to be given the opportunity to work, but also to be allowed the exercise of personal initiative in the work he does.... The worker is likewise entitled to a wage that is determined in accordance with the precepts of justice. This needs stressing. The amount a worker receives must be sufficient, in proportion to available funds, to allow him and his family a standard of living consistent with human dignity ...

The right to live involves the duty to preserve one's life; the right to a decent standard of living, the duty to live in a becoming fashion; the right to be free to seek out the truth, the duty to devote oneself to an ever deeper and wider search for it. ...

Since men are social by nature, they must live together and consult each other's interests. That men should recognize and perform their respective rights and duties is imperative to a well ordered community. ...

Human society, as we here picture it, demands that men be guided by justice, respect the rights of others and do their duty. It demands, too, that they be animated by such love as will make them feel the needs of others as their own, and induce them to share their goods with others, and to strive in the world to make all men alike heirs to the noblest of intellectual and spiritual values. Nor is this enough, for human society thrives on freedom, namely, on the use of means that are consistent with the dignity of individual members, who, being endowed with reason, assume responsibility for their own actions.[27]

While many may view this as a fair approximation of the ideal society envisioned by Jesus (and Marx), there are sharp controversies over whether this really is consistent with the actual teachings of Jesus. In his classic *The Quest of the Historical Jesus* (1906), Albert Schweitzer argued that "the Jesus of Nazareth who came forward publicly as the messiah, who preached the ethic of the

Kingdom of God, who founded the Kingdom of Heaven upon earth, and died to give his work its final consecration, never had any existence." Some historical commentators (including Schweitzer) insist that "Jesus as a concrete historical personality remains a stranger to our time" and suggest that the actual Jesus was a fanatical Jewish fundamentalist, expecting the immanent end of the world through the intervention of God, and having little in common — religiously or otherwise — with Pope John XXIII or anyone else in the modern world.[28]

Yet Leonardo Boff, in seeking to reconcile Church and Jesus, speaks for many in sharply questioning whether "a rupture between the historical Jesus and the Christ of faith [can] be sustained." John Dominic Crossan has added that "each Christian generation must write its gospels anew, must first reconstruct its historical Jesus with the fullest integrity and then say and live what that reconstruction means for present life in this world." In fact, there are indications in some of the innovative research in recent decades that the actual views advanced by Jesus and the earliest Christians may have more in common with those expressed by Tillich or Soelle than with those of the Inquisition, the Crusades, and any champions of Divine or secular violence and authoritarianism among present-day fundamentalists of whatever specific denomination.[29]

The key to the riddle of what Jesus thought may be the fact that he was a Jew. "It was the Torah and the prophets that Jesus himself expounded, preached about," as Abraham Joshua Heschel pointed out, which meant that — because "the place and power of the Hebrew Bible is so important," for Jesus (and for Christians being true to him), "God is Judge and Creator, and not only Revealer and Redeemer." Geza Vermes suggests that the interpretation of "the kingdom of God" most relevant to Jesus the Jew might be one in which "a pure and sanctified Israel was to draw the Gentiles to God. The manifestation of God's sovereignty over his own was to serve as a magnet to the rest." Irving Zeitlin insists that "Jesus envisaged an immanent, divine intervention in the world, a dramatic world-renewing judgment," hoping that "his own words and deeds of healing would hasten its realization," and that the coming of God's kingdom on earth would overcome "poverty, illness, sin, wickedness and oppression."[30]

Alan F. Sigal writes that Jesus "lived among people who looked to Scripture to understand how God would vindicate the downtrodden righteous," that "he was the chief inspiration in a religious movement against oppression, the likes of which we can sometimes see today among oppressed groups wherever a traditional worldview is being deeply challenged by a different and usually oppressive religious, political, or economic system" — that, in short, "Jesus lived and died as a Jew for his Judaism, and some of his Jewish convictions evidently impressed Rome and possibly some of the Judean ruling class as politically dangerous." The implications of this have been stressed by many — for example, the noted black theologian Howard Thurman, writing on the eve of the rise of the modern civil rights movement:

> The basic fact is that Christianity as it was born in the mind of this Jewish teacher and thinker appears as a technique of survival for the oppressed. That it became, through the intervening years, a religion of the powerful and the dominant, used sometimes as an instrument of oppression, must not tempt us into believing that it was thus in the mind and life of Jesus. "In him was life; and the life was the light of men." Wherever his spirit appears, the oppressed gather fresh courage; for he announced the good news that fear, hypocrisy, and hatred, the three hounds of hell that track the trail of the disinherited, need have no dominion over them.[31]

Of course, it was only after the death of Jesus that members of the early Christian movement — most notably Paul — consistently sought to reach out beyond the Jewish community. "Paul's dream of a united mankind in which tribal and creedal differences would finally be obliterated was consistent with a compelling strain in Jewish thought that has persisted from the days of the prophets to our own time," comments Richard Rubenstein. "Nowhere is Paul more prototypically Jewish than in his strenuous pursuit of this universalist vision."[32]

The implications of this were explosive. Walter Rauschenbusch, writing a Social Gospel classic in 1907, has not been the only one to insist that "there was a revolutionary consciousness in Jesus," although he adds that "Jesus was not a social reformer of the modern type .... He saw the evil in the life of men and their sufferings, but he approached these facts purely from the moral, and not from the economic point of view. He wanted men to live a right life in common, and only in so far as the social questions are moral questions did he deal with them as they confronted him." Nonetheless, "Jesus knew that he had come to kindle a fire on earth." Rauschenbusch adds that "this revolutionary note runs even through the Beatitudes," pointing out: "Now the poor and the hungry and sad were to be satisfied and comforted; the meek who had been shouldered aside by the ruthless would get their chance to inherit the earth," and — openly challenging the authority of religious and secular power structures — he manifested "a revolutionary consciousness emancipated from reverence for things as they are." The fact that "he bore within him the germs of a new social and political order" comes through in the story of the Gospels:

> Jesus was not a child of this world. He did not revere the men it called great; he did not accept its customs and social usages as final; his moral conceptions did not run along the grooves marked out by it. He nourished within his soul the ideal of a common life so radically different from the present that it involved a reversal of values, a revolutionary displacement of existing relations. This ideal was not merely a beautiful dream to solace his soul. He lived it out in his own daily life. He urged

others to live that way. He held that it was the only true life, and that the ordinary way was misery and folly. He dared believe it would triumph. When he saw that the people were turning from him, and that his nation had chosen the evil way and was drifting toward the rocks that would destroy it, unutterable sadness filled his soul, but he never abandoned his faith in the final triumph of the kingdom of God for which he had lived. For the present, the cross; but beyond the cross, the kingdom of God. If he was not to achieve it now, he would return and do it then.[33]

The revolutionary implications reverberate generation after generation. "Christianity is essentially a theology of liberation," according to James H. Cone, writing from Union Theological Seminary more than half a century after Rauschenbusch. "The function of theology is that of analyzing the meaning of that liberation for the oppressed community so that they can know that their struggle for political, social, and economic justice is consistent with the gospel of Jesus Christ." Insisting on *A Black Theology of Liberation*, he concluded: "Any message that is not related to the liberation of the poor in the society is not Christ's message. Any theology that is indifferent to the theme of liberation is not Christian theology."[34]

A Revolutionary Movement?

Simply pointing to a positive vision of Jesus hardly settles the matter of Christianity's meaning. Some critics of Christianity (and of other religions) take a "by their fruits you shall know them" approach — arguing that negative aspects of institutions and practices that have been associated with a religion stand as a proof that the religion was flawed at its very inception. This has a "commonsense" appeal, but reality is not so simple. A more serious approach is to examine the inception and early development of the religion in its specific historical, socio-economic, and cultural contexts, and to consider how it may have evolved, been altered, and even distorted as other contexts have come into being. Crimes committed in the name of Christ do not necessarily invalidate the lives or beliefs of the early Christians.

Karl Kautsky's description of the bureaucratic-authoritarian degeneration of the Christian movement over its first three centuries is worth considering. Kautsky — developing a Marxist critique of a powerful opponent of and rival to the socialist labor movement in which he was a prominent figure — is hardly an unbiased source. Nonetheless, his *Foundations of Christianity* provides an appreciation of the early Christian community that "originally contained proletarian elements exclusively, and was a proletarian organization." He adds that "the class hatred of the modern proletariat has hardly reached such fanatical forms as did that of the Christian." More than this, he praises "the communistic form of organization" described in The Acts of the Apostles: "And the multitude of them that believed were of one heart and of one soul:

neither said any of them that ought of the things which he possessed was his own; but they had all things in common .... Neither was there any among them that lacked. ..."35 Before considering Kautsky's account of the alleged degeneration of Christianity, however, we should consider whether there is validity to his claim that early Christianity represented some kind of revolutionary movement.

Aside from being somewhat dated (it was published in 1908), Kautsky's classic has been widely accused of "reductionism" — of reducing theological and religious complexities to presumed "deeper" conflicts involving economics and social classes. Far from being exclusively "proletarian," it can be demonstrated that the social composition of the early Christian movement reflected a cross-section of the various social strata existing in the larger society, with the apparent exception of both the wealthiest and the most destitute social layers. Indeed, some — scoffing at the notion of early Christianity as involving "unlearned evangelist and unwashed people" — argue along with Robert H. Smith that "Jesus himself was a skilled worker from the middle class" and that "the Galilean fishermen called by Jesus were independent owners of family businesses" — indeed, that the majority of early Christians "up to [the Roman emperor] Constantine ... were members of the middle class of antiquity. They were primarily free workmen, craftsmen, small businessmen, and independent farmers; and as time passed more and more members of the upper classes entered the church, although it was not until after the conversion of the emperor that the aristocracy converted in any numbers, which is easy enough to understand in a hierarchically organized society."36

Yet this is contested terrain. Significant numbers of Christian scholars — with Catholic theologian Hans Küng — assert that "at the beginning" the history of the Jesus movement was "the history of the lower classes: fishermen, peasants, craftsmen, little people who normally have no chronicler." He adds that "the first generation of Christians did not have political power and did not strive for positions in the religious and political establishment. They formed a small, weak marginal group of the society of their time, under attack and discredited." More than this, "Jesus himself, who came from an artisan family and spoke Aramaic, had addressed his message provocatively to the 'poor,' whom he blessed, along with those who wept, were hungry and downtrodden." Küng rejects the notion that Jesus preached the dispossession of the rich, or proletarian revolution, but he tells us that, nonetheless, "Jesus' opponents belonged above all to the narrow petty-bourgeois urban middle class ... and the thin layer of the upper class."37

Important contributions have been made to this topic by John Dominic Crossan. Drawing from work by sociologist Gerhard E. Lenski and political scientist John H. Kautsky (grandson of Karl) on the nature of peasant cultures and the social structure of the Roman Empire, Crossan has insisted that such (landless) artisans as carpenters — far from being a "middle-class" stratum between "lower-class" peasants and "upper-class" landowners and merchants — are actually of a class that is lower, not higher, than the peasant farmers of that time. The upper classes in such agrarian societies as those of the ancient Roman Empire included the ruler and the governing class (not more than 2 percent of the population), the retainer class (military and bureaucratic hierarchies — 5 percent), and the merchant class and priestly class (also small percentages). These upper classes — which appropriated at least 65 percent of the agricultural product of society — were separated by a vast gulf from the lower classes. These lower classes consisted of four groups: the peasant class, making up the vast majority of the population, an artisan class made up of dispossessed peasants and noninheriting sons (perhaps 7 percent), beneath which was "the unclean and degraded class" (porters, miners, prostitutes), and "the expendable class" (petty criminals, outlaws, beggars, underemployed itinerant workers, etc.). The early Christians, founded by Jesus and his followers, constituted "communities of resistance ... whose style of communal life was a calculated rejection and replacement of the entrepreneurial greed of Roman commercialization."[38]

Thanks to his own experience in the rural Ireland of his childhood, Crossan is better able than Kautsky or Rauschenbusch to imagine the specifics of the revolutionary agitator's interaction with his audience in Galilee. "He is watched by the cold, hard eyes of peasants living long enough at subsistence level to know exactly where the line is drawn between poverty and destitution," Crossan envisions. "He looks like a beggar, yet his eyes lack the proper cringe, his voice the proper whine, his walk the proper shuffle." With magic and parables, healing and shared meals, he and his fellow agitators bring an utterly subversive message:

> That ecstatic vision and social program sought to rebuild a society upward from its grass roots but on principles of religious and economic egalitarianism, with free healing brought directly to the peasant homes and free sharing of whatever they had in return. The deliberate conjunction of magic and meal, miracle and table, free compassion and open commensality, was a challenge launched not just at Judaism's strictest purity regulations, or even at the Mediterranean's patriarchal combination of honor and shame, patronage and clientage, but at civilization's eternal inclinations. It did not invite a political revolution but envisaged a social one at the imagination's most dangerous depths. No importance was given to distinctions of gentile and Jew, female and male, slave and free, poor and rich. Those distinctions were hardly even attacked in theory; they were simply ignored in practice.[39]

Eduardo Hoornaert — drawing from substantial scholarly and theological and religious labors in his native Belgium and his adopted Brazil — has likewise provided corroboration of the fundamental thrust in Kautsky's account of the early Christians. He is able to cite, of course, the point made by Paul to the Christians of Corinth: "Not many of you are wise, as men account wisdom; not many are influential; and surely not many are well-born. God chose those whom the world considers absurd to shame the wise; he singled out the weak of this world to shame the strong. He chose the world's lowborn and despised, those who count for nothing, to reduce to nothing those who were something; so that mankind can do no boasting before God."[40]

Indeed, Roman contemporaries made similar points. In his anti-Christian polemic *True Discourse*, Celsus explained that Jesus was a child of peasants, a mere carpenter, whose followers were from "the dregs of the people," people who lived "in cobblers' tents and fishermen's huts," and "such vulgar, dirty folk" as "shoemakers, stonemasons, and metal-workers" who — "glorying in their common execration" — were "imbued with prejudices against the rich." Hoornaert extends the list: "slaves, freedmen and their families, dancers, singers, prostitutes, women, and children. It was among these that the Christians were to be found." The "marginalized masses" — the urban poor and the illiterate peasantry, "the social classes lumped together under the name of 'am ha 'arets" — were the dominant social base of the Jesus movement. The domination, exploitation, and oppression of these masses by Roman imperialism and by their own ruling classes centered in Jerusalem made them seek salvation through "the Christian communities [that] acquired the implicit character of an organized social protest, a line of defense against the social atomization" generated by their exploiters and oppressors, communities in which they would share all they had, living in communion as brothers and sisters, sharing all that they had so that no one might be in need. This is the prelude to "the new heavens and new earth, the place where righteousness will be at home."[41]

The triumph of the marginalized masses is at the very heart of Christianity. There is another key element we must note. "Only when we place the Jesus stories about women into the overall story of Jesus and the movement in Palestine are we able to recognize their subversive character," Elisabeth Schlusser Fiorenza emphasizes. "In the discipleship of equals the 'role' of women is not peripheral or trivial, but at the center, and thus of utmost importance to the praxis of 'solidarity from below.'" Linking the past with the present, she adds: "The 'church of the poor' and the 'church of women' must be recovered at the same time, if 'solidarity from below' is to become a reality for the whole community of Jesus again."[42] Hoonaert offers this elaboration:

> We could draw up a lengthy catalogue of the symbols of marginality employed by the first Christians to express their experience.... In the evangelists' accounts, Jesus is not born in a "house," but in a stable, and among beasts, as he is on a journey. His birth is witnessed by the marginalized: shepherds and itinerant Oriental magi. When he is brought to the temple, only two marginalized persons — on the point of death — grasp the importance of his coming life. Unlike his contemporaries he does

not marry. He enrolls in none of the theological schools of Judaism. He prefers the company of fishers and other folk of humble social standing. His first public appearance is in the company of another individual who lives on the margin of Judaism, John the Baptizer. His concern is for the popular masses, the 'am ha 'arets rejected by the dominant society. He is not fond of the rich. He is tempted by power, but he resists. In the "beatitudes," those who live on the margin of society are called "blest." He replaces the law of reciprocity ("eye for eye, tooth for tooth" is society's law) with the law of charity ("turn the other cheek"). The master becomes a domestic slave and washes his disciples' feet. His journeys in the area of Jerusalem are only on the "margins" of the city. Neither the Upper Room, nor Calvary, nor Lazarus' house, nor the Garden of Gethsemane are within the holy city with its mighty temple. And when he finally does enter Jerusalem, he rides an ass and not some royal mount. The words inscribed on the head of his cross proclaim his royalty, but his real crown is a crown of thorns. Jesus' resurrection overthrows the laws of death, and the first to see him after the resurrection are not men, but women. Jesus proclaims an inversion of the most radical character: "The first shall be last, and the last first," he says. The symbols of the inversion of the "normal," of what is accepted by the norms of society, are to be found on every page of the gospel narratives.[43]

Triumphant Degeneration

Of course, Christianity became triumphant throughout the Roman Empire — eventually "official favor and even wealth could be hoped for where formerly persecutions … [had] tended to give pause to all but those impressed by the truth of the faith," historian Kenneth Scott Latrouette has put it. Why the triumph? As Rome was experiencing its decline, "the institution which Christianity possessed in the churches proved an attraction," with strong and inclusive organizations that cared for the poor and provided a system of mutual aid for all believers. According to Latrouette, Christianity benefited from a "combination of flexibility and uncompromising adherence to its basic convictions. … It availed itself of Greek philosophy to think through its theology. It took over and adapted much Judaism. In its organization it fitted into the patterns of the Empire."[44]

The organization question was of special interest to Kautsky: "Jesus was not merely a rebel, he was also the representative and champion, perhaps the founder, of an organization that survived him and kept growing stronger and more powerful." According to Kautsky, "it was not belief in the resurrection of him who was crucified that created the Christian community and lent it strength, but the converse: the vitality of the community created the belief in the continued life of their Messiah." The early and growing networks of Christian communities — animated by a radical egalitarianism and a significant subculture of shared meals, mutual aid, and support to members of the persecuted communities (the sick, those who were jailed, widows and orphans, etc.) — soon generated a division of labor. "The apostles were therefore relieved from acting as waiters in the people's house, something they must previously have done along with the propaganda work, and that became onerous as the community grew." With the passage of time and the growth of the movement, "there was gradually formed a community bureaucracy headed by the bishop, and it became increasingly independent and powerful. ... The apostles were pushed into the background by the prophets in the second century. Both, however, apostles as well as prophets, could often clash with the bishop, who would not hesitate to make his financial and moral power felt."[45]

Kautsky's description of the triumphant degeneration of Christianity as a radical social movement has the ring of authenticity, not least because this described aspects of a process he was observing first-hand (and resisting without success) in the bureaucratizing and deradicalizing socialist movement of the early 20th century (not to mention the Communism-turned-despotism of later years).

From the camp of critical Catholicism, Eduardo Hoornaert identifies similar tendencies. "The third century ushered in ever clearer indications of an important change of mentality in the Christian communities," he comments. "The theology of marginality, always under assault at the hands of the elite, was gradually relegated to secondary status." This coincided with a transition from the Christian communities' being based on a communion of goods to increasingly hierarchical institutions overseeing resources (utilized, to be sure, for the benefit of the needy) representing considerable wealth and power. Such influential church figures as "Clement of Alexandria, with his easy urbanity in the milieus of the Alexandrine bourgeoisie and his open door for the rich to enter the church without major difficulties of conscience," helped to alter the culture of the church — pushing toward securing church institutions from radical pressures. Increasingly, the church as "shared power, at the service of the lowly, and exercised in community" gave way to "the bureaucratization of popular religion at the hands of an organizing (and profiting) elite."[46]

"Sober, business-like practical men," the bishops were increasingly inclined to foster an "opportunistic revisionism in the Christian community" to "tone down the doctrines of the community in a way that would make it pleasanter for wealthy people to remain within it," according to Kautsky. With the further passage of time, "the bishop became the center both of the economic and propaganda work of the community," and "there now grew up an official doctrine, recognized and propagated by the bureaucracy of the community; views that differed from it were put down by all the means at their disposal." The growth of an enormous apparatus as well as growing economic inequality among the burgeoning membership fostered not only more rigid orthodoxy, but more restrictive practices. "Soon nobody dared to speak in the community assembly, the church, without previous permission from the bishop; that is, nobody outside the community bureaucracy directed by the bishop, the clergy, which set itself more and more apart from the mass of the fellows, the laity, and above them." As the Catholic Church crystallized, it became increasingly centralized, hierarchical, and authoritarian.[47]

Subsequent developments were — in hindsight — not surprising:

> So long as the church was a democratic organization, it was completely opposed to the essence of the imperial despotism in the Roman Empire; but the Episcopal bureaucracy, absolutely ruling and exploiting the people, was quite useful for imperial despotism. It could not be ignored; the emperor had to come to terms with it, because otherwise it threatened to grow too strong for him.
>
> The clergy had become a force which every ruler of the empire had to reckon with. In the civil wars at the beginning of the third century the victor was Constantine, the candidate to the throne who had allied himself with the clergy.
>
> The bishops were now the lords who along with the emperors ruled the Empire. ... The victorious Christian community was in every respect the exact opposite of that community that had been founded three centuries before by poor fishermen and peasants of Galilee and proletarians of Jerusalem. The crucified messiah became the firmest support of that decadent and infamous society which the messianic community had expected him to destroy down to the ground. ...
>
> When the Church became the State Church, an instrument of despotism and exploitation, on a scale of wealth and power that history has never yet known, the end of all its communistic tendencies seemed to have arrived.[48]

"It should be obvious that in this victory of Christianity was also something of a defeat," writes Latrouette. "The victory had been accompanied by compromise, compromise with the world which had crucified Jesus." Elisabeth Schlusser Fiorenza indicates the process of deradicalization, beginning well before the compromise with the Roman Empire, also seeking to return women to their subordinate place (although never with compete success).[49]

Hoornaet tells us about Eusebius, Bishop of Caesarea in Palestine, who — with support from Emperor Constantine — wrote a monumental *Ecclesiastical History* that helped to codify the early doctrines of the Roman Catholic Church. While an impressive contribution in many ways, it projects the Roman Emperor Constantine as "a liberator, a kind of new Moses." It presents "an 'imperial theology,' a theology of empire." Eusebius "abandons the tradition of Law, the prophets, and the liberation of the lowly and marginalized, and replaces it with the tools of recollection precisely of an imperial church that sees in the emperor the successor of Moses and David." The enemies are various religious competitors and heretics, "and not the structures of the empire, not the power of the rich who exploit the peasantry through heavy tribute and the urban slave population through forced labor." The church is identified "with one of its parts, merely: its organizers," that is, the leaders and hierarchy, with nothing about the "organized" except in the accounts of some of the martyrs. "The memory of the hopes and struggles of a Christian people striving to resolve urgent problems of survival, health, or basic human rights finds no room in the *Ecclesiastical History* of Eusebius of Caesarea."[50]

Catholic historians sometimes describe the triumph while denying the degeneration. While acknowledging that this "alliance with the state" meant "the Church would never be the same again — for better or worse," Thomas Bokenkotter emphasizes that the triumph was due to "the simple force of the Church's incomparable organization with all its ramifications," but also due to the fact that, "in a time of extreme social decay, it provided a refuge for the oppressed and acted as an agent of social justice." Bokenkotter goes on to assert: "There is no better illustration of the perennial vitality of the papacy than its behavior in the crisis engendered by the fall of Rome. Confronted by the collapse of the imperial administration in the West, the disintegration of the Roman social order, and its attendant chronic insecurity, the Popes refused to despair." The Church's new mission — "a labor of centuries" — was now "to convert the barbarians and incorporate them into a peaceful Christian society." He concludes: "Slowly their vision of the future began to take shape, and out of the wreckage of the Roman Empire in the West a new social order came into being: Christendom." By the 12th century, the power of the popes was consolidated in Church and society throughout Western Europe, becoming "one of the grandest, most integrated, and best-developed systems that has ever been devised for the conduct of human life." Bokenketter tells us: "the popes became the busiest men in Europe; their interventions reached down into the lowest strata of society."[51]

There is truth to this. Yet this is precisely the period, we should recall, in which (according to Simone Weil) the Church became a "totalitarian" force. This involved the Albigensian heresy arising in the 12th and 13th centuries, described by Homer W. Smith as "an ascetic cult which sought to purge the church of sacerdotalism, simony and superstition." Its growing number of followers "abstained from eating flesh or killing animals, ...wished to read the Bible for themselves, ... condemned tithes, ... opposed prayers for the dead, ... preached peace and nonresistance, practiced ordination but refused to take an oath and used a system of sacraments technically different from that of the church, and aimed, in principle at least, to return to the Pauline ideal of poverty and simplicity. ... Above all, the Albigenses denied the authority of the pope and the supernatural power of his priests." Simone Weil asserted that this widespread religious current developed in an area "where a high level of culture, tolerance, liberty, and spiritual life prevailed."[52]

Later scholars have challenged this general interpretation as an inaccurate idealization. The Albigenses are more commonly known as Cathars. (The first name refers to the Albi region in southern France, and "Cathar" means pure.) They denied that "an omnipotent and eternal God could have been responsible for the material world; for them this was the work of an evil creator," notes historian Malcolm Barber. Making a sharp distinction between the evil material world and the goodness of the spiritual world, they established an alternate Cathar Church, which stood in "total opposition to the Catholic Church, which was viewed by the Cathars as a false and fraudulent organization which had prostituted itself for power and ill-gotten wealth." In fact, the Catholic Church was unusually corrupt in this region. (This helps explain why it was precisely here that the reforming Dominican and Franciscan orders would arise.) In addition to southern France, the Cathars were strongest in northern Italy and the north of Spain. Latrouette adds that "their views were by no means uniform."[53]

Whatever the specifics of the heresy, it was seen as utterly incompatible with the Catholic faith, and it was destroyed by many years of denunciation and conflict topped by two decades of religious and military crusading, which included slaughtering an estimated one million of its adherents. At one point, when the Cathar region was invaded by powerful and pitiless Catholic armies, there was a moment of indecision — it was not clear how to distinguish between Catholics living in the region and Cathars who, to save themselves, were pretending to be Catholic. The decision: "Kill them all, for God knows his own." This was only the beginning. "The crusade against the Albigenses was so well received that violent repression thereafter became the established policy of the Church," Smith recounts. The Inquisition was established, unleashing terror, heresy hunts, rigged trials, torture, and — down to the 18th century — millions of executions. There were also two centuries of the Great Crusades to "save" the Holy Land from its Islamic inhabitants, generating the worst crimes and waves of mass murder, destroying millions more innocent men, women, and children. Hundreds of thousands of people in each European country were also slaughtered in the name of stamping out witchcraft. There was wave after wave of lethal anti-Jewish pogroms. A series of religious wars between Catholics and Protestants — with persecutions and horrendous atrocities on both sides — killed millions more (though issues of wealth and power were generally blended with questions of religious authority).[54]

Similar developments can be found throughout history. When examining how the revolutionary socialism inspired by Marx and Lenin gave rise to the horrors of bureaucratic authoritarianism of Stalinism, one must examine the specific historical circumstances facing revolutionary Russia and the early Soviet Union (as we will seek to do particularly in Chapter 4). Such circumstances of history, more than some alleged "original sin" in Marxism (or Christianity), can help us understand the failure of Communism. If there is an "original sin," it may be in humanity itself — the sin of pride, of self-righteousness, of arrogance, that enables one to do violence to others — and also something that could be called "the sin of the world." These are matters to which we will return at the conclusion of this chapter.

Marxist Faith

One can still argue, however, that the heroes and heroines of the Bolshevik Revolution of 1917, who struggled with such passionate idealism and selflessness during the brutal and brutalizing Civil War years of 1918 to 1921, were poorly equipped to avoid certain disastrous mistakes. Even the best of them were not able to avoid losing their moral balance at certain moments during the desperate Red Terror. This generated precedents and preconditions that contributed to the later rise of what became known as Stalinism.

Some continue to find Lenin persuasive, in his 1917 classic *State and Revolution*, on the desirability and practicality of the libertarian-communist vision of Marx and Engels. However, there will always be immense and unexpected problems and difficulties facing those seeking to create the new society. It is all too easy in such circumstances to lose one's way, which validates considerations raised by Muste and Tillich, who point us toward the transcendent "vertical line" of religion. One might respond, however, that within the revolutionary Marxist tradition of the Russian Bolsheviks, it is possible to find something akin to this transcendent "vertical line."

Of course, there is a very strong tradition — among Marxists as well as anti-Marxists — of seeing militant atheism as being at the heart of Marxism. This has been a point of sharp controversy for many years. As independent Marxist V.F. Calverton stressed, "the history of Marxism has been the history of revolutionary advance, whereas the history of religion has been the history of reactionary retreat." Emphasizing the scientific quality of Marxism, he added: "The conflict between Marxism and religion ... is as irreconcilable as the conflict between science and religion." Reinhold Niebuhr insisted, to the contrary, that "religion per se cannot be called either reactionary or revolutionary because it is the primary and the ultimate act of faith by which life is endowed with meaning." He urged that it would be wrong "to destroy the religious qualities of Marxism. That would destroy its vigor. It must find a way, as all religions must, to learn that its myths are great truths which contain many little lies. It must learn not to insist on these little lies as part of the great truth." Sidney Hook, defending the integrity of Marxism, weighed in on the side of Calverton: "If there are any two attitudes which from a logical and historical point of view may legitimately be opposed to each other they are the attitudes of Marxism and religion."[55]

Among the foremost U.S. Marxists of the late 20th century, Paul Sweezy and Harry Magdoff have articulated a somewhat different notion:

Clearly Marx thought of religion not as an evil but as a necessary human reaction to oppression and misery. For him religion was a symptom of an unacceptable state of affairs, of a world that had to be changed. Whether or to what extent religion fulfills other deep-seated human needs are questions Marx never addressed. ... It is sufficient to recognize that Marx was in no sense an enemy of religion as such, and the same goes for those who can reasonably claim to be Marxists.[56]

Beyond this, there have been, in the revolutionary socialist movement, conscious and purposeful attempts to fashion a form of Marxist religion — perhaps the most notorious being the efforts of some in and around the Bolshevik party in the 1907–1912 period (Anatoly Lunacharsky, Maxim Gorky, and others) to formulate a "new religion of Man." *Mother* (1907), Gorky's novel inspired by the abortive 1905 revolution, contains substantial religious imagery. By the end of the novel the words of Palegea Nilovna, the impoverished mother of the recently arrested working-class hero, Pavel, says to one of her son's female comrades:

> Our children have gone forth into the world — that is how I see it — into the whole world, coming from every corner of it and moving towards a single goal. The purest in heart, the finest in mind are moving against evil and trampling falsehood under strong feet. ... They have gone forth to do away with human sorrow, to wipe misfortune off the face of the earth, to conquer ugliness — and conquer it they will! ... To unite the broken-hearted — and unite them they will! ...
>
> Our children are treading the path of truth and reason, bringing love to the hearts of men, showing them a new heaven and lighting up the earth with a new force — the unquenchable fire of the spirit. From its flames a new life is springing, born of our children's love for all mankind. Who can extinguish this love? Who? What force can destroy it? What force oppose it? The earth has given it birth, and life itself longs for its victory. Life itself! ...
>
> It is as if a new God has been born to man! Everything for all — all for everyone! That is how I see it. In very truth we are all comrades, all kindred spirits, all children of one mother, who is truth![57]

Lenin warmly embraced Gorky's novel. At the same time, along with most Russian Marxists, he uncompromisingly rejected the trend toward poetic-mystical "God-building" as being inconsistent with the frank materialism that permeates the Marxist approach. But he did not favor the persecution or forcible repression of religion, calling instead for the defense of oppressed religious minorities and for united fronts with genuine religious activists who struggled against tyranny and injustice. Lenin supported the separation of church and state, which put him at loggerheads with the dominant hierarchy of the Russian Orthodox Church, a central pillar of the oppressive tsarist order. Given its support for the counter-revolution after 1917, he and his comrades advanced policies brutally targeting that institution. Some in the new Communist regime extrapolated this into a more general anti-religious crusade. Most important for Lenin, however, was opposing any attempt to infuse into Marxism itself what he believed to be the muddying and disorienting outlook of religious mysticism.[58]

Yet Julius Hecker, a supporter of the Russian Revolution and Professor of Social Ethics at the Moscow Theological Seminary in the 1920s, concluded an interesting study of *Religion Under the Soviets* with the following words:

> Whether ultimately the Communist materialistic philosophy of life will triumph over the religious emotions and practices of the people will, in the final analysis, depend upon human nature itself. If the religious emotion is a real, integral, basic part of human nature which cannot be supplanted by science, art, and social activities untiringly developed by Communists, if religion is a spirit of universal reverence and communion with God (known or unknown) then there will be religion in the U.S.S.R. If there is no living God in the universe and religion is a self-delusion, then this delusion will be exposed in the fires of materialistic criticism; if, however, atheism is an error, the Communist philosophy will undergo a metamorphosis and either become a religion itself or narrow down to functions of politics and economics very much like the other political organizations of the world.[59]

Elements of religious thought can be found, often more explicitly stated, in much of the socialist tradition outside of the Soviet Union. "There is no antagonism between the Cross and socialism!" proclaimed Irish revolutionary James Larkin, who helped establish the American Communist Party while also contributing substantially to the labor and nationalist movements of his native Ireland. "A man can pray to Jesus the carpenter, and be a better socialist for it. Rightly understood, there is no conflict between the vision of Marx and the vision of Christ. I stand by the Cross and I stand by Karl Marx. Both *Capital* and the *Bible* are to me Holy Books."[60]

Coming from a radical Protestantism that was an essential ingredient of the early British Labor Party, founder Keir Hardie emphasized: "I first learned my socialism in the New Testament, where I still find my chief inspiration." A U.S. socialist of the same period, John Spargo, argued a point that many of his comrades in various countries accepted: "The Marxian theory of historical materialism deals only with observed forces and tendencies in social evolution. It has nothing to do with those ultimate problems which lie beyond the realms of science and belong peculiarly to the realm of philosophy and religion." He warned that "the Golden Rule of Jesus will be crushed by the rule of gold," as long as capitalism existed, concluding that "in a very real sense, therefore,

Socialism is the emancipator of religion."[61] The revolutionary socialist James Connolly (appealing particularly to Irish Catholic workers) wrote:

> The day has passed for patching up the capitalist system; it must go. And in the work of abolishing it, the Catholic and the Protestant, the Catholic and the Jew, the Catholic and the Freethinker, the Catholic and the Buddhist, the Catholic and the Mahometan [Muslim] will cooperate together, knowing no rivalry but the rivalry of endeavor towards an end beneficial to all.[62]

In fact, what Einstein has chosen to call "cosmic religious feeling" can be shown to be an important element in the outlook of a number of revolutionary Marxists who were in no way shy about proclaiming their atheism.

We find this in Lenin himself, who reflected on the fact that "nature is infinite, but it infinitely exists" independently of humanity (which is, of course, a part of nature) and independently of some supernatural force (which, on the other hand, flows from human imagination). He embraced Engels' view that "the individual thought of many billions of past, present and future ... human beings ... is ... able to know the world as it exists, if only mankind lasts long enough and insofar as no limits are imposed on its knowledge by its perceptive organs or the objects to be known." As Engels stressed, this "should make us extremely distrustful of our present knowledge, inasmuch as in all probability we are but little beyond the beginning of human history, and the generations which will put us right are likely to be far more numerous than those whose knowledge we — often enough with a considerable degree of contempt — are in a position to correct." Combined with this modesty imposed by a scientific sense of the infinite cosmos, however, is a passionate human-centered morality grounded in the determination, above all else, to eliminate human oppression: "Our morality is derived from the interests of the class struggle of the proletariat .... We say: Morality is what serves to destroy the old exploiting society and to unite all laboring people around the proletariat, which is creating a new communist society .... Morality serves to help human society rise to a higher level and get rid of the exploitation of labor."[63]

Examining the anticipated Communist future described in Lenin's 1917 classic *State and Revolution*, theologian Reinhold Niebuhr found "a significant secular vision of the 'Kingdom of God,' where even the highest form of equal justice is transcended in an uncoerced and perfect mutuality."[64]

If we look at the farewell letter of Adolf Joffe — a prominent Communist who committed suicide in 1927 to protest the bureaucratic-authoritarian degeneration of the USSR under the Stalin regime — we find the following:

> More than thirty years ago I embraced the philosophy that human life has meaning only to the degree that, and so long as, it is lived in the service of something infinite. For us humanity is infinite. The rest is finite,

and to work for the rest is therefore meaningless. Even if humanity too must have a purpose beyond itself, that purpose will appear in so remote a future that for us humanity may be considered as an absolute infinite. It is in this and only this that I have always seen the meaning of life.[65]

We find within revolutionary Marxism, then, an element that encompasses a sense of awe and wonder over the infinite and intricate universe, while at the same time giving meaning to the life of every individual human being — a meaning that involves a sense of community with others as well as a sense of how one's own passionate and creative impulses can be fulfilled in advancing a higher purpose. This "cosmic sense" and moral passion are also at the heart of the great world religions. To Lenin's consternation, his friend Maxim Gorky sometimes sought to magnify such things in his fictional works: "The People … had always in the past lifted individual men to power, who always betrayed and oppressed them. Only when they realized that all must rise to the heights, and when many men of good-will wove together thoughts of justice and equality, there emerged the living God, the gentle child of the People — Jesus Christ." Lenin and most other Bolsheviks rejected such terminology with irritation. Yet it could not be denied that Gorky gave poetic-mystical expression to the outlook and aspiration inherent in the Communist ideal: "When the People splintered into slaves and rulers, into bits and pieces, when it tore asunder its thoughts and will — God perished. But when the People again flow together as one, an irresistible strength will rise in it, and God will be resurrected."[66]

Nonetheless, Lenin and his comrades — in their determined efforts to advance human society to what the more religiously inclined might call "the Kingdom of God" — proved capable of contributing to the creation of a state of affairs that culminated in the opposite of what they intended. The approximation of a transcendent "vertical line" in their perspective proved no more of a barrier to this than was the case with the early Christians.

Sin and Redemption

In his most mature reflections, Walter Rauschenbusch offered a definition of sin as selfishness, elaborating that "in the higher forms of sin it assumes an aspect of a conflict between the selfish Ego and the common good of humanity; or, expressing it in religious terms, it becomes a conflict between self and God." Yet sin can assume a different form in those seeking to advance "the common good of humanity." During his most radical Christian-Marxist period in the 1930s, Reinhold Niebuhr commented: "The social problem is complicated rather than solved when finite men make a final effort to transcend their finiteness and set themselves up as unqualified arbiters over the issues of life." He added that "the same man who touches the fringes of the infinite in his moral life remains imbedded in finiteness, that he increases the evil in his life if he tries to overcome it without regard to his limitations." Pulling away from his earlier revolutionary hopes, he deepened this insight during the 1940s into a notion of sinfulness inherent in human beings, applicable to the powerful leaders and passionate militants of the early Church and of the early Communist movement. "Sin is occasioned precisely by the fact that man refuses to admit his 'creatureliness' and to acknowledge himself as merely a member of a total unity of life. He pretends to be more than he is." This was the sin of pride (manifest in pride of power, pride of knowledge, pride of virtue, pride of self-righteousness), which amounted, as Abraham Heschel observed, to the existence of "evil within good."[67]

Those claiming to speak for God and to be doing God's work (as well as those replacing the word "God" with the word "Humanity") have more than once shown that they are pretending — often in their own minds and hearts, often with lives and actions animated by a complete sincerity — to be more than they really are. Niebuhr's elaboration is apt:

> Man is insecure and involved in natural contingency; he seeks to overcome his insecurity by a will-to-power which overreaches the limits of human creatureliness. Man is ignorant and involved in the limitations of the finite mind; but he pretends that he is not limited. He assumes that he can gradually transcend finite limitations until his mind becomes identical with the universal mind. All his intellectual and cultural pursuits, therefore, become infected with the sin of pride. Man's pride and will-to-power disturb the harmony of creation.[68]

Sometimes very terrible things have resulted, particularly as those so afflicted have been seeking to establish the Kingdom of God. A despairing withdrawal from struggles to change the world has often seemed the best alternative (as was the case, to some extent, with Niebuhr and others who embraced his "neo-orthodox" theology).

Some thoughtful Christians have disagreed with such withdrawal. "If self-deceit is an incurable defect of the human mind and spirit, then the neo-orthodox theologians themselves are also subject to it," commented A. J. Muste. Withdrawal from the struggle for a better world is no less worthy of critical examination than a commitment to that struggle. "If the criticism has validity and point," Muste argued, "it is precisely because the possibility of rising above it exists and men ought, therefore, to accept and utilize the criticism." Emphasizing the centrality of redemptive love to the Christian message, he noted that "the abandonment of human 'pretension' to which Niebuhr summons us is the 'moment' in which we experience the transforming power of God and are born anew in his spirit." At the same time, in the face of a society and world marked by oppression and violence, "the individual *must* be able to believe in his own essential dignity and in his ability somehow to assert it." Despite the moral complexities and ambiguities emphasized by Niebuhr, "moments come that require a moral decision," which include acquiescing to a corrupt and oppressive status quo or struggling against it.[69]

The "sin of pride" cannot by itself explain the authoritarian degeneration nor the fiercely repressive and murderous policies that all too often became associated with Christianity. The "profane" social, economic, and political developments discussed by Karl Kautsky are decisive for understanding the degeneration — although the "sin of pride" has surely facilitated the process. The same can certainly be said when we reflect on the path "between Lenin's complete sincerity and Stalin's cynical statecraft."[70]

In addition to the individual "sin of pride," there is for many Christians a deeper sense of "original sin" that could be understood as *the cumulative effect of sins* (actions against people, the natural world, God) *over generations that get embedded or embodied in social customs and structures that we are all born into.* Catholic theologian Karl Rahner points out: "In order to arrive at a real understanding of original sin, we begin with the fact that the situation of our own freedom bears the stamp of the guilt of others in a way which cannot be eradicated." This is an inescapable part of the human condition: the life of each person has been nurtured within a complex of relationships and actions in which terrible violence has been done to many, many others historically and down to the present moment. Citing "a very banal example," Rahner notes that when someone buys a banana, he or she does not reflect on the fact that its price is based on "the pitiful lot of banana pickers, which in turn is co-determined by social injustice, exploitation, or centuries-old commercial policy," and that the person enjoying the banana "now participates in this situation of guilt to his [or her] own advantage." This must be multiplied many, many times over to approximate the violence, oppression, and inhumanity layered in the historical and existential "situation" to which Rahner alludes.[71]

The fact that such "original sin" encompasses all of humanity, in one way or another, logically means that even those human entities dedicated to transcending such historical and contemporary dynamics cannot be free from them. Indeed, we can see in the history both of Christianity and Communism the terrible replication, manifestation, and "justification" of such dynamics. We can also see, in both traditions, an elemental resistance, the never-ending effort to create something better, something that remains true to the sacred injunction of the Golden Rule. Religious and secular manifestations that are consistent with self-centered arrogance and fear are contested by powerful counter-trends consistent with the "cosmic feeling" identified by Einstein, connecting people with each other, with creativity and freedom and genuine community.

In applying Marxism's historical materialist analysis to the Christian tradition (within which we find some of Marxism's roots), we have demonstrated that the teachings of Jesus cannot be equated with the evils committed in his name. The overlapping *Kingdom of God* associated with Jesus and *vision of socialism* associated with Marx may or may not be realizable, but they are not inherently "totalitarian." The challenge for people of faith, whether of Christian or Marxist or other persuasion, is to face the evil within the good — inherent in all struggles worth waging, inherent in all of us — seeking to transcend that evil, time after time, while remaining deeply committed to the good fight.

In a Catholic Bible study group of Nicaraguan working people in the 1970s, the notion emerged that redemption comes through engagement with the kingdom of God:

REBECA   I think the kingdom is among us already, because the kingdom is love. When we have love, there's the kingdom ....

LAURGANO   The kingdom of God is inside you but you do have to make it come true. You can have love but you have to make that love come true with others: only then do you make the kingdom of God come true.

ALEJANDRO No matter how far a country has advanced in making love come true, it will never reach perfection. Then you can never say: there it is. You can always do something more ....

OLIVIA   ...In a country where there's justice, where there's respect for human rights and there's food and schools for everybody, there's the kingdom of love; and you can see it and notice it in a little community where we love each other and we all respect each other; it's already the kingdom of love, the kingdom of God ....

REBECA   The one who struggles for liberation is the one who has love, and that one will be taken to the kingdom of God and to the kingdom of love. The one who doesn't is the one who's locked up in selfishness and clinging to wealth: that one will be left behind ....[72]

3
Lenin — Who Cares?

Vladimir Ilyich Lenin died many years ago. Political scientist Alfred G. Meyer, in an anti-Leninist classic entitled *Leninism*, explained that "Leninism is a school within the Marxist movement that has manifested a degree of radicalism and unceasing activism matched only by that of Marx and Engels themselves." Writing in 1957, when the Communist Bloc seemed very much intact and formidable, he added: "Lenin's activity, however, seems much more dramatic and effective than that of the movement's founders, partly because of his great successes."[1]

Yet the success has turned to failure, for many bringing discredit not only to Leninism but to Marxism as such. As the new century opens, all that Lenin stood for and tried to accomplish — a working-class republic, a socialist society in which, presumably, "the free development of each would be the condition for the free development of all" — has been mockingly dismissed as "the road to nowhere."[2] The effort to overturn capitalism and usher in a new and better society led to a colossal failure, a bureaucratic tyranny that proved incapable, after much sound and fury, of even sustaining itself.

Why should one bother giving attention to this long-dead revolutionary?

Statues, Symbols, Poems

Monstrous statues of Lenin were constructed by a network of Communist dictatorships throughout Eastern Europe in the 1940s and 1950s. Lenin had a reputation back then as a successful revolutionary committed to the liberation of all the oppressed of the earth. This central founder of the Communist movement seemed a fitting secular god to symbolize the rule of Communist Parties claiming to represent the interests of the toiling masses. With the collapse of these dictatorships from 1989 through 1991, the statues were torn down, with considerable jubilation, it is reported, on the part of those who had experienced Communist Party rule as a form of oppression. Also jubilant were the boosters of global "free enterprise," who hated Lenin not because his image was utilized by bureaucratic tyrants, but because he represented a challenge to the inexhaustible appetites of the lions of capitalism. Some of the bizarre complexity of it all was captured by émigré poet Andrei Codrescu, visiting his native Romania as a U.S. journalist of sorts at the moment when Communist rule was being overturned. Childhood memories blended with the swirl of new realities:

> I often looked up at the brass statue of Lenin in front of the printing house and felt my insignificance. In January [1990] an enthusiastic crew worked for three days to pull Lenin off his pedestal. The crew originally hoped to bring him down in an hour. But like other bulky monuments of the ceremonial Communist past, he was more stubborn than originally thought. Three trucks carted him away to be stored for either an auction, a new lease on symbolism or — my favorite — the "dustbin of history." All through my school years things the Communists didn't like were always thrown into the "dustbin of history." Everything interesting and fun was there: Henry Ford, Winston Churchill, Leon Trotsky. Now Lenin joined them.[3]

At the very least, then, it may be worth looking at Lenin because he *is* interesting.

Of course, "interesting" does not necessarily mean "nice" — and there are many who agree with Stefan T. Possony, one of many biographers who disliked Lenin: "Self-righteous, rude, demanding, ruthless, despotic, formalistic, bureaucratic, disciplined, cunning, intolerant, stubborn, one-sided, suspicious, distant, asocial, cold-blooded, ambitious, purposive, vindictive, spiteful, a grudgeholder, a coward who was able to face danger only when he deemed it unavoidable — Lenin was a complete law unto himself and he was entirely serene about it." Here, certainly, is a magnificent symbol of all the evils of the 20th century. Yet another biographer who has shown more affection for capitalism than for Lenin, Robert Payne, explained: "Once Lenin had decided that all means were permissible to bring about the dictatorship of the proletariat, with himself ruling in the name of the proletariat, he had committed Russia to intolerable deprivations of human freedom." In the words of Possony, Lenin initiated "the great world struggle between freedom and totalitarianism," and Payne elaborated that "his power was naked power; his weapon was extermination; his aim the prolongation of his own dictatorship." Indeed, it has been argued that Lenin's example helped inspire (and is thus responsible for) not only Stalin and other Communist tyrants, but also such anti-Communist tyrants as Benito Mussolini and Adolf Hitler. Almost everything wicked can be laid at the doorstep of his mausoleum.[4]

So here's a reason for looking at Lenin — to determine the extent to which all this is true. If Lenin *is* responsible for such evil, it would help to explain much of the history that has shaped our own time.

Of course, there have been other opinions. The eloquent anarchist martyr Bartolomeo Vanzetti, halfway through an imprisonment in the United States that led to the electric chair, expressed strong feelings about Lenin upon hearing of his death in 1924. "Lenin has passed away," he wrote. "I am convinced that unintentionally he has ruined the Russian Revolution."[5]

The anarchist movement in Russia had made common cause with the revolutionary socialists (many of whom soon labeled themselves Communists), an alliance not only in the 1917 overthrow of the tyrannical monarchy but also in the second revolution of 1917 that replaced a pro-capitalist Provisional Government with a socialist republic of workers' and peasants' councils (soviets). Within a short period of time, however, the Communists following Lenin were in sharp conflict with most of the anarchists (and with the Left Socialist Revolutionaries who had also been their allies in 1917) over the appropriate path to the future society. Lenin's Communist regime, Vanzetti noted, "has imprisoned and killed many of my comrades."

A convergence with Possony and Payne is blocked by the anarchist's next comment, that Lenin "has suffered much and toiled heroically for what he believed to be the good and the truth, and I felt my eyes filled with tears in reading of his passing and his funeral." For good measure Vanzetti added another thought, not dissimilar in spirit, perhaps, with the irreverent attitude that seems second nature to the poet Codrescu: "And to the prostitute scribes of the capitalist system, who are twisting and falsifying facts and truths, and throwing the mud of their miserable souls on the fresh grave of my great adversary — I roar with a mute gesture all my disgust and contempt."

It might be worth knowing more about why Lenin stirred, at one and the same time, such negative and positive feelings in the heart of this social rebel. That might also give us some insights into the dynamics of our history and of our own time.

Throughout much of the 20th century, Lenin, in fact, symbolized the struggle for liberation throughout the world. Far from making individuals feel insignificant or frightened, Lenin was seen as a good friend of all who struggled for freedom. A young Vietnamese militant visiting Moscow at the time of Lenin's death lamented: "In his life he was our father, teacher, comrade, and adviser. Now," Ho Chi Minh concluded, "he is our guiding star that leads to social revolution. Lenin lives in our deeds — he is immortal."[6] As African-American poet Langston Hughes noted: "Lenin walks around the world./ Black, brown, and white receive him./ Language is no barrier./ The strangest tongues believe him." Greater complexity is captured in Chilean poet Pablo Neruda's lines:

> Lenin, your hands kept on working
> And your mind never knew any rest
> Until all across the horizon
> a radiant image arose
> like a statue covered with
> blood:

> Victory clad in tatters,
> A woman lovelier than sunshine
> all scarred, enveloped in smoke.
> Men from the furthermost countries
> looked up:
>
> Yes, it was she, undoubtedly,
> It was the Revolution.
> The Universe's old heart struck
> a new rhythm.[7]

In the sweeping vision of such poets — just as in the hearts and minds of thousands and millions of others in many lands — Lenin represented the notion that a better world, free from all exploitation and oppression, was a practical goal to be achieved through applying the revolutionary's tough-minded perspectives. It is certainly worth looking at Lenin to determine to what extent this might be true.

1917

Of course, it would be ahistorical to imagine that it was simply this particular personality — whether great or evil or some of each — who accomplished this immense overturn. Here, we can simply and safely rely on a recent synthesis of scholarship provided in Rex A. Wade's excellent study *The Russian Revolution, 1917*. The revolutionary triumph of Lenin's Bolsheviks cannot be understood apart from the rich, complex historical context that Wade sums up in this way:

> The Russian revolution of 1917 was a series of concurrent and overlapping revolutions: the popular revolt against the old regime; the workers' revolution against the hardships of the old industrial and social order; the revolt of the soldiers against the old system of military service and then against the war [i.e., World War I] itself; the peasants' revolution for land and for control of their own lives; the striving of middle class elements for civil rights and a constitutional parliamentary system; the revolution of the non-Russian nationalities for rights and self-determination; the revolt of most of the population against the war and its seemingly endless slaughter. People also struggled over differing cultural visions, over women's rights, between nationalities, for domination within ethnic or religious groups and among and within political parties, and for fulfillment of a multitude of aspirations large and small. These various revolutions and group struggles played out within the general context of political realignments and instability, growing social anarchy, economic collapse, and ongoing world war. They contributed to both the revolution's vitality and the sense of chaos that so often

overwhelmed people in 1917. The revolution of 1917 propelled Russia with blinding speed through liberal, moderate socialist and then radical socialist phases, at the end bringing to power the extreme left wing of Russian, even European, politics. An equally sweeping social revolution accompanied the rapid political movement. And all this occurred within a remarkably compressed time period — less than a year.[8]

According to Wade, "central to the history of the revolution, key players in all stages of its development, were the urban, especially industrial workers .... The revolution began as a demonstration of industrial workers and they never relinquished their leading role in both political and social revolution in 1917. They represented a potent force for further revolutionary upheaval if their aspirations were not met — as they almost certainly would not be, at least not in full." Wade tells us that "while their own economic, working, and personal conditions were their most pressing concern, broader political issues also animated the workers." A thick organizational network — involving trade unions, factory committees, local and district soviets, cultural and self-help groups of various kinds, workers' militia groups, etc. — all were means through which workers sought "to use their newfound freedom and power to obtain a better life for themselves and their families." He notes that these and other developments "had the effect not only of solidifying working-class identity, but also of broadening the circle of those who identified themselves as workers." Previously unorganized elements outside of the factories — cab drivers, laundry workers, bath house workers, restaurant waiters, bakers, barbers, retail clerks, lower-level white collar workers such as office clerks and elementary school teachers — all now identified themselves as part of the working class, organized unions, and sent representatives to the soviets.[9]

After the fall of the Tsar's autocratic regime, when a Provisional Government of traditional politicians coexisted uneasily with revolutionary-democratic councils (soviets), the failure of the new *status quo* increasingly generated mass discontent that resulted in the working class's shifting in an ever more radical direction. "Although historical attention has, for reasons having to do with later developments, focused primarily on the Bolsheviks, the history of 1917 cannot be understood without recognizing the importance of the emergence of a radical left bloc," Wade insists. Along with Lenin's Bolsheviks there were "Left SRs [Social-Revolutionaries], Menshevik-Internationalists, anarchists, and others" who forged throughout Russia "broad leftist alliances [with] influence in or even control of local soviets and institutions earlier than in Petrograd."[10]

It was Lenin's Bolsheviks, however, who became the undisputed keystone of the 1917 movement of the revolutionary working class. The Bolsheviks had once been a faction ("majority-ites") of the Russian Social Democratic Labor Party — more intransigent in their revolutionary orientation than their Menshevik ("minority-ite") comrades. In 1912, they split away to form their own dynamic party. By 1917, their political program was increasingly in harmony with mass disappointment over the nonrevolutionary policies of the Provisional Government. "Their politics of sweeping change, of a revolutionary restructuring of society, aligned them with popular aspirations as the population turned toward more radical solutions to the mounting problems of Russia," Wade tells us. "Lenin and the Bolsheviks became the most vigorous advocates of 'All Power to the Soviets,' a slogan of great popularity among the masses, signifying not only radical social and economic reform, but a new, if ill-defined, political system." Even when Lenin was forced into hiding during the tumultuous months leading up to the October/November revolution, "Lenin, 'Leninists,' and 'Leninism' were major commodities in the political life of July–October, the symbol of radical change both for those opposed and for those in favor of it."[11]

Raphael Abramovitch, one of the leading Mensheviks, later lamented that from August, when the attempted right-wing coup of General Kornilov had been foiled, "great masses were drawn irresistibly toward Bolshevism. In the army [made up overwhelmingly of peasants] and among the workers, the Bolsheviks captured one important position after another in September and, particularly, in October," when they won control of the soviets and initiated the soviet seizure of power. Abramovitch contended that "chance and contingency … had been largely responsible for the Bolshevik victory."[12] But it was the convergence of the various elements Rex Wade has identified and described — a deep and widespread political and social crisis, a dynamic and radicalizing working class, a diverse revolutionary vanguard layer, and a cohesive revolutionary organization well-rooted in this class and vanguard layer — that culminated in the Bolshevik revolution of 1917.

A Personality in Historical Context

Louise Bryant confessed, in her 1918 work *Six Red Months in Russia,* that "if a reporter were to interview two representative Russians, Lenin and Kerensky, he might easily throw all the weight of his argument in favor of Kerensky because he *liked* him best." Bryant obviously felt more at ease with Kerensky, the moderate-socialist lawyer who briefly headed the 1917 Provisional Government before Lenin's Bolsheviks overthrew it. Kerensky "has 'personality plus,' as Edna Ferber would say; one cannot help but be charmed by his wit and his friendliness; he is a lawyer and a politician. On the other hand, Lenin is sheer intellect — he is absorbed, cold, unattractive, impatient at interruption." And yet Bryant's pragmatic sensibilities weighed more heavily than her personal comfort level as she noted, "Here are the facts: Kerensky is spokesman for the defunct Provisional Government; he is discredited; he has no power in Russia …. Lenin has tremendous power; he is backed by the soviets."[13]

Not all who had contact with Lenin reacted in the same way. A somewhat different image comes through in the account of sculptor Claire Sheridan (Winston Churchill's radical cousin) as she observed Lenin in animated conversation with a comrade: "Never did I see anyone make so many faces. Lenin laughed and frowned, and looked thoughtful, sad, and humorous all in turn." Seventeen years later, his widow Nadezhda Krupskaya offered similar recollections: "His voice was expressive, not monotonous .... He always spoke with animation, whether it was a public speech or a private conversation .... The need to put a thing into words, to clarify it, was always very strong in him .... He liked listening to people recounting things. He listened very seriously, attentively, eagerly .... Generally he was very emotional. He took things to heart .... The usual, predominant mood was tense concentration .... He was gay and noisy .... He had good control over himself .... His passionate nature was obvious when he spoke, even if he was outwardly calm .... A desire to delve deep into a question, to examine it scientifically was very pronounced.... He always had what I would call an organic connection with life.... Had a capacity for colossal concentration .... He was a fighter...."[14]

"Lenin always liked a fight," affirmed Orlando Figes in his eloquent and valuable narrative *A People's Tragedy*. "It was as if the whole of his life had been a preparation for the struggle that awaited him in 1917." There is truth in this, and yet it is not entirely true. It is certainly the case, as Figes recounts, that the series of political struggles Lenin engaged in from the 1890s to 1916 were "defining moments in his life" — and in the development of the Bolshevik organization capable of leading the 1917 revolution: "the campaign against the Populists, the campaign against the Economists, the campaign for the organization of the party along centralist lines, the campaign for the boycott of the Duma, the campaign against the Menshevik 'liquidators,' the campaign against Bogdanov and Mach, the campaign against the war." There is ample documentation, however, that many of these fights were not struggles that Lenin "liked" to engage in. He sometimes found them to be extremely troubling, difficult, depressing, stressful — particularly when they resulted in ruptures with comrades and the loss of valued friends.[15]

Figes and many others project an image of Lenin that has the aesthetic purpose of showing a correspondence between the inhumanity of the Revolution and the inhumanity of the revolutionary leader. But this does not do justice to the complexity (particularly certain elements of tragedy) to be found in both Lenin and the Revolution.

Consider the use that is sometimes made of an anecdote in Maxim Gorky's recollections. Lenin, after they had listened to a performance of Beethoven's Appassionata Sonata, told him: "I can't listen to music too often. It makes me want to say kind stupid things, and pat the heads of people. But now you have to beat them on the head, beat them without mercy." Even those who don't attribute to Lenin the desire to physically assault people (which he never did) instead of engaging in fierce polemics with political opponents (which he often did), have utilized this anecdote to buttress sweeping but ill-considered assertions. Lenin was so "downright obsessive" about avoiding distractions from politics that he "denied himself chess, Beethoven and the lovely Inessa," as Lenin biographer Robert Service puts it (who almost in the same breath petulantly denounces him as a "spoilt child"). The revolutionary leader "had no place for sentiment in his life," according to Figes. Indeed, Figes insists that "as a private man there was nothing much to Lenin: he gave himself entirely to politics. There was no 'private Lenin' behind the politician."[16]

This curtailment of Lenin's human qualities was not Lenin's doing — it is the "doing" of those who describe him in this way. Those who actually knew him could not honestly agree. According to so sharp a political opponent as the prominent Menshevik Raphael Abramovitch, who knew him personally and spent time visiting with him and his companion Nadezhda Krupskaya in their 1916 Swiss exile, "it is difficult to conceive of a simpler, kinder and more unpretentious person than Lenin at home." Another Menshevik leader, Julius Martov, concurred that there were not "any signs of personal pride in Lenin's character," that he sought, "when in the company of others, an opportunity to acquire knowledge rather than show off his own." Writing in 1924, Isaac Don Levine — a Russian-born U.S. journalist who was uncompromisingly critical of Lenin but quite familiar with the details of his life — commented that the Communist leader "derived genuine pleasure from associating with children and entertaining them," and that he had an "effeminate weakness for cats, which he liked to cuddle and play with." The knowledgeable Levine reported that other enthusiasms included bicycling, amateur photography, chess, skating, swimming, hunting — though Lenin was sometimes not inclined to actually shoot the animals he hunted ("well, he was so beautiful, you know," he said of a fox whose life he refused to take). According to one acquaintance, British diplomat Robert Bruce Lockhart, he was "the father of modern 'hiking' ... a passionate lover of outdoor life." And, of course, Lenin loved music. "During his life in Switzerland Lenin immensely enjoyed the home concerts that the political emigrants improvised among themselves," the journalist reported. "When a player or singer was really gifted, Lenin would throw his head back on the sofa, lock his knees into his arms, and listen with an interest so absorbing that it seemed as if he were experiencing something very deep and mysterious." This corresponds closely with a later memoir by one of Lenin's younger comrades and one-time secretary Lydia Fotieva, who recalled that "of the piano pieces I played, Vladimir Ilyich's favorite was Beethoven's Pathetique Sonata," and that he encouraged her to return to musical studies. "All his life," Lenin's brother Dmitry insisted, "Vladimir Ilyich loved music and always appreciated its finer points," although his sister Maria recounted: "In emigration he kept away from operas and concerts. Music had a strong effect on his nerves, and when these were frayed, which happened quite often during the stress and strain of factional struggle and emigrant life, sometimes he could hardly bear it."[17]

All of these elements cannot be separated from the qualities emphasized by the shrewd anti-Communist Levine — Lenin was a personality "concise in speech, energetic in action, and matter-of-fact," with an unshakable faith in Marxism, although "extraordinarily agile and pliant as to methods," with an "erudition" that could be termed "vast." His "capacity to back up his contentions [was] brilliant." While he had an ability "to readily acknowledge tactical mistakes and defeats," he was never willing to consider "the possible invalidity of his great idea" (i.e., revolutionary Marxism). Levine concluded: "The extraordinary phenomenon about Lenin is that he combined this unshakeable, almost fanatic, faith with a total absence of personal ambition, arrogance or pride. Unselfish and irreproachable in his character, of a retiring disposition, almost ascetic in his habits, extremely modest and gentle in his direct contact with people, although peremptory and derisive in his treatment of political enemies, Lenin could be daring and provocative in his policies."[18]

But we must move beyond personality traits to comprehend how Lenin came to represent the "tremendous power" mentioned by Louise Bryant. Bryant's friend and colleague Bessie Beatty, in her own 1918 account *The Red Heart of Russia*, provides a vivid portrait of Lenin speaking at a contentious session of the Central Executive Committee of the All-Russian Soviet. This council contained a variety of working-class parties, among which Lenin's group only three months previously became the dominant force — and quickly moved forward to engineer the overthrow of Kerensky's Provisional Government under the banner of "all power to the soviets." He was now defending the decision to dissolve the recently elected Constituent Assembly, which had proved to be a more conservative body than the soviets. Beatty offers a vibrantly described moment of history worth quoting at length. One of the members of the body, upon Lenin's arrival, angrily jeered: "Long live the dictator!" This set off a commotion of insults and counter-insults among the delegates.

> When the chairman had calmed them, Lenin took his place. He stood quietly for a moment, surveying his audience, his hands in his pockets with an appraising expression in his brown eyes. He knew what was expected of him. He must win the wavering members of his own flock. He must reach out to the larger audience spread over the vast areas of Russia. He must speak so that he would be heard beyond the confines of his country, in that world whose attention was focused for the time on this group of strange new actors in the international drama. Lenin began quietly tracing the historical developments of the Soviet as an institution. He made a critical analysis of the workings of various parliaments, declaring that they had become merely a sparring-place for the verbal contests of socialists.

"In Russia," he said, "the workers have developed organizations, which give them power to execute their aspirations. You are told that we ask you to jump a hundred years. We do not ask you to do anything. We did not organize the Soviets. They were not organized in 1917: they were created in the revolution of 1905. The people organized the Soviets. When I tell you that the government of the Soviets is superior to the Constituent Assembly, that it is more fundamentally representative of the whole of the mass, I do not tell you anything new. As long ago as April 4, I told you that the Soviets were more representative of the people than this Constituent Assembly which you wanted to organize."

He explained in detail the political break in the Social Revolutionary Party, and said:

"When the people voted for delegates of the Constituent Assembly, they did not know the difference between the Right S.R.'s and the Left. They did not know that when they voted for the Right Social Revolutionaries they voted for the bourgeoisie, and when they voted for the Left they voted for Socialism."

At first he spoke quietly, but before long his hands had come out of his pockets. These, and his brown eyes alternately snapping and smiling, and his eyebrows humorously expressive, all vigorously emphasized his phrases.

It was evident from the faces of the men before him that he was justifying himself and them to their satisfaction.

"The February Revolution was a political bourgeois revolution overthrowing Tsarism. In November a social revolution occurred, and the working masses became the sovereign authority. The Workmen's and Soldiers' delegates are not bound by any rules or traditions to the old bourgeois society. Their government has taken all the power and rights into its own hands. The Constituent Assembly is the highest expression of the political ideals of bourgeois society, which are no longer necessary in a Socialist state. The Constituent Assembly will be dissolved.

"If the Constituent Assembly represented the will of the people, we would shout: 'Long live the Constituent Assembly!' Instead we shout: 'Down with the Constituent Assembly!'" he finished.

In the seat next to me was a little Bessarabian with black beady eyes and a short, bristling mustache. He had a merry face that crinkled when he smiled. Every now and then he gave his head a queer little shake of amazed admiration and whispered:

"He's a wise man. He's a wise man."[19]

Despite angry counter-arguments and denunciations from Lenin's opponents in the soviet, Beatty reported, he won a great majority of the votes.[20]

While Lenin's revolution began with majority support among workers and peasants, and generated high hopes among millions of people inside and outside of Russia, a tidal wave of civil war and foreign intervention was unleashed against it. An economy already severely damaged by World War I and further weakened by an international capitalist blockade designed to kill the revolution began to collapse. Some fruits of the stewardship of Lenin and his comrades are described by yet another colleague of Bryant and Beatty, Albert Rhys Williams, in his 1921 classic *Through the Russian Revolution*:

"Repressions, tyranny, violence," cry the enemies. "They have abolished free speech, free press, free assembly. They have imposed drastic military conscription and compulsory labor. They have been incompetent in government, inefficient in industry. They have subordinated the Soviets to the Communist Party. They have lowered their Communist ideals, changed and shifted their program and compromised with the capitalists."

Some of these charges are exaggerated. Many can be explained. But they cannot all be explained away. Friends of the Soviet grieve over them. Their enemies have summoned the world to shudder and protest against them....

While abroad hatred against the Bolsheviks as the new "enemies of civilization" mounted from day to day, these selfsame Bolsheviks were straining to rescue civilization in Russia from total collapse.[21]

Of course, Williams, Beatty, and Bryant were part of a remarkable team of U.S. left-leaning journalists whose most famous member was John Reed, author of the 1919 masterpiece *Ten Days That Shook the World*. Reed's respect for Lenin was immense. Quoting the conclusion of the revolutionary's speech after the Soviet seizure of power (which asserted that "the labor movement, in the name of peace and socialism, shall win and fulfill its destiny"), he had commented: "There was something quiet and powerful in all of this, which stirred the souls of men. It was understandable why people believed when Lenin spoke."[22]

In the opinion of Reed, the Russian Revolution showed the way forward for the workers and the oppressed of all countries, whom he urged to "unite with the Russian workers and peasants, who overthrew their capitalists and whose Red Army conquers the troops of the foreign imperialists." He shared Lenin's view that the spread of revolution would help to end the isolation of revolutionary Russia and usher in a socialist world economy. He helped establish the Communist movement in the United States, which proclaimed itself "in full harmony with the revolutionary working class parties of all countries and stands by the principles stated by the Third [Communist] International formed at Moscow," going on to propose "the organization of the workers as a class, the overthrow of capitalist rule and the conquest of political power by the workers. The workers, organized as a ruling class, shall, through their government, make and enforce the laws; they shall own and control land, factories, mills, mines, transportation systems and financial institutions."[23]

Some commented on how odd and sad it was for such a dashing figure and talented writer as John Reed to have become entangled in such earnest efforts to build such a little left-wing sect — it was then called the Communist Labor Party — in the most powerful and prosperous capitalist economy in the world. But Reed was powerfully influenced by the romantic and heroic struggles of American radicals — the Socialist Party of Eugene V. Debs and especially the Industrial Workers of the World led by "Big Bill" Haywood — during the Progressive era. And he was convinced that this substantial labor-radical current in the United States could be made more effective if it was fused with the political program and the organizational perspectives developed by Lenin.

"The essential expression of Lenin's genius," explained Reed's friend Max Eastman several years later, "was the creation of an organization of purposive revolutionists" who would be utterly committed, through real and practical work, to a working-class revolution while at the same time being capable of an extreme tactical flexibility. "Lenin's party was an organization of a kind that never existed before. It combined certain essential features of a political party, a professional association, a consecrated order, an army, a scientific society — and yet was in no sense a sect. Instead of cherishing in its membership a sectarian psychology, it cherished a certain relation to the predominant class forces of society as Marx defined them. And this relation was determined and progressively readjusted by Lenin, with a subtlety of which Marx never dreamed."[24]

The desire to create such parties in one's own country and throughout the world, and to help defend and advance the cause of socialist revolution as initiated in Russia of 1917, was something that John Reed shared with millions of people who became part of the worldwide Communist movement inspired by the ideas and example of Lenin.

Those who have some concern with the actual history of Russia should want to know something about Lenin, then, but so should those who are concerned with the history (and future) of the labor and radical movements around the world — including in the powerhouse of global capitalism, the United States of America.

The Failure of Socialism

Some insights into the meaning of Lenin emerge from the trajectory of an American who began as one of the most ardent admirers of Lenin and the Russian Revolution — but who became one of their severest critics.

Max Eastman was a brash young radical, under many of the same influences as his friend John Reed. He was a decent poet, a fine writer, and brilliant editor of the groundbreaking magazines that blended left-wing socialism with serious journalism and avante-garde art and literature — *The Masses* and its successor *The Liberator*. His commitment to socialism lasted somewhat more than three decades, then was replaced by an almost three-decade commitment to capitalism and extended stint as "roving editor" with *Readers' Digest*. His engagement with Lenin was intense, and insights can be gleaned about the meaning of "Leninism" if we review some of Eastman's own experience, perceptions, and evolving ideas.

Eastman first heard Lenin speak in 1922 at the fourth congress of the Communist International. He described Lenin as "the most powerful man I ever saw on the platform," adding that "I do not know how to define the nature of his power, except to say that he is a granite mountain of sincerity." The charm of Eastman's word portrait is worth savoring: "His gestures are extraordinary in their variety and grace, but otherwise he is not distinguished-looking. He is a little bit funny-looking, perhaps, with his wide small eyes and broad nose and black-painted brows under a great bald head. I could almost think he was 'made-up' to look funny." Eastman's next comment comes as a jolt: "But if a man ever walked across my vision that I would trust to the edge of doom, that is Lenin." His explanation: "He is simple in his heart like a peasant who knows proverbs, but in his mind subtle and mighty. And this you feel while he is talking. You feel that he is all there for you — you are receiving the whole of the man."[25]

A few years later, not long after Lenin's death, Eastman was dismayed when such key leaders of the Russian Communist Party as Joseph Stalin, Gregory Zinoviev, Lev Kamenev, and "the easy to influence" Nikolai Bukharin — largely driven by "their own thirst for power," and "against whose domination Lenin warned the party" — had "succeeded in deceiving, or bewildering, or bull dozing, or otherwise silencing, or scattering to the ends of the earth, all those who might oppose them" — especially the brilliant and intractable Leon Trotsky, but thousands of others as well. "They were establishing and solidifying to an extremely dangerous degree a dictatorship of the officialdom within the Communist Party, entailing a separation of the party from the mass," and "inculcating, in place of the flexible and concrete realistic thinking of Lenin, a bigoted religious devotion to a supposed abstract canon of Leninism."[26]

By 1936, Eastman was writing that although "Lenin guided the Russian workers' and peasants' revolution to victory and laid the foundations of socialism" — which Eastman defined as "the society of the free and equal" — the Soviet Union was now "not only remote from socialism, but from sane human kindness and sound reason in any of its forms .... Under Stalin's leadership the power has been withdrawn completely from the workers and peasants. The soviets have become but the relic of a rough-draft of proletarian self-government. The power is in the hands of a dictator and an organization of bureaucrats." He wrote of the super-exploitation of workers, the murderous collectivization squeeze on the peasantry, state regimentation of cultural life, and the brutal purge, imprisonment, and slaughter of many Communists, including those who had been among Lenin's closest comrades.[27]

And by 1940, while asserting that "no other extreme revolutionist in history ever possessed Lenin's moral and intellectual endowment," Eastman finally expressed a thoroughgoing disillusionment: "The swiftness with which the collapse of his plans followed upon his death, the impotence of his colleague, Trotsky, to stem the tidal reassertion of crude power-thirsty human nature, revealed ... the flaw in those plans." [28] As the new decade unfolded, Eastman made clear his conclusion that "socialism was amateur; we must be expert" — and more specifically, that "the dream of universal freedom under a state-owned economy ... produced the most perfect tyranny in all history." The great socialist experiment, even under the direction of a Lenin, had demonstrated the impossibility of socialism — and the terrible dangers of trying to achieve it. In 1948, speaking at a convention of the American Federation of Labor, he took the opportunity to deliver a lecture to the working class:

> *Don't kill the goose that lays the golden eggs.* Capitalism is something of a goose from the standpoint of abstract reason and the ideal of perfection. It's easy to make game of that goose, and it's a lot of fun when you stay up in the sky. But she's the only creature on this earth that ever laid golden eggs, and in my humble but mature opinion she's the only one that ever will. My advice to organized labor is: Grab all the eggs you can lay your hands on — of course — but watch out. Don't kill the goose![29]

The Triumph of Capitalism

Max Eastman's disillusionment with socialism drew him deep into the capitalist orbit. He hailed such conservative "neo-liberal" economists as F. A. Hayek and Ludwig von Mises for showing "that the competitive market and the price system are the basis for whatever real political freedom exists." He claimed that Karl Marx himself had "observed that all our freedoms had evolved together with, and in dependence upon, private capitalism with its free competitive market." Yet even his sympathetic biographer William O'Neill complained that "Eastman's capitalism was all theory and no fact." O'Neill adds that "when writing about socialism, Eastman strained other people's ideas through the cloth of his own knowledge and experience. In writing about capitalism, he merely brought up stale ideas he had swallowed whole." He concludes: "The difference shows. Socialism had been the one grand passion of his political life, an affair of the mind and heart. With free enterprise he made a marriage of convenience."[30]

Although Eastman threw himself fully, if again somewhat abstractly, into anti-Red conservatism at home and full support for U.S. Cold War anti-Communism abroad, as time went on he found himself to be increasingly uncomfortable with his newfound political allies. Freda Utley (an old friend to whom Eastman first confessed his disillusionment with socialism and with whom, many years thereafter, he shared a "basic rapport") ultimately reported what Eastman himself had discovered — that the anti-Communist cause had largely been "taken over by reactionary forces who confused the quest for social justice with Communist treason" and was infested with "unscrupulous careerists." More than this, the conservative camp to which they belonged in the 1950s and early '60s contained many "who would have us go back to the bad old days when the power of capitalists and imperialists was as ruthlessly used and as uncontrolled as that of the ruling hierarchy in a Communist state." Neither Utley nor Eastman found a way to a coherent political orientation — although in his final years he broke with the conservative journal *National Review*, quietly dropped his belief in associating freedom exclusively with capitalism, and came to oppose the U.S. war in Vietnam.[31]

Eastman's late-in-life commitment to capitalism was never abandoned. The aggressiveness and selfishness that he saw as inherent in human nature had made a shambles of Lenin's "socialist experiment," in his opinion — but Eastman wanted to believe that these elemental human dynamics would be channeled and transformed by capitalism's market mechanisms to provide the freedom, democracy, and decent life for all that had been socialist goals of his youth. He explained to his readers that "in placing the major economic decisions in the hands of the whole people as consumers, recording those decisions automatically through the mechanism of price, the market makes freedom possible in a complex industrial society." He insisted that the economic competition of "free market" capitalism — although both presuming and generating certain social and economic inequalities — need not get out of hand:

> There is no conflict between freedom so conditioned and a humane regard on the part of the state for people who fail utterly in the competitive struggle. No one need starve, no one need be destitute, in order to preserve the sovereignty of the market. The principle of collective responsibility for those actually in want can be maintained without violating the principle of competition.

More than this, capitalism was creating the possibility for all people in society to have lives of freedom and abundance:

> Though it led off with the new-fashioned sufferings described by Marx in *Das Kapital* — not greater in degree, but different in kind from what had preceded — the market economy he thundered against has, in its full development, lifted the toiling masses of mankind to levels of life never dreamed of in all past history.... Whether or not it is true, as Von Mises asserts, that "capitalism ... deproletarianizes all strata of society," it is at least true that it makes possible their deproletarianization.[32]

Asserting that "the average real wage of the American worker rose, between 1840 and 1951, from eighteen to eighty-six cents an hour," he argued that if this rate of increase "continued for another hundred years," and if advancing technology continued to generate dramatic increases in productivity, and if (with birth control policies and techniques) this was "matched by a decline in the production of people," then it would be possible to achieve a society, in the United States and presumably on a global scale, in which "free citizens are normally found to be possessors of land or capital or both" — a capitalist version of the classless society that, until the age of 57, he had hoped would be achieved through socialism.[33]

Naturally, this vision of benevolent capitalism, if it reflects reality, would add up to a fundamental obsolescence of Lenin's orientation. Indeed, according to contemporary conservatives, this is very much the case. David Horowitz (whose journey across the political spectrum was similar to Eastman's) has enthused: "It was, in fact, this dazzling prospect of American progress in the era that stretched from Eisenhower to Reagan that lay at the heart of the demoralization and collapse of socialism's empire, whose own populations had been condemned to permanent grinding poverty by Marx's [and presumably Lenin's] impossible economic schemes."[34]

And yet, as Lenin was fond of saying, facts are stubborn things.

The perspectives advanced by Eastman appeared in his 1955 volume *Reflections on the Failure of Socialism*. Half a century later, the stark realities of our time might give rise to reflections on the failure of capitalism — at least if we use Eastman's generous expectations as a measure. Some of the specifics of this failure are elaborated elsewhere in this volume. Here, it will suffice simply to baldly state some of the most obvious points to be made.

Since Eastman's time, there has been a dramatic widening of the gap not only between the rich and the poor, but between the rich and the working-class majority. Specifically, a global power elite that owns and dominates our planet's economy has gotten richer at the expense of most of the world's peoples, for whom there has been a general decline of living conditions. Wealth is power. Economic power translates inevitably into political power. Even in countries claiming to be democratic republics (where "rule by the people" is supposed to be exercised through elected representatives controlled by the electorate), the political system and governmental apparatus are dominated by wealthy and powerful minorities that control the economy. All of this is easily documented.[35]

Nor is it difficult to document that — contrary to Eastman's hopeful speculations — the laboring population has absolutely *not* been increasingly "deproletarianized." If anything, more and more occupations and economic strata have undergone a process of proletarianization (as Harry Braverman documented in his classic *Labor and Monopoly Capital*). Meaningful business ownership has not been diffused throughout the larger population — instead, there has been an increasing concentration of ownership. The natural tendency of the capitalist economy has involved dynamics leading to increased productivity, with remarkable technological developments being utilized to cut labor costs. This is achieved through de-skilling and driving down wages and salaries, finding ways to eliminate overly "expensive" occupations, eroding or brutally rolling back working-class gains made through unions and "welfare state" reforms.[36]

Capitalist development has always been a global process. In the 19th and 20th centuries, an essential dimension of this global process was labeled "imperialism" — involving businesses expanding beyond the borders of one country with government aid, in order to secure ever more markets, raw materials, and investment opportunities. With new technologies, particularly impacting on communication and transportation systems, the ongoing global structuring and restructuring of capitalist enterprise has been able to proceed with increased efficiency and velocity — to the detriment of the expanded working classes of all countries.[37]

Even where capitalism has appeared to score its most dramatic triumph — winning the global economic contest with Communism — the Eastern European shift toward the market economy has had troubling, even dreadful consequences for the laboring majorities of that region, as we have documented in Chapter 1. And the "new world order" resulting from the collapse of Communism, rather than leading to the global peace and prosperity that Eastman would have anticipated, may involve a divided, turbulent, and ugly future, leading to the rise of other more threatening "isms," not least the global specter of "terrorism." Efforts to make the world safe for multinational corporations seem to generate an accumulation of state breakdowns and popular revolts. Economic stagnation and mounting social degradation in various areas could lead to rising xenophobia and neofascist currents. It is quite possible that there could be a reappearance of economic depression and intensified class struggle. It is also quite possible that a failure to move beyond the capitalist system could result in the degradation of our planet's environment to the extent that human life will no longer be possible.[38]

In the face of such realities, it is not surprising that so hostile a modern-day Lenin biographer as Robert Service has felt compelled to warn his readers that "it is not even impossible that his memory might again be invoked, not necessarily by card-carrying communists, in those parts of the world where capitalism causes grievous social distress. Lenin is not quite dead, at least not yet."[39]

Leninist Implications

Because Max Eastman's vision of a benevolent capitalism runs contrary to the reality of our times, both in the United States and globally, Lenin's orientation — which stands as a clear and uncompromising alternative to the capitalist status quo and claims to pose a practical and tough-minded answer to the question of "what is to be done?" — certainly *does* appear to have continuing relevance. Even if we find that its results were, as Eastman eloquently insisted, horrendously inconsistent with what Lenin and his comrades were hoping to achieve, it is something from which we should learn. This is a central focus of the next chapter.

Of course, there is still Eastman's late-in-life conclusion that nothing better than capitalism is possible, that the very idea of socialism is inconsistent with the aggressive and possessive drives of human nature.

This notion is challenged, however, by a point made by more than one Marxist: for most of humanity's existence, the norm, in hunting and gathering societies and early agricultural societies, has involved human communities characterized by people's collective rule over their own economic life — a "moral economy" of sharing and helping each other. Powerful elements of this persisted throughout the existence of pre-industrial class society among the peasantry and early working classes. It permeates the values found in many currents of the Christian, Judaic, Islamic and other religious traditions. It was absorbed into the blood stream and thought patterns of the modern socialist movement.[40]

Responding to this, David Horowitz has insisted that the socialist goal is reactionary, that it "belongs to the dark prehistory of mankind" (primitive societies in which domestic groups and tribes shared in the labor and in the fruits of their labor). "Socialism belongs to a social stage based on the simple economy of small groups, a stage that had to be overcome in order to realize the great wealth-making potential of the market system," he argues. "Far from being a progressive conception, the socialist ethic is atavistic and represents the primitive morality of preindustrial formations: the clan and the tribe." Horowitz tells us that "capitalist democracy (a system as flawed as humanity is flawed) is … the highest stage of social evolution." But as we can see from our survey of the actuality of capitalism in our time, "progress" for some — wealthy and powerful elites — may come at the expense of masses of people whose lives and labor are the basis for society's existence. The "progress" of capitalism may be inconsistent with *rule by the people*. In fact, from Horowitz's standpoint, it may be that real democracy is also a reactionary throwback to the dark and primitive tribalism of early humanity.[41]

Two essential elements are at the core of Lenin's outlook. One is the Marxist notion of class struggle between, in capitalist society, a minority class (the capitalists or bourgeoisie) who own the economy and a majority class (the working class or proletariat) whose lives and labor are used (exploited) to enrich that minority. The other essential element is that rule by the people over the political and economic life of society — democracy — must be established in reality. This will exist, in Lenin's words, when "all members of society, or at least the vast majority, have learned to administer the state *themselves*, have learned to take this work into their own hands." It will become "more complete" when "*all* have learned to administer and actually do independently administer social production, independently keep accounts and exercise control over the parasites, the sons of the wealthy, the swindlers and other 'guardians of capitalist traditions.'" Lenin believed it would culminate in a society where the democratic "observing [of] the simple, fundamental rules of the community will ... become a *habit*."[42] The need for a government apparatus, separate from and above the people, to maintain "law and order" would evaporate under such conditions. This most radical and stateless form of economic democracy is what Lenin meant by the word "communism."

One hardly needs to be a Lenin to be aware of the destructive realities of capitalist society and the reality of the class struggle, or even to project the goal of the working-class majority struggling for a classless society. The prominent and absolutely non-Leninist U.S. philosopher Richard Rorty has insisted on "the need to realize that the last hundred years of our country's history have witnessed a brutal struggle between the corporations and the workers, that this struggle is still going on, and the corporations are winning." Rorty (whose criticisms of Lenin we will cite in Chapter 4) has emphasized that "social justice in America owes much more to civil disobedience than to the use of the ballot," and that "the deepest and most enduring injustices, like the unending humiliation of African Americans and the miserable wages paid to unorganized workers, are always played down by the political parties and by most of the press." Calling on workers, intellectuals, and students to join together to "help bring our country closer to the goal that matters most: the classless society," Rorty emphasized: "It is time to revive the kind of leftist politics that pervaded American campuses from the Depression through the early 1960s — a politics centered on the struggle to prevent the rich from ripping off the rest of the country."[43]

Discussing mass demonstrations of students, workers, and social activists against the ravages of corporate capitalist globalization as the 21st century opened, economist William Tabb has emphasized that "the struggle for economic justice in the twenty-first century will be international," adding: "As the drive by transnational corporations and transnational finance to impose their rule over the working people of the world comes to be seen for what it is, some old ways of thinking will come back into vogue."[44]

The harsh economic realities of capitalist globalization transform the majority of human beings, the working classes of all countries, increasingly into units of labor and also consumption digits in the worldwide market place. "If capital conceives them to be one exploitable mass, that is how they must conceive of themselves," labor economist Michael Yates has argued. He repeats some of the old slogans of the working-class movement:

In unity there is strength.
An injury to one is an injury to all.
The working class and the employing class have nothing in common.
Workers of all countries, unite.

"As workers come to see themselves as an undifferentiated mass, they take action, forming unions that strike, picket, and boycott, and constituting political parties that vie for state power," Yates concludes. "Marxists believe that this propertyless mass of men and women, of all shades of color, and of every nation, is nothing less than the historic agent of the overthrow of capitalism and the beginning of communism."[45]

Such things are at the very heart of Lenin's life and thought and work. "The theory of the vanguard party, of the one-party state, is not (repeat not) the central doctrine of Leninism," C. L. R. James insisted many years ago. "It is not the central doctrine, it is *not* even a special doctrine. It is not and it never was." The truth of this assertion is matched by the truth of James's next point:

> Bolshevism, Leninism, did have central doctrines. One was theoretical, the inevitable collapse of capitalism into barbarism. Another was social, that on account of its place in history, its training and its numbers, only the working class could prevent this degradation and reconstruct society. Political action consisted in organizing a party to carry out these aims.[46]

This is as condensed as diamond. But a gem-like summary is not enough to resolve the many questions raised here. To do that, it is worth looking more carefully and critically at the specifics of Lenin's thought and practice.

At the conclusion of the next chapter, the specifics of Lenin's political thought are summarized. Central to it all, however, is the organizing of "a party to carry out these aims." James's comment that this is not a "special doctrine" of Leninism can be documented not only by reference to the *Communist Manifesto* (which projects an organized current of communist workers who are "the most advanced and resolute section of the working class of every country, that section which pushes forward all others"), but also to the writings of Rosa Luxemburg — closer to Lenin in temper and perspective than is often acknowledged. She saw such a party as (in her words) "the most enlightened, most class-conscious vanguard of the proletariat," interacting with "every spontaneous people's movement" to "hasten the development of things and endeavor to accelerate events," and she called for a "social-democratic centralism" that would be "the 'self-centralism' of the advanced sectors of the proletariat."[47]

Lenin agreed that "the Party, as the vanguard of the working class, must not be confused ... with the entire class," arguing that a "varied, rich, fruitful" interrelationship with the working class as a whole must be facilitated by what he called "the full application of the democratic principle in the Party organization." Nothing could be further from the truth than the common misrepresentation of Lenin's party as an internally authoritarian elite. He explained that "the principles of democratic centralism" involved "guarantees for the rights of all minorities and for all loyal opposition, ... the autonomy of every [local] Party organization, ... recognizing that all Party functionaries must be elected, accountable to the Party and subject to recall." In his opinion, working-class socialist organizations "must be united, but in these united organizations there must be wide and free discussion of Party questions, free comradely criticism and assessments of events in Party life." The interplay of vanguard with masses — he emphasized in the wake of the 1905 revolution — was a key to making possible the revolutionary upsurge, asserting: "The working class is instinctively, spontaneously Social-Democratic, and more than ten years of work put in by the Social-Democracy has done a great deal to transform this spontaneity into consciousness."[48]

Lenin emphasized the central importance of substantial working-class socialist educational and cultural work to counteract the immense predominance of capitalist and reactionary ideology, but he believed that this must be integrated into practical political activity that would connect with the lives and struggles of masses of working people. In the years before 1917, some of his more sectarian comrades, following Alexander Bogdanov, broke with him over this, viewing mass struggles for reforms as inconsistent with the struggle for socialist revolution. "A Bolshevik, they declared, should be hard and unyielding," Lenin's companion Nadezhda Krupskaya later recalled. "Lenin considered this view fallacious. It would mean giving up all practical work, standing aside from the masses instead of organizing them on real-life issues. Prior to the Revolution of 1905 the Bolsheviks showed themselves capable of making good use of every legal possibility, of forging ahead and rallying the masses behind them under the most adverse conditions. Step by step, beginning with the campaign for tea service and ventilation, they had led the masses up to the national armed insurrection. The ability to adjust oneself to the most adverse circumstances [in which only reform struggles were possible] and at the same time to stand out and maintain one's high-principled positions — such were the traditions of Leninism."[49]

Lenin did not have a romantic notion of the working class as being born with a Marxist-influenced class consciousness or being instinctively ready for revolution. Rather, a majority of workers would have to be won to this by a minority of their class that had developed such revolutionary class consciousness. The bulk of these initial Marxist revolutionaries were working-class intellectuals and activists from the more skilled occupations, working with intellectuals from university and professional milieus. These working-class revolutionaries were interested not in becoming a privileged layer in society, but instead believed that their interests and the interests of all society were bound up with the fortunes of the working class as a whole, especially those more oppressed than themselves. Lenin believed that they must be interested not only in wages, hours, and working conditions, but also in broader social and political questions — especially questions of democracy, opposing the oppression of racial and national and religious minorities, opposing the oppression of women, opposing violations of academic freedom and of civil liberties, and so on. Concern for such "non-economic" issues should not be left to bourgeois liberals, he insisted. Instead, the working class as a whole must see such things as essential elements of its own liberation. Real, practical struggles around such things would increase the number of the so-called "conscious workers," the vanguard layer of the working class that could provide leadership to the class as a whole in the struggle for a better world.

Orlando Figes sees this struggle for a better world as an "experiment" that went "horribly wrong, not so much because of the malice of its leaders, most of whom had started out with the highest of ideals, but because their ideals were themselves impossible." Bolshevik intellectuals, "with their own idealized vision of what the workers were supposed to be," were destined to be foiled by "the workers' actual tastes — vaudeville and vodka, for the most." Even though this does not describe the actual tastes of all workers (an immense human group reflecting an almost infinite variety of identities, ideologies, and inclinations), the point about an idealized vision of the working class's being common among Marxist intellectuals is not untrue. The struggle to mobilize the working class to take political power in order to usher in a glowing socialist democracy was, Figes concludes, doomed from the start: "The state, however big, cannot make people equal or better human beings."[50]

This brings us back to the agonizing image projected by George Orwell of the immense majority of the laboring classes — the Low — being permanently ruled by the High, and when the Middle entices them to help make a revolution, the result will never be emancipation but merely a change in masters. One of the most thoughtful of Leninists, Antonio Gramsci, grasped the dilemma as he recognized that the formation of a Communist Party added up to the creation of a new stratum of leaders: "In the formation of leaders, one premise is fundamental: is it the intention that there should always be rulers and ruled, or is the objective to create the conditions in which this is no longer necessary?"[51]

The process of creating such conditions must not commence once the Revolution is achieved, however, but through an extended prerevolutionary process similar to what Krupskaya (and Lenin) projected — with an immersion of the revolutionary party in "real-life issues" involving masses of workers in order "to construct an intellectual–moral bloc," as Gramsci put it, "which can make politically possible the intellectual progress of the mass and not only of small intellectual groups." Although the party must absorb "traditional intellectuals" who have been won to Marxism, Gramsci stressed that it must facilitate the development of "organic intellectuals" who are (and remain) part of the working class, and the revolutionary organization must "work incessantly to raise the intellectual level of ever-growing strata of the populace, to give a personality to the amorphous mass element." It must be "linked organically to a national-popular mass," seeking to "stimulate the formation of homogeneous, compact social blocs, which will give birth to their own intellectuals, their own commanders, their own vanguard — who will in turn react upon those blocs in order to develop them."[52]

For all the insight and intellectual coherence of Gramsci's Leninism, however, we are left with the brutal fact that the 20th century turned out the way that it did, not the way that Lenin, Krupskaya, Luxemburg, Gramsci, and James hoped it would. If we are to retain any hope for changing the world, we must struggle to understand the earlier momentous efforts — and momentous failures.

4
From Lenin to Stalin — and Back

"Leninism is as dead as a doornail everywhere other than among the sects that are reminiscent of antagonistic amoeba fighting each other to death in a drop of water." This wonderful imagery — which is not entirely true, but not entirely devoid of truth — was recently offered by the thoughtful left-wing scholar Stephen Eric Bronner in the midst of a controversy with his fellow editors and readers of the socialist journal *New Politics* over whether *revolutionary* socialism is irrelevant to the realities of the 21st century.[1]

Bronner for many years portrayed Rosa Luxemburg as "a revolutionary for our time." But times change. Now one must restrict oneself to working for humane, socialist-inspired reforms and policies, Bronner argued, within the framework of a liberal republic and through institutions that are "intertwined with capitalist interests."[2]

While gently disassociating himself from Luxemburg's politics, however, Bronner unleashed harsh polemical invective on Lenin. This would be logical if for no other reason than the fact that Lenin represents, in some ways more dramatically than Luxemburg (given his seeming success in 1917), the commitment to *revolutionary* socialism. But beyond such polemical logic, Bronner emphasized anti-Lenin objections (advanced by others many times before) that claim to offer a sober account of the actual historical experience. "Whatever the usefulness of Lenin's theory of the party with respect to fostering revolution, it stinks as a theory of rule," he wrote. "Every concrete experience of movements committed to Leninism has produced a one-party state with a varying, if generally horrible, set of authoritarian consequences. Every one!"[3]

As is often the case in polemics of this sort, reality is simplified and points are overstated. There are many movements committed to Leninism that have not produced a one-party state. Those associated with anti-Stalinist orientations (whether the various Trotskyist organizations, or those associated with Amadeo Bordiga in Italy, or the dissident German Communists around Heinrich Brandler), as well as the massive and Stalinist-influenced Italian Communist Party, for example, and the well-organized and influential South African Communist Party, not only did not establish one-party states (a prerequisite of which is taking political power), but don't quite measure up to the general description offered by Bronner. Those parties that actually did take power were organizations permeated by the Stalinist version of "Leninism." There is also the exception, of course, of the Communist Party of India (Marxist), taking and for many years holding power (rather benignly) in the state of Kerala, and other local examples can also be cited.[4] In any event, Bronner sees Stalinism as genuine Leninism — a matter to examine later. But it would be possible to acknowledge significant differences between Leninism and Stalinism while at the same time rejecting Leninism as inherently undemocratic. Many defenders of Lenin have argued that he was profoundly democratic, but Bronner responds:

> For my part, I simply don't see the democratic moment in Lenin: he never thought about placing constraints on the power of the party; he never valued civil liberties or an independent judiciary; and he never treated any actor outside the party other than in terms of pure expediency. His vanguard organization was, from the first, hierarchical and militaristic and his notion of "democratic centralism" always lacked any notion of institutional accountability to those whom the party was to represent. Rosa Luxemburg already underscored all of this in "The Organizational Questions of Social Democracy" (1904).[5]

Luxemburg's Challenge

For anyone concerned about the human condition, it is worth following Bronner into an examination of the profound challenge represented by Rosa Luxemburg. While many have used her simply as a club with which to beat Lenin, it must be admitted that her critique of capitalism was even more severe than her critique of Lenin (whom she did, after all, consider to be a comrade).

Applying the dialectical approach to her economic studies, Luxemburg understood capitalism as an expansive system driven by the dynamic of capital accumulation. Its accelerating and increasingly voracious dynamic caused capitalist economies of the more "advanced" societies to pour across national borders, brutally dominating the peoples of Asia, Africa, and Latin America, while at the same time throwing the more powerful capitalist nations into increasingly aggressive and menacing competition — leading to global warfare.[6]

The realities of capitalism in its increasingly violent and destructive imperialist form, Luxemburg felt, gave an urgency to the need for the replacement of global capitalism with a worldwide socialist democracy. Central to her strategic orientation for achieving global justice were the struggles of the working class in countries with industrially advanced capitalism. Those whose lives and labor keep society running are the ones who should run society. It is the great majority of the people who must shape the future. "Socialism cannot be made and will not be made by command, not even by the best and most capable Socialist government," she insisted. "It must be made by the masses, through every proletarian individual."[7]

Luxemburg's views on the labor movement corresponded to those of Karl Marx. She embraced (as did most German Social Democrats) the orientation presented in the *Communist Manifesto* — that the workers should struggle for various reforms to expand democratic rights and improve immediate economic and social conditions, that they should build increasingly effective and inclusive trade unions to secure better working conditions and higher living standards, that they should build their own working-class political party, finally winning political power in order to make "despotic inroads" (rule by the people) into the capitalist economy for the purpose of bringing about the socialist reconstruction of society.

An aspect of this dilemma was discussed by Luxemburg in the 1904 essay cited by Bronner in the following manner:

> The international movement of the proletariat toward its complete emancipation is a process peculiar in the following respect. For the first time in the history of civilization, the people are expressing their will consciously and in opposition to all ruling classes. But this can only be satisfied beyond the limits of the existing system.
>
> Now the mass can only acquire and strengthen this will in the course of the day-to-day struggle against the existing social order — that is, within the limits of capitalist society.
>
> On the one hand, we have the mass; on the other, its historic goal, located outside of existing society. On one hand, we have the day-to-day struggle; on the other, the social revolution. Such are the terms of the dialectical contradiction through which the socialist movement makes its way.
>
> It follows that this movement can best advance by tacking betwixt and between the two dangers by which it is constantly being threatened. One is the loss of its mass character; the other, the abandonment of its goal. One is the danger of sinking back into the condition of a sect; the other, the danger of becoming a movement of bourgeois social reform.[8]

That dilemma relates to a crisis that developed in the German Social Democracy — the *Sozialdemokratischen Partei Deutschlands* (SPD). A strong tendency developed among the national trade union leadership, who were members of the SPD, but who led relatively strong union organizations — the majority of whose members were not SPD members — organizations whose primary goal was to secure higher wages and better working conditions within the context of the capitalist economy. These trade union leaders wanted to bring the SPD under the control of the unions, to prevent revolutionary-minded socialists from leading the unions in a more radical direction, and instead getting the SPD to advance the moderate trade union agenda. A layer of the SPD functionaries wanted to go in this moderate direction, which they hoped would help the party accumulate votes of non-radical (and to some extent non-working-class) layers of the population.[9]

The tension between revolutionaries and reformists cropped up over and over with greater intensity. While the SPD was committed to replacing Germany's militaristic monarchy, headed by the Kaiser, with a fully democratic republic, there were some comrades who confused "patriotism" with accommodating themselves to the foreign policy of that regime. The revolutionaries in the SPD insisted on more radical politics. Luxemburg believed that the very workings of capitalism would periodically generate spontaneous upsurges — for which she used the catch-all phrase "mass strike" — among the working class, including among those layers that had remained untouched by trade union and socialist organization. Organized Marxists must, she believed, be prepared to respond to and supportively interact with such upsurges in order to build the workers' movement and prepare it for the eventual revolutionary overthrow of both the monarchy and capitalism. The divisions within the German labor movement came to a head in 1914, when the imperialism that Luxemburg had analyzed generated a horrendous World War, as she had predicted. A majority of the German socialist leadership — whose gradual-reform approach integrated them into the political and economic status quo — gave full support to the Kaiser's war effort. Opponents of the imperialist slaughter were either intimidated or, as in Luxemburg's case, arrested.

In 1917, Lenin and the Bolsheviks, thanks to the working-class and peasant upsurge in their own country, and thanks also to years of serious organizational development, had succeeded in establishing a revolutionary workers' government in Russia and appealed for the spread of revolutions throughout Europe, and beyond Europe, but in highly industrialized Germany most of all. Increasing numbers of German workers and war-weary soldiers responded with enthusiasm. So did Rosa Luxemburg, who soon was released from prison in the wake of the German monarchy's collapse. Although she helped to form the German Communist Party shortly before being murdered by right-wing death squads, Luxemburg turned her critical attention to grave mistakes being made, in her opinion, by Lenin and the Bolsheviks. Faced with ferocious counter-revolutionary threats, they proclaimed (and celebrated) a "proletarian dictatorship" under exclusive control of the Communist Party. "But the remedy which Trotsky and Lenin have found, the elimination of democracy as such," she warned, "is worse than the disease it is supposed to cure; for it stops up the very living source from which alone can come the correction of all the innate shortcomings of social institutions. That source is the active, untrammeled, energetic political life of the broadest masses of the people."[10]

The Democratic Imperative

Rosa Luxemburg therefore stands, in the minds of many, as a stark contrast to the elitist and authoritarian orientation of Vladimir Ilyich Lenin. It is difficult not to be impressed with the uncompromisingly democratic qualities that emerge from the following very long but very rich quotation of 1915. To attain an understanding of the indissoluble link — for serious Marxists like Luxemburg — between democracy and socialism, this entire passage should be read carefully and thoughtfully:

> The proletariat cannot become victor save through democracy, i.e., through introducing complete democracy and through combining with every step of its movement democratic demands formulated most vigorously, most decisively. It is senseless to contrast the socialist revolution and the revolutionary struggle against capitalism to one of the questions of democracy, in this case the national question. On the contrary, we must combine the revolutionary struggle against capitalism with a revolutionary program and revolutionary tactics relative to all democratic demands: a republic, a militia, officials elected by the people, equal rights for women, self-determination of nations, etc. While capitalism exists, all these demands are realizable only as an exception, and in an incomplete, distorted form. Basing ourselves on democracy as it already exists, exposing its incompleteness under capitalism, we advocate the overthrow of capitalism, expropriation of the bourgeoisie as a necessary basis both for the abolition of the poverty of the masses and for a complete and manifold realization of all democratic forms. Some of those reforms will be started prior to the overthrow of the bourgeoisie, others in the process of the overthrow, still others after it has been accomplished. The socialist revolution is by no means a single battle; on the contrary, it is an epoch of a whole series of battles around all problems of economic and democratic reforms, which can be completed only by the expropriation of the bourgeoisie. It is for the sake of this final aim that we must formulate in a consistently revolutionary manner every one of our democratic demands. It is quite conceivable that the workers of a certain country may overthrow the bourgeoisie before even one fundamental democratic reform has been realized in full. It is entirely inconceivable, however, that the proletariat as an historical class will be able to defeat the bourgeoisie if it is not prepared for this task by being educated in the spirit of the most consistent and determined revolutionary democracy.

This quotation not only gives a sense of how a revolutionary like Luxemburg approached things, but it gives an even better sense of how a revolutionary like Lenin approached things — *because this happens to be a quotation from Lenin.*[11]

What distinguishes the approach of many critics of Lenin is either an appalling ignorance of, or an almost inexplicable refusal to deal with, a considerable amount of primary sources and major scholarship that fundamentally challenge their interpretation of what Lenin and his revolutionary party actually represented. Consider the easily available work of the highly respected historian Moshe Lewin. Lewin provides an account diametrically opposed to the picture Bronner paints of the Bolsheviks in 1917. By then they had assumed an organizational form "that comes nearest to the tightly knit vanguard party of 'professional revolutionaries,' as Lenin's *What Is To Be Done?*, written in 1902, seemed to have anticipated." But, Lewin tells us, "this text did not intimate any mechanical authoritarianism in internal arrangements, despite the insistence on discipline and unity of action. Conferences and congresses, debates and platforms, continued to be part and parcel of the Bolshevik as much as the Menshevik faction, and were considered normal party procedure." His conclusions are consistent with a significant number of primary sources and capable secondary studies. The Bolsheviks made a transition from being "a rather small party of political cadres working clandestinely, [and] became a legal, democratic mass party, strongly led by outstanding leaders, relying on an influential second-echelon leadership well-connected with its rank and file and its following in the factories and barracks." Lewin notes:

> The documents concerning this period show convincingly that factions — left, right, and several in between — were not only active but were also accepted as the party's modus operandi, including by Lenin. The decision concerning the taking of power was reached only after a long and serious internal political battle. Almost all the top leaders of the party admired Lenin and accepted his leadership. However, they did not hesitate to take up cudgels against him over small and even major questions of policies and strategies. Lenin had to get what he wanted through the normal procedures of party institutions: by gaining the majority of votes. He had to accept defeat, or threaten to resign, if majorities did not support him.[12]

This has nothing in common with the "hierarchical and militaristic" Leninism described by Bronner, which allegedly "always lacked any notion of institutional accountability to those whom the party was to represent." Those holding this view of an authoritarian pre-1918 Lenin are certainly entitled to disagree with Lewin and others, but they have a responsibility to indicate why — to refute Lewin's interpretation and demonstrate the flaws in his evidence (as opposed to acting as if none of this evidence exists).

For backup, Bronner could point to Orlando Figes's thoughtful and splendidly panoramic account of the Russian Revolution, which baldly asserts: "Lenin had never been tolerant of dissent within his party's ranks." To document this, Figes cites two eyewitnesses and an important incident. Let us first consider the eyewitnesses. Nikolai Bukharin: Lenin "didn't give damn for the opinions of others." Anatoly Lunacharsky: Lenin deliberately "surrounded himself with fools" who would not dare question him. In fact, Bukharin's complaint is from one of the periods in which he was crossing swords with

Lenin in open dispute within the Bolshevik party. Bukharin's biographer has carefully documented that, at the conclusion of one of these disputes, Lenin acknowledged that he *had* been influenced, to some extent won over, by Bukharin. When the emotional Bukharin made the comment in question, Lenin had just succeeded in winning a Bolshevik majority to his own position on signing the Brest–Litovsk peace treaty in 1918 (and Bukharin's near-majority position for waging "revolutionary war" had been voted down after sharp debate). Once again, hardly proof that Lenin did not tolerate dissent. Lunacharsky's comment is undoubtedly from the period (1907–1910) in which he and others around Alexander Bogdanov engaged in a fierce factional struggle *within* the Bolshevik organization and then definitively split from Lenin. Several years later, the still-opinionated Lunacharsky rejoined Lenin and became one of those with whom the Bolshevik leader "surrounded himself" in the Soviet regime.[13]

The important incident involved "Lenin's struggle for the April Theses" of 1917 inside the Bolshevik party (this is the sharp debate concerning the taking of power referred to by Moshe Lewin), in which Lenin displayed what Figes calls "a domineering attitude" — that is, he argued fiercely for his own minority position and worked tirelessly (and democratically ... and successfully) to win a majority of his party to it. Figes's evidence seems to prove the opposite of what he and Bronner assert. In fact, Figes himself goes on to provide a picture of a far more democratic (and human) organization: "The idea that the Bolshevik Party in 1917 was a monolithic organization tightly controlled by Lenin is a myth — a myth which used to be propagated by the Soviet establishment, and one which is still believed (for quite different motives) by right-wing historians in the West." Basing himself on a considerable amount of recent social history, he seems to offer a more libertarian image of Bolshevism than even that provided by Lewin: "In fact the party was quite undisciplined; it had many different factions, both ideological and geographical; and the leadership, which was itself divided, often proved unable to impose its will on them."[14]

The argument that Lenin was authoritarian finds clear support only in what happened after 1917. There is the irrefutably authoritarian nature of the Russian Communist Party by 1921 (still in the period of Lenin's and Trotsky's leadership). This too is discussed quite knowledgeably by Lewin, who describes the transformation of Communist and Soviet politics in this "period of vicious war and of particularly highhanded and coercive methods of solving problems," as one that drew into Communist ranks new layers that "did not have the culture, general or political, which most of the old guard shared, and what they brought into the ranks was of necessity a new and different political culture characterized by strong militaristic overtones and, quite naturally, by deep authoritarianism."[15]

Murderous Violence

The analysis offered by Lewin has the advantage of factoring in elements that many ignore — the active, murderous, brutalizing hostility of the governments of the United States, France, Britain and other countries toward the Soviet republic. As U.S. Secretary of State Robert Lansing commented to President Woodrow Wilson, the Bolsheviks were appealing "to the proletariat of all countries, to the ignorant and mentally deficient, who by their numbers are urged to become masters. Here seems to me to lie a very real danger in view of the present social unrest throughout the world." The Bolshevik challenge was inconsistent with the focus of U.S. foreign policy — promoting an Open Door Policy that would enable U.S. business interests to secure markets, raw materials, and investment opportunities in a stable world environment.[16]

The U.S. ambassador to Russia during the revolutionary period, David R. Francis, wrote that the dictatorship of the proletariat "is a worse form of tyranny than any absolute monarchy." The ambassador offered two specific points to back up his generalization. First, "no man or woman is allowed to vote who does not perform manual labor." (In fact, those performing other forms of labor were also accepted as voters — but not, it is true, landed nobles and wealthy businessmen such as Francis.) The second problem the ambassador cited was that "the decrees of Bolshevism made marriage and divorce so easy that they were to be had for the asking." Warning of "the effect of Bolshevism already seen on the uneducated of every European country," Francis argued (writing in 1921) that "all of the unrest throughout Europe and in this country and in every country on the Western hemisphere can be traced back to the Bolshevik experiment in Russia." Here he seems to refer not to an international conspiracy, but to a very bad international example to workers and oppressed peoples of all countries.[17]

Arguing against "a temporizing policy with Bolshevism," he advocated "the eradication of Bolshevism in Russia because it is a blot on the civilization of the Twentieth Century, and for the additional reason that it is to our interest to exterminate it in the land of its birth." For this last thought, Francis offered two reasons. "First: If Bolshevism is permitted to thrive in Russia it will promote unrest in all countries. Second: It is our duty to the Russian people to relieve their country of the injury and disgrace inflicted upon it by Soviet Rule."[18]

This 67-year-old Missouri businessman and politician cannot be dismissed simply as an opinionated bigot. He was also the chosen representative of the Wilson administration in a sensitive position. The experienced U.S. diplomat George F. Kennan has commented that Francis's "simple, outspoken, American pragmatism provided a revealing contrast to the intensely theoretical controversies that raged around him, and one comes away from the reading of his memoirs with the feeling that America could have been in some ways worse served, if in other ways better." (It is worthy of note that Kennan, a dedicated public servant and man of keen intellect who helped to shape U.S. foreign policy in the early Cold War years following the Second World War, was himself a man "of decidedly anti-populist, even anti-democratic attitudes," in the words of Walter Isaacson, senior editor of *Time* magazine.)[19]

Hostility to Bolshevism was hardly unique to the government of the United States. French Prime Minister Georges Clemenceau — noting in 1918 Bolshevik "dreams of setting up soviet regimes first throughout the old Russian territories and then in the rest of Europe" — advocated an "economic encirclement of Bolshevism" using military forces "to establish around Bolshevism, not only a *cordon sanitaire* to isolate it and kill it by starvation, but also the nuclei of friendly [anti-Communist] forces around which the healthy elements of Russia will be able to organize, and bring about the restoration of their country under the aegis of the Entente [i.e., Allied forces of Britain, France, the U.S., etc.]." Britain's War Minister Winston Churchill, determined to block any Bolshevik threat to the far-flung interests of the British Empire, wryly commented: "Were they [the Allies] at war with Soviet Russia? Certainly not; but they shot Soviet Russians at sight. They armed the enemies of the Soviet Government. They blockaded its ports and sunk its battleships. They earnestly desired and schemed its downfall."[20]

Powerful economic interests in Britain saw an opportunity in European, Asian, and Middle Eastern areas threatened by revolutionary infection — if the Bolshevik threat was vanquished — "for the peaceful penetration of British influence and British trade, for the creation of a second India or a second Egypt." So stated a London meeting of the Bibi-Eibet Oil Company in December 1918, and such views were common among Britain's upper classes. Prime Minister David Lloyd-George, however, pulled back from War Minister Churchill's enthusiastic interventionism in Russia, in part because of radical ferment and anti-intervention activities among British workers, many with socialist sympathies and Labour Party affiliation. The oil magnates bitterly complained that "the feeble voices of our politicians, under the heel of democracy, drown all such aspirations" to add such "a valuable asset to the Empire."[21]

While the downfall of the Bolshevik regime was not achieved, the material aid given the counter-revolutionary White forces under General Denikin and Admiral Kolchak, among others, prolonged the incredibly bloody and brutalizing civil war long after it would otherwise have sputtered out. (As it was, more than 19 million deaths resulted from the combined effects of foreign intervention, economic blockade, and civil war, if one includes those who perished from the related waves of famine and disease.) "The Bolsheviki were absorbed during the whole of 1919 in the conflicts with Kolchak and Denikin," Churchill noted with satisfaction. "Their energy was turned upon the internal struggle." This made a shambles of the much-vaunted "workers' republic" and helped to block the spread of the revolution — creating "a breathing-space of inestimable importance" for the creation of anti-Communist regimes (generally in the form of right-wing dictatorships) throughout Eastern Europe that "were able during 1919 to establish the structure of civilized states and to organize the strength of patriotic armies."[22]

An Austro-Hungarian soldier of decidedly non-Communist predilections, Hans Kohn (later an academic authority in the United States on nationalism), witnessed the carnage as a prisoner of war in Russia. Musing that "even the restraints of international agreements valid in war do not prevail in times of bitter revolutionary and counterrevolutionary conflicts when both sides are locked in a fanatical life-and-death struggle," Kohn emphasized: "Compromise is out of the question and any act, no matter how barbaric, is permissible." His observations on those whom Churchill supported are not without interest:

> The "Red" terror during the Russian civil war was frightening, yet the "White" terror, with its disregard for human values, was even more savage and more depressing because it was not motivated by even the dedication to a universal cause that moved the Bolsheviks. Many people shuddered at the execution of the Tsar's family; but few of them cared about the countless other victims on both sides. Looking back on history, I am inclined to believe that this double standard has been the general rule. The brutalities of the country people in the Peasants' Wars [of the 1500s] could be explained by their long suffering and ignorance; their even more brutal repression by their masters was more revolting because this cruelty was deliberate and was undertaken in the name of order, civilization, and religion. The same was the case when ruling classes suppressed colonial uprisings, or when the government of [Adolph] Thiers savagely put down the Paris Commune [of 1871]. The ruling classes have never attributed human dignity to peoples in revolt, nor did they ever for a moment believe that the life of one of the subject people could be equal to the life of one of their own class or race.[23]

Kohn "witnessed much of this inhumanity" at close range in Siberia, where he was imprisoned, and where the "White" armies were operating under the command of Admiral Kolchak, "an ostensibly honorable and capable officer." The dominant element among these forces, he observed, were "old-fashioned reactionaries who did not understand the need for change, much less a social revolution, and wished to restore the vast estates seized by the Bolsheviks to their former owners, and to reinstate Russian domination over its subject peoples." Kohn concluded: "The desperate effort to restore a discredited *ancien regime*, the refusal to see its villainies and follies, and to grant the Russian masses' longing for equality and dignity, doomed the 'White' armies in spite of their initial great advantages."[24]

By blaming Lenin and his comrades for the failure to realize the radical-democratic goals to which they were committed, without giving any weight to such factors as these, is not something that we should expect from someone so thoughtful as Stephen Eric Bronner. But in his defense, one must acknowledge that he is hardly alone.

The notion of Lenin as a leading representative of radical democracy remains inconsistent with the notions of a great many influential scholars and thoughtful intellectuals. Some of them share the biases of such great men as Woodrow Wilson and Winston Churchill, and therefore are naturally inclined to interpret reality in like manner. But this is not true of Bronner, nor can it be said of the noted philosopher Richard Rorty. Coming from a quite different intellectual background than Bronner, nonetheless Rorty has a political orientation (and expresses a total rejection of Lenin) that is similar. Not long ago, Rorty wrote an autobiographical fragment in which he noted that he had been brought up in a home influenced by Trotskyism but that, as he puts it, "most of us who were brought up Trotskyite now feel forced to admit that Lenin and Trotsky did more harm than good, and that Kerensky [their liberal semi-socialist opponent during Russia's revolutionary days of 1917] has gotten a bum rap for the past 70 years."[25]

Yet the Russian workers' and peasants' revolution led by Lenin and Trotsky offered hope, in a way that Kerensky never did, among many millions of people for a life and a world without poverty, without oppression, without war. The violence of the status quo — which Lenin and Kerensky both failed to overcome — threatens billions of people, and our entire planet, today. It will not do simply to shrug off the failures of these two. What one immediately finds, however, is that (bum rap or not) Kerensky offered little in the way of political theory or practice for us to consider and utilize as we confront the violence of today's global capitalist status quo. Lenin constitutes a far greater source of analyses, strategies, tactics, and practical advice on how to struggle for a society of "the free and the equal" characterized by popular sovereignty.

Two Lenins

Lenin's critics fall into two categories: those who have rejected his revolutionary socialist goals, and those who share those goals. Ironically, if we wish to find a pioneering critic on each end of the spectrum, we can put forward a single name: Bertram D. Wolfe. Historian E. H. Carr once described him as having "a life-long love–hate affair with Lenin."[26] It may be worth taking a moment to remind ourselves of who he was.

Wolfe was one of the most talented intellectuals and writers involved in the founding of the U.S. Communist Party. A leading theoretician and educator in the early Communist leadership, he aligned himself with the faction headed by Jay Lovestone. In the late 1920s, Lovestone, Wolfe, and a handful of others rebelled against some of Stalin's policies and were expelled from the Communist mainstream. By 1941, the Lovestone group disintegrated and many of its members became increasingly conservative.[27]

During the 1940s, however, Wolfe continued to adhere to important elements of his earlier orientation. As he was writing his 1948 classic study of Lenin and the Bolsheviks, *Three Who Made a Revolution*, he was in the process of critically reexamining his previous commitments to the Communist movement — but had not yet fully broken from those commitments. He thought that the Bolshevik revolution had paved the way for Stalinist totalitarianism, but that (to use Wolfe's own words) "as late as the autumn of 1917 Lenin had no idea of outlawing all other parties and creating a one-party system."[28]

Up to this point, according to Wolfe, "Lenin in his own mind remains a democrat. That is to say, ... he believes himself to be a democrat, though it must be clear ... that in temperament, in passion, and in a number of decisive actions he has already unconsciously rejected or acted against the outwardly held democratic doctrines. ... His temperament and power-centered convictions, and tactical and organization methods, will come into open conflict with his democratic formulae." Wolfe concludes: "I find Lenin (before he takes power) advancing many democratic views. It is the moment of taking power, the method of holding power, and other subsequent choices that finally determine the character of his regime and the sum of his own character."[29]

Wolfe concludes that there are two Lenins, just as there are two Marxes. In the early 1850s, according to Wolfe, despite all his appeals for working-class rule, Marx demonstrated a definite authoritarian streak. After the Paris Commune of 1871, however, Marx's writings became more "de-centralist, anti-authoritarian, and democratic" — and Lenin follows in this spirit until 1917, when he "reverses the process."[30]

But in the 1950s, when Wolfe served as a Cold War ideologue employed by the U.S. government, he explicitly abandoned any pretense of being a socialist. In the same period, he developed a deep hostility to Lenin's life and ideas, helping to propagate the notion that Lenin was the architect of totalitarianism and that it would have been best if the Russian revolutionary had never been born.[31]

Within Wolfe the residual elements of the thoughtful revolutionary he once was remained locked in debilitating conflict with the increasingly conservative government employee and Cold War ideologist that he had become. Wrenching himself away from his commitment to the ideas of Marx and Lenin, he came to view the Russian Revolution as "a convergence of the irresistible force of a messianic and Manichaen belief system with the iron will of an all-powerful and demonic leader," as Arno Mayer has put it, and Mayer's judgment is apt: "Ultimately such over-ideologized and over-personalized explanations are obsessively monocausal. ... Unlike the lawyer, who pleads a case, and the judge, who holds the scales, the critical historian asks 'why,' and realizes that the answer will not be simple."[32]

The "mature" Wolfe was unable to finish the scholarly examination begun in his classic *Three Who Made A Revolution*, which took the story of Bolshevism only up to 1914. In the last two and a half decades of his life, before his

1977 death, his writing rarely rose above the level of anti-Communist polemics and Cold War propaganda. The historian most successful in producing actual scholarly works that are in the spirit of the latter-day Wolfe is probably the neo-conservative Harvard professor Richard Pipes, a veteran of the Reagan administration (proud sponsor of Central American dictators and death squads, not to mention weapons of mass destruction, in the crusade against Communism), who is far more sympathetic to the intolerant and inept Tsar Nicolas II, the sinister "holy man" Rasputin, and especially the reactionary General Lavr Kornilov than to any working-class, peasant, socialist, or democratic forces.[33]

What's Wrong with Lenin

In stark contrast, there are others who are closer in spirit to the earlier Bertram Wolfe, offering incisive criticisms of Lenin that have been consistent with a genuinely democratic and socialist standpoint. Among such works are Samuel Farber's 1990 study *Before Stalinism: The Rise and Fall of Soviet Democracy*, Neil Harding's 1996 critique entitled *Leninism*, and Robert Service's three-volume study *Lenin: A Political Biography*. These and other such works merit serious consideration by those seeking to learn from the accomplishments but also from the grave mistakes associated with the revolutionary socialist project.[34]

One can identify tendencies toward arrogance, theoretically and sometimes practically, in Lenin's orientation. What is seen as arrogance by Lenin's critics, of course, may be a source of strength for a serious revolutionary. How can a relatively small number of people hope to bring about fundamental political, social, and economic transformations — especially in the face of vast impersonal forces as well as powerful elements in society and the state that are opposed to such transformations? There is a need for a body of theory that helps to make sense of reality, as well as a strong will to utilize such theory to bring about the desired changes. The clear and self-confident political orientation of both Lenin and of his party were necessary elements in rallying the most conscious layers of the working class, and, for a time, majority sections of the population, to the revolutionary cause.

On the other hand, such sweeping self-confidence can contribute to an inadequate understanding of the revolutionary process. In combination with the complex of objective difficulties over which Lenin had no control (such as the brutal political and cultural inheritance of tsarist Russia, plus intense military and economic assaults by world capitalism), such inadequate understanding can pave the way for devastating mistakes.

Another common criticism of Lenin's orientation involves its relationship to the question of democracy. Actually there are two seemingly contradictory points that are made by critics: first, that Lenin was too radically democratic (that is, he theorized a radical form of super-democracy that was utopian and unrealizable); and second, that Lenin was radically undemocratic.[35]

Lenin's unfinished theoretical symphony, *The State and Revolution*, constitutes — first of all — a significant contribution to Marx scholarship. But building on the excavation of the actual views of Marx and Engels, Lenin projects the vision of a workers' state in which government is directly and genuinely a manifestation of "rule by the people," a modern Marxist version of Athenian democracy.[36]

Of course, the disastrous conditions already facing the new soviet republic, and the horrific intensification of difficulties guaranteed by powerful internal and external enemies, ensured the destruction of any necessary pre-conditions for a democratic order. "The faith which Lenin had placed in the Soviets was rendered altogether illusory by the circumstances of revolution and civil war," Ralph Miliband has noted, adding: "Whether they could have fulfilled even some of his expectations had circumstances been more favorable is an open question."[37]

Far more serious is the other side of the coin. In the face of the multiple and murderous catastrophes of a brutal and brutalizing civil war, a rapid succession of foreign invasions, a vicious economic blockade, and the collapse of industry and agriculture, the radical soviet democracy of 1917 was destroyed. "The Bolshevik project was an inconstant amalgam of ideology and circumstance, of intention and improvisation, of necessity and choice, of fate and chance," as Arno Mayer has put it — although it seemed that "the brazen daring of the Bolsheviks ... kept being vindicated by altogether improbable successes which legitimated and strengthened their tenuous and beleaguered regime." From 1918 through 1922, a one-party dictatorship was established that used extreme violence against active enemies and large numbers of potential and imagined enemies. This was a far cry from what had been promised in 1917. The absence of working-class and peasant self-government — Lenin's defenders can argue — was the result of horrendous social and economic disintegration that destroyed all necessary preconditions for democracy. The fact remains that, by the summer of 1918, Lenin's government had become an authoritarian regime that increasingly and systematically violated human rights.[38]

Such things were sometimes reported and struggled against by a number of Bolsheviks — but also were defended by many, sometimes including Lenin and Trotsky. "Lenin's writings of the time show his military-authoritarian strain," Robert C. Tucker points out, "despite the fact that his overall legacy to the movement was the idea of the preferability of persuasion in the party's relations with the masses."[39] In a 1920 address, as Red Army troops were about to engage with powerful military forces led by counter-revolutionary General Denikin, Lenin said:

What is better? To ferret out, to imprison, sometimes even to shoot hundreds of traitors from among the Cadets, non-party people, Mensheviks and Socialist-Revolutionaries, who "come out" (some with arms in hand, others with conspiracies, others still with agitation against mobilization, like the Menshevik printers and railwaymen, etc.) *against* Soviet power, in other words, in favor of Denikin? Or to allow matters to reach such a pass that Kolchak and Denikin are able to slaughter, shoot, and flog to death tens of thousands of workers and peasants? The choice is not difficult to make.[40]

In the same period Trotsky argued that "the Red Terror" works in the same way as a war — "it kills individuals and intimidates thousands …. This is inhumane, but no one ever considered war a school of humanity — still less civil war." Rejecting "the Kantian priestly and vegetarian-Quaker prattle about the 'sacredness of human life,'" he asserted: "We were revolutionaries in opposition, and have remained revolutionaries in power. To make the individual sacred we must destroy the social order which crucifies him. And this problem can only be solved by blood and iron."[41]

Notions of defending the Russian Revolution and of the need for "Red Terror" could sometimes be intertwined with a seemingly compelling logic. Yet there were things done that perhaps can be understood and explained but cannot be defended. Isaac Deutscher puts it well:

Then comes the great tragedy of the isolation of the Russian Revolution; of its succumbing to incredible, unimaginable destruction, poverty, hunger, and disease as a result of the wars of intervention, the civil wars, and of course the long and exhausting world war which was not of Bolshevik making. As a result of all this, terror was let loose in Russia. Men lost their balance. They lost, even the leaders, the clarity of their thinking and of their minds. They acted under overwhelming and inhuman pressures.[42]

"Lenin, Trotsky, and their supporters have already been poisoned by the corrupting virus of power," complained Maxim Gorky, "which is evident from their disgraceful treatment of freedom of speech and person, and all of those rights for which democracy has struggled." More than this, Lenin and his comrades were increasingly inclined to defend what they were doing by putting forward "authoritative" assertions and theorizations that were arrogant and destructive. This included a false identification of Marx's notion of "dictatorship of the proletariat" not with its actual meaning (political domination of the state by the working class, in fact a *workers' democracy*) but rather with one-party rule by the Bolsheviks (renamed "Communists" in 1918).[43] As Trotsky put it in 1920:

> The road to Socialism lies through a period of the highest possible inten-
> sification of the principle of the State.... Just as a lamp, before going out,
> shoots up in a brilliant flame, so the State, before disappearing, assumes
> the form of the dictatorship of the proletariat, i.e., the most ruthless
> form of State, which embraces the life of the citizens authoritatively in
> every direction.[44]

Another problem in the Leninist tradition involves the premature economic "nationalization" of the economy. Initially, Lenin, Trotsky, and some of
the more astute Bolsheviks had not favored rapid nationalizations that would
quickly eliminate the capitalist mode of production from revolutionary Russia. Instead they called for a "mixed economy" ruled by a democratic workers'
state in which the socialized sector of the economy would make "despotic
inroads" (in the words of the *Communist Manifesto*) into the private sector
as conditions made this feasible. Under the impact of civil war and foreign
intervention in the summer of 1918, this policy was reversed. Victor Serge
described the results this way: "This expropriation of industry, verging ever
closer to a total nationalization, placed an increasingly numerous population
of workers within the responsibility of the Socialist State, and compelled it
hastily to establish a body of functionaries, managers, and administrators
who could not be recruited straight away from among the working class. The
bureaucracy was born, and was rapidly becoming a threat."[45]

Also, during this period of "war communism," the government adopted
policies toward the masses of Russia's peasantry that were often violent and
destructive, frequently permeated with arrogance and based on ignorance.
The results were summarized, after the bloody repression of a number of peasant uprisings, by high-level Bolshevik stalwart Vladimir Antonov-Ovseenko
in a lengthy report. A few sentences give a sense of the realities:

> The peasant uprisings develop because of widespread dissatisfaction, on
> the part of small property-owners in the countryside with the dictator-
> ship of the proletariat, which directs at them its cutting edge of implacable
> compulsion, which cares little for the economic peculiarities of the peas-
> antry and does the countryside no service that is at all perceptible.... The
> peasantry, in their majority, have become accustomed to regarding the
> Soviet regime as something extraneous in relation to themselves, some-
> thing that issues only commands, that gives orders most zealously but
> quite improvidently.... [The Soviet regime] is a force which issues instruc-
> tions from the outside and not the acknowledged guide of the peasant
> farmer; in the eyes of the peasants it is tyrannical and not a system that,
> before all else, organizes and ministers to the countryside itself.[46]

In an important comparative study of violence and terror in the French
and Russian revolutions, Arno Mayer outlines the dialectic of revolution and

counter-revolution, economic chaos and international intervention, breeding violence and terror. Unlike many who simply condemn the murderous violence of Lenin and the Bolsheviks, Mayer sees the no less murderous violence of the powerful anti-Bolsheviks as an essential element in the equation. He comments that Bolsheviks "were unprepared for the enormity of the crisis," and also were "caught unawares by its Furies, which they were not alone to quicken." At the same time, he reflects: "It may well be that by virtue of its eventual costs and cruelties, this resolve to fight a civil war became the original sin or primal curse of Bolshevik governance during the birth throes of the Russian Revolution."[47]

Others have made similar observations. Years before the Bolshevik Revolution, Jean Jaures had insisted in his monumental *Socialist History of the French Revolution*: "Revolutions are a barbarous means of progress." His countryman Boris Souvarine would quote this while trying to make sense of Russian realities. "Bolshevism could not escape the psychosis of systematized murder," he observed. "At the end of the Civil War it was soaked in it. Its principles, practice, institutions, and customs had been turned into new channels by the weight of the calamities it had endured. It was its misfortune rather than its fault."[48]

With the "New Economic Policy" of 1921, Lenin and his comrades finally ended the repressive and destructive policies toward the peasant majority and stepped back from some of the over-centralization of the economy. But there was an initial blindness in Lenin's perspective to dangers that contributed directly to the emergence of what came to be known as "Stalinism." There had developed within the regime a subculture of brutality, an authoritarian dismissal of democracy and human rights, and a rise of bureaucracy that rapidly overwhelmed the Soviet republic.

"Revolution from Above"

While Lenin's policies during the desperate civil war years contributed to the rise of Stalinism, the brutal authoritarianism of "war communism" did not flow uninterruptedly into Stalinist totalitarianism. With the conclusion of the civil war, there was an essential interlude initiated in 1921, associated with the New Economic Policy (NEP).

There was, of course, the consolidation of the Communist Party dictatorship. "There is room for all kinds of parties in Russia," joked one Communist leader, Mikhail Tomsky, in the 1920s, "but only one of them is in power and all the rest are in prison." The logic of this is that only one specific party should *ever* be allowed to be in power — which meant that the slogan of the 1917 Revolution "all power to the soviets" (government by democratic councils) now added up to *all power to the Communist Party*.[49]

This was the crystallization of political realities emerging from the civil war. Hannah Arendt, in her classic *The Origins of Totalitarianism*, wrote: "There is no doubt that Lenin suffered his greatest defeat when, at the outbreak of the civil war, the supreme power that he originally planned to concentrate in the Soviets definitely passed into the hands of the party bureaucracy; but even this development, tragic as it was for the course of the revolution, would not necessarily have led to totalitarianism."

Arendt's point hinges on the developments Lenin sought to foster under the banner of NEP — seeking to regenerate the economic, social, and cultural life of the newborn Soviet republic. "Lenin seized at once on all possible differentiations ... that might bring some structure into the population, and he became convinced that in such stratification lay the salvation of the revolution." He sought to secure the development of an independent peasant class, Arendt argued, tried to strengthen the working class by encouraging independent trade unions, even facilitated the reappearance of businessmen, and he helped to generate a significant degree of cultural freedom and artistic diversity. "He introduced further distinguishing features by organizing, and sometimes inventing, as many nationalities as possible, furthering national consciousness and awareness of historical and cultural differences even among the most primitive tribes in the Soviet Union." Arendt went on to explain:

> At the moment of Lenin's death [in 1924] the roads were still open. The formation of workers, peasants, and [in the wake of the New Economic Policy] middle classes need not necessarily have led to the class struggle which had been characteristic of European capitalism. Agriculture could still be developed on a collective, cooperative, or private basis, and the national economy was still free to follow a socialist, state-capitalist, or free-enterprise pattern. None of these alternatives would have automatically destroyed the new structure of the country.[50]

Vladimir Brovkin, a relentless critic of the Bolsheviks (and author of perhaps the most sophisticated and plausible argument for the continuity between Leninism and Stalinism) makes a similar point about the situation that developed in the 1920s: "If peasants had received a fair price and a Peasant Union; workers been allowed an unaffiliated party and free trade unions; women had received equal pay and respect; and students, teachers, and professors had been granted their academic freedoms, Russia would have continued to evolve towards a normal country. It would have been a triumph of civil society."[51]

The Soviet Republic's continued economic backwardness and global isolation generated growing tensions and crises, and the authoritarianism that marked the civil war period once again came to the fore. This crystallized under Joseph Stalin, whose tactical shrewdness and political pathology were greatly underestimated by others in the Bolshevik and Communist leadership, enabling him to concentrate considerable power in his hands. In the newly created position of general secretary of the Russian Communist Party, Stalin oversaw the growing bureaucratic apparatus that was supposed to help carry out the decisions of the old Bolshevik leadership and the Soviet workers' state.

But the apparatus, concentrating in its hands power and material privileges, became dominant over both party and state. One after another, old Bolshevik leaders found themselves outmaneuvered by the party's general secretary, whom they had initially taken for granted.

Stalin was "a formidable master of the techniques of accumulating power," writes Robert C. Tucker. "His secretiveness, capacity to plan ahead, to conspire, to dissimulate, and to size up others as potential accessories or obstacles on his path, stood him in good stead here." Tucker's portrait reveals the lethal element of idealism entwined in Stalin's increasingly neurotic personality — "power for power's own sake was never his aim," but rather "a never-ending endeavor to prove himself a revolutionary hero." From his "commanding position in the party oligarchy by the end of 1927," Tucker recounts, "Stalin manipulated events in 1928 to make it appear that Soviet Russia was in a state of external and internal emergency that required a policy of revolutionary advance in the construction of socialism, for which speedy collectivization of the peasants was a necessity. He thereby steered the state into the revolution from above."[52]

The impact of this state-imposed "revolution" was not anticipated. "So habituated was the collective party mind to the idea that building socialism would be an evolutionary process," explains Tucker, "that Stalin's party colleagues apparently did not divine what the apostle of socialism in one country was saying" when he first hinted at what he had in mind in 1926. It was certainly alien to Lenin's orientation. From 1918 through 1922 the Bolshevik leader had shown that he would not hesitate in "repressing real or suspected enemies of the new state. But the idea of the construction of socialism in a revolution from above employing repressive means against large elements of the Revolution's social constituency, especially in a terror-enforced collectivization of the peasantry, never entered his mind." From 1928 through the 1930s, Stalin's "revolution from above" pushed through the forced collectivization of land and a rapid industrialization that remorselessly squeezed the working class, choked intellectual and cultural life, and killed millions of peasants, culminating in purge trials, mass executions, and a ghastly network of prison camps brutally exploiting its victims' labor.[53]

There was a method in the madness. What Marx called *primitive capitalist accumulation* — involving massively inhumane means (which included the slave trade and genocide against native peoples, as well as destroying the livelihood of millions of peasants and brutalizing the working class during the early days of industrialization) — had created the basis for modern capitalist industrial economy.[54] Marx had expected that this capitalist economic development would provide, after a working-class revolution *from below*, the basis for a democratic, humane socialist order. But if Soviet Russia, so incredibly backward economically, was to build socialism in a single impoverished country, then there would be the need to create a modern industrial order through what some had theorized as *primitive socialist accumulation*.[55] This flowed from the conclusion of Stalin and those around him that — contrary to the initial expectations of Lenin and the Bolsheviks — socialist revolutions in other countries would not come to the aid of the Soviet Republic. Socialism would be built in a single country, the Union of Soviet Socialist Republics. What came to be known as "Stalinism" flowed inexorably from these premises.

For many, the essence of the Stalinist order is symbolized by three syllables: labor camps. This network of camps, whose name has become known internationally as "the gulag," has been immortalized in the writings of the great Russian novelist Alexander Solzhenitsyn, most poignantly in his novels, but most monumentally in the three-volume work of nonfiction *The Gulag Archipelago*. The strange term "comes from the official language of the state organization called GULAG — *Glavnoye Upravleniye Lageryei* [Central Administration of Camps] — a powerful, far-reaching organization to supply the labor force for the construction of socialism," explains former camp inmate Mikhail Baitalsky. The reference to "socialism" is a bitter tongue-in-cheek comment from this Communist survivor of the gulag. By World War II, the camps contained masses of underfed and ragged forced laborers, policed by armed guards and snarling dogs. Baitalsky bitterly highlights a sign at the Vorkuta Camp Number 12 that bore the glowing words of Stalin: "Every day, going to work and returning from it, accompanied by vicious, handsome, well-cared-for German shepherds, we read the words of the leader directed at us: 'Life has become better, comrades; life has become more joyful.'"[56]

Vitally important as a source of information, Solzhenitsyn's remarkable study was also conceived of as an anti-Communist polemic — a fact that introduced more than one unfortunate distortion. There is, first of all, the point made by Baitalsky, who went to the gulag years before Solzhenitsyn was consigned there, and who endured the ordeal for much longer. "I notice that for him a Communist is an unredeemable individual, barely a person at all," Baitalsky has commented. "To him, a person's moral character is determined by his political views: A devoted 'orthodox' Communist is a degenerate, while a devoted Christian is an uplifted soul." Baitalsky objects that "ordinarily, a person's moral character develops before he or she chooses a set of ideas to adopt, not afterward." He observes that Solzhenitsyn "does not deny himself the right to develop but others who are on his list of ideological deadbeats — former or present Communists — he summarily dismisses." Baitalsky insists that "in the camps, people matured and found themselves. Solzhenitsyn was among them. I, too, matured, as did tens of thousands of others."[57]

Related to the great writer's blindness to the humanity of Communists in these three volumes is another serious distortion. A central theme of Solzhenitsyn's account is that Lenin and the Bolsheviks had from the very beginning, and intentionally, established the systematic state terror and forced labor camps — that this orientation "had been advanced in the first month after the October Revolution." Stalin was simply Lenin's loyal heir. Although the gulag was formally established in 1930, after Lenin's death, it has become common-place even for reputable historians to refer to "the millions committed to the gulag under Lenin and Stalin."[58]

David Dallin and Boris Nicolaevsky (two of Lenin's severest Menshevik opponents) tell us that "the Communist party came to power as the great heir to an age-old revolutionary movement in which lofty ideals and humanitarian goals were the inspiring stimuli to self-sacrifice and devotion to the political cause." In their opinion, there was in the early Soviet period a "struggle of the two tendencies — humanitarianism and terrorism — [in which] the latter was the winner. After the first decade of the Soviet system the new trends were definitely victorious." But they note that systematic state-sponsored forced labor had been maintained in Russia years before Lenin was born (with 30,000 as the maximum on the eve of World War I, although the number shot up to 50,000 by 1917, just before the revolution). The camps of the Soviet period rep-resented what they termed the "reappearance of the Old Russia."[59]

While this suggests disturbing continuities between the old Russia and the new, it was in the years 1928–1934 that what they term "the great upheaval" took place. As late as 1928 (according to Robert Conquest's *The Great Terror*), the populations of the Soviet Union's "correctional" camps was 30,000. In 1990, Conquest asserted that Stalin's vicious "revolution from above" — the forced collectivization of land and rapid industrialization — sent the population of the gulag sky-rocketing to 7 million by 1935, and well beyond that in later years. Other scholars, using newly-released materials from secret police archives, have found the figures to be somewhat lower — rising from the tens of thousands in the 1920s to the hundreds of thousands in the early 1930s, soaring to at least 1.3 million by 1937. Death helped keep the number of pris-oners down. "In 1930–40, at least 726,000 people were shot, most of them in 1937–38," comments the widely-respected Russian historian Oleg Khlevniuk. "Executions, along with the high mortality rate during investigation and en route to and within prisons and camps, reduced the ultimate number of inmates." It has been estimated that 936,766 additional prisoners died in the camps between 1934 and 1947.[60]

The incredible increase in the number of prisoners and deaths suggests a qualitative change in the system as such. There was certainly a qualitative dif-ference in the conditions of those sentenced to prison camps before and after "the great upheaval." The first Soviet penal code actually called for maximum penalties to be five years (raised to ten years in 1922 — then to 25 years in 1937) and called for prisoners' conditions to be "humane and liberal in the best sense of the word" (according to Dallin and Nicolaevsky). In the "internal isolators" to which many political prisoners were initially sent, there was "a certain degree of individual freedom," and even in the harsher labor camps in which a number of Mensheviks, Socialist-Revolutionaries, and anarchists found themselves — where individual camp commanders perpetrated abuses (sometimes in conflict with policies of the Soviet government) — there persisted a "liberal tradition" that allowed for certain freedoms and a degree of self-organization, making it possible for them to organize, sometimes successfully, against instances of brutality and for better conditions. During the 1920s, however, conditions deteriorated, and the 1930s saw the dramatic expansion and deepened brutality of the forced labor system. Stalin's favorite jurist, Andrei Vyshinsky, denounced the "sentimental" humanitarianism of the earlier Soviet penal code: "Punishment cannot be reduced to education, and let us not pretend that prisons are no different from schools!" Eugene Shirvindt, another top figure in the Soviet criminal justice system, concurred: "We must overcome the sugary liberalism and a sympathetic attitude toward the offender." And as the commander of one of the camps put it: "We are not trying to bring down the mortality rate."[61]

Elinor Lipper, a German Communist swept up by the purges in the late 1930s, indicates how the change affected prisoners at the forced labor camp of Kolyma in northeastern Siberia:

Henceforth there was no more fur clothing for the prisoners. The standard equipment became wadded jackets and trousers which soon hung like torn rags upon the bodies of the gaunt prisoners. The felt boots were replaced by shoes made of canvas, and practically every mine worker suffered from frozen feet. ... The wretched rations of the prisoners were deficient in fats; the major component was bread [in contrast to what had previously been a meager but more substantial diet]. But the quantity of bread in all Soviet camps is governed by the amount of work the prisoner performs. ... It is impossible for a person unaccustomed to physical labor to fulfill the quota. He quickly falls into a vicious circle. Since he cannot do his full quota of work, he does not receive the full bread ration; his undernourished body is still less able to meet the demands, and so he gets less and less bread, and in the end is so weakened that only clubbings can force him to drag himself from camp to gold mine.[62]

"These people might die!" objected a nonprisoner on the scene (who soon lost his own life for such interventions), and was told by a camp administrator: "What people? These are enemies of the people." This is the portrait of the "classic" gulag — where the mortality rate doubled between 1933 and 1938, and 90 percent of the camp inmates arrested before World War II were destined to perish.[63]

In addition to the greater scale and more brutal conditions, there is a qualitative difference also between the contexts of Leninist and Stalinist repression. "Lenin's Terror was the product of the years of war and violence, of the collapse of society and administration, of the desperate acts of rulers precariously riding the flood, and fighting for control and survival," Conquest points out. "Stalin, on the contrary, attained complete control at a time when general conditions were calm …. It was in cold blood, quite deliberately and unprovokedly, that Stalin started a new cycle of suffering."[64]

Surveying the horrendous scale of deaths of the "red terror" under Lenin and Trotsky in 1918–21, Arno Mayer has judged that they are not higher than those during the "reign of terror" of the French Revolution (and proportionately lower when one factors in the difference in overall population between France and Russia) — in each case, estimates (depending on "a mixture of incomplete or flawed data and informed conjectures") seem to range from 200,000 to 500,000. Mayer adds: "In pondering the bloodletting in the civil war, which needs to be doubled to take account of the White Terror, it is worth noting that unlike the terror in the French Revolution, it was set in a time when violence was invading every European nation and every other home: in the Very Great War [i.e., World War I] between 10 and 13 million men were killed and close to twice that number wounded."[65]

Like Conquest, Mayer emphasizes the "world of difference between the first terror of 1917–22 and the second terror of the 1930s" when the Stalin regime "was involved in neither civil war nor foreign war, and the internal resistance was of [little] consequence." The most modest estimates of outright executions during the 1930s purges number in the hundreds of thousands, and deaths in the labor camps (not to mention peasant deaths through government-induced famines in the early 1930s) pushes even the modest estimates into the millions.[66]

To declare that "Stalinism was the outcome of Leninism," Hannah Arendt has argued, obscures "the sheer criminality of the whole regime" that actually made the gulag its centerpiece. Whittaker Chambers once made a similar point: "To become the embodiment of the revolutionary idea in history Stalin had to corrupt Communism absolutely …. He sustained this corruption with a blend of cunning and brute force. History knows nothing similar on such a scale." Of course, propagandists of the Stalin regime — through doctored histories, airbrushed photographs, and fictional films, through paintings and poems and polemics — proved to the world that Stalin was Lenin's most apt and loyal pupil, and innumerable anti-Communist propagandists have been pleased to concur. In fact, "Lenin was only slightly acquainted with Stalin before the revolution," historian Roy Medvedev points out, and "an analysis of Lenin's speeches and articles during 1917–1920 shows that he did not assume the existence of a one-party system in Soviet Russia nor a complete ban on other left and socialist parties. On the contrary, he said that after basic revolutionary changes had been carried out, free elections should be held."[67]

History turned out differently. Yet the balance of evidence suggests that — whatever the contradictory and problematic elements to be found in the orientation and actions of Lenin and the Bolshevik organization leading up to the 1917 revolution — they represented a "revolution from below." By 1919, this "revolution from below" had badly degenerated under the hammer blows of civil war and socioeconomic collapse, with the Communist party dictatorship attempting to salvage the Revolution amid the wreckage of soviet democracy. But the revolutionaries' ideology was still marked by the pre-civil war Bolshevik norms, fundamentally at odds with the future "revolution from above" represented by Stalin and his totalitarian regime. A remarkable reflection of the early Communist conception of what was meant by "dictatorship of the proletariat," still containing the earlier democratic residue, can be found in the 1921 eyewitness report of U.S. Communist William Z. Foster. He gave two quite different descriptions, reflecting a deep ambivalence:

1. "The present government of Russia is what the Communists term a dictatorship of the proletariat. This means that the workers have become the ruling class in Russia, and the intention is that they shall remain such until, through the operations of the new Communistic institutions, social class lines are wiped out by all the people physically fit becoming actual producers."

2. "The dictatorship of the proletariat, as expressed by the small, strongly organized Communist Party, came into existence because of the general unripeness of the masses. Since the various social institutions, made up in the main of these knowing elements, could not function spontaneously in a revolutionary manner, the Communist minorities in them were compelled to find a way, through organization, discipline, and militancy, to make them do so."

Foster emphasized that the Communist dictatorship was temporary — the elimination of "ignorance and general social backwardness" would make "the dictatorship gradually disappear," and in time the ultimate Communist goal of "a non-government society would be arrived at." While political parties of "the capitalists, aristocrats, and their many hangers-on ... are outlaws," however, he recorded milder treatment toward "proletarian parties," among whom he counted the Left-Socialist Revolutionaries, the Mensheviks, and the anarchists. They had been subjected to restrictions and, in some cases, outright repression. "No one deplores more than the Communists this rigid suppression of the opposition, especially the honest working class opposition," he wrote. "But it is a supreme necessity of the revolution, something without which the latter could not survive." This was because of the life-and-death struggle against the counter-revolution. "Organized opposition to the Government is forbidden, but individuals talk as freely as in any country in the world," he stressed. "In Russia I heard people criticize the Government more freely than in any country I have ever been in." He made explicit reference to Menshevik, anarchist, and Socialist-Revolutionary delegates at the Moscow Soviet denouncing the mistreatment of some of their comrades in the wake of the Kronstadt rebellion, and a Russian anarchist vigorously polemicizing against Communist policy at a session of the Red Trade Union International.[68]

By 1932, under the rule of Stalin, everything was much simpler for Foster: "The leader and organizer of the proletarian dictatorship is the Communist Party," he explained. "In a socialist society, based upon workers and farmers and where the aim of the government is to advance solely the interests of these toiling masses, there is room for only one Party, the Communist Party …. The toiling masses of the Soviet Union know that the Communist Party is their great leader and they give it their enthusiastic support." There was no mention of the right to criticize the government, or of some future disappearance of Communist Party rule.[69] Communists around the world (aside from handfuls of critical-minded dissidents) learned to see Stalin's regime in this way, harmonizing it with their idealistic aspirations by refusing to comprehend the camps and the other horrors, by justifying the repressions, by denying or rationalizing the growing inequalities.

The growing inequalities are a key. There was an underlying material dynamic in the Stalinist system: rapid industrialization and forced collectivization of land, at the expense of workers and peasants, and growing material privileges for those who were part of the regime.

"We Communists of the first decade after October did not delude ourselves with rosy hopes for an immediate substantial rise in the workers' standard of living," recalled veteran Bolshevik Aleksandra Chumakova. "In the wake of the world war of 1914–17 and the civil war of 1918–22, the economy we inherited from the capitalists and landlords of defeated tsarism was in ruins," yet the Communist Party "saw the salvation of the working class and of workers' power in speeding up the industrialization of the country" — but not in the manner of Stalin's "revolution from above." According to the original Bolshevik conception, it must take place along with at least "a minimal improvement in the life of the workers," but instead it was being carried out in tandem with "the horrifying unrelieved poverty of the workers," with wage cuts accompanying rising production quotas. Chumakova's 1932 argument that the workers needed "immediate government relief" in the form of food, clothing, household goods, and other necessities, put her at loggerheads with the man overseeing industrialization, Stalin's loyal lieutenant Lazar Kaganovich. She soon lost her job and found herself under arrest.[70]

Left-wing journalist Anna Louise Strong wrote of losing one of her best friends in the same period — a saintly woman identified simply as "Yavorskaia" in Strong's memoirs. In a sense, she died of the deep idealism that had drawn her to the Bolshevik revolution. She had been working for years at an orphanage that by the early 1930s was overwhelmed with emaciated little survivors of the ghastly famine that killed millions of peasants, thanks to the forced collectivization of the land. Strong's friend "died raving of inequality."

She had been among the most steadfast supporters of Soviet power, but she had never joined the Communist Party and under the new circumstances was adamant about not joining: "I care more for the party's success than for anything in life, but I cannot honestly join while their speed of change makes children homeless. For me they go too fast." Exhausted, refusing special food privileges, she succumbed to typhus. Her adopted daughter, "choked with tears," described her mother's last moments to Strong:

> Do you know what she said: "There is no equality! There will never be equality! Some will always have special meals while others hunger." Then just before she became unconscious she said: "Do not regret if I die. I am so worn out and so disappointed by people that I want some place in the country where there are only trees."[71]

The inequality was not a hallucination. Joseph Berger, secretary of the Palestine Communist Party who spent much time in the USSR in the 1920s and 1930s (before being arrested and sent to the gulag), has offered a lucid account of the development:

> In the early years of the regime the ascetic tradition of the revolutionaries was maintained. One of its outward manifestations was the "party maximum" — the ceiling imposed on the earnings of Party members. At first this was very low — an official was paid scarcely more than a manual worker, though certain advantages went with a responsible job. Lenin set the tone by refusing an extra kopeck or slice of bread. Later the ceiling was raised, more money for expenses was allowed and it was possible to earn extra on the side by writing. Some people slipped into bourgeois ways, but this was frowned on as a sign of "degeneration." NEP struck a further blow at the tradition, but as long as Lenin was alive something more than lip service was paid to it. A man might earn 120 roubles a month and use the special shops and restaurants opened for the privileged, but he was still not completely cut off from the rank and file of the Party or from the masses. The change came with Stalin and his high material rewards to his supporters. In preparation for the final struggle with the Opposition [in 1926-27], the struggle against privilege was finally given up.[72]

In 1932, as workers' protests were being fiercely repressed, according to Berger, "fairly high local officials were punished as well as the strikers." The reason was that, outraged by the workers' plight, "some party officials were not satisfied with protesting to Moscow but insisted on sharing these conditions themselves. They and their wives boycotted the special shops, wore workers' clothes and stood in the food queues." Berger recounts Kaganovich's explanation for their punishment: "the use of special shops by the privileged was party policy — to boycott them was therefore aggression against the Government.

It was a sign of aping the workers and following their lead — a dangerously subversive attitude." In his incisive study *The Birth of Stalinism*, Michel Reiman emphasizes that "while political terror played an important part, the real core of Stalinism … was social terror, the most brutal and violent treatment of very wide sectors of the population, the subjection of millions to exploitation and oppression of an absolutely exceptional magnitude and intensity." The implementation of this "revolution from above" required a ruling stratum "separated from the people and hostilely disposed toward it" — and so "elements within the ruling stratum that tried to represent or even consider the interests of the people were suppressed."[73]

In his meticulous study of workers in a Moscow metal factory spanning 1912 to 1932, Kevin Murphy comments that now "the relationship between rulers and ruled had become firmly entrenched and there would be no return to workers' militancy." Instead, there would be "the dull drone of uninterrupted productivity drives and the seemingly endless demands for more sacrifice and austerity." Documenting propaganda extolling "socialist competition" that pitted workers against each other as well as top-down Five Year Plans, combined with intensifying repression of dissident protests, Murphy goes on to suggest that "rather than propaganda or terror, in the factories Stalinism relied more heavily upon the weapon of hunger — on its control of food distribution — and on its success in enlisting a loyal minority to police the shop floor on behalf of the state."

Such "Communism" more than rivaled the worst abuses of the "robber baron" era of industrial capitalism. Fred Beal, a U.S. Communist living in Russia in the early 1930s, later described a banquet in Tashkent ("the most sumptuous feast I ever attended") held in his honor as a leader of the famous strike that had been savagely repressed in Gastonia, North Carolina:

> Twenty-five guests were present, all Soviet officials and trade union leaders. Even before the meal began, hundreds of people had gathered at the windows to stare at us. At first I thought they had come to see me, as foreigners were seldom seen in these parts. But it soon became clear that the people were hungry, fiercely hungry. They grumbled at the sight of the rich food the like of which they had probably never tasted. They became menacing in their attitude and the leading Communists gave orders to have them sent away. Soon the police were driving the hungry crowd in all directions. An official drew the curtains together so that no one could look in on that lavish meal. He smiled at me and apologized for the interruption. I kept thinking: How much this scene is like a *Daily Worker* cartoon of capitalists stuffing themselves while the starving workers are looking on.[74]

While Beal soon fled from the Soviet Union and broke with the Communist movement, he expressed the conviction "that there is another road to a free and classless humanity, a road which is worth the quest, and which can be found only by minds liberated from the worship of false gods and spirits strong enough to face the truth in the quest for truth." Yet there were many in and around the Communist movement who could not so easily break from what Leopold Trepper has termed "God-the-party and His prophet Stalin." Trepper, a heroic Communist militant who was active in Poland, Palestine, and France, continued to demonstrate his courage during the Second World War as the leader of "the Red Orchestra," the legendary anti-Nazi spy network. Nonetheless, his awareness of profound problems in the USSR did not enable him to overcome (until many years later) the cult of Stalin's party: "The party cannot be wrong, the party never makes a mistake; you cannot be right if you oppose the party. The party is sacred. Whatever the party says — through the mouth of its secretary general — is the gospel truth. To question it is sacrilege. There is no salvation outside the party: and if you are not with the party, you are against it."[75]

Many idealistic activists — including the young Trepper — were prepared to commit themselves to the Communist order under Stalin's leadership, not because they believed in privileges, inequalities, and labor camps, but because they believed in a better world.

In a survey of "ordinary life in extraordinary times" of Soviet Russia in the 1930s, Sheila Fitzpatrick comments that "people understand and remember their lives in terms of stories," personal narratives that "make sense out of the scattered data of ordinary life, providing a context, imposing a pattern that shows where one has come from and where one is going." The Stalin regime "had a keen interest in shaping such stories," she notes, and this was "the function of agitation and propaganda, a basic branch of Communist Party activity." This influenced the self-perceptions of many Soviet citizens, helping to shape three basic story lines that Fitzpatrick identifies.[76]

1. *The Radiant Future.* "A person who did not know the story might look at Soviet life and see only hardship and misery, not understanding that temporary sacrifices must be made in order to build socialism." Fitzpatrick observes that writers and artists under Stalin were pressured to "develop a sense of 'socialist realism' — seeing life as it was becoming, rather then life as it was," and she comments, "socialist realism was a Stalinist mentalité, not just an artistic style." This fit naturally with the next narrative.

2. *Out of Backwardness.* "*Then* workers' and peasants' children had no chance of an education; *now* they could become engineers. *Then* peasants had been exploited by gentry landlords; *now* the landlords were gone and they held the land collectively. *Then* workers had been abused by their masters; *now* workers themselves were masters. *Then* the people had been deceived by priests and lulled by the

opiate of religion; *now* their eyes had been opened to science and enlightenment."[77]

3. *If Tomorrow Brings War*. "The capitalists would try to overthrow the Soviet Union militarily as soon as a good opportunity presented itself, just as they had done in the Civil War." Survival would depend on how well socialism was being built, "measuring socialism in the most concrete way possible as numbers of new blast furnaces, tractor and tank factories, hydroelectric dams, and kilometers of railroad track." The point of the break-neck industrialization, according to Stalin, "was that without it the country would be vulnerable to its enemies and 'go under' within ten years."[78]

Such narratives were compelling for a broad stratum of people inside the USSR and beyond. Even the friend and humane critic of Lenin, novelist Maxim Gorky, decided to return from his self-imposed exile in 1933 to spend his last three years in what he perceived as the place where socialism was heroically being forged through the proliferation of factories. While it has justly been said that Gorky consequently "stood on the throat of his own song," he was also joining with millions who saw the Soviet Union as a humanistic beacon of hope in a world where global capitalism had sunk into a devastating depression, and where the forces of fascism and Nazism were gaining power.[79]

Throughout the USSR, significant numbers of workers felt that the story lines suggested above corresponded to the realities of which they were an organic part. While they were hardly blind to deficiencies and inequalities, and to bureaucratic stultification, some believed that the problem lay with lower- and middle-level party leaders, and they looked to the top leadership layer around Comrade Stalin for relief. Ironically, this contributed to the purges whirling out of control — especially when the Stalin leadership initiated, for example, a so-called "democratization" campaign in the state-controlled trade unions. "For Stalin and his supporters, democracy was a way to rebuild working-class support, and to forge a united Party, purged of opposition and corruption," writes Wendy Goldman. "They viewed the personal fiefdoms that had developed around regional elites as obstacles to these aims." The reality was fraught with contradictions. Stalinism "was undergirded by bureaucracy," Moshe Lewin has commented, "but it considered bureaucracy both indispensable (hence the pampering of the upper layers) and unreliable." The purges were, in part, an effort to deal with "malfunctions of the bureaucracy," but also reflected Stalin's "pathological sociology that suggested to him where enemies might come from," and — in addition — his "need to furnish himself with a new historical alibi" to put onto others responsibility for the gap between present-day realities and the promise of the revolution's "heroic years." There was a powerful compulsion to mobilize working-class support for and complicity in such lethal shake-ups. Goldman has observed that this top-down push for trade union "democracy" helped accomplish this goal. Yet the resulting charges and counter-charges of these contending forces, often interlarded with personal animosities, as well as accusations of corruption and "wrecking" activities, and also of covert oppositionist "treason," served to "create a toxic brew" that could send both middle-level bureaucrat and temporarily triumphant rank-and-file dissident to the gulag.

The fact remained that a significant layer of the rapidly growing Soviet working class — in some cases inspired by social improvements, in some cases inspired also by variants of socialist idealism — labored to build up the USSR.

The spectacular industrialization was a decisive factor in the USSR's survival and triumph over Hitler. While hardly an industrial power like Germany, Great Britain, or the United States, it was in the process of becoming one when World War II began. Historians of the Second World War note two principal features on the Soviet home front that allowed for the spectacular defeat of Germany: "the rigors which an authoritarian government (aided by an appeal to patriotism) could impose on the people, and the adaptability of the Soviet economy, which partly made up for its technical weakness by its ready response to central planning and direction." They add that, after the horrendous German onslaught of 1941, "once the corner was turned and production resumed [by 1942], expansion was astonishingly rapid. ... Russian production of tanks and aircraft surpassed German production in 1943." Out of a Soviet population of 200 million, at least one-tenth died — but out of the 13.6 million German soldiers killed, wounded, or missing during World War II, 10 million met their fate on the Eastern Front. This was decisive for Hitler's defeat.[80]

The fact remained that "the Stalinist regime did little to improve the life of its people in the 1930s," and this was reflected in confidential reports developed by the NKVD (the secret police) on public opinion, that "the regime was relatively though not desperately unpopular in Russian towns," while in the villages — especially in the early 1930s — it was very unpopular, although this dissatisfaction assumed "fatalistic and passive" forms. Despite the massively promoted Stalin cult, the tyrant "was compared unfavorably with Lenin." Active supporters for the regime could be found among "the young, the privileged, office-holders and party members, beneficiaries of affirmative action policies, and favored groups like Stakhanovites [privileged workers who set high production norms by working harder than the bulk of the workers]." Fitzpatrick adds that despite dissatisfactions, "many workers retained a residual feeling of connection with the Soviet cause, especially in cities with strong revolutionary traditions like Leningrad."[81]

Fitzpatrick's summary of key ideological elements of early Stalinism: "In the October Revolution of 1917, the proletariat, headed by the Bolsheviks, had overthrown the exploiting capitalists, whose concentration of wealth in a few hands had left the majority to poverty and deprivation. Socialism was the predetermined outcome of proletarian revolution." Communists "meant to transform and modernize Russian society, a process they described as 'building socialism.'" This was in "the long-term interests of the people," and "the Communists' sense of mission and intellectual superiority was far too great to allow them to be swayed by mere majority opinion. ... It was the Communists' task to turn backward, agrarian, petty-bourgeois Russia into a socialist, urbanized, industrialized giant with modern technology and a literate workforce." Yet by the 1930s, she acknowledges, the Communists' mode of operation was "acquiring some ... features that few would have predicted in 1917."[82]

The "Leninism" That Stalin Made

The *revolutionary* party of Lenin — one could argue — began to decline when it came to power in 1917. The Russian Communist Party was, unlike the Bolshevik party, a ruling governmental party, not a party of revolutionary opposition. This resulted in significant shifts in the functions and the composition of the organization. More than this, the calamities that befell revolutionary Russia after 1917 — civil war, invasion, economic blockade, and collapse — resulted in intense stresses that introduced authoritarian "expedients" and distortions. Much of this influenced the organizational norms promoted within the Communist International, to which Communist parties in all countries were affiliated.

On the other hand, there was a concern to overcome such distortions among enough of the early Communists so that an explicit warning was written into a resolution on democratic centralism adopted at the 1921 congress of the Communist International against "formal or mechanical centralization [which] would mean the centralization of 'power' in the hands of the Party bureaucracy, allowing it to *dominate* the other members of the Party or the proletarian masses which are outside the party." Instead, democratic centralism was to be "a real synthesis, a fusion of centralism and proletarian democracy" that would facilitate "the active participation of working people" in the ongoing class struggle, in an eventual working-class revolution, and in the effort to create a socialist society.[83]

Precisely the danger this resolution was warning against, however, is what increasingly came to characterize the functioning of the Communist movement in Soviet Russia and throughout the world. Stalin's 1927 interpretation of the essentials of Lenin's theory of the party is less consistent with the revolutionary realities leading up to 1917 than with a trend to centralize power — both in the Communist Party and among the masses outside of the Communist Party — into the hands of the leadership. According to Stalin, Lenin's theory showed:

(a) that the Party is a higher form of the class organization of the proletariat as compared with the other forms of proletarian organization (labor unions, cooperative societies, state organizations) and, moreover, its function was to generalize and direct the work of these organizations; (b) that the dictatorship of the proletariat may be realized only through the party as its directing force; (c) that the dictatorship of the proletariat may be complete only if it is led by a single party, the Communist Party; and (d) that without iron discipline in the Party, the tasks of the dictatorship of the proletariat to crush the exploiters and to transform class society into socialist society cannot be fulfilled.[84]

"The Party is governed by leaders," explained one Stalinist propagandist, V. G. Sorin, in the early 1930s. "If the party is the vanguard of the working class then the leaders are the advanced post of this vanguard." Sorin emphasized that "the special feature of the Communist Party is its strictest discipline, i.e., the unconditional and exact observance by all members of the party of all directives coming from their Party organizations. Discipline, firm and unrelenting, is necessary not only during the period of underground work and struggle against tsarism, not only during civil war, but even during peaceful times." Sorin concluded: "The stricter the discipline, the stronger the party, the more dangerous is it to the capitalists."[85]

Vladimir Brovkin captures important aspects of the reality when he notes that "intellectual debates between high-ranking Bolsheviks on the meaning of socialism were of no special interest to the new ruling elite, as long as they held the reins of power and privilege." As early as 1924, one party intellectual was commenting that "people who had set themselves a goal of changing the world and fighting against prejudice must be brave, fearless, and revolutionary themselves in deeds and thoughts as the Bolsheviks used to be." In contrast, "the party today" was becoming "nothing but a herd of sheep, not daring to have opinions but only trying to please, fearing any independent act." He feared that the Communist Party would "turn into a caste" in which only "careerists, thieves, opportunists, and conservatives would remain." There were acid comments about "officials and bureaucrats, people who … despite their party cards live not for Communism but on Communism." By the late 1920s, an angry Communist worker complained in a letter to a friend that a "majority of those who hold the levers of the dictatorship of the proletariat here in Moscow … live in luxurious apartments and regularly commute to their country-houses." While "one part of the proletariat — entire families — sleep on bare floors and plead for a piece of bread, hungry, cold, and barefoot," the so-called "other part of the proletariat" were able "to glut themselves in restaurants."[86]

The revolutionary poet Vladimir Mayakovsky, not long before his despairing suicide, wrote in "Talk with Comrade Lenin" (1929) that

> Some people
> without you
> got out of hand.
> Many a rogue,

many a scoundrel
rove
to and fro
and around our land....
Chest thrown out
they stalk along
proudly,
all decked with badges
and fountain pens....
Thus the day has passed
and faded away
We are two in the room:
I
And Lenin –
On the whitewashed wall
His lifelike portrait[87]

In 1932, Trotsky wrote from exile: "On the foundation of the dictatorship of the proletariat — in a backward country, surrounded by capitalists — for the first time a powerful bureaucratic apparatus has been created from among the upper layers of the workers, that is raised above the masses, that lays down the law to them, that has at its disposal colossal resources, that is bound together by an inner mutual responsibility, and that intrudes into the policies of a workers' government its own interests, methods, and regulations." Trotsky was merciless in describing the ex-working-class functionary: "He eats and guzzles and procreates and grows himself a respectable potbelly. He lays down the law with a sonorous voice, handpicks from below people faithful to him, remains faithful to his superiors, prohibits others from criticizing himself, and sees in all of this the gist of the general line." In the same period, a dissident Communist in Soviet Russia, M. N. Riutin, was complaining that "the main cohort of Lenin's comrades has been removed from the leading positions, and some of them are in prisons and exile; others have capitulated, still others, demoralized and humiliated, carry on a miserable existence, and finally, some, those who have degenerated completely, have turned into loyal servants of the dictator."[88]

A one-time leader of the Communist Party in Moscow, associated for a time with Bukharin, but expelled in 1930 for opposing the forced collectivization of land, Riutin covertly circulated a document that asserted that "the rule of terror in the party and the country under the clearly ruinous policy of Stalin has led to a situation in which hypocrisy and two-facedness have become phenomena." He went on to assert that "the most evil enemy of the party and the proletarian dictatorship, the most evil counterrevolutionary and provocateur could not have carried out the work of destroying the party and socialist construction better than Stalin has done." But this was all being done under the banner of Communism: "Stalin is killing Leninism, [killing] the proletarian revolution under the flag of the proletarian revolution and [killing] socialist construction under the flag of socialist construction."[89]

Stalinist ideological twist and mode of operation became a defining aspect of Communist parties throughout the world, and shaped how millions of people would interpret "Leninism" throughout the 20th century. Yet, in his final years (beginning in 1922), Lenin himself had become aware that the mode of operation represented by Stalin threatened the socialist future to which he had devoted his life. His struggles against it came too little and too late. The triumph of an apparatus permeated by bureaucratic-authoritarian viciousness eventually would unleash — in the late 1920s and early 1930s — the so-called "revolution from above" that would kill millions of people and destroy what was left of the 1917 "revolution from below," blossoming into what some political theorists would label totalitarianism.[90]

"As Stalin became master of the party, he decisively changed the interpretation of the principle of party unity," historian Roy Medvedev has noted. "Conscious discipline was replaced by blind obedience to the will of the Leader. Party members were instilled with the conviction that Stalin and his leadership could make no mistakes and that any opposition was the work of petty-bourgeois and bourgeois-imperialist circles." As one seasoned member of the Communist Party of the Soviet Union commented many years after: "Lenin foresaw that Stalin, little by little, would make himself master of the party and transform it into a throne."[91]

Historian Robert Thurston has labored creatively and somewhat persuasively to suggest how Stalin and others in his inner circle may have believed, quite sincerely, in the delusion that a conspiracy of one-time "left oppositionists" and "right oppositionists" to Stalin had drawn together into a sinister and murderous threat to the Soviet regime.[92] The sources and consequences of this sincere belief were shaped, however, by structures and ideological perspectives that were qualitatively different from those that characterized Lenin and his comrades. At the shocking public show trials of such one-time Bolshevik leaders as Zinoviev, Kamenev, Bukharin, and others, the defendants were forced to "confess" to such things and to call for their own execution. This was alien to the "Leninism" of Lenin.

Consider the prominent Italian Communist Vittorio Vidali's recollection of the account given to him in 1957 by another trusted veteran of the Communist movement. She had been a young comrade of Rosa Luxemburg and Karl Liebknecht in the earliest beginnings of the German Communist movement, then moved to Moscow to be active in the apparatus of the Communist International. Arrested on false charges in 1937 and sent to the Siberian gulag until the early 1950s, then "rehabilitated," she told this story:

I always believed that our Party was a democratic organization, faithful to traditions of dynamic vitality, in which one could discuss, engage in polemics, dispute, but where nobody could be punished for so doing by being dismissed, pushed to one side, expelled, isolated, jailed, shot. We discussed everywhere: in the trade unions and in the soviets, on the street, in the offices and in factories where everybody wanted to express his own opinion. The very foundation of democracy was constructive criticism. The party organizations, the trade unions, the government bodies had authority and enjoyed universal trust. Then came the rule of bureaucracy; polemics were eliminated and criticism was suppressed. They began to talk about "enemies of the people," "fascist agents," "traitors." The purges began, the trials, deportations, executions. You know that after Kirov was assassinated [in 1935], the death penalty was applied, the Old Guard was liquidated, and tried and tested political and military leaders began to disappear. Stalin, our great and dearly beloved Stalin, wanted to be alone in a vast cemetery. ... The Party, the state power, the bureaucracy are all one and the same thing. I don't believe that the end of Stalin means the end of Stalinism. A caste of bureaucrats and technocrats has replaced the state, the Party and the trade unions. Even our internationalism has weakened. Lenin was right when he insisted on the dangers inherent in bureaucracy, on the need to combat these dangers with specific measures to prevent the bureaucrat from becoming professional, cynical, shameless.[93]

The determination to struggle against fascism, exploitation, poverty, war, and all forms of oppression drew many into the Communist movement, and the same determination became a justification for some to deny or to minimize the brutalities of Stalinism. Characteristic in their revolutionary eloquence were Vidali's words employed to rally forces for the defense of Madrid against the fascist onslaught on November 7, 1936, during the Spanish Civil War:

Madrid cannot fall. ... Men and women, young and old are rushing to the trenches to defend their city, their lives and their future. ... Long live the Spanish Revolution! ... Today is the anniversary of the Russian Revolution. Our Russian brothers, surrounded by millions of enemies, starving, without planes and without tanks, and besieged on all sides, won their battle, because they had faith and confidence in the future. ... We too have faith ... and for that reason we shall conquer.[94]

Interwoven with such a vision, Stalinist brutalities could be rationalized as part of a "tough-minded" pragmatism justified by the immense brutalities of capitalism and imperialism. Vidali, long engaged in Comintern activity, later recalled a discussion with a superior who, regarding a delicate situation, instructed him that "this is a ticklish proposition and it calls for a lot of tact, a great deal of prudence. We must be very, very wily. ... Don't forget that word even in the most difficult moments. We must be open-minded and wily." He also recalled "a 'theory' concerning the 'usefulness' of people, of the masses," commenting that "even a movement can be considered useful or useless. As long as it remains useful, it is utilized; when it no longer serves its purpose it is rejected, or suffocated, or destroyed." Vidali concluded "that Stalin himself taught people to be cynical, unscrupulous without any limit, Machiavellian in the most subtle manner, hypocritical."[95]

Even so, Vidali was unable to shake off the belief — nourished over decades — in Stalin's "strength as a revolutionary, his ability as a statesman, the strategy adopted to lead a great country through terrible storms, in peace and in war."[96] Another revolutionary who, like Vidali, had fundamentally compromised himself by adapting to Stalin was the great philosopher and theorist Georg Lukács, who nonetheless by 1968 was adamant that, although "Stalin's propagandistically proclaimed unanimity with Lenin was hammered deeply into the consciousness of the Communists," this was a "historical legend" that must "be torn to pieces," because "Leninism, in which the spirit of Marx lived, was converted into its diametrical opposite" by the apparatus under Stalin.[97]

One could argue that in the massive Communist Party of the Soviet Union in the 1930s and after, and in the Communist parties throughout the world, many remained who believed passionately in the ideals that had inspired the early Bolsheviks. They are described by the Italian Vidali: "We have believed and continued to believe in an idea which inspires us and for the fulfillment of which we have been tenacious and stubborn, we have passionately struggled and worked, we have suffered [fascist and capitalist] prison, torture and exile, and have faced death. Many of our people have fallen but up to the last moment they were sure that the road we have chosen leads to the triumph of social justice and the progress of mankind."[98]

Eugenia Ginzburg, a Russian Communist who ultimately turned to Christianity to help her survive the gulag, remembered hearing someone unseen — an escapee from the land of Mussolini who found refuge in the USSR — swept up in 1937 purges, being dragged to a punishment cell in a Soviet prison, her screams "piercing, uterine, almost incredible," punctuated with cries of "*Comunista italiana, Comunista italiana!*"[99] Vidali may have found it difficult to include such comrades in his list of martyrs, but, of course, this woman, and many others like her, must be included among those who were drawn to the inspiring vision — suddenly and brutally tormented by doubts about where the road to which they had committed themselves was actually leading.

Surely there was accumulating evidence that the leadership of the Communist movement was dictating policies fundamentally inconsistent with the original high ideals. As Vidali himself describes at the conclusion of one incident, receiving instructions (including the admonition "we must be very, very wily") from a Soviet Communist official, "I stood there with a nasty taste in my mouth." Indeed, he was assured after the fact, by knowledgeable people in the Soviet Union, that the undisputed leader of the world Communist movement was worse than Ivan the Terrible "because he spread death around him, destroying all those who knew more than he did, surrounding himself with mediocrities, spineless clowns. Whoever spoke up was silenced by arrest, 'confession,' death, Siberia. His accomplices are still with us."[100] Indeed, the USSR and the world Communist movement — despite vigorous "de-Stalinization" campaigns — never recovered from this.

The question faces us: if Stalinism is the opposite of "the Leninism of Lenin," how and why did the one give way to the other *inside* the party of Lenin? Two aspects of the answer, stressed by Trotsky in his 1937 essay "Stalinism and Bolshevism," merit close examination.

[1] Bolshevism … is only a political tendency closely fused with the working class but not identical with it. And aside from the working class there exist in the Soviet Union a hundred million peasants, various nationalities, and a heritage of oppression, misery, and ignorance. The state built up by the Bolsheviks reflects not only the thought and will of Bolshevism but also the cultural level of the country, the social composition of the population, the presence of a barbaric past and no less barbaric world imperialism.

[2] Let us remember the prognosis of the Bolsheviks, not only on the eve of the October revolution but years before. The specific alignment of forces in the national and international field can enable the proletariat to seize power first in a backward country such as Russia. But the same alignment of forces proves beforehand that without a more or less rapid victory of the proletariat in the advanced countries the workers' government in Russia will not survive. Left to itself the Soviet regime must either fall or degenerate. More exactly: it will first degenerate and then fall. … Lenin stressed again and again that the bureaucratization of the Soviet regime was not a technical or organizational question, but the potential beginning of the degeneration of the workers' state.[101]

We have already taken note of the first point. The second point is no less decisive, and it was central to Lenin's orientation.

Arrogance

"Doubt is out of the question," wrote Lenin in September 1917 as he labored to rally the forces of socialist revolution in Russia. "We are on the threshold of a world proletarian revolution." This was an idea he repeated over and over as World War I was devastating Europe: "Imperialist war is the eve of socialist revolution." He argued persistently that the Russian working class should follow Bolshevik leadership in "taking power and retaining it until the triumph of the world socialist revolution." After the 1917 seizure of power, as he helped to shape the political program of the Russian Communist Party, Lenin argued for "an analysis of imperialism as the highest stage of the development of capitalism and also an analysis of the era of the socialist revolution."[102]

Lenin was consistently linking the fate of the transition to socialism in Russia with the spread of socialist revolution outside of Russia. He emphasized repeatedly that "there would doubtlessly be no hope for our revolution if it were to remain alone, if there were no revolutionary movements in other countries. ... When the Bolshevik Party tackled the job alone, it did so in the firm conviction that the revolution was maturing in all countries and that in the end — but not at the very beginning — no matter what difficulties we experienced, no matter what defeats were in store for us, the world socialist revolution would come — because it is coming; would mature — because it is maturing and will reach full maturity. ... [I]t is indisputable that all the difficulties in our revolution will be overcome only when the world socialist revolution matures ...." In his *Letter to American Workers*, he gave expression both to the desperate situation of an isolated revolutionary Russia and to the revolutionary-internationalist optimism that had been at the core of the Russian Revolution: "We are now, as it were, in a besieged fortress, waiting for the other detachments of the world socialist revolution to come to our relief .... We are invincible, because the world proletarian revolution is invincible."[103]

The economic disaster, the authoritarian and bureaucratic degeneration, the violence and brutality that overwhelmed Lenin's revolution can be traced to the isolation resulting from the failure of socialist revolution in countries outside of Russia. To this some critics have responded with the charge (which is difficult to refute) that Lenin had an inadequate understanding of the difficulties involved in transforming revolutionary situations in the various countries into actual revolutions that would end the isolation of revolutionary Russia. Yet it is certainly worth considering the recollections of 1919 by someone who lived in this time, Bertram D. Wolfe:

> The opportunities for American radicalism of all varieties seemed immense in that year of interregnum between all-out war and what was supposed to be all-out peace. Millions of soldiers were being demobilized and hundreds of thousands of those who had risked their lives at the front were finding that there were no jobs waiting for them at home. Europe was in turmoil: crowns were tumbling and ancient empires falling; there were revolutions, still not defined in their nature, in Russia, Germany, Austria-Hungary, then a Communist revolution in Hungary itself and another in Bavaria; soldiers were carrying their arms from the front and imposing their will insofar as they knew what they willed. A strike wave unprecedented in our history swept through America: the Seattle General Strike grew out of a protest at the closing down of

the shipyards; the Lawrence Textile Strike; the national coal strike; and, wonder of wonders, the Boston police strike; the great steel strike involving 350,000; the battles of the workers in many industries to keep wages abreast of the high cost of living, and of the employers to end the wartime gains of the labor movement [and] to establish or restore the [anti-union] open shop. Not until the Great Depression [of the 1930s] would the labor movement again show so much militancy.[104]

It has been argued persuasively that socialist revolution was a distinct possibility in Germany during the 1917–23 period. This might have helped generate revolutionary gains elsewhere, and could have blocked the rise of Stalinism (and of Hitlerism). But those who stress this possibility are also compelled to explain how Leninist expectations in Germany were so utterly disappointed.[105]

There is no way to satisfactorily resolve this dispute of what might have been. Partisans praise Lenin and the Bolsheviks for responding to the degrading, violent realities of capitalism and to the revolutionary possibilities in the way that they did. Critics tell a different story. Lenin and the Bolshevik elite — believing they knew what was best for the workers and peasants of Russia and the world, and animated by a colossal arrogance (convinced that their "scientific" understanding enabled them to know more than, in fact, they could know) — initiated a train of events that led to disastrous and brutalizing consequences for millions of workers and peasants, and for most of the Bolshevik elite.[106]

And yet, when one criticizes Lenin for arrogance and elitism that led to inhumanity, one should not pretend that such qualities were stronger in him than in other major political figures and world leaders of the early 20th century. U.S. presidents Theodore Roosevelt and Woodrow Wilson — in their own outlooks and in the orientations of their administrations — were no less arrogant and elitist. Not to mention Winston Churchill, and other champions of the British Empire. Indeed, Lenin never came close to sharing their prejudices against those in the "lower classes" and "weaker races."[107]

One should consider the policies associated with "dollar diplomacy" that were autobiographically and self-critically described in 1935 by Smedley Butler (by then Major General, U.S. Marine Corps, Retired):

I spent 33 years and 4 months in active service as a member of our country's most agile military force — the Marine Corps. I served in all commissioned ranks from a second lieutenant to Major-General. And during that period of time I spent most of my time being a high-class muscle man for Big Business, for Wall Street and for the bankers. In short, I was a racketeer for capitalism.... I helped make Mexico and especially Tampico safe for American oil interests in 1914. I helped make Haiti and Cuba a decent place for the National City Bank boys to collect revenues in. I helped in the raping of half a dozen Central American republics for the benefit of Wall Street.... I helped purify Nicaragua for the international banking house of Brown Brothers in 1909-12. I brought light to the Dominican Republic for American sugar interests in 1916. I helped get Honduras "right" for American fruit companies in 1903. In China in 1927 I helped see to it that Standard Oil went its way unmolested.[108]

Such arrogance and elitism by no means passed out of existence after the early decades of the 20th century.[109] Consider the blunt explanations of James Burnham, Cold War ideologue, awarded the Medal of Freedom by President Ronald Reagan:

The present candidates for leadership in the World Empire are only two: the Soviet Union and the United States.... Now it is obvious, as well as confirmed by historical experience, that carrying out the imperial responsibilities requires certain characteristics in the imperial citizens, or at least in the leading strata; confidence in both their rights and in their ability to perform the imperial task; resoluteness; perseverance; a willingness to assure the strength — that is, the military force — to fulfill the task; and finally (it must be added) a willingness to kill people, now and then, without collapsing into a paroxysm of guilt.[110]

Two other authors also influential among U.S. conservatives of the 1960s and 1970s, Nathaniel Weyl and Stefan Possony, projected what they believed to be a scientific conception of human nature:

When we consider man as conditioned, together with other animals, by the principles of territory, dominance and hierarchy, when we view him as the lineal descendant of a highly successful line of killer-apes, when we consider that the growth of his brain may well have been due in large measure to natural selection for adaptation to his predatory role, much of his instinctual psychology seems to become clear.

They suggested that "the hierarchy of dominance" provides status and security for all people, that even those who are "unsuccessful" prefer "lowly status to lack of status," adding: "Rank not only satisfies the ambition of the strong, but the insecurity of the weak. One danger of the egalitarian society is that, by destroying all status, it creates anxiety among the masses. The logical transition is from the egalitarian hell of insecurity to the Communist hell of unfreedom." Weyl and Possony warned that "the contemporary mania to legislate equality among nations, classes and races and to impose democracy upon all of mankind may stumble against formidable instinctual urges for private property, for dominance over one's brothers, for the hierarchic security of status and for the opportunity to release violent emotions."[111]

The systematic arrogance and commitment to violence of these various and impeccably anti-Leninist figures more than match all such qualities that we can find in Lenin. On the basis of "elitist" similarities, it would make little sense, however, simply to equate Lenin with his global adversaries. We must examine not only means, but ends. What were the goals? The question posed by Antonio Gramsci has relevance: "Is it the intention that there should always be rulers and ruled, or is the objective to create the conditions in which this division is no longer necessary?"[112]

Indeed, Gramsci and Lenin were far closer to the Christianity of A. J. Muste than to the "scientific" secularism of Weyl and Possony. "The cardinal sin is separating oneself from others with whom as a matter of fact we are in every way identical," Muste insisted. "Biologically we are of one blood. Culturally we are products of the same influences .... We are one family, one community." The Marxist revolutionaries might not have agreed with Muste's religious terminology but would certainly have accepted the spirit of this insistence: "Above all, we are children of one divine Father. Setting oneself apart from anyone is the key mistake, the most hideous sin." In commenting on Lenin's "genius," Muste's Christian pacifist comrade Dorothy Day elaborated: "His life followed the pattern of all great men — a single-mindedness, a purity of heart, a search for the new society for man."[113]

What Lenin Knew

One distorts the reality of Lenin by denying the profound good that he believed in and devoted "the whole of his life" to achieving. But one cannot honestly deny what Abraham Heschel termed the "evil within good" that was also part of what he represents. For all of his personal modesty and sincerity, we see in him the sin of pride that Niebuhr stressed, especially a pride of knowledge: the false belief that he understood more than he could actually understand, and basing life-or-death decisions (ultimately for millions of people) on what he believed he knew. And at a certain point, although he continued to cling to intellectual and political "certainties," and to political power, he lost his way. He helped to create preconditions for a reality that was the opposite of what he believed in and had devoted his life to.

To overstate this can also distort the realities. The negative developments of the civil war period do not define the whole of Lenin — his last seven years (particularly the three years of desperate civil war) cannot be used to obliterate the first 47 years of his life. Here was someone so serious about his revolutionary socialism that his contributions to theory and practice culminated in an effective revolutionary challenge.

Lenin is important for serious-minded socialists because of what Georg Lukács stressed as the core of his thought — a deep belief in "the actuality of revolution." In contrast to so many would-be socialists, he does not see the capitalist status quo as the solid and unshakable ground of our being. Rather, his starting point is the opposite — that the continuing development of capitalism creates the basis for working-class revolution. This means not that revolution is about to erupt at every given moment, but that every person and every issue can and must be seen in relationship to the fundamental practical problem of advancing the struggle for revolution. What this means, for a Marxist like Lenin, is utilizing his revolutionary Marxism, as Lukács put it, "to establish firm guide-lines for all questions on the daily agenda, whether they were political or economic, involved theory or tactics, agitation or organization." James P. Cannon elaborated: "Lenin believed that for victory the workers required a party fit to lead a revolution; and to him that meant a party with a revolutionary program and leadership — a party of revolutionists." He cited "Big Bill" Haywood of the Industrial Workers of the World (IWW): "The essential thing is to have an organization of *those who know*."[114]

What did Lenin "know"? We can identify, in highly compressed form, at least ten major components that are at the heart of Lenin's thought.[115]

1. *Connecting socialism with the working class.* Lenin's starting-point is an understanding of the necessary interconnection of socialist theory and practice with the working class and labor movement. "By directing socialism towards a fusion with the working-class movement, Karl Marx and Frederick Engels did their greatest service," the young Lenin stressed, because the previous "separation of the working-class movement and socialism gave rise to weakness and underdevelopment in each," the one remaining abstract theorizing, the other remaining a fragmented and limited movement. The task of organized socialists "is to bring definite socialist ideals to the spontaneous working-class movement, to connect this movement with socialist convictions that should attain the level of contemporary science, to connect it with the regular political struggle for democracy as a means of achieving socialism — in a word, to fuse this spontaneous movement into one indestructible whole with the activity of the revolutionary party."[116]

2. *Dealing with diversity within the working class.* Inseparable from this is a basic understanding of the working class as it is, which involves a grasp of the incredible diversity and unevenness of working-class experience and consciousness. (In one analysis he distinguished between "advanced" workers who might become members of the revolutionary party, "average" workers interested in immediate struggles as well as socialist ideas, and "the mass of the lower strata.") This calls for the development of a practical revolutionary approach: seeking to connect, in serious ways — utilizing various forms of education, agitational literature and speeches, and practical struggles — with the various sectors and layers of the working class. It involves the understanding that different approaches and goals are required to reach and engage one or another worker and especially to engage a sector

or layer of workers. The more "advanced" or vanguard layers must be drawn not to narrow and limited goals (such as "pure and simple" trade unionism), but to a sense of solidarity and common cause with all workers.[117]

3. *Political independence of the working class.* Another essential ingredient of Lenin's outlook is the insistence on the necessity of working-class independence and hegemony in political and social struggles, as opposed to relying on pro-capitalist liberals. "The very notion that 'our' demands, the demands of working-class democracy, should be presented to the government by the liberal democrats is a queer one," he argued. "On the one hand, precisely because they are bourgeois democrats, the liberal democrats will never be able to understand 'our' demands and to advocate them clearly, consistently, resolutely." More than this, as he puts it, "if we are strong enough to exercise serious influence on the bourgeois democrats in general," then "we are also strong enough to present our demands to the government independently." In fact, he insisted, "it is the business of the working class to widen and strengthen its organization among the masses tenfold," and "to conquer by force for themselves that which Messieurs the liberal bourgeoisie promise to give them as charity — the freedom of assembly, the freedom of the workers' press, complete political liberty for the wide and open struggle for the complete victory of socialism."[118]

4. *Working-class struggle against all forms of oppression.* Lenin also distinguished himself with his stress on the necessity for active socialist and working-class support for struggles of all who suffer oppression. "Working-class consciousness cannot be genuine political consciousness unless the workers are trained to respond to all cases of tyranny, oppression, violence, and abuse, no matter what class is affected," Lenin emphasized, explaining that even "average" workers must concern themselves not only with factory conditions and workplace struggles, but also with "the brutal treatment of the people by the police, the persecution of religious sects, the flogging of peasants, the outrageous censorship, the torture of soldiers, the persecution of the most innocent cultural undertakings, etc." He went on to discuss the need for "even the most backward worker" to "understand, or ... feel, that the students and religious sects, the peasants and the authors are being abused and outraged by those same dark forces that are oppressing and crushing him at every step of his life." The socialist ideal, he concluded, "should not be the trade union secretary, but the tribune of the people, who is able to react to every manifestation of tyranny and oppression, no matter where it appears, no matter what stratum or class of people it affects."[119]

5. *A party of the working-class vanguard.* Inseparable from the analytical and strategic orientation that Lenin developed was the development of an organizational approach "to facilitate the political development and the political organization of the working class" in a manner that would "ensure that these demands for partial concessions are raised to the state of a systematic, implacable struggle of a revolutionary, working-class party, against the [tsarist] autocracy" as well as "against the whole of capitalist society." Lenin insisted that "we must train people who will devote the whole of their lives, not only spare evenings, to the revolution; we must build up an organization large enough to permit the introduction of a strict division of labor in the various forms of our work."[120]

Contrary to the assertions of many critics, Lenin believed that although "the Party, as the vanguard of the working class, must not be confused ... with the entire class," it was the case that a "varied, rich, fruitful" interrelationship with the working class as a whole must be facilitated by "the full application of the democratic principle in the Party organization." This meant that the organization should function according to "the principles of democratic centralism." The unity and cohesion of the party must be permeated with "guarantees for the rights of all minorities and for all loyal opposition ... the autonomy of every [local] Party organization ... recognizing that all Party functionaries must be elected and subject to recall," and that "there must be wide and free discussion of Party questions, free comradely criticism and assessments of events in Party life." This would help the proletarian vanguard to link up "and — if you wish — merge, in a certain measure, with the broadest masses of working people," but only (as Lenin explained in 1920) "through a prolonged effort and hard-won experience" that would be "facilitated by a correct revolutionary theory which ... is not a dogma but assumes final shape only in close connection with the practical activity of a truly mass and truly revolutionary movement."[121]

6. *Struggles for reforms and democracy linked with revolutionary socialist strategy.* The "Leninism" of Lenin also involves an approach of integrating reform struggles with revolutionary strategy and, combined with this, a remarkable understanding of the manner in which democratic struggles flow into socialist revolution. As we have already noted, at the heart of Lenin's orientation was a "democratic imperative" interweaving "the revolutionary struggle against capitalism with a revolutionary program and revolutionary tactics relative to all democratic demands: a republic, a militia, officials elected by the people, equal rights for women, self-determination of nations, etc. ... Basing ourselves on democracy as it already exists, exposing

its incompleteness under capitalism, we advocate the overthrow of capitalism, expropriation of the bourgeoisie as a necessary basis both for the abolition of the poverty of the masses and for a complete and manifold realization of all democratic forms."[122]

7. *A worker–peasant alliance.* Related to this revolutionary-democratic approach to revolutionary strategy, especially in such a predominantly peasant country as Russia, was Lenin's insistence on the development of a worker–peasant alliance. "To avoid finding itself with its hands tied in the struggle against the inconsistent bourgeois democracy, the proletariat must be class-conscious and strong enough to rouse the peasantry to revolutionary consciousness, guide its assault, and thereby independently pursue the line of consistent proletarian democratism," he wrote amid the 1905 revolutionary upsurge. "Only the proletariat can be a consistent fighter for democracy. It can become a victorious fighter for democracy only if the peasant masses join the struggle."[123]

8. *The united front tactic.* As early as 1905 he was also an articulate partisan of what would later be called the united front tactic — different labor, socialist, and sometimes even liberal organizations joining in specific coalition efforts. He insisted on "the preservation of complete independence by each separate party on points of principle and organization" in the context of "a fighting unity of these parties" in favor of democratic demands, as well as specific social and economic reforms, or for even overthrow of tsarism. Lenin believed that through the united front the most revolutionary of the parties (his own) would be able to prove its superiority and ultimately win majority support for a revolutionary socialist strategy. For this reason he warned: "We must be very careful, in making these endeavors, not to spoil things by vainly trying to lump together heterogeneous elements. We shall inevitably have to ... march separately, but we ... can strike together more than once and particularly now," that is, when there are compelling common goals.[124]

9. *Comprehending imperialism and nationalism.* A central element in the Leninist perspective, as it crystallized amid the fires of the First World War, were profound analyses of imperialism and nationalism. Lenin argued that as capitalism evolved into its modern imperialist phase it became transformed. The way he discusses it has special resonance in our own age of "globalization." While he emphasizes that "commodity production still 'reigns' and continues to be regarded as the basis of economic life, it has in reality been undermined and the bulk of the profits go to the 'geniuses' of financial manipulation." Lenin perceived that "the 20th century marks the turning point from

the old capitalism to the new, from the domination of capital in general to the domination of finance capital."

His notion of finance capital was not some crude conception of big banks calling the shots, but instead was defined as "the concentration of production; the monopolies arising there from; the merging or coalescence of the banks with industry." He identified this period as one in which "a monopoly ... inevitably penetrates into every sphere of public life, regardless of the form of government and all other 'details'" — with a tendency by the state to identify the needs of the massive capitalist firms with the national interest. But the "national" increasingly became enmeshed in the global, in ways that were different from the old forms of trade and colonialism.

Under the old capitalism the export of goods was typical, while under the new capitalism the more important dynamic is the export of capital. The logic of the capital accumulation process leads Lenin to conclude that "surplus capital will be utilized not for the purpose of raising the standard of living of the masses in a given country, for this would mean a decline of profits for the capitalists, but for the purpose of increasing profits by exporting capital to the backward countries." He explains that "in these backward countries profits are unusually high, for capital is scarce, the price of land is relatively low, wages are low, raw materials are cheap."

But for Lenin imperialism involved not simply the quest for profits in formally colonized areas (such as the British Empire), but also the drive to invest in independent countries — sometimes "semi-colonies" for all practical purposes but sometimes enjoying even greater autonomy than that — creating "diverse forms of dependent countries which, politically, are formally independent but, in fact, are enmeshed in the net of financial and diplomatic dependence." This involved "not only agrarian territories, but even the most highly industrialized regions ... because (1) the fact that the world is already partitioned obliges those contemplating a re-division to reach out for every kind of territory, and (2) an essential feature of imperialism is the rivalry between several great powers in the striving for hegemony."

This view of the imperialist evolution of capitalism shaped Lenin's understanding of the nature of nationalism. A traditional Marxist view had been that nationalism was a progressive force that had challenged feudal traditions and monarchist empires with a vision of the self-determination of a people over the land in which they lived. But the more industrialized capitalist economies of some nations, advanced by powerful military establishments, were now dominating and exploiting the peoples of other regions, rationalized by a new conservative form of nationalism used to mobilize popular support for imperialism. Lenin believed that "imperialism is the period of an increasing oppression of the nations of the whole world by a handful of 'great' nations," and emphasized the need for socialists to oppose the nationalism of "oppressor nations" and to support the nationalism — the right of self-determination — of "oppressed nations." He also believed that such national liberation struggles would be a key in advancing the struggle for socialism worldwide.

In a recent analysis developed by Kevin Anderson, it is argued that under the impact of the First World War (and a deeper study of Hegel's dialectical philosophy) Lenin developed a "view of social revolution as a living phenomenon" that included "not only the revolt of the industrial working class but also 'revolts by small nations in the colonies and in Europe,' as well as peasant revolts against landowners." Lenin believed that "to imagine that social revolution is conceivable without" this diverse and international insurgency "is to repudiate social revolution."[125]

10. *Revolutionary internationalism.* Lenin advanced a vibrantly revolutionary internationalist approach that stressed the necessity of workers and oppressed peoples of all lands to make common cause. He noted that the conditions generated by the First World War had "brought the whole of humanity to an impasse, and faced it with the dilemma of either permitting the extermination of more millions of lives and the complete extinction of European civilization, or handing over power to the revolutionary proletariat and achieving the socialist revolution in civilized countries." More than this, he insisted on the need for a "union between revolutionary proletarians of the capitalist, advanced countries, and the revolutionary masses of colonial countries." This meant the need for revolutionary forces of various countries to strengthen each other in the face of global capitalist power, but it meant something more. Capitalism as a global system must be replaced by an international socialist order. A long-term "live-and-let-live" coexistence on the same planet of the imperialist system and socialist democracies would be impossible.

In 1920 Lenin rejoiced that the Communist International "unites white, yellow, and black-skinned working people in brotherhood." He insisted: "World imperialism shall fall when the revolutionary onslaught of the exploited and oppressed workers in each country ... merges with the revolutionary onslaught of hundreds of millions of people who have hitherto stood beyond the pale of history, and have been regarded merely as the object of history." More than this, Lenin's revolutionary internationalism involved the mutual strengthening — shared experiences and insights that would become part of the revolutionary arsenal of ideas — of revolutionary forces in each country. Victories in one sector of the world would, not only theoretically but materially, make possible victories in other parts of the world. The Russian Revolution pointed the way for the workers and oppressed of all countries, Lenin believed, but at the same time he noted that the Soviet republic was "a besieged fortress waiting for the other detachments of the world revolution to come to our relief."[126]

Too little relief came, and it came too late, leading to the bureaucratic degeneration, the viciously authoritarian corruption, and the eventual collapse of the Soviet republic. This outcome has caused many to reject what Lenin and his comrades represented. Yet even some of his severest critics would agree with Robert Service that these uncompromising revolutionaries "were responding to the conditions of distress, social and political, in their own countries," and that "in most societies these conditions have not been improved in the years after Lenin's death." The fact that so many of the oppressive conditions that Lenin and his comrades were confronting also confront us today raises questions about the wisdom of dismissing the contemporary relevance of his ideas and example.[127]

History Is Tricky

Taken together, the points outlined in the previous section constitute an orientation that provides a comprehensive and coherent approach to the problems of capitalism and the struggle for a socialist alternative. Whether one ends up embracing him or not, the point that C. Wright Mills once made about Marx is also true about Lenin: "To study his work today and then come back to our own concerns is to increase our chances of confronting them with useful ideas and solutions." One is reminded of the argument advanced by existentialist philosopher Jean-Paul Sartre many years ago, that Marxism remains "the philosophy of our time" because the fundamental realities that generated it have not been transcended.[128]

Sartre pointed out something else that we must also remain aware of — "the fact that history is 'tricky,' as Lenin said, and that we underestimate its tricks."[129] While the fundamental realities faced by Marx and Lenin have not been transcended, the realities have not remained the same from their time to ours. The failure to understand this contradictory reality has been the undoing of countless revolutionary activists, particularly when it comes to building revolutionary organizations.

The initial growth of revolutionary socialism — including the bodies of thought and experience associated with such figures as Marx, Luxemburg, Lenin, and Trotsky — took place in a broad framework of industrial capitalist development and working-class formation/evolution stretching from the 1860s through the 1930s. It was in this context that labor movements and labor-radical sub-cultures flourished that gave meaning and relevance to the perspectives of Lenin and of the various political movements influenced by him.

In multiple ways the massive violence and upheaval of the Second World War and its aftermath, and subsequent developments in the global capitalist economy, altered and obliterated much of the social and economic basis of those labor movements and of the mass sub-culture of labor radicalism. (This is discussed at the end of Chapter 5 and also in Chapter 7.) The relevance of Marxism, in all of its varieties, as a *political strategy* for changing the world (as opposed to being merely a mode of historical, economic, or cultural analysis for understanding the world) is dependent on the existence of such mass labor movements and mass labor-radical sub-cultures. It is these movements and sub-cultures that make possible the kind of class consciousness and class struggle that are required for posing a serious challenge to capitalism.

Underlying the decomposition of the traditional Left has been the decomposition of the traditional working class. While many knowledgeable analysts have consequently — at various moments since 1940 — bade "farewell to the working class," the fact is that a more widespread process of proletarianization throughout the world (both in more highly developed and less highly developed capitalist economies) has been unfolding. The decomposition has been accompanied by a dramatic recomposition of the working class.

But this has not meant any automatic revival or duplication of traditional labor movements, labor-radical sub-cultures, or class consciousness. The relative decline of class as a central organizing principle and primary point of self-identification has meant that discontent and social struggle have found more widespread and vibrant expression around specific issues (such as opposition to war and imperialism, defense of human rights and democratic rights, defense of the environment, opposition to hunger and poverty, etc.), and also around various nonclass identities: race and ethnicity, gender, generation, sexual orientation, etc. Struggles around such issues and identities have come to the fore not simply because of the decline of the traditional working class and labor movement, but also because capitalist development has dynamically and often disastrously impacted in ways that have disrupted traditional economic, social, and cultural patterns.

In the youth radicalization of the 1960s and 1970s, as many young activists were seeking to develop a coherent understanding of capitalist realities that had radicalized them, and a coherent strategy for dealing with those realities, they naturally turned to one or another version of what they took to be revolutionary Marxism. But the effort to absorb the ideas of Marx, Luxemburg, Lenin, Trotsky, Gramsci, and others — abstracted from the actual class-struggle contexts in which those ideas had developed and been given relevance — often resulted, certainly in the United States, in an idealist and superficial understanding of those ideas. The result was often a pathetic misapplication of those ideas, as well as disorientation, disappointment, disillusionment. (This and related matters are explored in the final chapter of this volume.)

For reasons discussed earlier in this chapter, there is an especially yawning gap between the historical reality of Lenin's party leading up to the revolution of 1917 and how this party has been perceived by latter-day activists. One must clear away not only distorted understandings of what such a party is (what it represents, how it comes into being, how it functions) that were introduced by Stalinism, but even distortions introduced during the heroic period of early Communism (1917–1925) — which involved seeking to build an allegedly Leninist "party of a new type" that was qualitatively different from the actual party of Lenin and the Bolsheviks up to October 1917. Leaders of the Communist International (or Comintern) in the 1920s glorified Lenin's "party of a new type" as they sought to "Bolshevize" Communist parties around the world. But it is not clear that such hyper-centralized organizations would have been capable of leading the 1917 workers' and peasants' revolution in Russia. (Recall the actualities of that revolution discussed in Chapter 3.)

The Bolshevik party in the period of 1912–1917 — from the time it became an organization independent of non-revolutionary socialists up to the moment when it helped bring about the revolution — was committed to a revolutionary working-class program infused with Marxist perspectives. It blended democratic functioning with activist coherence, a unified political orientation with substantial autonomy for activists in various locales. It was rooted in and powerfully influenced by politically advanced layers of the working class. Because of such things, it was capable of playing a decisive role in advancing the struggles of workers and the oppressed. The policies of the Comintern, and the organizational norms that it fostered (shaped by methods and habits of the civil war period and then Stalinism), increasingly undermined the development of such parties as instruments of effective revolutionary struggle.

Getting clear on the reality of Lenin's revolutionary party — as opposed to Stalinist and "Cominternist" distortions — is only a first step for contemporary scholars and political activists. One must get clear on the relationship of such authentic Leninism to the realities of the early 21st century.

The Leninist party came into being within a context: as part of a broad global working-class formation, as part of a developing labor movement, and as part of an evolving labor-radical sub-culture. That earlier reality no longer exists. To try to duplicate some variant of the Leninist party today will create something that cannot function as the Bolsheviks functioned in prerevolutionary Russia, nor can it function in the way the early Communists functioned in the 1920s or in the 1930s. Our experience from the 1950s down to the present demonstrates that efforts to create Leninist parties (certainly in advanced capitalist countries) generally tend to degenerate into political sects.

A layer of the working class that is permeated by a sub-culture helping to nourish a certain level of class consciousness must exist if something like the "Leninism of Lenin" is to come into being. A genuinely revolutionary vanguard organization cannot exist abstracted from such a reality. Only through the development of that broad vanguard layer and sub-culture could the context be created that will allow for the development of an effective revolutionary vanguard party — a 21st-century variant of what the Leninist party was, but also reflecting some of the difficult lessons of the post-1917 period.

Before exploring what this might mean, however, it is worth giving critical attention to other components of the revolutionary tradition.

5
The Red Decade

Eugene Lyons, a one-time partisan of Communism and the USSR, bitterly disillusioned by his 1930s experiences as a journalist in the Soviet Union, termed the 1930s in the United States "the Red Decade," involving "a grotesque and incredible revolution" that — while led by the American Communist Party — was "neither communist nor revolutionary, in the normal sense of these words," but that "penetrated, in various degrees, the labor movement, education, the churches, college and non-college youth movements, the theatre, movies, the arts, publishing in all its branches," as well as boring "deep into the Federal government and in many communities also into local government." He described the dynamics as follows:

> The distinguishing mark of the Red Decade was hypocrisy, manifest in false-front societies, secret inner-caucus controls, duplicate and triplicate names, high-minded lying and deceptions....
>
> At the core of the incredible revolution was a small group of leaders, some known to the public, others obscure but no less powerful, still others — the official resident agents of the Moscow hierarchy — secret but most powerful of all. Around them was the solid ring of the Communist Party members, the mass of them acknowledging their allegiance but an effective minority concealing their membership under fake names and even protesting with outraged vehemence when accused of being members. Beyond them were deployed more diffuse and vastly more numerous fellow-travelers, consciously working within the movement, though obeying a moral rather than an organizational discipline. And farther out were concentric rings of wholly or partly innocent camp-trailers....
>
> At its highest point — roughly 1938 — the incredible revolution of the Red Decade had mobilized the conscious or the starry-eyed, innocent collaboration of thousands of influential American educators, social workers, clergymen, New Deal officials, youth leaders, Negro and other racial spokesmen, Social Registerites, novelists, Hollywood stars, script writers and directors, trade-union chiefs, men and women of abnormal wealth. Its echoes could be heard, muted or strident, in the most unexpected places, including the supposed citadels of conservatism and respectability.[1]

There is much truth in the story that Lyons sketches here, but the whole truth is much larger, more complex, more contradictory. One of the complexities is the fact that there was a rich variety of "Red" organizations in the 1930s aside from (and in competition with) the Stalinist-led Communist Party — although this was unquestionably the largest and most influential of these. But even if combined with all of its smaller competitors — the Communist Party Opposition (Lovestoneites), the Communist League of America (Trotskyists), the American Workers Party (led by A. J. Muste),[2] the Socialist Party (led by Norman Thomas), and the scattering of other left-wing groups — the number of organized "Reds" added up to a small percentage, less than a quarter of a million people, in a population of 123 million.

It is also undeniable that the great majority of people in the categories identified by Lyons — rich people and exploited laborers, social workers, New Dealers, clergymen, trade union leaders, Hollywood figures, etc. — were indifferent, dismissive, suspicious, or hostile when it came to Communism. As Granville Hicks, a prominent ex-Communist intellectual, put it:

> Even in the early thirties, when millions of people were hungry and desperate, the Communists polled barely 100,000 votes. Even in the later thirties, when the Popular Front had captured the allegiance of many intellectuals, the party made almost no impression on the solid anti-Communism of the great majority of the American people. Even when Communism tried to disguise itself as Twentieth-Century Americanism, the party could not count more than a hundred thousand members and a few hundred thousand sympathizers. A hundred thousand disciplined Communists might have been something to think twice about, but most sympathizers were as far from the Leninist ideal as most churchgoers are from the Christian ideal, and they soon found plenty of reason for backsliding.[3]

Another aspect of the complexity involves the fact that a mass radicalization took place in the 1930s. It was not the case that millions of people in the United States joined the Communist Party or embraced Marxist theory or became conscious socialists. But they were profoundly changed in the face of the economic collapse of the Great Depression, in the face of the overseas expansion of Italian fascism and German Nazism and Imperial Japan, in the face of the approach of another global war. In their thoughts and feelings and — sometimes, for some of them — in their actions, they questioned authority, they broke with established norms and traditions, they challenged existing power structures.[4]

The impact of the Great Depression, devastating millions of lives, generated a profound change in consciousness. Opinion polls in the mid-1930s found that overwhelming majorities among lower-income groups believed that the wealthy had too much influence over the nation's affairs, that what the wealthy want of the government is generally not good for the country, that government should provide full employment, and that the government should provide free medical and dental care for all — indicating a clear "tendency of the lower and middle classes toward a value system different from acquisitive individualism," as Robert McElvaine has noted. "Most working- and middle-class Americans in the Depression were not socialists in any strict ideological sense, but certainly they were leaning to the left."[5]

There was complex and dynamic interplay of *organic intellectuals* who were part of the working class majority (that is, particularly thoughtful, critical-minded, creative people influential among sectors of that majority), intellectuals of other social strata, as well as "non-intellectual" layers of these various social strata, organized left-wing parties, the organized labor movement, and a variety of influential "mainstream" political and cultural forces. And the result of that amazing interplay approximates — to a significant degree — the tag that Eugene Lyons put on the 1930s: the Red Decade.

What Lyons' comments do not convey, however, is the richness and excitement characterizing much of the "Redness" of these times.

In this chapter we will look at the cultural and social dynamism of this decade and the centrality of the Communist Party, with special reference to labor and black liberation and the struggle against fascism. At the same time, we will need to deal with the complex impacts of the USSR and Stalinism in shaping American Communism — inspiring it, splintering it, helping it grow, and subverting it from what it might have been.

Crossroads and Cradle

A fascinating moment in the history of U.S. cinema has captured important aspects of this moment in history of the United States — Tim Robbins's motion picture "Cradle Will Rock" (1999), which deals with two cultural struggles during the Great Depression of the 1930s. The two struggles involve the fierce 1933 controversy over Diego Rivera's mural "Man at the Crossroads" and the no less fierce controversy over Marc Blitzstein's musical "The Cradle Will Rock" (1937). These cultural controversies reflected a momentous power struggle that shook the country in that period, involving millions of militant workers, led or influenced by Marxist-oriented activists, in collision with some of the country's leading business interests. Looking first at the cultural conflicts may highlight possibilities inherent in the social conflicts.

Diego Rivera's magnificent 1933 fresco for Rockefeller Center would focus, he explained beforehand, on the blending frontiers of "ethical evolution" and "material development." It would involve "the Workers arriving at a true understanding of their rights regarding the means of production, which has resulted in the planning of the liquidation of Tyranny, personified by a crumbling statue of Caesar, whose head has fallen on the ground. It will also show the Workers of the cities and country inheriting the Earth." At the intersection-point of microscopic and celestial bodies, and also at the intersection-point of two counterposed realities — poverty, war, fascism *versus* workers struggles, the flowering of youth, abundance for all — would be an image of Man guiding the forward development of humanity. Dominating would be "the image of a Popular Movement, the result of high aspirations created by Ethical Development, but unsuccessful without an accompanying parallel material development of Technical Power and Industrial Organization, either already existing or created by the movement itself."[6]

This was Rivera's description to Nelson Rockefeller and his family (at that time the epitome of liberal, broad-minded, forward-looking capitalists) who were hiring him. They knew he was a Marxist artist, but they were determined to have someone with his fame decorate their new modern building in New York City, and they undoubtedly assumed they could come to an understanding. "It was perfectly clear from the outset that he was planning a Communist — that is, a revolutionary socialist — mural," wrote Rivera's friend Bertram Wolfe, one involving "the denunciation of capitalism as breeding war, crisis, and unemployment; a 'popular movement' based on ethics and modern industry; all looking 'with certainty but hope towards … a New, more Humane and Logical Order.'" As the mural increasingly became a vibrant and colorful reality, complete with an image of Lenin clasping hands with a multiracial cluster of workers, Nelson Rockefeller protested that Lenin's image "might very easily offend a great many people."[7] Rivera refused to eliminate it. The Rockefellers took the position that the wall in question belonged to them, halted work on the fresco, and banned Rivera and his assistants from the building. There were protests and demonstrations in favor of Rivera's artistic freedom.

But more was at stake than simply that. "We all recognize," Rivera insisted, "that in human creation there is something which belongs to humanity at large, and that no individual owner has the right to destroy it or to keep it solely for his own enjoyment."[8] The balance of power was such that Rivera and his supporters were defeated, and the mural was smashed to pieces by order of the Rockefellers. This was, however, only an early episode in the confrontation during the 1930s between defenders of the status quo and insurgent forces striving for a new humane order. One year later, the issues dramatized in Rivera's mural were exploding across America's industrial landscape.

In 1934, the country was rocked by three violent strikes — the Toledo Auto-Lite Strike, the Minneapolis Teamsters Strike, and the San Francisco Longshoremen's Strike. In Ohio the strikers were led by the left-wing socialists of A. J. Muste's American Workers Party. In Minnesota, Vincent Raymond Dunne and other Communist-dissident followers of Leon Trotsky were in the leadership. In California, radical leader Harry Bridges was backed by militant activists of the "mainstream" Communist Party. In each city, violence from the employers was met and pushed back with intransigent working-class resistance, resulting in troops being brought in. Yet working-class solidarity reached a crescendo in each city with a general strike that finally resulted in sweeping union victories over what had once seemed the overwhelming power of big business. This propelled one-time labor anti-radicals such as John L. Lewis onto the path of militancy — with the Congress of Industrial Organizations breaking off from the conservative American Federation of Labor to initiate aggressive organizing drives and strikes to organize industrial workers. Of course, this impacted back onto the cultural front.[9]

"Negro writers can seek to unite blacks and whites in our country, not on the nebulous basis of an interracial meeting, or the shifting sands of religious brotherhood, but on the solid ground of the daily working-class struggle to wipe out, now and forever, all the old inequalities of the past." So argued Langston Hughes at a left-wing writers conference in 1935.[10] Increasing numbers of people believed that the best place to carry on such a struggle — in the midst of the Great Depression and in the face of the rising threat of fascism — was in the ranks or the swelling periphery of the Communist Party.

Opposition to fascism was not simply rhetorical posturing — when a right-wing military uprising (with support from Mussolini and Hitler) attempted to overthrow the left-liberal Spanish Republic, the Communist Party mobilized 2,800 young Americans to join the International Brigades (consisting of 40,000 volunteers from 53 countries) to defend the Republic. "They were students, teachers, writers, trade unionists; most were communists, some were socialists," was how Harry Fisher described the International Brigades. "They all shared a hatred of fascism, a love of liberty." Describing his own decision to join up, this working-class Communist explained:

I knew the fascists were in control in Germany and Italy, with close ties to the governments of Britain and Portugal, and with many powerful friends in the United States and France. Soon it became clear that Germany and Italy were behind the rebellion in Spain. If they won, what a boost to fascism all over the world, including the United States! ... I could not forget those newsreels of Nazi storm troopers stomping and spitting on those poor helpless people. I also knew it could happen here. My anger was so strong, I knew I had to go. Fascism simply had to be stopped.[11]

By the time that the U.S. volunteers of the multiracial Abraham Lincoln Battalion were withdrawn, just before the final defeat of the Republic and on the eve of World War II, "nearly one-third were dead," notes historian Peter Carroll, and "virtually every military survivor had been wounded at least once." And for the most part, "they returned from Spain with a feeling of responsibility to remain loyal to each other and to the cause that had brought them together." The fact that the USSR was one of only two countries (Mexico was the other) sending aid to the beleaguered Republic also had a powerful impact — and not only on Communists. Stalin's call for a "collective security" coalition against Germany, Italy, and Japan, and for a People's Front in each country to advance a "progressive" agenda — despite a dark underside unseen by many — seemed a bulwark of democratic hope.[12] The heroic role of the young American activists — the survivors as well as the dead — in the struggle against fascism in Spain gave a poignant and radical edge to all of this that profoundly affected consciousness and culture in the United States, perhaps most dramatically reflected in Ernest Hemingway's novel *For Whom the Bell Tolls*, but also in the poetry of Langston Hughes:

> Proud banners of death,
> I see them waving
> There against the sky.
> Struck deep in Spanish earth
> Where your dark bodies lie
> Inert and helpless –
> So they think
> Who do not know
> That from your death
> New life will grow.
> For there are those who cannot see
> The mighty roots of liberty
> Push upward in the dark
> To burst in flame –
> A million stars –
> And one your name:
> Man
> Who fell in Spanish earth:
> Human seed
> For freedom's birth.[13]

The left-wing cultural impact in the United States of the 1930s resulted in what Michael Denning in a brilliant, richly informative study has described as "a deep and lasting transformation of American modernism and mass culture." He utilizes a rather labored formulation — "the *laboring* of American culture" — but captures an essential reality touched on some years before by literary critic Alfred Kazin regarding the Depression era. There was a style and sensibility attributable "to the toughness of the times, to the militant new wind, to the anger which was always in the air, and in whose name you only had to point to a soup kitchen, a picket line, the Dust Bowl, the Memorial Day Massacre in Chicago" to challenge those resistant to the sort of class-struggle appeal voiced by Langston Hughes to the left-wing writers conference.[14]

But there was more to it, as Kazin explained:

> Trouble was in the air every day now, and whatever else you could say about them, the "new" writers looked as if they had been born to trouble — as in fact they had been, for they were usually the products of city streets, factories and farms. More than the age of the ideologue, of the

literary revolutionary and the "proletarian" novelist, roles usually created within the Communist movement, the Thirties in literature were the age of the plebes — of writers from the working class, the lower class, the immigrant class, the non-literate class, from Western farms and mills — those whose struggle was to survive.... It was a time of such endless storm, of such turbulence every day of social crisis, that the drama of the depression and of Hitler's coming to power was immediately documented for me in the savage unleashed hope with which the banked-up experience of the plebes, of Jews, Irishmen, Negroes, Armenians, Italians, was coming into American books. The real excitement of the new period was in the explosion of personal liberation which such writers brought in from the slums, farms and factories.[15]

There was a radical upsurge not only in literature but in theater — which in the 1930s gained a popularity not achieved in the United States before or since, in part, as Annette Rubinstein suggests, because it is a medium involving "a shared experience, appealing to a common emotional denominator in its audience," and this was in harmony with the spirit of the decade. In a fine history of the Group Theatre, which so powerfully affected the performing arts and popular consciousness, Wendy Smith effectively demonstrates the interrelationship between social struggles and the new social theater, and the essential influence of the Communist Party on both. "The discipline and solid organizing capabilities of party members won them a respected place at the left end of a broad consensus of progressive opinion that encompassed everyone who believed fascism overseas must be fought, hungry people in America must be fed, workers had a right to trade-union representation, and black people deserved equal treatment." She added: "The discipline the Communist party imposed was not so different from the commitment the Group [Theatre] demanded: subjugation of the ego to the collective will, hard work and financial sacrifice in service of a greater goal, whether it was a classless society or a serious American theatre. To want both at once didn't seem contradictory at the time."[16]

Alfred Kazin described Clifford Odets' play "Waiting for Lefty" (put on by the Group Theatre in early 1935), which presented a left-wing interpretation of political and social themes on a bare stage, "but Odets worked with human samples, not abstractions. A husband and wife were suddenly revealed by the spotlight, and they were talking." The dialogue goes like this: "JOE: It's conditions. EDNA: We're at the bottom of the ocean .... We're stalled like a flivver in the snow ... My God, Joe, the world is supposed to be for all of us." Kazin commented: "Art and truth and hope could come together — if a real writer was their meeting place .... I had never seen actors on the stage and an audience in the theater come together with such a happy shock." At the end of the play, when it is discovered that the working-class hero "Lefty" has been murdered, the taxi drivers stand up both to their corrupt union officers and their exploitative employers — with various actors, including a few planted in the audience, calling out, "Strike!" As Wendy Smith recounts:

> Suddenly the entire audience, some 1,400 people, rose and roared, "Strike! Strike!" The actors froze, stunned by the spontaneous demonstration. The militant cries gave way to cheers and applause so thunderous the cast was kept onstage for 45 minutes to receive the crowd's inflamed tribute .... The actors were all weeping. When [Director Harold] Clurman persuaded Odets to take a bow, the audience stormed the stage and embraced the man who had voiced their hopes and fears and deepest aspirations.[17]

A similar experience was generated by Marc Blitzstein's left-wing musical "The Cradle Will Rock," whose John Houseman/Orson Welles production for the Federal Theatre Project was, thanks to right-wing pressure, suppressed by the government — only to be audaciously "liberated" and presented by a radical-minded coalition of writer/composer, producer, director, actors, and audience. These rebellious, truly subversive performances of 1937 electrified audiences, who hung on a sister's lament for a fallen union militant —

> Listen, here's a story.
> Not much fun, and not much glory;
> Low-class ... low-down...
> The thing you never care to see,
> Until there is a showdown.
> Here it is — I'll make it snappy:
> Are you ready? Everybody happy?
>
> Joe Worker gets gypped;
> For no good reason, just gypped.
> From the start until the finish comes ...
> They feed him out of garbage cans,
> They breed him in the slums!
>
> Joe Worker will go,
> To shops where stuff is on show;
> He'll look at the meat,
> He'll look at the bread,
> And too little to eat sort of goes to the head.
> One big question inside me cries:
> How many fakers, peace undertakers,
> Paid strikebreakers,
> How many toiling, ailing, dying, piled-up bodies,
> Brother, does it take to make you wise?

Joe Worker just drops,
Right at his workin' he drops,
Weary, weary, tired to the core;
And then if he drops out of sight
there's always plenty more!
Joe Worker must know
That somebody's got him in tow....
Yet what is the good
For just one to be clear?
Oh. It takes a lot of Joes
To make a sound you can hear!
One big question inside me cries:
How many frame-ups, how many shakedowns,
Lockouts, sellouts,
How many times machine-guns tell the same old story,
Brother, does it take to make you wise?[18]

As the play closes, a militant steel strike is beginning to "rock the cradle" of the big-business tycoon Mr. Mister and his various hired hands, admirers, and hangers-on. The radical union organizer taunts them, almost surrealistically:

Outside in the square they're startin' somethin'
That's gonna tear the catgut outa your stinkin' rackets!
That's *Steel* marchin' out in front!
But one day there's gonna be
Wheat ... and sidewalks ...
Cows ... and music ...
Shops ... houses ...
Poems ... bridges ... drugstores ...
The people of this town are findin'
out what it's all about ...
They're growin' up!
And when everybody gets together
Like Steel's gettin' together tonight,
Where are you then? ...
When the storm breaks...
The cradle will fall![19]

The show "raises a theatre-goer's metabolism and blows him out of the theatre on the thunder of the grand finale," confessed *New York Times* theatre critic Brooks Atkinson.[20]

The fact that this musical was written, the fact that it was produced and — despite great obstacles — presented to the public, and the enthusiastic public response all attest to the radical spirit of the Red Decade. Much of the social radicalism of the time was unquestionably influenced by the Communist Party.

While its membership was no more than 80,000, a quarter of a million people passed through the Communist Party and Young Communist League, and many hundreds of thousands were conscious and active sympathizers. "Through the party's activities in unions, and in organizations of the unemployed, youth, farmers, Negroes, veterans, professionals, intellectuals, cultural workers, and anti-fascist activists, its 'private' advocacy of socialism (in addition to public propaganda activities) was vastly more pervasive than the socialist agitation of the relatively isolated Socialist Party and the sectarian Socialist Labor Party," commented ex-Communist Max Gordon. "The wide association of party members with others in common causes, and the respect won by many for their leadership and dedication, gave their advocacy considerable weight."[21]

Labor Insurgency

Central to the 1930s radicalization was the rise of the new industrial unions brought into being through heroic organizing drives and hard-fought strikes. The result was the Congress of Industrial Organizations (CIO), in which Communists and other radicals often played a key role. "The influx of Communists into the CIO reached such proportions that the CPUSA determined it was being stripped of its best cadres at the expense of Party activities," notes historian Fraser Ottanelli, who points out that much of the approximately 4 million-member union federation was led by "labor leaders around the country who had various degrees of alliance to the Party." He elaborates:

> Among them were "Red Mike" Quill of the Transit Workers; Joe Curran of the Merchant Seamen; Ben Gold of the Fur and Leather Workers; Julius Emspak and James Matles, of the Electrical Workers; Harold Pritchett, president of the Woodworkers union; and Donald Henderson, head of the Cannery Workers. [Communist leader Earl] Browder later estimated that Communists and their allies led unions representing one-third of the CIO's membership and played significant roles in another third.[22]

Without question, non-Communists and anti-Communists were predominant in the CIO. The three outstanding personalities — David Dubinsky of the International Ladies Garment Workers Union, Sidney Hillman of the Amalgamated Clothing Workers of America, and most of all John L. Lewis of the United Mine Workers of America — had faced and smashed strong Communist factions in their unions during the 1920s. Dubinsky and Hillman identified with the moderate wing of the Socialist Party (and were gravitating to the left wing of the Democratic Party), while Lewis — temporarily supporting Franklin D. Roosevelt — had been a registered Republican.

As undisputed leader of the CIO, Lewis was not your typical Republican. Although an anti-radical autocrat in his own union, in the 1930s his gravel-voiced eloquence and uncompromising glare became the national symbol of insurgent working-class radicalism. "Of all my teachers in power and mass organization, he was the greatest," commented the effective radical organizer Saul Alinsky. "His defiance of every power from the White House out was a note of reassurance for the security of the democratic idea, that his dissonance was part of our national music." Years later, the far more conservative George Meany of the AFL-CIO mused: "Frankly, I think John was dreaming of being the leader who led the working class to the control of society. He was that ambitious." Ultimate goals aside, the commitment to organizing the mass-production workers in the steel, auto, electrical, and other industries in the country's major industrial centers would involve something akin to open warfare with the country's most powerful big-business corporations. These were opponents that in years gone by had proved quite adept at employing their immense wealth, their social and cultural influence, and their extensive political influence to crush strikes and break unions. "Lewis and his associates embarked on the fight of their lives — as they well understood," notes Bert Cochran. "Consequently, Lewis was not merely disposed to accept whatever allies were available in the desperate war that was in the offing. He could not do without the support of the radicals — and in the 1930s, radicals meant primarily the Communists."[23]

Communists and other organized radicals made the difference between labor's victory and defeat. The successful union battles represented a significant power shift in the United States, which included a distinct leftward tilt in the social and political landscape. "Due to the prestige Communists gained in labor struggles of that period, the Party's influence and acceptance among workers grew, as did the toleration of its activities," Ottanelli commented, adding that in 1938 alone — when CP membership rose from 37,000 to 60,000 — half of the new recruits were union members, with the following new members represented in basic industry: 603 marine workers, 552 steelworkers, 474 miners, 415 metal workers, 426 autoworkers, 269 transportation workers. Labor historian Robert H. Zieger, by no means uncritical of the Communists, has summarized aspects of their role in the CIO in this way:

> The overall record of Communist-influenced unions with respect to collective bargaining, contract content and administration, internal democracy, and honest and effective governance was good. Rank-and-file Communists exhibited a passionate commitment to their conception of social justice. As a group Communists and their close allies were better educated, more articulate, and more class conscious than their counterparts in the CIO. Communist-influenced unions ... were notable for fair and efficient administration, innovative cultural and educational programs, and positive responses to the distinctive problems of minority

and female workers.... In regard to race and gender the Communist-influenced CIO affiliates stood in the vanguard.[24]

Related to this is the point made by Anne Braden regarding the racist-dominated South. "Yet another force impinging in the Southern police state, although many people don't want to admit it now, was the work of radical political groups, especially the Communist Party," she commented in 1965. "In the South, they faced the danger of jails and mobs, but so did the CIO and NAACP organizers, and Communists were not considered any more outlaw in the South than these were." She adds that "often the CIO would send its Communist organizers into the South because they were the only ones who were willing to go and risk getting their heads beat in. ... Thus Communists moved and worked freely in the South, and their attack on the economic causes of Negro oppression opened new doors of thought for many people and contributed to the general ferment."[25]

It is hardly the case that most of the insurgent workers and radical activists were members of the Communist Party. In some cases, non-Communist radicals — left-wing Christians, anarchists, socialists of various kinds, Trotskyists — played essential and decisive roles in leading struggles and advancing consciousness among broad sectors of the working class. At the same time, among the left-wing forces, the Communists were far more powerful and influential than the others.[26]

Left-wing activist Len De Caux served as an aide to John L. Lewis and editor of the *CIO News*, and was in a position to monitor the temper of the times. He later recalled:

> As it gained momentum, this movement brought with it new political attitudes—toward the corporations, toward police and troops, toward local, state, national government. Now we're a movement, many workers asked, why can't we move on to more and more? Today we've forced almighty General Motors to terms by sitting down [in factory occupations] and defying all the powers at its command, why can't we go on tomorrow, with our numbers, our solidarity, our determination, to transform city and state, the Washington government itself? Why can't we go on to create a new society with the workers on top, to end age-old injustices, to banish poverty and war?[27]

This kind of fundamental social change — the working-class majority taking political power and transforming the socioeconomic order — would not be brought about through magnificent murals or musicals, nor even by union organizing drives or strikes. Such revolutionary change, necessarily emerging out of a multifaceted and coherent tactical and strategic plan, would require serious, clear-minded coordination. The only force in the United States at that time even remotely capable of providing such leadership would have been the Communist Party.

In fact, while Communists played a key role in moving certain aspects of the class struggle leftward in the 1930s, they also played a key role in deflecting that struggle in a non-revolutionary direction. To understand this anomaly, and much else, we need to take a closer look at the complexities of American Communism.

Red and Black

It is often argued that it is the Russian influence that subverted and ruined American Communism, even as it was bringing it into being and shaping it. But a careful examination of the realities reveals something that is more complex — certainly in regard to the question of race. One of the most promising aspects of the Communist impact on U.S. radicalism had to do with a commitment to bridge the gap between black and white workers and to undermine — radically and irrevocably — the incredibly deep racism that had been so central to so much of the history of the United States.

Black radical poet Claude McKay, visiting revolutionary Russia in the pre-Stalinist period of the early 1920s, commented on a spontaneous upsurge of enthusiasm and affection among everyday Russians whenever he appeared in public. He symbolized for them the world's oppressed peoples, whose liberation struggles would bring strength to the USSR. This, in turn, inspired in him similar feelings for them. "Never in my life did I feel prouder of being an African, a black, and no mistake about it," he later wrote. "I was carried along on a crest of sweet excitement. I was like a black ikon in the flesh." When the Communist leadership made available resources to make his stay comfortable, McKay noted that "for the first time in my life I knew what it was like to be a highly privileged personage. And in the fatherland of Communism!"[28]

The type of experience described by McKay also impacted on Lovett Fort-Whiteman, the first African-American Communist to receive training in Moscow. He was a capable writer and speaker, with experience in the Industrial Workers of the World (IWW) and Socialist Party, and also in the secret African Blood Brotherhood, which consisted of black radical intellectuals committed to black self-defense, black pride, and black self-determination. In addition to Fort-Whiteman, its leading members (such as Cyril Briggs, Richard B. Moore, Grace Campbell) were also drawn into the Communist Party. A Communist since 1921, Fort-Whiteman created a considerable stir upon returning from his crash course in leadership training in Moscow. Another black activist who became a Communist only slightly later, Harry Haywood, has recalled:

> Fort-Whiteman was a truly fantastic figure. A brown-skinned man of medium height, Fort-Whitman's high cheekbones gave him somewhat of an Oriental look. He had affected a Russian style of dress, sporting

a *robochka* (a man's long belted shirt) which came almost to his knees, ornamental belt, high boots and a fur hat. Here was a veritable Black Cossack who could be seen sauntering along the streets of Southside Chicago. Fort-Whiteman was a graduate of Tuskegee and, as I understood, had had some training as an actor. He had been a drama critic for *The Messenger* and for *The Crusader*. There was no doubt that he was a showman; he always seemed to be acting out a part that he had chosen for himself. Upon his return from the Soviet Union, he held a number of press conferences in which he delineated plans for the American Negro Labor Congress, and as a black communist fresh from Russia, he made good news copy.[29]

Such things exasperated some of the others in the small but growing cadre of African-American Communists such as Richard B. Moore, who saw him as "far removed from the workers he was expected to organize," although Moore was appreciative of a recognition of "the semi-colonial features of the condition of Afro-Americans" that was developing in Moscow. Nonetheless, all leading black Communists were united in supporting policies emanating from Moscow in 1925 for the "Bolshevization" of the U.S. Communist Party — designed to create more centralized organizational norms and closer ties to the Moscow-led Communist International. "From their point of view, any program which increased Soviet control of the Party seemed *positive*," writes historian Mark Naison, "since the Soviets had been the strongest force in the movement pressing for recruitment of black members and emphasis on black issues."[30]

In fact, the Bolsheviks were decisive in helping white radicals of the United States realize the centrality of "the Negro question" to the American class struggle. Claude McKay, who had worked on the left-wing magazine *The Liberator* under Max Eastman, complained to his friend in a 1923 letter that "the files of the magazine are available to show what you, as chief editorial writer, said about the problem of the Negro in the Revolution. Nothing at all." This critical-minded poet, associated with the African Blood Brotherhood and, briefly, with the early U.S. Communists, felt a powerful kinship with the Bolsheviks. "There is magic in the name of Lenin, as there is splendor in the word Moscow," he wrote. The life of this Russian revolutionary "was devoted to the idea of creating a glorious new world," he explained in prefacing his poem "Moscow" —

> My memory bears engraved the strange Kremlin,
> Of halls symbolic of the tiger will,
> Of Czarist instruments of mindless law . . .
> And often now my nerves throb with the thrill
> When, in that gilded place, I felt and saw
> The simple voice and presence of Lenin.[31]

McKay's enthusiasm was related to the Russian Communists' alertness to the importance of racism and antiracist struggles in the United States. He had substantial discussions with prominent Bolsheviks on this and was invited to present an incisive informational and analytical report to the 1922 fourth congress of the Communist International. While in the Soviet Union he also wrote a short study at the request of the Soviet government, *The Negroes in America*, published in 1923, whose perspective was that "the Negro question is an integral part and one of the chief problems of the class struggle in America." A brief work peppered with unusual insights (for example, that "the Negro question is inseparably connected with the question of women's liberation"), it notes that among U.S. Communists of this time "some white comrades would sooner agree to go to the barricades than look squarely at the reality of the Negro question in America." This was related to the fact that "to go to the very heart of the Negro question for Communists means to incur the violent anger of American public opinion in the North as well as the South."[32] In a substantial article appearing in the NAACP magazine *Crisis* in the same year, McKay wrote:

> When the Russian workers overturned their infamous government in 1917, one of the first acts of the new premier, Lenin, was a proclamation greeting all the oppressed peoples throughout the world, exhorting them to organize against the common international oppressor — private capitalism. Later on in Moscow, Lenin himself grappled with the question of the American Negroes and spoke on the subject before the second congress of the Third International. He consulted with John Reed, the American journalist, and dwelt on the urgent necessity of propaganda and organizational work among the Negroes of the South.[33]

In fact, the first substantial organizing among African Americans was in Northern urban areas, to which millions of blacks, from the beginning of the First World War onward, were migrating. During the mid-1920s, "Bolshevization" of the U.S. Communist Party, notes Mark Naison, black Communists "found themselves in much closer contact with rank-and-file white Communists," because "black Communists, like all other Party members, were required to join street units in their neighborhoods or shop units where they worked. Following the logic of bolshevization, which defined ethnic solidarity among Communists as an obstacle to party unity, Party leaders encouraged, and later required, these units to be interracial."[34]

On the other hand, Robin Kelley stresses the interactive dynamic:

> Far from being a slumbering mass waiting for Communist direction, black working people entered the movement with a rich culture of opposition that sometimes contradicted, sometimes reinforced the left's vision of class struggle. The party offered more than a vehicle for social

contestation; it offered a framework for understanding the roots of poverty and racism, linked local struggles to world politics, challenged not only the hegemonic ideology of white supremacy but the petit bourgeois racial politics of the black middle class, and created an atmosphere in which ordinary people could analyze, discuss, and criticize the society in which they lived.[35]

A significant element brought by African-American contacts and recruits in the urban and rural South was the radical interpretation of Christianity, which was, historically, an essential ingredient in the African-American community. "The Bible was as much a guide to class struggle as Marx and Engels's *Communist Manifesto*," according to Kelley. "Rank-and-file black Communists and supporters usually saw nothing contradictory in combining religion and politics." The Communist message was seen by many as being the same thing that "Jesus Christ himself told us," and that, as Communists, "our burden was gonna be heavy like his." A black Baltimore minister in 1933 commented that large numbers of laboring and poor blacks "are shouting happy over what Communism has done for them, and praising God for what they expect it to do."[36]

Yet there were systematic efforts among black comrades to mesh "an African-American culture of opposition" with "a Stalinist version of Marxism-Leninism." Stalin's 1913 work *Marxism and the National Question* was lavishly promoted and widely distributed in the newly Stalinized Communist movement of the early 1930s. Combined with the theorization by the Communist International that blacks in the U.S. constituted an oppressed "nation," this was utilized to provide "a Marxist justification for black Communists to join the search for the roots of a national Negro culture," as Kelley has observed:

> As William L. Patterson wrote in 1933, the African American nation was bound by a common culture: "The 'spirituals,' the jazz, their religious practices, a growing literature, descriptive of their environment, all of these are forms of cultural expression. ... Are these not the prerequisites for nationhood?" Black party leader Harry Haywood traced the roots of a "national Negro culture" in "ancient African civilization [and] Negro art and literature reflecting the environment of oppression of the Negroes in the United States."[37]

Not everyone was inclined to embrace the transplanting of Russian Bolshevism to American soil. Reflecting on his Chicago experience in the U.S. Communist Party of the 1930s, Richard Wright commented: "The American Communists, enjoying legality, were using methods forged by the underground Russian Bolshevik fire, and therefore had to have their followers willing to accept all explanations of reality, even when the actual situation did not call for it." The inclination to copy the Russians even affected the mannerisms of black Communist speakers in Chicago's Washington Park — they copied things "they had seen Lenin or Stalin do in photographs." He scoffed: "Though they did not know it, they were naively practicing magic; they thought that if they acted like the men who had overthrown the czar, then surely they ought to be able to win their freedom in America."[38]

Deeper critiques were offered by such black radicals as Claude McKay, who in later years denounced "the Stalin terror" as well as the Communist-influenced League of American Writers because "it fights Fascist totalitarianism, but proscribes as Fascists, Trotskyists and Reactionaries the writers who are opposed to Communist totalitarianism." Asserting in 1937 that he did not "accept the official version of the Moscow trials," McKay expressed "a high respect for Trotsky as a thinking man and none for Stalin," although he insisted that he did not consider himself any sort of Communist. Expressing solidarity with two Soviet poets — Vladimir Mayakovsky and Sergei Yesenin — who had committed suicide in the face of the rising bureaucratic dictatorship, he commented that they "had wholeheartedly embraced Communism, but ... ominously preferred the way out by self-purge, just before the great purge liquidated scores of their fellow writers and artists." Arguing that "any regime is bad under which people were afraid to think and talk independently," he stressed: "I believe in the social revolution and the triumph of workers' democracy, not workers' dictatorship."[39]

More systematic was the critique developed by Afro-Caribbean intellectual C. L. R. James, who would have a significant presence on the American scene. His 1936 study *World Revolution* explained that, on the one hand, "by 1932–1933 collective ownership [in the USSR] had demonstrated its capacity for increasing production on a scale unprecedented in the most expansive periods of capitalist economy," providing the basis for the modernization of the Soviet Union. On the other hand, "a workers' state rests on the workers, and any plan which did not in fact improve their conditions from year to year was thereby condemned .... But the Stalinist regime was based on bureaucracy; its only idea of fighting bureaucracy was to admit workers into its ranks and create more ill-educated and incompetent bureaucrats." And "the errors of the bureaucracy were paid for by the workers," in the form of "cut wages, low standards of living and remorseless speeding-up." What's more, workers accused of participating in or organizing strikes to defend their conditions could be imprisoned or, in some cases, executed.

More brutal, James emphasized, were actions taken against peasants to "collectivize" agriculture through state confiscation of their lands. "Civil war raged in the countryside," he reported. "The peasants refused to produce; they ate the seed rather than plant it, they slaughtered the livestock rather than take them to collective farms. Thousands were shot, and these and those deported [to labor camps] were the more successful farmers." The result of such "maladministration and brutality" was the devastation of Soviet agriculture — "a ghastly famine seized the country," and millions died in the early 1930s. "To the mass shootings of workers and peasants were now added a series of proscriptions against professors, secretaries, collective-farm officials, workers, all who dared to utter a word of criticism, while, in a vain attempt to drown the somber rattle of the bullets, Stalin and the Soviet Press sang unceasing panegyrics to the brilliant and amazing victories of ... Socialism." He concluded that "the social contradictions, and the contradiction between the promises of the bureaucracy and its actions, all could only be met by an increasing terror."[40]

Some chose to see a different reality. The bright shining star guiding the Communists was the victorious revolution in Russia, where — they were convinced — socialism was now being created through immense sacrifices. Through "years of revolution, civil war, and blockade [that] must have taken a fearful toll," in the words of black lawyer William L. Patterson, "one thing stood out: the people led by Communists had taken power." Visiting the Soviet Union in the late 1920s, he found "a new world in the making. This called for the making of a new man, a new people." It seemed an immense and spectacular undertaking. "How long would it take us to make a new man in Mississippi, and a new Black man in the ghettoes of the United States? How long to humanize millions of whites?" Patterson found a "heartwarming" response reminiscent of that given Claude McKay several years before. He concluded: "There was in the treatment accorded me a wholesomeness born of the new freedom they were experiencing and wanted for others."[41]

This could not erase the fact, however, that many of its inhabitants found repression and death in this "new world" during the 1930s, including Americans.

There is the case of Lovett Fort-Whiteman, in the mid-1920s — as we've seen — one of the most prominent African-Americans in the U.S. Communist movement. His "excessive flamboyance" had alienated such prominent black comrades as Richard B. Moore, Cyril Briggs, Otto Huiswood, William L. Patterson, and Harry Haywood. The American Negro Labor Conference, which he headed — according to James Ford, the leading black Communist of the 1930s — remained "almost completely isolated from the basic masses of the Negro people." He lost further credibility by opposing the position developed by Comintern officials in collaboration with Harry Haywood that African-Americans constituted a nation whose claim to self-determination was grounded in the Black Belt region of the U.S. South.

Fort-Whiteman was pushed out of his positions of authority, but an exciting consolation for him was a 1930 assignment in the Soviet Union to work for the Communist International. While there, he married a Russian, went on speaking tours to raise support for anti-racist struggles in the U.S., and sought to be an "ideological mentor of other black Americans living in Moscow," in part by initiating Marxist discussion groups in his apartment. In 1933, he asked to return to the United States, but was not permitted to do so. In 1935,

Fort-Whiteman was the subject of a Comintern subcommittee (including U.S. comrades Earl Browder, Sam Darcy, and William Schneiderman) to investigate his "reported efforts to mislead some of the Negro comrades," and by 1936 — the year of the Moscow trials — he was publicly arguing with William L. Patterson over leftist criticisms Fort-Whiteman leveled at Langston Hughes' book *The Ways of White Folks.*

Soon afterward, U.S. Communist reports asserted that he "has showed himself for Trotsky." More to the point, he was accused of "anti-Soviet agitation" by the Stalin regime in 1937, and his banishment to "internal exile" was soon expanded into a sentence of five years' hard labor at the Sevotlag labor camp. He didn't last more than two years. According to one account, "he died of starvation, or malnutrition, a broken man, whose teeth had been knocked out."[42]

This was not typical of African-American experience in the USSR, however.

No one was more eloquent in extolling the Soviet Union than the great singer, intellectual, and political activist Paul Robeson. Courageously and eloquently challenging racism and capitalism in the United States and everywhere else, Robeson insisted on the need to "fight for the right of the Negro people and other oppressed, labor-driven Americans to have decent homes, decent jobs, and the dignity that belongs to every human being," pointing to "the connection between the problems of all oppressed people and the necessity of the artist to participate fully" in the struggle for a better world. In Robeson's opinion, "for all mankind a socialist society represents an advance to a higher stage of life — that it is a form of society which is economically, socially, culturally, and ethically superior to a system based upon production for private profit."[43] As with so many others, he viewed the USSR as the promising beginning of that better future.

Soviet Inspiration

In a 1935 interview in the *Daily Worker*, Robeson asserted: "I was not prepared for the happiness I see on every face in Moscow. I was aware that there was no starvation here, but I was not prepared for the bounding life; the feeling of safety and abundance and freedom that I find here, wherever I turn." He added (after the mysterious assassination of prominent Leningrad Communist Sergei Kirov, but before Stalin's murderous purge trials took place): "From what I have already seen of the workings of the Soviet Government, I can only say that anybody who lifts his hand against it ought to be shot!"[44]

One year later, Robeson and Gustav Regler (a German Communist preparing to join the International Brigades to fight against fascism in Spain) were in a Moscow radio station when news came of the arrest of Lenin's old comrades Kamenev and Zinoviev on charges of treason (for which they would soon, after forced confessions at public show trials, be shot). Regler later wrote:

He loved the land of Pushkin — "The only country in the world where we can feel at home. Here there is no segregation, no foolish ban — we are all brothers." They were the words he had just uttered over the microphone, and he had sung the same message amid shacks on the Mississippi, through Texas and Arkansas and to the colored soldiers of France. Now his sensitive nostrils caught the scent of death, fratricide, the ugly smell of Judge Lynch. There was a look of such torment in his eyes that for a moment I forgot my own troubles; and a brief sentence broke from his lips as though it were a groan — "It must not be!" As he turned to go the man on the panel called to him, reminding him of his promise to sing. Robeson looked sadly up at him, clearly marveling at so little perception, and politely refused. It was no time for singing.[45]

Robeson's ten-year-old son attended school in the USSR in this period, and the parents of some of the child's schoolmates were swept up in the purges. "My father warned me not to question what was happening and to accept things as they were," Paul Jr. later recounted. "When I asked him whether the executions were justified, he replied that, as foreigners, it was not for us to judge — only the Russians themselves could decide." A year later, when the Robesons were safely outside of the USSR, the artist was prepared to talk with his son more frankly:

He acknowledged that "terrible" things had been done, and that innocent people had been "sacrificed to punish the guilty." But the Soviet Union felt it was already in a situation that was to them "the equivalent of war." They felt they could not tolerate any kind of dissent. Sometimes, he added, great injustices may be inflicted on the minority when the majority is in the pursuit of a great and just cause.[46]

Robeson refrained from public criticism, still believing that "the Soviet Union is the bulwark of civilization against both war and fascism." According to his biographer Martin Duberman, "he resisted every pressure to convert any private disappointment he may have felt in the Soviet experiment into public censure."[47]

"But there was the other side," historian Arno Mayer has commented, echoing what Robeson, Patterson, and many others had argued. "In the city and, to a lesser extent, in the countryside, the educational system developed rapidly at all levels, fostering upward social mobility alongside advancement by geographic relocation and on-the-job training." Terming Stalin "a radical modernizer," he notes that during the 1930s the USSR "became a major industrial power, with gigantic metallurgical complexes, hydroelectric power stations, and tractor plants." Soviet heavy industry caught up with that of Western Europe (in quantity if not in quality), with the number of industrial workers rising from fewer than 3 million to more than 8 million, and the urban population rising by almost 30 million — and this in a period when most of the world was in the throes of the Great Depression. (The immense and heroic role played by the USSR in resisting and overcoming Hitler's onslaught during World War II also "fostered the legitimacy of the regime" among Communists and sympathizers around the world.) Drawing on insights from Roy Medvedev, Mayer captures contradictory elements in the Soviet reality: "Clearly the situation was simultaneously closed and open, terrifying and full of promise." Purges, executions, and labor camps were obscured for many by the fact that "new schools, factories, and palaces of culture were rising everywhere." Scientific, cultural, and intellectual life were being terrorized and regimented — and yet "Soviet science ... developed rapidly with the party's support," while literacy and education were being made available throughout the USSR. And "while leaders in the minor republics were being arrested as nationalists ... the formerly oppressed nationalities were improving their lot." The positive developments were projected as the achievements of socialism and of its primary architect Joseph Stalin.[48]

For the great majority of American Communists, therefore, Stalin was the personification of revolutionary patience combined with a practical-minded commitment to creating a better future — a symbol of all the progress in the USSR that would some day be spread throughout the world.

Yet Medvedev has insisted that it was not Stalin but "the October revolution that opened the road to education and culture for the Soviet people," adding that the USSR would have "traveled that road far more quickly if Stalin had not destroyed hundreds of thousands of the intelligentsia, both old and new." He adds that the system of forced labor "accomplished a great deal, building almost all the canals and hydroelectric stations in the USSR, many railways, factories, pipelines, even tall buildings in Moscow. But industry would have developed faster if these millions of innocent people had been employed as free workers." Medvedev also notes the devastation of Soviet agriculture that resulted from the use of force and violence against the peasants. He concludes that "Stalin's cruel recklessness" resulted in unnecessary sacrifices that "did not speed up but rather slowed down the overall rate of development that our country might have enjoyed." What were seen as "victories" for the USSR during the 1930s "turned out in fact to be defeats for socialism," fatally undermining the USSR's future.[49]

Most U.S. Communists, however, would allow themselves to see only the "victories," persuading themselves that the sacrifices were unavoidable and heroic. The brutal realities that Claude McKay and C. L .R. James pointed to at the time, and that Lovett Fort-Whiteman among so many others experienced, represented "the evil within the good." Both were central elements in the mainstream of American Communism.

Two Souls of American Communism

Idealistic delusion, commitment to a totalitarian order, betrayal of self and country — this is the story of Communism in the United States, according to many influential commentators. As anti-leftist historians Harvey Klehr and John Earl Haynes put it, the organization's leadership "knowingly and willingly assisted Soviet spies" and while the organization's "chief task was the promotion of communism" through a variety of educational and political activities, the Communist Party also functioned as a " fifth column ... inside and against the United States in the Cold War." With the collapse of the Soviet Union and the defeat of Communism in the decades-long Cold War, they could conclude quite simply: "American Communism is a sad tale of wasted commitment and wasted life."[50]

But the story is more interesting, in some ways more inspiring, and in some ways more tragic, than this. From the time of its founding, the Communist Party attracted many thousands of the most committed (and often among the most effective) political activists, who functioned with a remarkable discipline in a variety of causes and struggles. Despite efforts to minimize their influence at the time, and despite efforts by many historians and commentators to belittle their role, the Communists had a decisive influence on American life — in the labor movement, in anti-racist struggles, in women's rights efforts, in innumerable reform activities, as well as exercising quite substantial intellectual, artistic, literary, and cultural influence.[51]

The need to understand historical actualities, the need to deepen our understanding of the political and moral questions that we have been examining in this study, and the challenge to activists to learn from the past in order to be more effective in the struggle for a better future, all require that we take the story of American Communism seriously, being neither dismissive nor uncritical.[52]

If we allow ourselves to comprehend the meaning of what was represented by the example of the Russian Revolution of 1917 led by Vladimir Ilyich Lenin, we can also comprehend the kind of organization that the Communist Party of the United States — inspired by the Leninist model — sought to be. Rooted in the multicultural U.S. working class and American labor movement, it sought to bring together a critically conscious and activist element that would be animated around a revolutionary interpretation of the socialist theories of Karl Marx. It would draw added strength — in developing analyses, strategies, and tactics — through its connection with an international movement, giving aid to and receiving assistance from liberation struggles in other lands. Functioning as a cohesive, disciplined collectivity of such activists, it would seek to apply the theories to living realities. As part of the ongoing experience and struggles in U.S. society, and learning from that experience, it would be enabled to make the theories more relevant, and also help bring about significant social and political changes. This dialectical interplay would allow the revolutionary organization to grow in numbers and influence, impacting powerfully upon the intellectual, cultural, and political life of the United States. Eventually, the conscious activist element organized in the Communist Party would have sufficient weight in the working-class majority to pose a serious challenge to the capitalist system, and initiate a revolutionary struggle leading to socialism.

The formation of the U.S. Communist Party was the culmination of half a century of experience since the Civil War, involving the cumulative development of a vibrant labor-radical sub-culture, and the corresponding evolution of three generations of labor-radical activists. This formation was uneven, full of contradictions and sometimes absurdities. At first, there were three rival Communist parties emerging from the Socialist Party, with many Socialists also deciding decisively against going Communist. (This included the beloved and heroic leader Eugene V. Debs, who had warmly supported the Bolshevik revolution but was critical of the Communist Party dictatorship in the Soviet Republic and of the Communist International.) In addition to much of the Socialist left wing, however, a layer of militants from the colorful and uncompromisingly radical "one big union," the IWW, were attracted to what many perceived as "the red dawn." By the early 1920s, a unified Communist Party had taken shape in the United States, with a membership fluctuating between 7,000 and 12,000 that exercised significant influence in labor, radical, and even liberal circles.[53]

Under William Z. Foster's leadership, an influential network was created in the AFL through the Trade Union Educational League (TUEL). Progressive union leaders and activists rallied to many of the TUEL's perspectives, and a number of unions were influenced by the TUEL program, as were central labor councils in Chicago, Minneapolis, and other cities. The Party was also involved in defending human rights and civil liberties in the United States, particularly those of workers, through the International Labor Defense (ILD), which was conceived of during discussions among the legendary IWW leader "Big Bill" Haywood, Rose Karsner, and James P. Cannon, who became its national secretary when it was set up in 1925.[54]

There were many other components of the Communist movement — focusing on the rights of oppressed racial and national groups, women's rights, immigrant rights, the interests of young people and aspirations of students, the opposition to war and imperialism and militarism. Significant attention was given to educating around and building support for the Soviet Union, where many felt a bright socialist future was being built. There was a variety of publications, educational efforts, cultural activities, and more.

The Communists' subordinate relationship with an increasingly bureaucratic and authoritarian USSR weakened both the Communist Party and the American Left, as many people came to see Communism as a force, not for liberation, but as representing a new tyranny, and often blurred together with all

"Reds," whether Stalinist or anti-Stalinist. Yet the vision of Communism — the inspiring goal, the comprehensive view of history that gave it meaning, the serious commitment to opposing present-day injustices as part of reaching for the ultimate goal, the expansive integration of world politics with national and local struggles, the tough-minded organizational approach — had a powerful impact not only on the hundreds of thousands of people who were in or around the Communist Party at one point or another, but on many more, particularly in the 1930s.

"Few Communists have ever been made simply by reading the works of Marx or Lenin," commented Whittaker Chambers. "The crisis of history makes Communists; Marx and Lenin merely offer them an explanation of the crisis and what to do about it. Thus a graph of Communist growth would show that its numbers and its power increased in waves roughly equivalent to each new crest of crisis." In a thoughtful analysis of "objective factors" in the United States that made specific social groups "susceptible to Communist influences," conservative anti-Communist (and ex-Communist) Frank Meyer explained that three related peaks in recruitment could be found for workers and intellectuals:

1. The early 1920s, "when in the mass-production industries and in a megalopolitan New York the foreign-born workers, stimulated by the war-time disorganization of society and the Russian Revolution, surged out against the caste-like barriers about them," while at the same time "the trauma of the first of the great modern wars interacted with a utopian glorification of the Russian Revolution;"
2. The early 1930s, as workers experienced the shocks of unemployment and dispossession, also threatening the economic status of intellectuals and professionals, shaking "the ideological and psychological underpinnings" of each;
3. From 1935 to 1945, "when a widespread movement of militancy and organization spread through great sections of hitherto unorganized American labor" and at the same time "the crusading spirit against fascism stirred the whole intellectual community — particularly during the Spanish Civil War and the World War II alliance with the Soviet Union."[55]

Whittaker Chambers joined near the end of the earlier influx of the mid-1920s. Two personifications of Communism stand out in Chambers' memoir from this earlier period. One is Kate Gitlow, the activist mother of Communist leader Ben Gitlow:

She was a short, sturdy Jewish woman, with shrewd eyes behind her glasses, suggesting a touch of earthy horse sense. She stood for a moment, waiting for the meeting to become quiet — an interval that she used

to roll up her sleeves as if for a brawl. Then she said in a tone of challenge: "Cumreds! The potato crop has failed in Ireland and thousands of
peasants are starving to death. Cumreds! What are we doing to help the
starving workers and peasants of Ireland?" ...

Mother Gitlow was Communism in action. That short, squat, bellig-
erent woman, pleading in a thick Yiddish accent for food for the hungry
Irish peasants, personified the brotherhood of all the wretched of the
earth. It made no difference that most Irish peasants would have hooted
her out of town. She knew that too. But she was a Communist. In her
worked the revolutionary will to overcome ignorance and prejudice in
the name of militant compassion and intelligent human unity.[56]

Another personification of Communism in Chambers' memoir is a Hungarian he came to know through a chance meeting, who was involved in secret
work for the Communist International, and was temporarily staying in the
United States. "He was short, dark, and dressed quietly with an air of extreme
tidiness," Chambers recalled. "His eyes were black, intelligent, friendly, fearless. ... He spoke quietly ... he seldom paused, laying out his thoughts like a
man turning the pages of a book. Sometimes, in summing up, he closed his
eyes, as if that way he could better see the order of the propositions on the
page." According to Chambers, "much of what he taught me I would later
find in Lenin's *What Is To Be Done* — the meaning of the professional revolutionist, the tasks, the discipline and duties of that modern secular secret
order which has dedicated its life and its death to initiating a new phase of
history for mankind." There was a "religious" quality to their conversations,
with the experienced Hungarian comrade "patiently sowing seeds, not knowing whether any would take root, but believing that they might." Chambers
remembered him as "a man simple yet sinuous, warm but disciplined, ascetic
but friendly, highly intelligent but completely unpretentious" — an embodiment of Chambers' own vision of Communism.[57]

Such luminous and vibrant human beings seemed to reflect the vision of a
communist future: a society of abundance, freedom for the full development
of each person, in which the state would gradually give way to the free association of individuals. This vision "was beautiful in concept and plausible,"
according to immigrant worker-writer, Sandor Voros: "In a Communist society every person would have an equal right to a full share of the products of
that society. With private profit eliminated, the productivity of such a society
would grow so plentiful that working time would be cut to four hours a day,
possibly even less."

Capitalism rested on the incentive of monetary reward and punishment by starvation. Yet even in a capitalist society it wasn't money that
drove men to perform the most valued, most respected, socially most
useful acts.

Does a mother nurse her child, change his diapers, because she expects pay for her services?

Does a father stay up all night with his sick child because he expects a cash bonus for it?

Does a volunteer rush into a burning building to save his neighbor's life because he expects to tender a bill for it later?

How much cash did the man who did not know how to swim demand in advance before he jumped off the dock to try to save a floundering child and who himself had drowned in the attempt?

What is the cash value of a Congressional Medal of Honor?

How much money did the early Christian martyrs demand for refusing to say "*Ave Caesar*" and for letting themselves be mangled to death by the hungry lions?

According to the Communist vision that Voros embraced, people "give their best for pride in achievement, for their inner satisfaction and peace of mind; to win the approval, praise, and admiration of their fellow human beings." This the Communist future would provide in abundance. "All unhappiness caused by poverty, by inequality and social discrimination, by lack of opportunity, by lack of freedom, would simply disappear when their underlying economic causes had been removed." No less important to Voros and many others was the belief that "this conception of an ideal society was no longer a dream. It was in the process of realization right then in the Soviet Union, under the leadership of the Communist Party, the elite guard of the proletariat. The Communist Party was destined to lead the downtrodden masses into similar revolts all over the world when the right historical moment arrived." For Voros, "this was the purpose in life I had been searching for — to help elevate mankind — and now I was offered a chance to participate in it." He responded with enthusiasm.[58]

Not only the existence of admirable Communists and the vision of an amazing future, but the existence of a vibrant collectivity was an essential ingredient. Another worker-writer, Richard Wright, emphasized the sense of community and comradeship: "It was not the economics of Communism, nor the great power of trade unions, nor the excitement of underground politics that claimed me; my attention was caught by the similarity of the experiences of workers in other lands, by the possibility of uniting scattered but kindred peoples into a whole. My cynicism — which had been my protection against an America that had cast me out — slid from me, and, timidly, I began to wonder if a solution of unity was possible." Wright viewed his comrades as "acting upon the loftiest of impulses, filled with love for those who suffer, urged toward fellowship with the rebellious, committed to sacrifice," asserting that regardless of serious problems he perceived in the Communist Party, "I felt they were moving in the right direction ... I was for these people. Being a Negro, I could not help it. They did not hate Negroes. They had no racial prejudices. Many of the white men in the [Communist Party meeting] hall were married to Negro women, and many of the Negro men were married to white women. Jews, Germans, Russians, Spaniards, all races and nationalities were represented without any distinctions whatever."[59]

Margaret Budenz and her husband joined in the mid-1930s, after experience in other radical groups. They "did not expect to find the degree of perfection" that some Communist friends had assured them of. "Some people and some decisions would not be to our liking — we kept reminding ourselves — but we must keep before us the reality of the Soviet Union where socialism was in progress, the one spot on the globe (and one sixth of the globe at that!) where society was undergoing radical change." By 1937, the USSR not only was surrounded by capitalist enemies, but particularly threatened by Hitler's Germany, Mussolini's Italy, and the threat of insurgent fascism in Spain, where the Popular Front government of liberals, Socialists, and Communists was threatened with defeat in the Spanish Civil War. A fascistic regime in Japan had also launched an invasion of China, which turned out to be the beginning of World War II in Asia. Against this rising threat, the Communist Party was engaged in the struggle against exploitation and for workers' rights, against racism and for the brotherhood and sisterhood of all. "The fabric of our lives was so interwoven with the Communist Party that it did not occur to us to question any twist or turn of the official line," she noted. "The ultimate discipline was to accept the line because the line is 'correct,' a favorite word in the Communist jargon. It was correct for the Party, for the United States, and for the future of our children. We had real concern for the life we would make for our little girls, a life, we hoped, without depressions or unemployment or fascism or war."[60]

Margaret's husband, Louis F. Budenz, explained the connection between the ultimate revolutionary goals and immediate non-revolutionary struggles. "The Communist Party stands for socialism," he wrote in a pamphlet designed to help overcome suspicion of Communism in the U.S. trade union movement. "It points out that the experiences of the workers will show them that the machine system cannot be run under capitalist control. Capitalism, in its effort to pile up more and more profits, brings on an inevitable crash or inevitable world war." On the other hand, "the Committee for Industrial Organization does not stand for socialism. It is a trade union movement, which of its very nature includes American workers of all races, creeds, colors, national origins and political beliefs. The great bulk of its membership has not yet come to accept socialism as their goal. Its leader, John L. Lewis, does not stand for socialism." Communists understand this, Budenz commented, but "are certain that the trade unionists will come to accept this view [about the need for socialism] out of their experiences." Because of this, the Communists "wholeheartedly and vigorously participate in the immediate struggles of all the workers, meanwhile emphasizing what lies ahead and those things with which other workers may not yet agree."[61]

All of the foregoing quotations on the attractions of the Communist Party were written by people who shifted from Communism to bitter anti-Communism. To comprehend this, we must consider other aspects of the Communist Party experience.

In addition to a deep idealism, a profound opposition to oppression and exploitation, and an uncompromising commitment to the creation of a society of "the free and equal," there swirled and jostled within the leadership of the Communist Party a variety of personalities, egos, ambitions, and "careerist" aspirations. It was in 1937 that Margaret Budenz and her husband — who had risen in the Communist Party's hierarchy — found themselves socializing with two Party higher-ups, Morris Childs and William Weiner. As she kept company with Mrs. Childs and the children in the kitchen, her husband sat with Childs and Weiner in the dining room in before-dinner banter. She was able to hear much of their conversation.

> That afternoon I learned more about Party functionaries than I had ever known before. As Weiner and Childs mellowed under the influence of alcohol and their tongues loosened beyond discretion, they began to indulge in careless jokes about "passing resolutions" that showed their real or imagined authority in the Party. They laughed about the orders they could give and the power they had over the "rank and filth" working-class members of the Party. I heard only what floated to me from the dining room. It was supposed to be funny, but Louis was not joining in the laughter. For the most part he seemed to be listening and smiling sheepishly from time to time …. What I thought I was hearing was a display of raw power over Party members who could easily be controlled by disciplinary measures, political orders, or threats of exposure or expulsion …. I was disgusted because I thought they were drunk, boastful, and unworthy of what I believed Party leadership to represent, in private as well as in public.[62]

There was certainly no shortage of negative human traits among U.S. Communist leaders in earlier years either. Looking back upon his experience in the 1920s, however, James P. Cannon argued: "Even if it is maintained that some of these leaders were careerists — a contention their later evolution tends to support — it still remains to be explained why they sought careers in the communist movement and not in the business or professional worlds, or in bourgeois politics, or in the trade-union officialdom." In Cannon's opinion, "the course of the leaders of American communism in its pioneer days, a course which entailed deprivations, hazards, and penalties, can be explained only by the assumption that they were revolutionists to begin with; and that even the careerists among them believed in the future of the workers' revolution in

America and wished to ally themselves with this future."[63] It is also the case that some prominent Communists, whatever their limitations or flaws, had admirable qualities. We must look to factors other than unworthy personalities to comprehend the fate of the Communist Party.

The goal of a workers' revolution that could bring socialism to the United States, the most developed and powerful of capitalist economies — particularly in "the Roaring Twenties" — was daunting. There were, naturally, serious differences on how best to build the Communist Party and to advance the struggles of the workers and the oppressed. Such dynamics intertwined with, and were influenced by, the workings of the Communist International, to which the U.S. Communist Party was affiliated. Although it was projected, when established under the leadership of the Russian Communists, to be a world party of socialist revolution in which all national sections and individuals would enjoy a comradely equality, it was the Russians (who had made a successful revolution and were the hosts and financiers of the Comintern) who were naturally seen as the leaders.[64]

"In the first days of the October revolution — that is the Bolshevik revolution — the Russians were leaders through prestige, through achievement, through the fact that they conquered one-sixth of the world for socialism," recalled Jay Lovestone some years later. "We had an attitude of almost religious veneration toward them.... But I must say in fairness to the Russian leaders at that time they did not advocate this, they did not nurture this." In fact, according to Lovestone, "they tended to treat us as equals, with equal respect: respecting our opinions, and we appreciated that. They were big men, and because they were big men they did not act in little or small ways, but nevertheless the Russian influence was decisive."[65]

According to Cannon, he and his comrades "learned to do away forever with the idea that a revolutionary socialist movement, aiming at power, can be led by people who practice socialism as an avocation. ... Lenin, Trotsky, Zinoviev, Radek, Bukharin — these were our teachers. We began to be educated in an entirely different spirit from the old lackadaisical Socialist Party — in the spirit of revolutionists who take ideas and program very seriously." Bertram Wolfe concurred, noting that before 1925 it was *not* the case that "all important decisions for the American Communist party were being made in Moscow" — rather, communications from Lenin, Zinoviev, and other Comintern leaders "were intended only as helpful suggestions, often exciting ones, and as successful examples to imitate after adapting them to American conditions, but not as categorical commands."[66]

Lovestone recalled that by 1924, however, when Comintern leader Gregory Zinoviev was allied with Joseph Stalin against Leon Trotsky, there developed "sharp, unprincipled factionalism — I would say suicidal factionalism — in the Russian party, [and] the Comintern policies began to be involved in and determined by factional struggles inside the Russian party .... First there was the beginning of slavishness and mechanical transference, and what I called the Byzantine court at Moscow — kowtowing before the potentates, but it was not yet worked up into a system. ... Then that culminated in the triumph of Stalin in Russia and thereafter the triumph of Stalin in the Communist International."[67]

"Everything had been settled behind the scenes," Cannon observed about a typical situation in the Comintern of the mid-1920s. "The word had been passed and all the secondary leaders and functionaries in the Comintern were falling into line." When radical intellectual Max Eastman complained to William Z. Foster of the highhanded action of Comintern leadership, Foster responded: "Max, a lot of things happen here that I don't like. But we can't do anything about it. They've got the prestige. No revolutionary movement anywhere, as things stand now, can prosper without their backing."[68]

The consequent factional struggles of the mid- to late-1920s undermined the moral fiber of the struggling party, particularly under the influence of the little-understood bureaucratic degeneration in the USSR. These developments, Cannon later recalled, were difficult "to live through without sliding into cynicism as did so many others — good companions in earlier endeavors." He reminisced that "many good militants succumbed to factionalism and lost their bearings altogether. It is only a short step from cynicism to renegacy. Betrayal of principle in little things easily leads to betrayal in bigger things."[69]

An anti-Trotsky campaign was being orchestrated throughout the Comintern, and under Lovestone's leadership — ably supported by Wolfe, Gitlow, and others — this campaign was advanced among the American Communists. Ludwig Lore, a prominent and talented German-American Communist, had been expelled in 1925, at Lovestone's initiative, in part for defending Trotsky. "I know everyone of our boys is solid with Stalin," Lovestone asserted proudly when Trotsky and Zinoviev established a united opposition to challenge the crystallization of the bureaucratic dictatorship in the USSR in 1926. But the party was shaken in 1928 when James P. Cannon and some of his closest associates (Max Shachtman, Martin Abern, Rose Karsner, and others) were brought up on charges and expelled for Trotskyism. Disgusted and disheartened by the factionalism and what he viewed as unprincipled maneuvering that seemed to characterize so much of the internal life of American Communism and the Comintern as such, Cannon had indeed been won over to Trotsky's critique of Stalinism. He and about 100 expellees promptly organized the Communist League of America in 1929, basing themselves forthrightly on Trotsky's revolutionary perspectives.[70]

But 1929 also saw a dramatic "leftist" zigzag in Stalin's policies inside the USSR and its Communist Party, and within the Comintern. Over the objections of his moderate-Communist ally Nikolai Bukharin (with whom Lovestone and his associates had nourished a close relationship), Stalin pushed through the brutal forced collectivization of the land and a rapid industrialization policy in the USSR that brought extreme hardship and death to millions of peasants and workers and was accompanied by an intensification of extreme dictatorial measures. Consummate factional infighter though he was, Lovestone was no match for Stalin's political machine. Lovestone, along with Bertram Wolfe, Ben Gitlow, Will Herberg, and 200 other unrepentant co-thinkers were expelled, and they reorganized themselves as the "Communist Party Opposition."[71]

A majority of American Communists had no patience for continued factional disputes, let alone critiques of the USSR and the Comintern — particularly when the Stalin regime insisted that a failure to fall in line would be grounds for expulsion. Many felt it was time to close ranks behind the leadership of Comrade Stalin, in the face of intensifying economic hardship, the rising tide of fascism, and the shadows of war. As Peggy Dennis later commented, "in our political naiveté … we younger comrades did not particularly connect our own internal struggle with that which had raged in the Comintern and the Soviet Communist Party," nor did many U.S. Communists comprehend that the Comintern's interventions into the affairs of the American Communist party were "part of Stalin's consolidation of his leadership within the Soviet party and the international movement, less than five years after Lenin's death." She added, "we eloquently echoed Stalin's published denunciations of Bukharinism and Trotskyism without even objecting to the fact that we were not allowed to read what Bukharin or Trotsky had said or written."[72]

Trotskyist membership generally fluctuated between 200 and 1,200, certainly never attracting more than 2,000 formal adherents, who sometimes existed in several competing organizations. Despite an exaggerated reputation for sectarianism, they were able to play an honorable role in the labor movement, especially when they provided impressive leadership in the 1934 Minneapolis general strike. Pockets of working-class militants in various unions and industrial centers, as well as in unemployed and community struggles, continued to do what they could to advance class consciousness and the class struggle, and to keep alive revolutionary socialist ideas. Trotskyist and Trotskyist-influenced intellectuals, writers, and artists made contributions to American culture, and some of the most prominent figures among the intelligentsia were part of this milieu (including — for a time — Max Eastman, Sidney Hook, Herbert Solow, James Rorty, Edmund Wilson, Mary McCarthy, Philip Rahv, Meyer Schapiro, James T. Farrell, and Irving Howe). Among the influential black intellectuals and activists in this group were C. L. R. James, labor organizer Ernest Rice McKinney, radical lawyer Conrad Lynn, and Detroit physician Edgar Keemer. One of the greatest legacies of the Trotskyists was their consistent anti-Stalinism — not only denouncing Stalin's crimes, but insisting that these were alien to Marxism, to the Russian Revolution of 1917, and to the goals and commitments of the early Communist movement. In later years, some were also able to play a significant part in antiracist, antiwar, feminist, and other struggles.[73]

The Lovestoneites have left a more complex legacy. They hoped to be recognized as having been right by the Comintern, and therefore persisted in defending many of Stalin's policies — until by 1937 they recoiled with horror as the bloody purges of the 1930s made it clear that there was no way back for them. One of their greatest contributions was having the fabulous Mexican revolutionary muralist Diego Rivera paint a magnificent left-wing mural history of the United States at their New Workers School in New York. Prominent writers Louis Adamic, Lewis Corey, Albert Halper, Grace Lumpkin, and Ben Stolberg were, at one point or another, in the Lovestone milieu. So were several black activists and intellectuals who rose to some prominence in later years — Edward Welsh, Abram Harris, Pauli Murray, Maida Springer, and Ella Baker. Lovestoneites also made significant contributions in certain union struggles. This included involvement in the historic sitdown strikes in the auto industry — but their role in unsavory union factional fights finally destroyed their credibility in the United Auto Workers.[74]

A prominent Lovestoneite, the popular Charles ("Sasha") Zimmerman rose in the leadership of the International Ladies Garment Workers Union (ILGWU), and Lovestone became a close associate of ILGWU chieftain David Dubinsky. Eventually he became an even more significant figure in the AFL (after Dubinsky assured other AFL leaders that "the son of a bitch converted" to their own anti-Communist outlook). This was after his organization formally dissolved in 1941, and Lovestone went on to help develop and implement Cold War foreign policy in collaboration with the State Department and Central Intelligence Agency. Bertram Wolfe became an anti-Communist authority on the USSR and a State Department employee. Another Lovestoneite, Will Herberg, became a prominent Jewish theologian and conservative intellectual. Ben Gitlow, who had broken with the group in the early 1930s, by the 1950s and early 1960s was associated with such ultra-right enterprises as Rev. Billy James Hargis's Christian Crusade and Dr. Fred Schwarz's Christian Anti-Communist Crusade.[75]

Much of this reaction is related to revulsion over the fact that the Russian Revolution, in which so many idealistic hopes were invested, gave way to the murderous dictatorship of the Stalin regime. This reality (and the defense or denial of the reality) is one of the most negative legacies of American Communism's mainstream. There were also those drawn into spy networks to assist the "homeland of socialism" — through the Comintern underground apparatus, the Soviet secret service, Soviet military espionage — in its battle against the capitalist enemy.

This was a very small minority of those who were Communists, and in some cases their stories did not end well. There was immensely talented labor educator Juliet Stuart Poyntz, who took on trusted "underground" assignments, became disillusioned with Stalinism, and suddenly disappeared (perhaps kidnapped and murdered) in the 1930s. There were Whittaker Chambers and "Red spy queen" Elizabeth Bentley, idealistically drawn into "secret work," then repelled by aspects of what they were doing. They turned on their comrades and became professional witnesses against Communism, fingering prominent figures in the U.S. government whose "progressive" sympathies had drawn them into one or another connection with the information-gathering networks of the USSR.[76]

The same trajectory was followed by Louis F. Budenz, who in the late 1930s (told that he was helping to thwart a plot to murder Stalin) had helped implant Communist Party members — under the discipline of the Soviet secret service — among the U.S. Trotskyists, and unknowingly facilitated efforts culminating in the 1940 assassination of Leon Trotsky. A related problematical legacy was the tendency for Communists in various social struggles to tailor their efforts to harmonize with the dictates of the Stalin regime, sometimes to the detriment of those struggles. Such things helped lead to Budenz's defection in 1945, also to his career as a "professional anti-Communist." The testimony of people like Chambers, Budenz, and Bentley fed into an anti-Communist hysteria as the Cold War era began in the late 1940s, and caused many to view American Communism as simply a treasonous conspiracy.[77]

Masters of Deceit

The fact remains that the legacy of American Communism cannot simply be reduced to this. Too many were heroically involved in the struggle for the economic betterment of the working class, for racial equality and human rights, against poverty, against imperialism and militarism, against fascism. There was certainly a vibrant idealism associated with the glowing example of the socialist future that was actually being created — many sincerely believed — in the USSR. Listening to a debate between Stalinist V. J. Jerome and Lovestoneite Bertram D. Wolfe, George Blake Charney later recalled: "I was in no position to judge the respective merits of their arguments on Marxism. Both were learned men. In the end I was drawn to the position of the [Stalinist] party because it was positive and forward-looking, whereas Wolfe was carping and negative and offered so little hope at a time when we needed so much."[78]

This uncritical attitude toward the USSR and toward the Stalin dictatorship — far more than passing information to that regime — was the fatal flaw of the Communist Party. This has relevance to the question of what kind of threat it posed to the established order.

One answer to this question was advanced in an anti-Communist classic of the 1950s. In *Masters of Deceit*, FBI Director J. Edgar Hoover commented on the Red Decade and the World War II period (during which the United States and the USSR were allies): "When the Communist Party was at its peak in the United States it was stronger in numbers than the Soviet Party was at the time it seized power in Russia."[79]

Of course, Hoover wanted to emphasize the anti-subversive importance of his own agency, and to secure substantial Congressional appropriations for the Federal Bureau of Investigation (FBI). But the insinuation that Communists might have come to power obscures the fact that even the thought of moving along this path was blocked by the Communists themselves. They were following the line of the 1935 Seventh World Congress of the Communist International, advanced with Stalin's full support by Georgi Dimitrov: "Now the toiling masses in a number of countries are faced with the necessity of making a definite choice, and of making it today, not between proletarian dictatorship and bourgeois democracy, but between bourgeois democracy and fascism." The task of Communists was to join together with socialists (except for those influenced by Trotsky, considered beyond the pale), and especially with pro-capitalist liberals to form reformist class-collaborationist governments. This Popular Front orientation adopted by the world Communist movement, under the leadership of the Stalin dictatorship, projected drawing back from the goal of socialist revolution. Instead, the goal was to maintain capitalist democracies outside of the Union of Soviet Socialist Republics that might join it in a global alliance against Hitler's Germany.[80]

This meant subordinating the class struggle to, and drawing radicalizing workers into support for, the liberal "New Deal" wing of the Democratic Party of President Franklin D. Roosevelt. As James Wechsler, at the time a leading member of the Young Communist League, later noted, although some right-wing critics were "under the impression that the communists of the thirties were telling Mr. Roosevelt what to do," the fact was that the Communist Party was "largely engaged in a new game of follow the leader and, until further notice, the leader was to be FDR."[81]

In line with Browder's slogan that "Communism is 20th Century Americanism," the Communists sought to avoid doing anything to alienate pro-capitalist liberals in the Democratic Party. According to Browder, "Roosevelt's programmatic utterances of 1937, when combined with the legislative program of the CIO (his main labor support), provides a People's Front program of an advanced type," adding that "we can completely agree with such non-socialist democrats upon the united defense of democracy under capitalism."[82]

Browder later boasted that his organization "relegated its revolutionary socialist goals to the ritual of chapel and Sundays on the pattern followed by the Christian Church. On weekdays it became the most single-minded practical reformist party that America ever produced." The problem was, as Leo Huberman commented, that "the New Deal was a reshuffle of the old deck of cards." FDR was nobody's fool, nor was he a political radical. Biographer James McGregor Burns noted: "Roosevelt, like Stalin, was a political administrator in the sense that his first concern was power — albeit for very different ends." Labor historian David Brody is hardly the first to take note of "the essential conservatism" of the New Deal, rooted in "Roosevelt's unreflective acceptance of America's basic institutions [which] guided him wherever he had a choice to make." Or as David Milton aptly put it, "Roosevelt would never grant labor the power or prestige that he showered on business."[83]

"For a time the CIO leaned toward the formation of a labor party," Brody notes, but this contradicted the People's Front strategy. Under the leadership of John L. Lewis, and with the full support of the Communist Party, the CIO became a decisive force in Roosevelt's reelection in 1936. While FDR certainly welcomed such support, he never shared Lewis's "claim that the CIO stood in a special relationship to the administration and could demand favored treatment from it," as Brody comments. And then, again with Communist complicity, "instead of Lewis's vision of labor as a pivotal independent political force, the CIO committed itself to the Democratic Party" in a thoroughgoing way. Lewis was sidelined by Sidney Hillman, cerebral chieftain of the Amalgamated Clothing Workers, as the Second World War unfolded. While initially Lewis partisans, the Communists would end up solidly aligned with the more moderate Hillman, a one-time socialist and key architect of both the CIO's subordination to the Democratic Party and the nation's first PAC (Political Action Committee), which played a such a powerful role in the 1944 elections.[84]

While the pro-labor policies of the New Deal, especially the 1935 Wagner Act (National Labor Relations Act), seemed to provide ample motivation for CIO loyalty to the Democratic Party, the identification of CIO militancy with government policy would have a "deadly effect" on labor radicalism, according to Brody:

> If New Deal labor policy helped draw any radical potential from the militancy of the early CIO, the day-to-day implementation of that policy — rounds of NLRB hearings and appeals, representation elections and certification of bargaining agents — inexorably stifled the spirit of militancy, not to say any genuine labor radicalism....
> The price of government protection for the right to organize and engage in collective bargaining was public accountability. Although that bill was not presented at once (thereby lulling traditional unionists into a false sense of security), it would come soon enough in the form of accumulating legislative constraints on labor's freedom to handle its internal affairs and its relations with employers as it saw fit.[85]

U.S. Communists proved to be their own "Masters of Deceit," fooling themselves into thinking that the Popular Front (by the late 1930s christened "the Democratic Front") was advancing them toward a socialist future. Sometimes projected as a "Trojan horse" designed to smuggle in Communist influence under the guise of democracy, the Popular Front actually transformed American Communism in ways that most party leaders hadn't bargained for.

"As the CP gained thousands of new members during the Popular Front years — very few of them 'revolutionary' in either Old Bolshevik or Stalinist styles — it began itself, internally, somewhat to resemble a Popular Front," Irving Howe has shrewdly noted. The Communist Party "managed to combine an extraordinary range of political and emotional appeals," with "a popular blend of New Deal outlooks and CIO militancy" and "the stirring cause of Loyalist Spain, under assault by General Franco's fascists." While there remained "an old skeletal 'vanguard' of three or four thousand," the party ranks contained many other components as well: "You could think of yourself as a revolutionary, you could think of yourself as a 'progressive,' you could even think of yourself as a liberal of sorts, and still lend support to the communist movement," even though the Popular Front as such, along with the Popular-Frontized Communist Party, "really signified a break from classical Leninism." Earl Browder, Howe points out, "not only accepted the Popular Front line; he warmed to it, he enjoyed it, and he came with evident sincerity to believe in it" — which is why he was removed from leadership and expelled from the organization, at Stalin's initiative, as the Cold War loomed on the horizon after the close of World War II.[86]

Some years later, James P. Cannon offered a critical Leninist assessment:

> My own opinion is that Roosevelt was the best political leader crisis-racked American capitalism could possibly have found at the time; and that his best helper — I would go farther and say his indispensable helper — was the Communist Party .... The CP ... played a major role first in promoting the expansion of a new labor movement and then in helping Roosevelt to domesticate it. To blunt its radical-revolutionary edge, and to convert it into his most solid base of support in both domestic and foreign policy.[87]

Maurice Isserman, an historian sympathetic to the Popular Front, comments that U.S. Communists "did blunt their criticism of capitalism" in favor of "fuzzy, Rooseveltian categories," adding: "The party increasingly came to rely on the goodwill, or at least the tolerance, of New Deal political leaders and mainstream union leaders." David Milton argues that such far-reaching compromises meant that "the future of the Communist Party of the United States ... was foredoomed by 1940" (although an anti-Red purge was briefly deferred thanks to World War II and the U.S./USSR alliance).

Especially problematical, according to Milton, was the pattern of decisions by Communist Party leaders, "divorced from the workers they claimed to represent," to prevent the rise of popular, effective Communist militants to central leadership in key industrial unions (including the United Auto Workers, the National Maritime Union, and — almost — the United Electrical, Radio and Machine Workers). One example: the Communist leadership "as early as 1938 ... abandoned [Wyndham] Mortimer and the class-conscious workers who had organized the auto industry for a spurious Left-center united front" with CIO moderates. A second example: sidelining "Blackie Myers, the most popular avowed Communist on the waterfront," to support and strengthen the dubious and (as it turned out) temporary Communist ally Joe Curran.

According to Milton, if the Communists had avoided such fatal compromises, and held to a more militant trade union policy, "Roosevelt would have found it a great deal more difficult to consolidate the power of the Democratic Party and the state bureaucracy it controlled." The alliance of the United States with the USSR during the Second World War not only gave the Communists a respite before the inevitable assault on them, but the war further facilitated the accumulation of government power that could be used against them: "With the war as his chief ally, Roosevelt mastered the emergency situation and real power soon resided in the executive branch of the government."[88]

Aftermath

During World War II, the Communist Party went far beyond adapting to non-Communist labor leaders and Franklin D. Roosevelt's Democratic Party. "From the moment this global war and our participation in it became inevitable, the Communist Party declared for the unconditional subordination of all issues to that one issue of winning the war," declared Earl Browder. He went further: "The freedom-loving nations, whether capitalist like the U.S.A. or socialist like the Soviet Union, or some intermediate forms that may appear, are pledging themselves to peaceful co-existence and collaboration in the post-war world." In fact, "if anyone wishes to describe the existing system of capitalism in the United States as 'free enterprise' that's all right with us, and we frankly declare that we are ready to cooperate in making this capitalism work effectively in the post-war period." According to Browder, "the Communist understanding of history, which is the school of Marx, Engels, Lenin, and Stalin," presents a "practical program ... which holds out a realistic perspective of an orderly world emerging out of the present war, and this is given us in the United Nations for peace as for war. ..."[89]

The peaceful postwar global order envisioned by Browder was rooted in large measure in his conception of changes taking place in the world capitalist system:

> It is easy to point out not one but a thousand undemocratic and imperialistic aspects of the policies, practices, and habits of mind that have long dominated the United States (and Great Britain) in violation of our democratic and anti-imperialist tradition and origin. But these things are no longer decisive as to the character of the war, although their modification and elimination will be decisive for victory in the war. These things are in the process of modification and elimination in the policies of the United Nations, because they are *obstacles to victory.* ... In its drive for world conquest, the Axis is forced by the logic of the struggle to more extreme enslavement of nations and peoples; on the contrary, the United Nations is by the same logic driven onto the path of universal national liberation.[90]

Following the agreements emerging from the 1943 meeting of Roosevelt, Churchill, and Stalin at Teheran, Browder proclaimed: "Teheran represents a firm and growing common interest between the leaders who gathered there, their governments, the ruling classes they represent, and the peoples of the world." He projected a "long-term confidence and collaboration between the capitalist democracies and the socialist democracies," predicting that the United States would emerge as "by far the strongest capitalist economy in the world." This economy "must have enormous post-war markets for its products," and the restrictive old form of colonialism would need to give way to "independent, self-governing nations [which would] provide expanding markets" in Asia, Africa, the Middle East, and Latin America. "Economic concord" between the U.S. and Britain, and between the two of them and "economically weaker" countries, would necessarily require a significant amount of global economic regulation. A program of economic development and industrialization in the less developed portions of the world (blessed with "great reserves of land, raw materials and manpower") would allow for additional investments from the stronger capitalist countries, leading to new opportunities and rising living standards for the peoples of the newly developing regions. "Such a program, in order to be really held in common, must reconcile the interests of each corner of the triangle" — the United States, Britain, and the developing nations.[91]

"As World War II was winding down" according to radical "global justice" analysts writing half a century later, "the Allies were beginning to consider how the new global economy should be ordered." Or as economist Michael Yates puts it, "the rich countries, led by the United States and to a lesser extent by Great Britain, established international organizations to help them manage the world economy in such a way as to ensure their dominance." In particular, the International Monetary Fund (IMF) and the World Bank were established at a historic 1944 conference at the Bretton Woods Hotel in rural New Hampshire. "The IMF was considered the base institution — a monitor of national economies which oversaw currency values, and a kind of credit union to which national governments contributed money and from which they could take short-term loans in the event of balance-of-payment difficulties." The World Bank was "designed to make loans for rebuilding war-torn countries and developing non-industrial countries like those in South America, the newly-independent countries of Asia and, later, Africa."[92]

It is interesting to note that the key architect of the IMF and World Bank was a left-wing New Dealer named Harry Dexter White. Assistant Secretary of the Treasury, White "had close ties to other individuals in the left wing of the New Deal who were, or had been, in the Communist party," according to sympathetic economic historian Fred Block. White would later be accused of passing classified information to Soviet agents — a charge that he strenuously and eloquently denied. After White's fatal 1948 heart attack, radical journalist I. F. Stone wrote that if White was a Communist then "Communists have reason to be proud," but added: "I do not think Harry White was a Communist, if the word is to be used correctly and without quotation marks."[93]

Particularly considering the views articulated by Earl Browder, however, "there was little in the relatively conservative Communist party line of that time that conflicted with the views of many non- or anti-communist economic planners," and it seems obvious that White accepted some of Browder's key notions: "peaceful co-existence" between the United States and the USSR was possible and desirable, the postwar world could be shaped by a relatively harmonious United Nations, and it was possible and desirable for the capitalist economies of the United States and Britain to establish economic institutions and policies that could help to rebuild and develop the global economy in a benign manner. As Block has documented, however, White's initial blueprints for the IMF and World Bank were modified by "two outside forces" — one being the British economist with whom he worked in developing the Bretton Woods blueprints, John Maynard Keynes, and perhaps more decisive, conservative forces in the U.S. Congress that would have to sign off on any such blueprints. "White considered himself a shrewd judge of the political mood; rather than risk rejection he would cut his plan to an acceptable pattern" — but on top of this, "subsequent alterations by financial conservatives would prevent the Fund from playing the role White had envisioned for it."[94]

Similarly, the consolidated United Nations — a primary architect of which was Alger Hiss, another left-wing New Dealer — was also to become more a tool and a battleground of contending global elites dominating the new institution's Security Council than the egalitarian guarantor of global liberty and justice for all envisioned by Browder and his co-thinkers. Predominant in the conceptualization of the UN, of course, were not the followers of Earl Browder, but followers of Woodrow Wilson and FDR — liberal internationalists who hoped for "a system committed to respect the sovereign equality of all nations," maintained "through the cooperation of the permanent members of the Security Council," as historian Steven Bucklin has put it. Some of its shrewdest supporters, such as Quincy Wright, viewed it as a necessary hybrid of political systems — "in some respects resembling an empire, with five great powers exercising control via the Security Council," in other ways resembling "a world federation with the General Assembly and the Economic and Social Council at the Center." Such partisans hoped for "a concert of powers — a Grand Alliance," that would facilitate a world peace grounded in positive global economic development. Yet by 1946, Hiss later commented, "the cold war had already led me to conclude that we could make little use of the UN" for such august purposes. Feeling that "my position as coordinator of our [State Department] policies toward the UN would no longer be rewarding," he left government service at the end of 1946 (to become president of the Carnegie Endowment for International Peace). Soon after he was the public target of espionage charges, compliments of ex-Communist Whittaker Chambers.[95]

In fact, the evaporation of imperialism anticipated by Browder was not to be. The IMF and World Bank were eventually to become notorious for imposing on the "developing countries" policies beneficial to the multinational corporations based in advanced capitalist countries, with growing debts and deteriorating conditions pressing down on the majority of people in various Asian, African, and Latin American countries.

Not long after the Bretton Woods agreement, Franklin D. Roosevelt's death had brought into the Presidency the more conservative Harry Truman, and the end of the Second World War was giving way to growing hostility between the United States and its former Communist ally. Former Vice-President Henry Wallace (also associated with the New Deal's left wing) later recalled Harry Dexter White's pulling him aside, in November 1945, to complain that Truman "always uses good words, but never does anything, or if he does act he acts weakly or on the wrong side." He felt that Truman's administration "was very rapidly going to pieces on both the domestic and the foreign front." White urged Wallace "to come out in the very near future and make a very forthright speech in order to dissociate myself as nearly as possible from the impending wreck."[96]

By 1946 Browder was disgraced and expelled from the Communist Party. But his former comrades were not in a good position to improve their situation. A growing number of liberal Democrats joined the anti-Communist (and anti-radical) crusade. The Communist Party and the rest of the Left had not developed a popular base and independent structures sufficient to survive as a political force. The moral authority of the Communist Party had already been seriously undermined for some by its defense of Stalinist authoritarianism and brutality, and by its two-year abandonment of the anti-Hitler cause with the 1939 Hitler–Stalin Non-Aggression Pact. The 1941 German invasion of the USSR, of course, had revitalized and intensified the Communists' Popular Front enthusiasm. But as the radical-tinged "people's war" unity against Hitlerism was giving way to a Cold War polarization between capitalism and Communism, radical labor and cultural activist Elizabeth Hawes voiced the concern of many on the Left: "If the majority of people do not immediately start toward peace and socialism, tomorrow we will have war and fascism."[97]

Time had run out. There was a hothouse effort — in ways heroic, in ways pathetically pale — by Communists and other radical allies to make up for a decade of subordinating socialist perspectives to Democratic Party liberalism: the 1948 Progressive Party campaign of Henry Wallace, which Communist stalwart Dorothy Healey described as "a very energizing campaign," but which netted a disastrously low one million votes. Labor historian George Lipsitz has suggested that "at the very moment when they most needed to rouse the rank and file [workers] in defense of their class interests, Communist labor leaders devoted their efforts to the presidential campaign of a disillusioned member of the ruling elite, whose main argument seemed to be that American capitalism could dominate the world without having to resort to encirclement of the Soviet Union." Yet Healey (among others) speculated: "Had Henry Wallace received anywhere near the five million votes expected by his supporters, the fallout from the [Communist] Party's single-minded emphasis on his campaign would not have been as serious — would not, that is, have left the Communists stripped of allies and vulnerable before the Right's vengeful counterattack."[98]

In 1942, a U.S. opinion poll done for *Fortune* magazine had discovered that socialism was opposed by 40 percent of respondents, with 25 percent being in favor and 35 percent having "an open mind" about it. By 1949, 61 percent had swung into opposition, according to another poll, with only 15 percent wishing "to move more in the direction of socialism." For many, a shrewd British journalist later observed, "the free enterprise system was seen as Americanism; social criticism, class solidarity, and radical politics were rejected as 'un-American.'"[99]

The "war and fascism" that Elizabeth Hawes anticipated came in modified form: the Cold War, punctuated by such deadly hot spots as Korea and Vietnam; and the ruthless destruction of left-wing influences in the country's labor movement, culture, and politics that had been such important forces in the 1930s and early 1940s. The onslaught of Cold War anti-Communism of the late 1940s rose to the crescendo of McCarthyism of the early 1950s, replacing the earlier period's vibrant critical challenges and radical protests with a blanket of fear and political conformity. Highly publicized government investigating committees; screaming headlines; intimidating inquiries and visits by agents of the FBI; large-scale firings and black-lists; the expulsion of "Reds" from some unions, and the expulsion of some "Red" unions from the CIO (and the systematic destruction of most of those unions); for some, arrests, trials, and imprisonments; sometimes vigilante and mob violence — all this and more destroyed innumerable careers, shattered thousands of lives, wrecked many painstakingly built organizations, intimidated millions, and broke the power and influence of the left in the political and cultural life of the United States.[100]

Among the forces that broke the leftist influence were vital elements within the left itself. A case in point was Father Charles Owen Rice, influenced by Dorothy Day's Catholic Worker movement and dedicated to the proposition that "we should feed the poor, spread the social gospel, and be engaged," adding: "A radical is one who goes to the root of matters, and we count on doing just that. We are dissatisfied with the present social and economic set-up; we want to see it drastically changed." Rice admitted that the Catholic Church had "the reputation, unfortunately, among all too many of being reactionary — the friend of the rich rather than the poor; the friend of the bosses rather than the masses." But he had insisted that "if the plain facts of Christian principles were known, it is just the opposite. The Church is the Church of the poor and must be. She is the friend of the oppressed against the oppressor." And yet it was precisely this eloquent and charismatic left-of-center activist who would

— in the words of his sympathetic biographer — play a central role in foment-ing "the crusade which expelled the left of the CIO." Rice "would counsel mighty union leaders of the day to disavow any apparent leftist entanglements and to drive the communists from their midst." His work in the Association of Catholic Trade Unionists (ACTU), the Americans for Democratic Action (ADA), labor schools, newspaper columns and radio programs were dedicated to this goal. He helped to organize anticommunist caucuses and rival unions, collaborating closely with the FBI and the House Un-American Activities Committee.

Father Rice — pulled in two directions by his radical Christian inclinations and by the accommodation of his Church superiors to fascism (convergent with its fiercely anti-Marxist inclinations, and definitively reversed only in the 1960s by "the good Pope" John XXIII) — found relief and resolution, from the late 1930s through the 1950s, by focusing on the evils of Stalinism. "I was very much influenced by the murder of Trotsky … and by all those trials," he explained. "I remember listening and watching very carefully the news of the Moscow trials. The people pleading guilty when it was absurd. And later one of the trials [in Communist Hungary during 1949] when they got [Car-dinal Jozsef] Mindzenty, they forced him, got him to say what obviously he didn't want to say." Rice's concern was not simply over what was happening in other parts of the world. "At the time I believed there was some chance of their taking over and messing things up for us in the United States, foolishly I think now, but that's hindsight." Years later, Rice self-critically described the vision that animated him and others in the anti-Communist crusade: "There was a feeling among many anti-communists that communism was irreversible. That when they took over that was it, and that as they took each little — or big — piece of territory, it moved under the monolith, the curtain shut down, freedom was ended. There was no variety, and they moved on to another piece and digested it. I really felt that."

Before the end of what radical journalist I. F. Stone described as "the Haunted Fifties," the Red Decade's aftermath was capped by the shattering crisis of the world Communist movement. It was a crisis long in the making. A growing number of liberals, radicals, ex-Communists, and others swept up in the radical turbulence of the Red Decade now embraced the anti-Communist cause — particularly as the Cold War power struggle between the capitalist democracy of the United States and Stalin's USSR seemed to give a new spin to the class-struggle question of the 1930s, "which side are you on?"

Many former leftists now agreed with Lionel Trilling's 1946 comment:

I live with a deep fear of Stalinism in my heart. A usual question at this point … is: And not of Fascism? Yes, of Fascism too, but not so *deep* — in one's fantasies one can imagine going out to fight one's Fascist enemies quite simply; but whenever I fantasy fight an enemy that has taken all the great hopes and all the great slogans, that has recruited the people who have shared my background and culture and corrupted them, I feel sick. I am willing to say that I think of my intellectual life as a struggle, not energetic enough, against all the blindness and malign obfuscations of the Stalinoid mind of our time.[101]

Yet even for many of the Communist hard-core, at this time consisting of about 20,000 members in the United States, the "malign obfuscations" were stripped away by 1956 revelations of USSR leader Nikita Khrushchev concerning Stalin's crimes. Chairing the National Committee meeting of the Communist Party, where a copy of the Khrushchev speech was read aloud to the assembled leadership, stalwart Steve Nelson recalled the shock:

> For twenty years we'd labeled the stories of Stalin's atrocities as lies and distortions. We'd suppressed every doubt, feeling that a Communist Party could never have perpetrated such crimes. Now the secretary general of the Communist Party of the Soviet Union confirmed all these accusations and added documentation of many more. ...
>
> The words of the speech were like bullets, and each found its place in the hearts of veteran Communists. Tears streamed down the faces of men and women who had spent forty or more years, their whole adult lives, in the movement. ...
>
> As chairman, I broke the deafening silence that followed the last sentence of the speech. I had made my sacrifices voluntarily and never thought of myself as a martyr, but now I felt betrayed. I said simply, "This is not why I joined the Party."[102]

The well-known novelist Howard Fast, in breaking from the Communist Party in 1956, spoke of devastating discussions he'd had with Eastern European Communists in the wake of Khrushchev's revelations: "They spread before my tortured eyes such a picture of terror, injustice, and sheer nightmare as to make the Khrushchev secret speech appear to be only a moderate outline of a never-to-be-itemized whole." One man spoke to Fast "in such quiet, simple tones" over a luncheon table:

> He spoke of the pall of fear over his land. He talked about the enshrinement of ignorance, the curse placed upon those who offer either disagreement or fresh opinion. He talked about how the Communist leaders who ruled his country lived — their sleek black limousines, their servants, country homes and bejeweled wives, their mistresses and passions. He talked about the crumbs that were left to the people.[103]

Such conditions generated the 1956 uprising against the Communist dictatorship in Hungary, which was replaced by a democratic coalition government of dissident Communists and non-Communists — and which was quickly drowned in blood by a massive invasion of Soviet troops. This, on top of the Khrushchev revelations, fed into a short-lived rebellion within the U.S. Communist Party led by *Daily Worker* editor John Gates (but defeated by hard-liners such as William Z. Foster), followed by an exodus of 15,000. As one thoughtful and talented (and blacklisted) Hollywood screenwriter, Walter Bernstein, described it: "I felt both sadness and relief. I would miss the connection to decent and committed people who believed as I did and were willing to risk much on those beliefs. ... Those who were friends would remain friends. The others would drop out of my life. I would not miss the dogma or the unthinking obedience to the Soviet Union." Like many of his comrades, Bernstein could add: "I reread those writings of Marx that had stirred me the most to bolster my faith and I found they held the same powerful truths for me. I had left the party but not the idea of socialism, the possibility that there could be a system not based on inequality and exploitation." But what is the political relevance of an idea that is not connected to an organization capable of advancing an effective struggle for that idea?[104]

Twenty years after the Red Decade, there seemed to be barely anything remaining except for faded and often distorted memories. The organized left was a shambles: a battered membership of less than 5,000 in the Communist Party, several hundred Trotskyists and Socialists, handfuls of others. American capitalism — while locked in a grim global power struggle with the USSR — seemed stronger and more prosperous than ever. Nor was this all.

By the early 1950s an immense change had taken place in the United States that is crucial for understanding the decline of the left.[105] It involved a double erosion of the radical working-class base that had provided the decisive context out of which, and in relation to which, the left in all of its varied components had emerged. One aspect of the erosion was the fading out of immigrant radicalism and of the vibrant working-class sub-cultures that had been so important to labor's left wing since the mid-19th century. The second aspect of this erosion was the fact that working-class struggles led by radicals had helped to make capitalist society a better place to live for many workers and their families, so they came to have much more to lose than the "chains" of capitalist oppression.

Communist organizer Steve Nelson commented that "increasingly, first and second generations [of working-class immigrants] not only spoke different languages but also opted for different life-styles" as profoundly "changing cultural patterns" transformed life and consciousness. "World War II was a watershed," he emphasized. "Sons who went to high school and then served in the armed forces thought in far different terms than their fathers. Daughters who worked in the shipyards and electrical plants were a world away from their mothers' experiences with domestic service and borders. Industrial workers after the war were no longer just pick-and-shovel men. Machine tenders who enjoyed the security provided by unions with established channels for collective bargaining could not appreciate the chronic insecurity of the pre-CIO era."[106] Another working-class activist who lived through this period, Frank Lovell, added another element:

> The war changed the world. It changed almost everything about the world that we had known. It changed class relations among people around the world. And of course it left vast destruction and devastation in its wake. But this was the very condition needed for the recovery and expansion of the capitalist system. Capitalism as a world system gained renewed strength from the process of rebuilding.[107]

Trotskyist leader James P. Cannon commented in 1953 that the sixteen years since the auto sitdown strikes had been years of "union security" that dovetailed with "thirteen years of uninterrupted war and postwar prosperity, [which] have wrought a great transformation in the unprivileged workers who made the CIO." He added that "the pioneer militants of the CIO are sixteen years older than they were in 1937. They are better off than the ragged and hungry sit-down strikers of 1937; and many of them are sixteen times softer and more conservative."[108]

The younger layer of workers represented an entirely different experience. "A new middle class arose which included a number of young people of working-class background," wrote sociologist John C. Leggett, noting that many prospering working people had moved out of traditional working-class communities to become homeowners in the suburbs. "The class struggle abated with the end of the post-World War II strikes, although repeated flare-ups between management and workers occurred during and after the Korean War." An important aspect of the new labor–management harmony involved "Governmental boards and labor unions [that] often helped minimize class conflict as unions grew more friendly toward companies which were willing to bargain with, and make major concessions to, labor organizations." He added that "even working-class minority groups [for example, some African Americans] improved their standard of living and sent sons and daughters into the middle class." A radical black autoworker named James Boggs asserted in 1963 that "today the working class is so dispersed and transformed by the very nature of the changes in production that it is almost impossible to select out any single bloc of workers as a working class in the old sense." By "the old sense" he meant the kind of class-consciousness that had made possible the Red Decade. "The working class is growing, as Marx predicted, but it is not the old working class which the radicals persist in believing will create the revolution and establish control over production. That old working class is the vanishing herd."[109]

There was from the 1950s through the 1970s, as Stanley Aronowitz has put it, a tendency "toward the replacement of all the traditional forms of proletarian culture and everyday life — which gave working-class communities their coherence and provided the underpinnings for the traditional forms of proletarian consciousness — with a new, manipulated consumer culture which for convenience's sake we can call mass culture." Despite the flattening and fragmentation of much that had sustained the old radical working-class consciousness, it is hardly the case that workers' minds simply turned to mush, or that they simply believed whatever their bosses or televisions told them. The distinctive philosophy of many disaffected workers, one participant-observer commented, was not any of the traditional left-wing ideologies, however, but cynicism: "Cynicism is a variant of anarchism — anarchism without ideals or ultimate illusions, apathetic, easy-going instead of strenuous, non-sectarian, hence more broadly appealing and far more suitable to the conditions and mentality of contemporary workers than the older tradition of militant idealism and self-sacrifice."[110]

Among the intellectuals who had, during the Red Decade, tended to rally to the left end of the political spectrum, the predominant perspective now was, as one shrewd observer later summed it up, "that American capitalism was a revolutionary force for social change, that economic growth was supremely good because it obviated the need for redistribution [of wealth] and social conflict, that class had no place in American politics." Noting that "the liberals were always more concerned about distinguishing themselves from the Left than about distinguishing themselves from conservatives" in this period, he concluded: "Organized labor, the intelligentsia, and the universities had become citadels of what was in effect a conservative liberalism."[111]

Yet the Red Decade cannot be erased from our history or culture. It is there forever. What was done during those ten years, and what the decade represented, continue — in innumerable ways — to be felt by us and to influence our still-unfolding history. More than this, the Red Decade provides much that we can learn from, including from the disastrous mistakes whose avoidance would have opened up amazing opportunities; and from actual opportunities that if they had been grasped (instead of being missed) would have changed the course of history.

As it was, the dramatically changed socioeconomic-cultural context that the traditional left-wing organizations found themselves in after devastating defeats from 1946 to 1956 precluded the possibility of their recovering their earlier vitality — at least in anything close to what had existed during the Red Decade. For in another sense, the reality of that decade (crackling with specific and exciting possibilities) was and is gone forever. What at least some of these organizations might have become was no longer a possibility. As subsequent years revealed, the left that took shape in the 1930s had been destroyed as a durable force in U.S. political life.

The destruction was not absolute, as will be seen in the final chapter of this book. But in order to flourish in later years, American radicalism had to draw from sources much further to the left end of the political spectrum.

6
The Anarchist Challenge

Anarchism has deep roots in the United States. "I heartily accept the motto — 'That government is best which governs the least': and I should like to see it acted up to more rapidly and systematically," declared Henry David Thoreau in 1849 (quoting Thomas Jefferson). He was disgusted by the role of the U.S. government in perpetuating slavery and in waging a dirty war against Mexico to seize much of its territory. "Carried out, it finally amounts to this, which I also believe — 'That government is best which governs not at all'; and when men are prepared for it, that will be the kind of government which they will have."[1] This stakes out a political stance far to the left of all others.

On the left/right political spectrum, the more one is committed to the principle of *rule by the people*, the further one is to the left. The more one is opposed to that fundamental principle, the further one is to the right.[2] On the extreme right are monarchist-absolutists, who favor unrestricted rule by kings and queens, and, in modern times, it includes fascists, Nazis, and theocratic fundamentalists, all of whom are completely opposed to democracy. A bit further to the left are conservatives, who grudgingly and often demagogically compromise in the direction of rule by the people — but primarily to better conserve the traditional power structures in their societies. In the middle of the spectrum are liberals, who favor rule by the people politically but not economically — favoring, or at least accepting, the economic oligarchy of capitalism. Further to the left are those who favor rule by the people not only over political institutions but also over the economy, with reform-socialists willing to compromise (in the United States of the early 1900s these were called "slowcialists" by their less patient comrades) and with revolutionary socialists further to the left, believing one must go deeper, further, faster toward the desired goal. Communism was the most militant and effective variant emerging from the revolutionary socialist orientation. But the Stalinist outgrowth of Communism, while articulating much of the rhetoric of the left, seemed to corrupt and betray the very essence of what the left represented.

Furthest to the left on the political spectrum, anarchists reject all the authoritarianism, compromises and corruptions to their right. For them, the principle "rule by the people" is best served by what Thoreau advocated: people ruling themselves, without accepting the right of any governmental apparatus — whether elected "democratically" or not — to rule over them.

The horror over a Communism gone very wrong has, as we have seen, pushed some of its disillusioned adherents further to the right on the political spectrum — but it also pushed others further to the left. To oppose totalitarianism (the state attempting to establish total control over all aspects of human life), there are some who have moved to a total opposition to the power of the state. "The inherent tendency of the State is to concentrate, to narrow, and monopolize all social activities," Emma Goldman asserted in 1923. "The nature of revolution is, on the contrary, to grow, to broaden, and disseminate itself in ever-wider circles .... The State idea killed the Russian Revolution, and it must have the same result in all other revolutions, unless the *libertarian idea prevail*."[3]

Many activists, rejecting the capitalist status quo and seeking a better world, identify with the views of Thoreau and Goldman. Commenting on the contemporary global justice movement of the early 21st century in which he was participating, David Graeber asserted: "Anarchism is the heart of the movement, its soul; from it has emerged most of what's new and hopeful about it." One can imagine Graeber, himself an anarchist, smiling as he wrote that "many of those who would, in fact, like to see revolutionary change might not feel entirely happy about having to accept the fact that most of the creative energy for radical politics is now coming from anarchism — a tradition that they have hitherto mostly dismissed with stupid jokes — and that taking this movement seriously will necessarily also mean an earnest and respectful engagement with it."[4]

The reality is more complex than this. "Within the movement, ever since Seattle, there has been a debate over the tactics of the anarchist Black Bloc, whose members have consistently used protests organized by others to trash shops, banks, and cars or, less frequently, to attack the police," commented Alex Callinicos from the Marxist end of the spectrum. Graeber responded that the "Black Bloc ... eschews any direct physical harm to human beings" as it initiates what he terms "non-violent warfare" (i.e., violence against property, not people) involving efforts to creatively "map out completely new territory" in the global justice struggle. The "non-violent warfare" that exploded in the Genoa global justice demonstrations of 2001 sharpened the debate. "Whether intentionally or not, the Black Bloc's violence — usually petty and sometimes downright childish (how did burning ATMs used by ordinary workers and cheap cars probably parked there by protestors along the Genoa waterfront in any way undermine global capitalism?) — certainly played into the police's hands by legitimizing a violent response." According to another socialist activist, David McNally, "not all anarchists identify with the approach of the so-called 'Black Bloc,'" which is a loose and fluid alliance whose "tactics have varied at different events" and whose participants "were more part of the widespread street resistance waged by thousands of people" in Quebec City protests. Challenging the so-called "non-violent warfare" approach, Belgian revolutionary socialist Francois Vercammen was critical of "minority violence which replaces mass action," explaining that "our movement aims at the emancipation through self-activity of the working and popular masses, solicits their active participation and applies democracy in its own ranks."[5]

The flare-up of tactical debates cannot be allowed to obliterate the truth that David Graeber highlights. If anything, it reinforces the need for "an earnest and respectful engagement" with the anarchist resurgence that has taken many by surprise at the beginning of the new century. It comes from a rich tradition that has both intersected with and challenged — in more than one way — the revolutionary Marxist tradition that has been our focus in this book.

Anarchism against Marxism

Twentieth-century U.S. anarchist Paul Goodman once commented that "the political program of libertarians is necessarily negative, for positive goods are achieved by other forces than (coercive) political institutions." Or as nineteenth-century French anarchist Sebastian Faure once declared: "Whoever denies authority and fights against it is an anarchist." Yet this is too simple. There are, first of all, many variants of anarchism. George Woodcock once referred to "the curve that runs from anarchist individualism to anarcho-syndicalism," and Daniel Guerin has commented that "some anarchists are more individualistic than social, some more social than individualistic," while adding that "one cannot conceive of a libertarian who is not an individualist." The fact remains that the essential element in anarchist thought is an absolute rejection of all forms of government that exist over and above the people. "To be governed is to be watched over, inspected, spied on, directed, legislated, regimented, closed in, indoctrinated, preached at, controlled, assessed, evaluated, censored, and commanded," protested Proudhon. Bakunin denounced the state as an "abstraction devouring the life of the people."[6]

From the time of Karl Marx down to the present moment, anarchism has posed a challenge to those with socialist commitments. Denouncing Marx as "authoritarian from head to heels" (although valuing his bearded rival's economic analyses), the great Russian anarchist Mikhail Bakunin thundered against all gods and governments, as well as aristocratic landowners and capitalist bosses, and projected the vision of a decentralized future in which the masses of people would govern and provide for themselves through networks of free communes. To achieve this goal, he was prepared to maneuver against Marx and others within the International Workingmen's Association (the First International of 1864–76) in a manner that helped to shatter it, amid mutual recriminations between its socialist and anarchist adherents.[7]

Anarchists have generally not fared well when discussed by socialists influenced by Marxism. In the pages of the revolutionary socialist *Masses* in 1914, Max Eastman commented that "anarchists do ... radiate that brotherly rebellious spirit which promotes the hope of industrial democracy," but added that the word anarchy "is a word that merely denies. When you grasp it, there is nothing in your hand." Three years later in the same magazine, cartoonist Art Young portrayed a portly capitalist probing the thoughts of a foppish young anarchist. The capitalist asks: "Of course, even anarchists have to get together and decide on certain laws and rules of procedure, do they not?" To which the young man replies: "Oh, yes, certainly — but you see we don't abide by our decisions."[8]

Several years earlier, an exasperated Eleanor Marx (Karl's bold and vivacious daughter) had denounced the "anarchist windbags" of her native England, lamenting that "there are many of the younger, or of the more ignorant sort, who are inclined to take words for deeds, high-sounding phrases for acts, mere sound and fury for revolutionary activity, and who are too young or ignorant to know that such sound and fury signify nothing." This was in the 1895 preface to her English translation of George Plekhanov's pamphlet *Anarchism and Socialism*, which (as Lenin later complained) "falls into two distinct parts: one of them is historical and literary, and contains valuable material on the history of the ideas of Stirner, Proudhon, and others; the other is philistine, and contains a clumsy dissertation on the theme that an anarchist cannot be distinguished from a bandit."[9]

Two Souls of Anarchism

A more sophisticated variant of the Marxist dismissal of anarchist thought has been that of Hal Draper, whose brilliant essay "The Two Souls of Socialism" described a revolutionary-democratic "socialism from below" (among whose representatives he included Marx and Engels, William Morris, Rosa Luxemburg, Eugene V. Debs, Lenin, and Trotsky) and a bureaucratic-elitist "socialism from above" (whose elitist representatives included the utopian socialists, Ferdinand Lassalle, Edward Bellamy, Eduard Bernstein, the moderate Fabian socialists, Stalin, and … the anarchists).

The key contribution of Marx, Draper noted, was a commitment to the self-emancipation of the working class (the majority class under capitalism) as the key to the struggle for socialism — which meant for him, and for those who embraced his perspectives, a fusion of democracy with the social ownership of the economy. Focusing on the pioneering anarchist theorists Pierre-Joseph Proudhon and Mikhail Bakunin, he finds that they were, in fact, "thoroughgoing authoritarians" having "a fierce contempt for the masses of people," with the banner of uncompromising liberty serving only as a veil covering their actual "schemes for dictatorship and suppression of democratic control." These are points that Draper is able to document in his examination of what Proudhon and Bakunin actually wrote and did. Others have made similar points — Paul Avrich describes Bakunin as "a libertarian with an irresistible urge to dominate others, … he could preach unrestrained liberty while spinning from his brain a whole network of secret organizations and demanding from his followers unconditional obedience to his will." In these and other ways — "his pathological hatred of Germans and Jews (Marx, of course, being both), his cult of violence and revolutionary immoralism," etc. — Bakunin was brought "uncomfortably close to later authoritarian movements."[10]

Draper generalizes this in a sweeping condemnation of anarchism as such:

Anarchism is not concerned with the creation of democratic control from below, but only with the destruction of "authority" over the individual, including the authority of the most extremely democratic regulation of society that it is possible to imagine.... The great problem of our age is the achievement of democratic control from below over the vast powers of modern social authority. Anarchism, which is freest of all with verbiage about something-from-below, rejects this goal. It is the other side of the coin of bureaucratic despotism, with all its values turned inside-out, not the cure or the alternative.[11]

There is more than one anarchist answer to Draper. One is the defiantly anti-democratic position articulated by Emma Goldman in 1910. She spoke of democracy contemptuously: "authority, coercion, and dependence rest on the mass, but never freedom of the free unfoldment of the individual, never the birth of a free society." She proclaimed the need "to repudiate the majority as a creative force for good ... because I know so well that as a compact mass it has never stood for justice or equality. It has suppressed the human voice, subdued the human spirit, chained the human body. As a mass it will always be the annihilator of individuality, of free initiative, of originality." Goldman insisted that "the living, vital truth of social and economic well-being will become a reality only through the zeal, courage, the non-compromising determination of intelligent minorities, and not through the mass."[12]

One can argue that Goldman's view (overlapping with aspects of the Leninist notion of the revolutionary vanguard) does not necessarily represent the authoritarianism of which Draper accuses all anarchism. It could be that various "militant minorities" will establish oases of liberty to which majorities would become increasingly accustomed, and whose positive influence would radiate outward to the benefit of more and more people. On the other hand, it is conceivable that what Goldman articulates could evolve into a self-absorbed politics of elitist self-expression, with "the militant minority" flaunting its contempt for the stupid and corrupt masses. Or it could evolve into a substitutionist politics, replacing the possibility of mass action with the heroic actions of small groups — an "anarchism from above." Or it could evolve into some variant of Bakuninism at its worst — manipulative, destructive, authoritarian just below the surface.[13]

Almost 20 years later, in *The ABC of Anarchism*, one of Goldman's closest comrades, Alexander Berkman, articulated a very different conception of what he called "anarchist communism" — distinguished from the Communist dictatorship that had arisen in the Soviet Union because "anarchist communism

... means voluntary communism, communism from free choice." In contrast to what Goldman had argued two decades earlier, Berkman saw this anarchism emerging precisely from the uprising of the masses of the exploited and oppressed of society. "The aim of the social revolution, in particular, is to enable the masses by their own efforts to bring about conditions of material and social well-being, to rise to higher moral and spiritual levels," he wrote. "The interest of the masses and their loyalty to the revolution depend ... on their feeling that the revolution represents justice and fair play. This explains why revolutions have the power of rousing people to acts of great heroism and devotion .... It was because of that spirit that the Russian masses so strongly triumphed over all obstacles in the days of February and October [1917]." Berkman believed that workplace committees, "elected by the workers on the job," would be the means through which the economy would be controlled by the people: "Shop and factory committees, organized locally ... and federated nationally, will be the bodies best suited to carry on revolutionary production, while "Local and State labor councils, federated nationally, will be the form of organization most adapted to manage distribution by means of the people's cooperatives." In Berkman's opinion, such a democratic communism is the necessary material basis for liberty: "In the profoundest sense liberty is the daughter of economic equality."[14]

It is possible simply to counterpose the perspectives (creative elitism vs. creativity of the masses) expressed by these two anarchist comrades, Goldman and Berkman, although it may be more accurate to see this as a dynamic tension within anarchism. We have seen a similar tension within the Leninist tradition. In any event, the reality of anarchism is far more interesting than Draper is inclined to allow. One can speak of "two souls of anarchism," certainly an *anarchism from above* demonstrating the qualities denounced by Draper, but also an *anarchism from below* that has much more in common with the "socialism from below" personified by Draper's heroes. Anarchists have proved capable of being as dogmatic, sectarian, arrogant, and irresponsible as anyone else. And yet many of anarchism's key elements seem to transcend such limitations.[15]

Vital Insights

Particularly in the work of Peter Kropotkin — in *Mutual Aid*, *The Conquest of Bread*, *Ethics*, and innumerable pamphlets and articles — a vision of a cooperative and stateless future (what he called "the no-government system of socialism"), based on the scientific study of cooperation among animals and within various stages of human society, provides the basis for an elaboration of a future society free from exploitation and oppression. Such work, in the opinion of Max Eastman, constituted the chief anarchist contribution to revolutionary theory: "Without investigating at least the abstract possibility of the society aimed at, its compatibility with the hereditary instincts of man, and thus the probability of its enduring if it were once established, no maturely scientific person would devote himself to the effort." Latter-day anarchist Murray Bookchin, who has contributed substantially to the kind of utopian theorizing often deemed "unscientific" by Marxists, later commented that "two things trouble me about Marx's mature writings: their pseudo-objectivity and the obstacle they raise to utopian thinking."[16]

As Noam Chomsky has suggested, the practicality of such utopianism is "that at every stage of history our concern must be to dismantle those forms of authority and oppression that survive from an era when they might have been justified in terms of the need for security or survival or economic development, but that now contribute to — rather than alleviate — material and cultural deficit."[17] Paul Goodman spelled this out for the 1960s: "Anarchism is grounded in a rather definite proposition: that valuable behavior occurs only by the free and direct response of individuals or voluntary groups to the conditions presented by the historical environment. .... Anarchists want to increase intrinsic functioning and diminish extrinsic power."[18] Goodman's anarchist critique of the modern "democratic" state of late 20th-century America is also worth pondering (and savoring):

> Concretely, our system of government at present comprises the military-industrial complex, the secret para-military agencies, the scientific war-corporations, the blimps, the horses' asses, the police, the administrative bureaucracy, the career diplomats, the lobbies, the corporations that contribute Party funds, the underwriters and real-estate promoters that batten on urban renewal, the official press and the official opposition press, the sounding-off and jockeying for the next election, the National Unity, etc., etc. All this machine is grinding along by the momentum of the power and profit motives and style long since built into it; it *cannot* make decisions of a kind radically different than it does. Even if an excellent man happens to be elected to office, he will find that it is no longer a possible instrument for social change on any major issues of war and peace or the way of life of the Americans.[19]

One is reminded of Lenin's comment in *The State and Revolution* that "to decide once every few years which member of the ruling class is to repress and crush the people through parliament — this is the real essence of bourgeois parliamentarism not only in parliamentary-constitutional monarchies, but also in the most democratic republics." This is anarchism. Lenin knew it, and insisted that "Marx agreed with Proudhon in that they both stood for the 'smashing' of the modern state machine," adding that the so-called "orthodox Marxists" who rejected revolutionary practice did not wish "to see the similarity of views on this point between Marxism and anarchism (both Proudhon and Bakunin) because this is where they have departed from Marxism."[20]

In this period of 1917–1921, revolutionaries who had been associated with anarchism and anarcho-syndicalism (in Russia, France, Spain, and a variety of other countries) connected with the Bolshevik-Leninist current.[21]

Anarchism with Marxism

This was hardly the first time that such things had happened. The United States in the 1880s had seen the rise of the International Working People's Association, which was formed in large measure from a blend of revolutionary Marxist and libertarian currents. In Chicago, this became a mass working-class movement, and careful examination of the thought of the most prominent of the Chicago Haymarket martyrs — August Spies and Albert Parsons — indicates that they were guided more by Marx than any of the anarchist theorists, but approached the question of the state in a spirit similar to that of Lenin's *State and Revolution*: they had rejected the idea that socialism could be achieved by an electoral politics through which the workers would simply take control of the existing state apparatus. They had concluded that the state was on the side of the rich and the bosses and must be overthrown along with capitalism. They were inclined to use the terms socialism, communism, and anarchism interchangeably.[22]

The opening of the 21st century has seen a similar creative intermixing. The fact that anarchism represents a dynamic force among particularly younger activists in the early years of the 21st century, however, does not wipe away the historical inability of any anarchist current to generate a theoretical and strategic orientation approximating the strength and coherence represented by the revolutionary Marxism to which Lenin and others adhered.[23]

This comes through in the self-critical evaluation by activists who had been involved in a revolutionary anarchist group called Love and Rage. "The lack of clarity about organizational method ... led to a lack of clarity about the distinction between a mass organization and a revolutionary organization," they commented. Organizational weakness characterizes much of historic anarchism. It was also related to a lack of clarity around strategy, theory, and purpose. It posed the question: what is the point of belonging to an anarchist group that has no clear notion of how to bring about an anarchist future? "Our attempts to develop a new theory from the lessons of our mass work were not always rigorous. This further blurred the distinction as members of the organization rightly asked what Love and Rage had to offer that they weren't getting in their mass work." Another problem involves what they termed "anarchism's persistent tendency to substitute a moral posture for a strategic political perspective." They elaborated:

> Ethical principles tend to offer better guidance on what not to do than on what to do. In Love and Rage, political positions were often judged not on terms of their validity, but on their appeal to righteousness. This

led to an over-eager embrace of the most strident formulations and a tendency to shut down debate when issues got complicated. The persistent refusal of the anarchist movement as a whole to learn any serious lessons from its defeats suggests to us the deep-rootedness of these theoretical weaknesses.[24]

Nonetheless, it seems likely that various strains of anarchism in our time will leave a positive imprint on new varieties of revolutionary socialism that will evolve in coming years. It is wrong to bend the stick too far in critically evaluating anarchism (just as it is wrong to do so in critically evaluating Christianity or Leninism). A good example of doing this can be found in the self-critical anarchist document we have been examining:

> The final test of any system is the results it produces in practice. We hold Christianity responsible for the Crusades, the witch hunts, and the intolerance of contemporary fundamentalism. We hold Leninism responsible for mass starvation resulting from forced collectivization in the Soviet Union and China, as well as for the anti-democratic practices of various Leninist groups today. Similarly, anarchism must be judged by its results. Anarchism has had its brief moments as a serious revolutionary movement, but they have been few and have all gone down to defeat. Anarchism has been almost completely marginalized for over half a century and shows no real signs of emerging from its current semi-comatose condition.[25]

Such comments are positive to the extent that they contribute to a critical-minded and self-critical approach, but they are not positive to the extent that they lead to an uncritical and relatively ahistorical dismissal of Christianity, Leninism, or anarchism — each of which represents far more than the stupidities and crimes committed in their names, and none of which should be shrugged off simply because it did not sustain itself as a powerful revolutionary force.

Anarchy Alone

There is another point to consider in response to the notion that "the final test of any system is the results it produces in practice." The failure to carry one's struggle for human liberation to a victorious conclusion, to get the right "results" (particularly from the vantage point of our own particular moment of existence) does not necessarily invalidate a revolutionary orientation. Consider the outlook of anarchist martyr Bartolemeo Vanzetti. In contrast to many optimists who believed in "progress," he concluded in a letter to a Chinese friend less than a month before his 1927 execution: "To my understanding, we are actually certainly dragged, with the rest of mankind, toward tyranny and darkness." Three quarters of a century later, this comment, reminiscent of George Orwell's later bleak warnings, has not lost its power. And yet, in the same letter, whose eloquence shines through his imperfect English, he reaffirmed his passionate anarchist commitment:

> Anarchy, anarchists alone, we only can break these deadly circles and set life in such a way that by a natural synchronism, produced by the very nature of the things which create the new order, more exactly, which constitute the new order, history will be streamed toward the infinite sea of freedom, instead to turn in the above said dead, close circles, as, it seems, it did 'til now.
>
> It is a titanic task — but humanly possible, and if we know, we will create the happy kingdom of Freedom when the fooled, misled, abused working class, and people of all classes will, most instinctively, join us for the greatest emancipation in history. But even then we will have to be at the brightness of our task, or else, only a new tyranny will be substitute to the present one as corollary of the immense holocaust.[26]

One need not share the conviction, in absorbing these words, that "anarchists alone" can break the deadly circles closing in upon a humanity trying to survive the blessings of capitalist civilization. Nor would it be right to pretend that Vanzetti's anarchism offered more than it actually did. Indeed, deeply rooted in even the best currents within the anarchist tradition are serious limitations to sustaining organizations and strategies capable of bringing about revolutionary victories.

This is best demonstrated, perhaps, if we look at the rich and vibrant Russian anarchist movement of the early 20th century — made up of diverse currents of anarchist-individualism, anarcho-syndicalism, anarcho-communism, and peasant-anarchism, each of which thought theirs was the only way. Paul Avrich has acidly commented on "their congenital inability to subordinate personal differences to the good of the movement," but there were efforts to do just that. One of the most prominent anarchist writers, Voline, insisted that organizational unity must be preceded by theoretical unity — at which he made a predictably unsuccessful attempt. "Ready to employ the most violent and destructive means to make a revolutionary transformation," writes Anthony D'Agostino, "Voline still rejected the most elementary organizational principles for fear that such organization would profane his ideal of natural freedom." Indeed, one can study Voline's monumental work on anarchists in the Russian Revolution, *The Unknown Revolution*, without obtaining a clear idea — under the circumstances described — of how the anarchist perspective, supposedly inherent in the Russian people, could have triumphed.[27]

Activists such as Nestor Makhno were critical of Voline as a "moralizing intellectual unconnected with social practice." Makhno led, among peasants in the Ukraine, the most powerful anarchist movement during the Russian Revolution and civil war, sometimes allied with the Bolsheviks, sometimes warring against them. He was particularly concerned that "the absence of a great specifically anarchist organization, capable of marshaling its resources against the revolution's enemies, left it powerless to assume any organizational role." Exasperated by an anarchism "walled up inside the parameters of a marginal thinking to which only a few tiny groups operating in isolation subscribe," Makhno advanced a devastating critique focused on why the Russian anarchists — who had played a not insignificant role in the events of 1917 — had been utterly defeated:

> Had anarchists been closely connected in organizational terms and had they in their actions abided strictly by a well-defined discipline, they would never have suffered such a rout. But, because the anarchists "of all persuasions and tendencies" did not represent (not even in their specific groups) a homogenous collective with a well-defined policy of action, for that very reason, these anarchists were unable to withstand the political and strategic scrutiny imposed upon them. Disorganization reduced them to impotence.[28]

Makhno's own efforts in Russia were impressive — although marked at times by the tragic brutality that on all sides characterized the civil war period. "But ultimately," notes Arno Mayer, "precisely because he exulted in the not inconsiderable support of the ambient peasantry, Makhno was blind to his weakness: lacking an overall strategic military and political vision, he remained, above all, fatally isolated." Paul Avrich concurs: "He never understood the complexities of an urban economy, nor did he care to understand them. He detested the 'poison' of the cities and cherished the natural simplicity of the peasant environment into which he had been born." Avrich adds that "Makhno's utopian projects ... failed to win over more than a small minority of workingmen, for, unlike the farmers and artisans of the village, who were independent producers accustomed to managing their own affairs, factory workers and miners operated as interdependent parts of a complicated industrial machine." Mayer concludes that it was never clear "how he proposed to fit his anarchist peasant republic of participatory democracy into either a nascent peasant post-tsarist Russia or an at best embryonically independent Ukraine."[29]

As soon as the various counter-revolutionary armies were decisively defeated by the Red Army, Makhno's forces were isolated and crushed — facilitated by the Bolshevik government's dramatic pro-peasant measures in the New Economic Policy. Avrich comments that some of the Russian anarchists "grudgingly admitted the truth" of a thoughtful critique by Bolshevik Karl Radek, "that romanticism and their instinctive hostility towards organization prevented them from facing the realities of contemporary industrial society, with its expanding population and its intricate division of labor, and doomed them to failure and defeat."[30]

In an effort to break free of this problem while in Parisian exile during the 1920s, Makhno allied himself with the ex-Bolshevik worker Peter Arshinov, who was arguing for the development of a highly organized anarchist party that would struggle for "workers' democracy." D'Agostino tells us that both "called for unified command and discipline in anarchist ranks, denouncing the study-circle character of the activity of city anarchists," although "Makhno only dimly perceived what Arshinov had been driven to accept: that anarchism basing itself on the idea of class struggle already has a strong impetus in the direction of Marxism." Arshinov finally decided to embrace Communism and returned to the USSR in 1931 — but although "he made reconciliation with the 1917 Lenin," he tragically "returned not to Lenin's Russia but to Stalin's." Makhno didn't follow him, and died of tuberculosis in 1934. Arshinov died in Stalin's purges not long after.[31]

Another location where anarchism manifested itself as a serious political force in a potentially revolutionary situation was in Spain during its civil war of 1936–39. Here the anarchists were organized into a far more powerful movement than existed in Russia, and one that enjoyed a significant base in the working class as well as among sectors of the peasantry. They also maintained more coherent organizational structures, particularly thanks to the anarcho-syndicalist influence that resulted in the formation of strong trade unions. Yet here too the limitations of anarchism came to the fore.

After a Popular Front coalition of liberals, Socialists, and Communists had won a narrow electoral victory in Spain in 1936, a murderous insurgency was initiated by a combination of conservatives, monarchists, fascists, military men, and conservative clergy to replace the democratic republic with an authoritarian order. Lending critical support to the Spanish Republic was the country's massive anarchist movement, whose largest organizational expressions were the National Confederation of Labor (the anarcho-syndicalist *Confederacion Nacional de Trabajo*, CNT) and the Spanish Anarchist Federation (*Federacion Anarcquista Iberica*, FAI).[32]

The anarchists had developed deep roots and a mass base among peasants and workers since the 19th century. In the peasant villages, Gerald Brenan commented in the 1930s, "rural anarchism is quite simply the attempt to recreate the primitive Spain in the sixteenth and seventeenth centuries," adding: "There has not been a peasant rising in Andalusia in the last hundred years where the villages did not form communes, divide up the land, abolish money and declare themselves independent — free that is from the interference of 'foreign' landlords and police." He went on to argue that "the anarchism of the industrial workers is not very different," explaining:

> They ask, first of all for self-government for their industrial village or syndicate and then for a shortening of the hours, a reduction in the quantity of work. They ask for more liberty and more leisure and above

all for more human dignity, but not necessarily a higher standard of living. After all, that is simply another way of saying that they wish for a return to the empty, leisurely conditions of the seventeenth century, when, at the expense of their stomachs, the workmen in the towns still retained their innate dignity and freedom and had not been crushed and dehumanized by factory life.[33]

In the elections of 1936, responding to repressive measures of the conservative government, the anarchists dropped their long-standing policy of abstaining from elections and voted overwhelmingly for the Popular Front coalition, which won by a narrow margin. With the Popular Front taking power, the forces of the right moved to overturn it — an effort blocked by a working-class mobilization of the left.

The CNT called an emergency congress. "Virtually all the speakers at the congress seemed to feel that Spain was entering into a revolutionary situation," Murray Bookchin has observed. "Their seemingly utopian discussions of how the future society that followed that revolution would be organized thus had practical, indeed, immediate significance." And this was indeed the focal point of discussion. An elaborate resolution was adopted that exuded "a liberty-loving generosity toward the capacity of people to manage society freely and directly." But the delegates dispersed without deciding on practical political issues regarding the policy the CNT should follow when — with the defeat of the military putsch — it found itself at the head of a mass revolutionary upsurge. Consequently, the actual political agenda for the country was defined by deadly battle between forces rallying to the left-liberal Popular Front government and the powerful forces of authoritarian-traditionalist reaction. The one side was committed to the notion that the Spanish Republic, and capitalism, should be reformed, not overturned. The other side was waging a brutalizing civil war to destroy the forces of both reform and revolution. There was no coherent anarchist alternative. The anarchist deficiency was covered over with rhetoric: "Only weak nations have strong governments," proclaimed the CNT newspaper. "Today Spain has a weak government with no influence because the people themselves are going into action."[34]

Yet the Popular Front government was not inclined to remain a weak government in the face of the rising fascist onslaught. If the anarchists were not going to put themselves forward as a revolutionary alternative to this government, what should they do? "The Anarchists, even militants such as Durruti, were slowly becoming clients of the creature they most professed to oppose: the state power itself," Bookchin comments. Indeed, they went further. Militant FAI leader Federica Montseny explained: "We were compelled by circumstances to join the government of the Republic in order to avoid the fate of Anarchist movements in other countries that, through lack of foresight, resolution, and mental agility, were dislodged from the Revolution and saw other parties take control of it." If this seemed a devastating refutation of anarchism's central tenet, there was even more. While one CNT leader explained that it was necessary "to participate in the government for the specific purpose of ... preventing an attack on the conquests of the workers and peasants," another explained that, to secure military aid from the "international bourgeoisie," it was necessary "to give the impression that not the revolutionary committees were in control but rather the legal government." In the opinion of Horacio M. Prieto, the foremost CNT advocate of collaboration, "the libertarians were not equipped psychologically or materially to impose their will in the Republican zone, even less to win the war against fascism."[35]

An exasperated Leon Trotsky, commenting from afar, critically contrasted what the anarchists were doing in Spain with what had happened in Russia of 1917 — where the Bolsheviks gave military support to the liberal-socialist coalition government to defeat the right-wing putsch attempt of General Kornilov in July, but remained politically independent to replace the moderate coalition with a revolutionary regime in October.

"No one could have prevented the Anarchists after the conquest of power [i.e., after defeating the initial fascist coup] from establishing the sort of regime they deem necessary, assuming of course that their program is realizable," Trotsky fumed. "But the Anarchist leaders themselves lost faith in it." Noting that "the renunciation of conquest of power inevitably throws every workers' organization into the swamp of reformism," he observed: "The Anarchist workers instinctively yearned to enter the Bolshevik road [of worker–peasant revolution] ... while their leaders, on the contrary, with all their might drove the masses into the camp of the Popular Front, i.e., of the bourgeois regime."

Pinpointing the problem in the abstractly anti-government principle at the heart of anarchist ideology, Trotsky commented that "the anarcho-syndicalists, seeking to hide from 'politics' in the trade unions, turned out to be, to the great surprise of the whole world and themselves, a fifth wheel in the cart of bourgeois democracy. But not for long; a fifth wheel is superfluous."[36]

Indeed, the Popular Front regime (particularly due to the rising influence of the Spanish Communists and of the USSR, the only major country to come to the aid of the Republic) moved to marginalize and suppress these unreliable partners who had such a radical vision and volatile mass base. Except for a few days of Barcelona street fighting in 1937, there was minimal resistance. This repression of the anarchists, however, combined with the even more savage repression of the revolutionary socialist POUM, seriously undermined the morale of the Spanish Republic. The moderate social and economic policies of the Republic — the failure to support workers challenging the power of their employers (workers morale sagged as economic exploitation continued as usual), the failure to allow land seizures and the creation of revolutionary communes by the peasants (sectors of which were rallying to the traditionalist clergy and conservative landowners), the refusal to adopt an anti-colonialist position in regard to Spanish Morocco (facilitating the use of Moorish mercenaries by the fascist military) — were restraints meant to appease and gain support from the "international bourgeoisie," as we have seen. But this was not enough to lure the "capitalist democracies" into coming to the aid of the Spanish Republic. In the meantime, Hitler and Mussolini were giving generous aid to their Spanish counterparts, and the Republic was overwhelmed in 1939.[37]

Violence and Authority

Anarchism as a distinctive political orientation, these experiences suggest, can be effective as a *vision* of what the future could be like, and as a *protest* — within existing society — against oppressive realities. Alone, by itself, it has never demonstrated a capacity to link such protest with the realization of the vision. Yet an appreciation of its insights and vision (along with a critical confrontation with some of its limitations) might be blended with other elements to provide more viable orientations.

Worth considering in all of this are issues engaged by the vibrant intellect of Simone Weil, whose life journey brought her through passionate yet fitful and successive connections with Marxism, Leninism, Trotskyism, anarchism, and Christianity.[38]

Before her final break from left-wing activity in the late 1930s, Weil was drawn from France to Spain, where the civil war was raging. It was in the ranks of this broad and vibrant anarchist current that Weil found her place as one of many international volunteers in the struggle of revolution against counter-revolution among the Spanish people. And it was here that she found "the natural expression of that people's greatness and of its flaws, of its worthiest aspirations and of its unworthiest." She elaborated:

> The C.N.T. and F.A.I. were an extraordinary mixture, to which anybody at all was admitted and in which, consequently, one found immorality, cynicism, fanaticism and cruelty, but also love and fraternal spirit and, above all, the concern for honor which is so beautiful in the humiliated. It seemed to me that the idealists preponderated over the elements of violence and disorder.[39]

An accident ended her stay in Spain, and she came reeling away from the conflict, reflecting that "in the agony of civil war every common measure between principles and realities is lost, every sort of criterion by which one could judge acts and institutions disappears," and later commenting that "the smell of civil war" means "the smell of blood and terror." She recounted that the heroic anarchist commander Buenaventura Durruti, confronting a teenage prisoner who had been with the fascists, lectured the boy for an hour on "the beauties of the anarchist ideal," giving the 15-year-old a choice between joining the anarchist militia or being shot. The youth chose death, and Weil later wrote that "the death of this little hero has never ceased to weigh on my conscience." She later recalled: "Men who seemed to be brave ... would retail with cheery fraternal chuckles at convivial meal-times how many priests they had murdered, or how many 'fascists,' the latter being a very elastic term." It seemed that "once a certain class of people has been placed by the temporal and spiritual authorities outside the ranks of those whose life has value, then nothing comes more naturally to men than murder." Remarking on the opening up between armed forces and civilians in Republican Spain of "an abyss, exactly like the abyss between the rich and the poor," she found between the people and the anarchist militia two different attitudes — "the one always rather humble, submissive and timid, the other confident, off-hand and condescending."[40]

Those associated with the fascist, militarist, and conservative side of the Spanish conflict were no less oblivious to the humanity of their enemies and victims, and were even more inclined toward a brutal authoritarianism (which — in contrast to the anarchists — was fully consistent with their own ideology). One is reminded of the point made by Victor Serge when confronted by excesses and atrocities of the Red Terror unleashed to defend the early Soviet Republic in 1919. He wrote: "Against how many hangings, humiliations, ruthless repressions, threatened reprisals, did these excesses have to be set? If the other side won would it be any more merciful?" If the "cabal of old generals, supported by the officers' organizations" had destroyed the Bolshevik regime, "Russia would have avoided the Red Terror only to endure the White, and a proletarian dictatorship only to undergo a reactionary one." (Indeed, the rise of fascist and Nazi dictatorships in Italy and Germany had been precisely in reaction to the possibility of the left's taking power — and was enabled precisely by the left's failure to do so.) Shifting from anarchism to Bolshevism, Serge did not abandon the anarchist-influenced view that the Bolsheviks were wrong "in their intolerance, in their faith in statification, in their leaning towards centralism and administrative techniques." But he saw the authoritarianism and violence of the regime as brought on "by civil war, blockade and famine, and if we managed to survive, the remedy would come of itself," particularly through the efforts of those committed to "freedom and the spirit of freedom" who were also very much part of the Bolshevik movement.[41]

Weil found herself unable to make a similar choice. Libertarians "loathe military constraint, police constraint, compulsory labor, and the spreading of lies by the press, the radio, and all the means of communication. We loathe social differentiations, arbitrariness, cruelty." But she noted that such things were part of the reality she found in Republican Spain, even among the anarchists, amid the civil war. Weil offered a striking comparative analysis with the earlier realities of revolutionary Russia. "In Russia, Lenin publicly demanded a state in which there would be neither army, nor police, nor a bureaucracy distinct from the population," she noted. "Once in power, he and his associates set about constructing, through a long and grievous civil war, the heaviest bureaucratic, military, and police machine that has ever burdened an unfortunate people." While it may be possible to question the good faith of Lenin and his comrades, she commented, "one cannot question the good faith of our anarchist comrades in Catalonia." Yet there too "we see forms of compulsion and instances of inhumanity that are directly contrary to the libertarian and humanitarian ideal of the anarchists. The necessities and the atmosphere of civil war are sweeping away the aspirations that we are seeking to defend by means of civil war."[42]

It is remarkable that in the same period, A. J. Muste was expressing similar thoughts to explain his return to earlier Christian pacifist convictions. This culminated in a distinctive variant of anarcho-pacifism that Weil herself failed to achieve.

The Leninist-Trotskyist movement to which Muste had been drawn had concluded, by the mid-1930s, that a second world war was inevitable — but that this would (as had been the case with World War I) generate global revolutionary upsurges. For Muste, this meant that it had become "involved in the contradiction of abhorring war as the ugliest fruit of an outworn economic order and yet 'welcoming' that war as giving them the opportunity to hasten the collapse of capitalism." This found expression in the revival of Lenin's World War I slogan: "transform the imperialist war into a civil war."

Muste's conclusion was that "war ... will indeed be both international and civil, fought not merely along certain national boundary lines, but inside every nation — in every city, every hamlet, every street — that war which can hardly mean anything except collective suicide." He also saw it as "a succumbing to the spirit which so largely dominates the existing social and political order and an acceptance of the methods of capitalism at its worst," which enshrines "the philosophy of power, the will to power, the desire to humiliate and dominate over and destroy the opponent, the acceptance of the methods of violence and deceit, the theory that 'the end justifies the means.'" Muste saw this as "in the end corrupting, thwarting, largely defeating all that is fine, idealistic, courageous, self-sacrificing in the proletarian movement," and he pointed to the Russian revolutionary experience to illustrate his point:

> You achieve a revolution by violence, though admittedly by a relatively small amount of it. You proceed to build the defenses of violence around your revolution. You create a great machine for war, repression and terrorism. You develop a Cheka [secret police], a system of espionage, numerous revolutionary tribunals. You exalt ruthlessness into a major virtue. You deliberately become — temporarily, you tell yourself, of course — callous about the individual human life. What do you get? Certainly something which is, as yet, far removed from socialism. And no one can deny that the machinery for repression which has persisted now gives evidence of becoming, like every machine, a vested interest.[43]

This "vested interest" had become the opposite of what had been intended — under Stalin abandoning "the basic Leninist concept of world revolution … the Leninist concept of fighting against war … the Leninist concept of party democracy," instead "wielding the machinery of a totalitarian state."[44]

After the cataclysm of the Second World War, from the late 1940s until his death (which came as he led a broad coalition against the war in Vietnam when he was in his 80s), Muste observed two power blocs facing each other in a Cold War confrontation, each wielding weapons of mass destruction. Muste insisted that "whatever the provocation or the danger, there is no justification in heaven or on earth for our arms indiscriminately wiping out any other people, men, women, the aged, and the babies," observing that "there is no difference between the leaders in the two rival power blocs" in regard to their willingness to risk the "politically irrational and morally … indefensible and hideous atrocity" of nuclear war.[45]

Even before the first atomic bomb made its appearance, Simone Weil, swept out of her pacifism and yet overwhelmed by tidal waves of violence consuming many millions of human beings during World War II (and feeling compromised by her association with General Charles De Gaulle's "Free French" movement), had starved herself to death. She was at one and the same time filled with an incandescent spirituality and tragically incapacitated in the face of evil. "We are living in times that have no precedent," she wrote, adding that "today it is not nearly enough merely to be a saint, but we must have the saintliness demanded by the present moment, a new saintliness, itself without precedent." She despaired: "I am an instrument already rotten. I am too worn out."[46]

In the wake of the war's devastation, under the shadow of possible nuclear annihilation, the Catholic writer Georges Bernanos — with whom Weil had corresponded in the wake of the Spanish Civil War — emphasized that it was neither anarchism nor Leninism nor any other radical insurgency that posed the greatest danger to humanity, but something quite different:

> I have thought for a long time now that if, some day, the increasing efficiency of the technique of destruction finally causes our species to disappear from the earth, it will not be cruelty that will be responsible for our extinction and still less, of course, the indignation that cruelty awakens and the reprisals and vengeance that it brings upon itself … but the docility, the lack of responsibility of the modern man, his base, subservient acceptance of every common decree. The horrors which we have seen, the still greater horrors which we have seen, the still greater horrors we shall presently see, are not signs that rebels, insubordinate, untamable men, are increasing in number throughout the world, but rather that there is a constant increase, a stupendously rapid increase, in the number of obedient, docile men.[47]

Muste concurred and called for "Holy Disobedience" toward all state-sponsored violence, warning against any conciliatory actions that would "help to build up or to smooth the way for American militarism and the regimentation that accompanies it." His sense of God and vision of Jesus Christ had something in common with aspects of Weil's later thinking — her notions that "the children of God should not have any other country here below but the universe itself, with the totality of all the reasoning creatures it ever has contained, contains, or ever will contain," that "our love should stretch as widely across all space, and should be equally distributed in every portion of it," and that "Christ has bidden us to attain to the perfection of our Heavenly Father by imitating his indiscriminate bestowal of light."[48]

And yet Muste's religious sense and vision seem more connected with the world around him and with the conviction that it was possible to struggle for a better world. The notion that "Jesus did not really expect His followers by ethical, social effort to strive for and achieve the Kingdom of God on earth," was implausible to him. In fact, "it is impossible to conceive of Him as a coherent personality at all if we suppose that He after all expected that it was by the intervention of … a magic-mongering Messiah that the Kingdom was in the end to come." Muste insisted:

> God is Father. God is Love. He cannot deny Himself, he cannot act otherwise than as a father dealing with his children …. God wills the coming of His reign among men. He will not cease his struggle to win men by His love to the way of love. All their efforts to build society on any other basis than fellowship are doomed to fail. Because they are His children and he will not let them go, they will at last join Him in building the Kingdom, the divine-human society.[49]

The practical meaning of this was anything but other-worldly. The necessity of confronting "the role which the United States is playing … to maintain Western economic, political, and military hegemony in Asia, Africa, and Latin America" was central to Muste's orientation. While "the United States conceives of itself as engaged in a global power struggle to contain Communist power," he commented, it was at the same time "a very rich and powerful nation … constantly in the position of trying to prevent revolutionary movements aiming at national independence and radical socio-economic change in the non-Western world, or at the least to push the brakes down heavily on them." Noting "the disparity, becoming greater rather than less, between the standard of living in the highly developed Western nations and the underdeveloped parts of the world where the non-white peoples live," he pointed out that "because of its preoccupation with the power struggle, the arms race and the economic interest of its corporations," the United States "is doing nothing substantial to bridge that gulf."[50]

Muste emphasized the poisonous role of "white supremacy" in the oppression and exploitation of nonwhite peoples around the world — including within the United States — which had created "the gulf between peoples" that is "the deepest and most significant we have to face," suggesting that "contemplation of it and awareness of its meaning are the chief essentials for dealing with contemporary problems."[51]

Struggles for peace and for "a true, racially integrated democracy here at home" should be combined with support for "the democratic revolutions in the underdeveloped countries," he argued. He also pointed to "the labor and socialist movement of a half century ago, which ... sought economic well-being, social justice, humaneness in all human relationships, equality and the end of war — all of these together. It believed in man's power to determine his own destiny and to build the beloved community." He mused: "We need such a movement in our own time and it is not easy to see how it can be gathered in such vastly changed circumstances."[52]

But integrated into this vision were the hard-won insights of the late 1930s, requiring a rejection of violent strategies and the creation of "a non-violent organization" that "would make full use of the energies a people feel under such circumstances arising from a sense of liberation and from the ancient yoke, the feeling of having entered the promised land." Muste stressed: "There is also at such moments a joyous sense of brotherhood among the masses, which causes them to embrace each other, to join in jubilant songs, to share their goods, to endure gladly the greatest sacrifices."[53]

A Muste admirer and ally, Paul Goodman, asserted that "pacifism is revolutionary: we will not have peace unless there is a profound change in social structure, including getting rid of national sovereign power." He also merged this with his own variant of anarchism, which rejected "the idea of 'getting into power in order to ...' or just 'getting into power' as an end in itself," and of thereby getting into the business of "managing and coercing." This meshed with the notion advanced by Alex Comfort (best known for his best-selling *The Joy of Sex*, but also a serious anarchist theorist) that a genuine revolution reflecting anarchist sensibilities "is not a single act of redress or vengeance followed by a golden age, but a continuous human activity whose objectives recede as it progresses." Or as Comfort's fellow Briton Nicolas Walter put it: "What is important is not the future, the strict adherence to a fixed ideal and the careful elaboration of a beautiful utopia, but the present, the belated recognition of a bitter reality and the constant resistance to an ugly situation." Writing in 1969, Walter added that "most anarchist activity is thought of as the action of a vanguard or at least scouts in a struggle which we may not win and which may never end but which is still worth fighting."[54]

Those approaching reality from a revolutionary Marxist perspective, and many others as well, may ask whether we can afford not to win — that the continued degradation and destruction of life, culture, and environment could sooner or later (but perhaps all too soon) cause such "never-ending struggle" to blink out of existence. If anarchism cannot provide a genuine alternative, then the insights it provides remain inadequate unless blended with perspectives whose application can make possible another, better world.

It is certainly the case, however, that A. J. Muste's vision found some measure of confirmation in the U.S. civil rights movement and some of the other struggles for peace and justice of the last half of the 20th century. A seemingly unsystematic mixture of anarcho-pacifism with elements from the Marxist and Christian traditions, its insights and spirit, have also flowed into the multifaceted struggles of the 21st century.

7
Tree of Life

"Theory, my friend, is gray, but ever green is the tree of life." This saying from Goethe was a favorite of Lenin's. It has relevance as we look at the meaning of key notions in the thought of Marx and Lenin for our own time: the centrality of the *working class* in bringing about meaningful change, and the central- ity of *organization* in the struggles of the working-class majority — topics to be explored in this final chapter. While traditional interpretations of these notions seemed woefully outdated in many parts of the world (such as the United States) by the late 1950s, they have retained their relevance when understood in non-traditional (non-dogmatic) ways, particularly as we face the impacts of globalization in the early years of the new millennium.

Coming out of the last century, it seems likely that some thoughtful activ- ists will feel a need to reach for a moral balance gained from blended traditions — secular and spiritual, and profoundly radical. Valuable insights may also be gleaned from thoughtful conservatives, contrasting sharply from the blandly conformist conservatism that enveloped American culture and politics in the 1950s, and which some — with tactics that are anything but bland — would like to reimpose today. Even in that conservative decade, however, there were, beneath the surface, strong and vital counter currents (perceived and cele- brated by a few maverick thinkers) that contributed to powerful, if sometimes problematical, eruptions of dissent and resistance in the 1960s.

The relevance of all such things for today, and for our dreamed-of tomor- rows, will be explored in these concluding pages.

The Spirit of Lenin and the Kingdom of God

An audacious blend of diverse ideological influences can sometimes yield remarkable analytical insights and practical breakthroughs that can help lead to a better future. This can be illustrated as we examine such instances in the past, particularly in regard to Marxism, which especially lends itself to such things because it came into being precisely as an audacious blend of diverse ideological influences — the Enlightenment, Romanticism, French political thought, British political economy, German philosophy, utopian socialism, working-class agitational influences, and more.

Another characteristic of Marxism lends itself to such further syntheses. More than one knowledgeable and perceptive person has commented that

Marxism is now part of our larger culture. It "has created new tools of criticism and research the development and use of which [have] altered the nature and direction of the social sciences in our generation," and "all those whose work rests on social observation are necessarily affected," as the decidedly non-Marxist intellectual historian Isaiah Berlin put it. "Not only conflicting classes and groups and movements and their leaders in every country, but historians and sociologists, psychologists and political scientists, critics and creative artists, so far as they try to analyze the changing quality of the life of their society, owe the form of their ideas in large part to the work of Karl Marx."[1]

Such influences are deeply embedded in American culture. Even the perspectives of conservative ideologists have been so polluted — hardly surprising given the influence among them of such one-time Marxists as James Burnham, Whittaker Chambers, Will Herberg, Frank Meyer, Irving Kristol, and so many others.[2]

To the extent that Marx's ideas are influential, this is often automatically the case for Lenin's as well, since Marx's perspectives were dramatically extended and shaped by Lenin's interpretation and utilization of them in the 20th century. Lenin's name was "linked with that of Karl Marx to designate the world philosophical and scientific view which is building the struggles of the oppressed to build a new world worthy of human beings," as Paul Sweezy and Harry Magdoff once put it. Lenin's thinking on the revolutionary party, on the state and revolutionary strategy, on imperialism and the national question, and even on philosophical questions has, for many people, been at the core of what they perceive as "Marxism." Leo Huberman pointed out in a best-selling book in 1936: "What had been theory with Marx was put into practice by his disciples — Lenin and the other Russian Bolsheviks — in their seizure of power in 1917. Before that time the teaching of Marx had been familiar to a small group of devoted followers; after that time the teachings of Marx had the spotlight of the world focused on them." Leninist influences have been absorbed — often unacknowledged or even unperceived — into quite diverse currents within the political culture of our times.[3]

Marxist and Leninist influences have often blended with other radical currents — one of the most distinctive being the Judeo-Christian tradition (which is not surprising because it is here that we can find some of Marxism's deepest roots). The prominent Anglican Reverend Hewlett Johnson, Dean of Canterbury, went much further than most with his comment that "Lenin's belief in personality as something alive, creative, originating, and dignified" in fact constituted the rejection of "a devitalizing and degrading materialism" and a recovery of "much of the core of real belief in God." America's foremost Protestant theologian, Reinhold Niebuhr, whose "Christian realist" classic *Moral Man and Immoral Society* (1932) was based largely on a shrewd utilization of texts from Lenin, hailed the Russian revolutionary as a resourceful and resolute "strategic genius" and made a point similar to Johnson's: "Lenin's insistence that the objective forces of history must be consciously directed toward a revolutionary goal by a revolutionary class seeks to preserve a proper 'dialectic' balance between 'religious' determinism and the voluntarism of an adequate moral theory."[4]

Such comments reflect a significant development among U.S. Christians in the Depression decade — although some of them were persecuted by their own churches at the time. "In the crisis before us, institutional religion will serve as chaplain to the forces of reaction, blessing its program, justifying its repression. It always has; it always will." This was the judgment of the experienced Methodist clergyman and left-wing faculty member at Union Theological Seminary, Harry F. Ward. He identified two other currents: "Liberal religion will pass resolutions against both fascism and communism, affirm moral generalities and defend free speech. Prophetic religion, in all our faiths, will recognize itself as one of the forces of social change. It will bring them hope and courage, sharing the dangers and persecutions that are the lot of those who break new paths in the social order."[5]

Very much in this last mode was Rev. Claude Williams, an idiosyncratic radical organizer in the South (and an excommunicated Presbyterian minister), who made a sharp distinction between "a religion of Jesus and a religion about Jesus." He displayed portraits of Jesus, the beloved U.S. socialist Eugene V. Debs, and Lenin in his parsonage, convinced (according to his biographer) that if "God was truth, and if there was truth in Marx and Lenin, then there was God in Marx and Lenin." Or as the well-known missionary and Young Men's Christian Association evangelist Sherwood Eddy explained, "the part played by Marx in the understanding and making of the modern world is even more epoch-making than the work of Copernicus and Darwin in their day," and while "Marx was the giant intellect and social philosopher, ... Lenin [was] the greatest practical revolutionary who ever lived."[6]

All such socially active Christians shared Kirby Page's commitment to "the Kingdom of God, to be sought faithfully and expectantly on this earth and to be fully consummated in the ages to come — God's reign in human hearts and in social relations in past, present, and future," which adds up to the "abolition of capitalism and the supplanting of the existing economic order with a society consistent with the religion of Jesus," which can be accomplished only if enough Christian activists "recognize the reality of the class struggle and throw the full weight of their influence on the side of the workers." Page, editor of *The World Tomorrow* (an influential Social Gospel magazine of the late 1920s and early 1930s), was one voice in a chorus of Christian socialism. As his friend Sherwood Eddy emphasized, it was a delusion for American Christians to think that a genuinely democratic community can be based on economic inequality, with appeals for "love and brotherhood" between workers and capitalists, because "what that really means is that we should all cooperate for the perpetuation of a system of organized injustice and exploitation." Eddy stressed that the state does not exist "to secure the interests of society as a whole," and that it was not "the well-being of the masses but of the privileged classes" that had become "the chief concern of the governing classes." He emphasized (writing in 1934): "The amended American Constitution guarantees the Negro freedom and the franchise, and the worker equal rights with the capitalist. But in certain areas the Negro dare not vote and the force of the state and its troops and police is habitually called out to defend the property of the employer rather than the rights of striking workers."[7]

Lenin's emphasis on the need to "base ourselves on democracy as it already exists" and to struggle "for a complete and manifold realization of all democratic forms" (quoted at length in Chapter 4) found an echo in comments of Rev. A. J. Muste. Urging that revolutionaries engage in "using to the full such, admittedly as yet imperfect, democratic machinery as men have developed," he added that "to argue ... that democracy has only been imperfectly realized, much so-called democracy is camouflaged dictatorship of a class, [and] therefore we must get rid of democracy and embrace some kind of dictatorship ... is neither good logic nor good politics." By this point (1940), Muste had himself seriously engaged in and then rejected Leninist politics — returning to his earlier Christian pacifism — but even as the executive secretary of the Fellowship of Reconciliation, his radical pacifism was sharpened by explicit reference to Lenin's analysis of imperialism as being organically rooted in the dynamics of the capitalist economic system and necessarily generating militarism and war. He also drew upon and adapted the Leninist conception of a revolutionary vanguard organization:

> Without a fellowship of those who have found the truth, who are in league with the universe, with the very heart of reality, who have surrendered themselves to the good and find all their joy in its service, who have taken up the Cross and are ready to lose their life so that they may find it; a fellowship which knows no bounds but is universal in character and intention; a fellowship of hope and faith which as all that men have relied on goes to pieces knows that thus the way is opened for a better order, that "the Kingdom of God is at hand" — without such a fellowship mankind is lost.

Muste affirmed that such a perspective "corresponds to ... the Leninist's idea of The Party or The Internationale."[8]

Sensibilities similar to those examined here animated U.S. activists who made a profound difference in the labor and civil rights movements of the South. Highlander Folk School was founded in rural Tennessee during the early 1930s by Myles Horton, Don West, Zilla Hawes, James Dombrowski, and others committed to establishing a progressive labor education center in the South. Blending religious perspectives with those of Marx and Lenin, they attracted support from such figures as Reinhold Niebuhr, Norman Thomas, and John

Dewey. Highlander was designed "to educate rural and industrial leaders for a new social order," particularly in union-organizing efforts that would advance what Horton called "conscious class action." West explained that Highlander "educates for a socialized nation" in which "human justice, cooperation, a livelihood for every man and a fair distribution of wealth" would replace the present system of "graft, exploitation, and private profit." Hawes noted the school's "revolutionary purpose" to help bring its students to an awareness of the need for, and the skills needed to struggle for, "a classless society."[9]

At the same time, as Horton later explained, it was informed by the insight that "people have to believe that you genuinely respect their ideas and that your involvement with them is not just an academic exercise." (His debt to Lenin was explicit. "Lenin helped me understand that the [gradualist] socialism of the Fabians, with its roots in the intellectual middle and upper classes, would never work, because the people have to win the revolution themselves before it's theirs," Horton later commented. "If it's given to them or if it's arrived at through compromise, then it's going to run on a compromised basis.")[10] From the early 1930s, the school viewed the necessity of cooperation among black and white workers to advance the needs of both. Historian John M. Glen offers this summary of the early Highlanders' efforts:

> Zilla Hawes covered "the story of the working class from Feudalism up to the present American scene" with the aid of charts, outlines, her own knowledge as an ACWA [Amalgamated Clothing Workers of America] organizer, and the experiences of students in recent strikes. Myles Horton's psychology class investigated "the prejudices and other psychological handicaps that weakened the Labor Movement," drawing examples from labor situations familiar to the students. James Dombrowski's lectures on Russia prompted an examination of capitalist and communist economic systems. Students also practiced the fundamentals of public speaking and parliamentary law, wrote short plays on the struggles of organized labor, and published a weekly newspaper.[11]

Highlander's central role as a school for CIO workers in the South from the late 1930s through the late 1940s was disrupted by the Cold War, when Communist-influenced unions were driven out of, and left-wing influences in general dramatically marginalized within, labor's mainstream. By the early 1950s, Highlander shifted "to extend its activities into wider fields of democratization," and, in the wake of the Supreme Court's 1954 decision on school desegregation, it became a center for education and training to assist the civil rights movement. Horton recognized the dynamics of that movement when he explained that "any white person who advises that Negroes share their leadership with white people is either naïve or a compromiser. The Negroes must furnish their own leadership, and the role of white people is to strengthen that leadership rather than to share it with them on an equal basis." On this basis,

Highlander would make substantial contributions in the rise and development of the civil rights movement of the 1950s and 1960s.[12]

Lenin's impact was enhanced through the influence of some of the best-known social theorists, cultural critics, artists, historians, economists, journalists, and creative writers of the 20th century, who embraced the "selfless tradition of Lenin" — in the words of U.S. literary critic F. O. Matthiessen — and saw "the Russian Revolution as the most progressive event in our century." This is a remarkable comment, coming as it does from one of the most perceptive American literary critics, whose penetrating and exciting exploration of some of the greatest U.S. writers of the 19th century — Ralph Waldo Emerson, Henry David Thoreau, Nathaniel Hawthorne, Herman Melville, and Walt Whitman — has yet to be surpassed. Matthiessen's "close response to the complexities of existence" in his classic *American Renaissance* brought him to a Christian/Marxist exploration of the meaning of tragedy and the meaning of democracy, and connections between the two, in 19th-century American culture.[13]

As a Christian, Matthiessen retained a vivid and sophisticated sense of human fallibility and sinfulness (especially the sin of pride and pitfalls of arrogance), and a sense of the mystery of existence that transcended what he saw as the naïve secularism of Marxists. Nonetheless, his approach was, in his words, influenced by "the truth we grasped through the theory and practice of Lenin" — that the extended wave of "political revolution [associated with the democratic upheavals of the English, American, and French revolutions] now can and must be completed by an economic revolution. It must be so completed because we have now learned that otherwise the immense concentration of wealth in a few hands makes for a renewed form of tyranny."[14]

This Leninist reaffirmation has particular significance for additional reasons. It was put forward by someone who — in contrast to Hewlitt Johnson or Harry F. Ward — was *not* inclined to embrace the Stalin regime as a healthy continuation of Leninist perspectives or as an initial reflection of "the Kingdom of God." Also, he expressed these thoughts in 1949 — as the Cold War was generating a domestic "anti-Communist" reaction. One year later, in a deep depression over the loss of close friends (including his long-time lover Russell Cheney), the accelerating rightward shift in American politics, a subpoena from the House Un-American Activities Committee that seemed about to destroy his career, and perhaps also the pressures of a homophobic culture, Matthiessen took his own life. But the magnificence of his work endures.

There were others who gravitated toward the sort of synthesis represented by Matthiessen and Muste. In the 1940s, the idiosyncratic Claude McKay — a writer of fierce polemics, fiery poems, insightful and searching commentaries, now, toward the end of his life, marginalized, isolated, and ill — converted to Catholicism. He explained to his astonished atheist friend Max Eastman:

After all Max, what is Truth? It seems to me that to have a religion is very much like falling in love with a woman. You love her for her color and the music and rhythm of her — for her Beauty, which cannot be defined. There is no reason to it, there may be many other women more gorgeously beautiful, but you love one and rejoice in her companionship.

McKay acknowledged that "sometimes I feel as if the Marxists are right when they say that every human thought, emotion and action is determined by dialectical materialism," but asserted that "I prefer the Catholic church and its symbolic interpretation of the reality of Christ Crucified." Acknowledging that "this is a new experience for me and, I suppose, the final stage of my hectic life," he explained to Eastman that "the Catholic church with its discipline and traditions and understanding of human nature is helping me a lot," and that "I am a Catholic because I believe that the Catholic church has a spiritual message for mankind's spiritual nature which we can get from no heads of state."

McKay asserted: "I am not the less a fighter." Still hostile to Stalinism, he saw the Catholic Church as "a bulwark against the menace of Communism," but he emphasized more than once his affinity with "a formidable left wing within the Catholic church," particularly represented by the Catholic Worker movement of Dorothy Day, whom he knew well and admired immensely. (He also identified with the Christian Anarchism of another friend, the former IWW activist Ammon Hennacy.) "The capitalists do not want me, and I don't want anything of them," McKay wrote, critical of his friend Eastman's rightward drift. "Whatever the Soviet nation has done is not worse than what the British empire has done in its 300 years," he emphasized. "I am certainly never going to carry the torch for British colonialism or American imperialism abroad."[15]

What we find in such dynamic interpenetrations as represented in McKay, Matthiessen, Muste, and the Highlander experience is suggestive of future possibilities. Even someone not inclined to embrace either the Marxist or the Christian component of such syntheses can learn something from each component, and from the syntheses as well.

Writing from a decidedly non-Christian standpoint, George Orwell gave expression to a similar perspective:

Socialists don't claim to be able to make the world perfect: they claim to be able to make it better. And any thinking Socialist will concede to the Catholic that when economic injustice has been righted, the fundamental problem of man's place in the universe will still remain. But what the Socialist does claim is that that problem cannot be dealt with while the average human being's preoccupations are necessarily economic. It is all summed up in Marx's saying that after Socialism has arrived, human history can begin.[16]

Conservative Interlude

The maverick conservative Garry Wills once put forward a political vision that suggested that our capitalist "democracy" (whose conservation he favored) vitally needs "prophetic" activists who will challenge it radically and periodically force it to make far-reaching changes that are necessary for its continued survival. His argument diverges from that of the present study on some points (for example, he does not seem to believe the "kingdom of God" can exist on earth), but dovetails with others.

As a conservative, Wills is naturally an elitist — but of a particular kind. "Businessmen are our material elite," he comments. "The saints constitute our spiritual elite." By "saints" he means the prominent radical activists who have challenged "the system" whose continuation he favors. He notes that it is a favorite stratagem of right-wing critics to mock such radicals for being privileged elitists. "Neat, isn't it, this argument used against 'elitists' who try to do anything except for themselves?" he comments. "Using privilege to bastion privilege is 'productive' and authentic. Using privilege to spread privilege is nonproductive and arrogant."[17]

But in our "democracy," positive change is dependent on these spiritual elitists. "Elections settle questions of legitimacy, not policy," he tells us. "They tell us who will govern, not how they will govern." How they will govern is largely shaped by those who have material power in society, which creates a sharp pressure for maintaining the *status quo*. "Change is initiated by the principled few, not the compromising many; by the 'crazies' in the streets, not by politicians on the hustings," he argues.[18]

"Intellectual risk comes first. The learned feel confident enough to question the social and religious myths," Wills writes — although he acknowledges that "most revolutions, even the nonviolent and evolutionary kind, need a mass with rising hopes and envisioned alternatives." Although he does not acknowledge it, it is unlikely that this close (if idiosyncratic) student of Whittaker Chambers, James Burnham, and Frank Meyer is unaware of the parallel between these notions and Lenin's conception of the revolutionary vanguard. Commenting on the "arrogance" of radical abolitionist William Lloyd Garrison and radical feminist Harriet Stanton Blatch, he notes:

> Garrison does not take a poll among the slaves, before denouncing slavery, to see if slaves dislike it. Mrs. Blatch did not survey housewives before saying that women should have the right to vote.... It is not the elite's job to go with the majority. Let politicians do that, to the extent they can get things muddled down for a majority to choose them. The elite's job is to be as good and as bright as it can, and give as much help as it can in the way of moral teaching and expertise.[19]

The uncompromising agitation and propaganda and organizing and protests mobilized by such radical "saints" force concession after grudging concession from the power-holders. "Change after change — the minimum-wage
law, the voting-rights act — has been admitted into our politics in order to
be 'tamed,' not enshrined," comments Wills. But rather than closing off the
radical demands, such concessions eventually lead to increasing expectations
among the oppressed groups, and the "sop that was meant to placate them
becomes a platform from which new urges can develop. Yesterday's radicalism
becomes today's common sense, from which radicalisms take their point of
departure." He continues:

> But the first proponents of that "common sense" must pay a terrible
> price. They are resented, since they ask for change, and people find
> change hard. They are put off as long as they can be, dismissed, treated
> at first as invisible and then as affronts. Such "fanatics" are mocked,
> threatened, jailed, beat up, shot at — think of Eugene Debs, Margaret
> Sanger, Mary Church Terrell, A.J. Muste, Dorothy Day, Cesar Chavez.
> Political change does not come easily, by way of campaign promises and
> congressional log-rolling. It begins with individual risk and heroism. By
> the time passage of the 1964 and 1965 civil-rights bills became feasible,
> they were eased through with sounding oratory by the politicians. But a
> lot of people had to die to make that oratory possible — James Chaney,
> Andrew Goodman, and Michael Schwerner; Herbert Lee, Louis Allen,
> Medgar Evers; Jimmie Lee Jackson, James Reeb, Viola Liuzzo; Addie
> Mae Collins, Denise McNair, Carol Robertson, Cynthia Wesley — to
> name some. Dr. King died in good company.[20]

Such perceptive observations, however, were possible for Wills to develop
only after the tumultuous events of the 1960s. Before that decade, the civil
rights martyrs listed by Wills were still alive, and possibilities for radical social
change seemed quite dead. The 1950s in the United States of America were
shaped by a conservatism far more bland, more shallow, less sensitive, less
humane than that offered by Garry Wills. A remarkable affluence that took off
soon after the end of World War II was to embrace a majority of Americans
(including major sectors of the working class) for well over three decades in
what seemed a fabulous "middle class" consumer culture.

The basis for this development was in part due to the "social compact" created by a post-World War II alliance of government, business, and labor. The
government would seek to create global "stability" through a foreign policy
beneficial to U.S. business (containing Communism and revolution in general). It would seek domestic "stability" through social programs that would
defend U.S. business interests and economic and social security for the bulk
of the population, maintaining — through Republican as well as Democratic administrations — much of the social safety net created by Franklin

D. Roosevelt's New Deal of the 1930s. The dominant sectors of the deradical-ized trade union movement — in the soon-to-be-merged AFL-CIO — would accept the basic foreign policies of business and government, and the right of private business to own and manage the economy, in exchange for high employment rates, plus paychecks and fringe benefits that would yield rising living standards, and social programs providing security to the young, to the unemployed, and to the elderly. This sense of well-being for many working-class families was enhanced by a market-driven consumerism that provided an increasing quantity of affordable, attractively packaged, alluringly adver-tised consumer goods to more and more people.[21]

Parallel to this was a Cold War confrontation between the so-called Free World led by U.S. capitalism and the totalitarian Communist Bloc led by the USSR — with massive doses of propaganda gushing from both sides, spying and "dirty tricks" on both sides, an exorbitant arms race on both sides, and the threat to all people on all sides of being killed by a surplus of nuclear weap-ons not once or twice, but several times — the accepted term for this haunting craziness being "overkill."[22]

In the United States, this generated a Cold War anti-Communism gone wild. Under the label of "McCarthyism" (named after its most flamboyant practitioner, conservative Wisconsin Republican Joseph McCarthy), it went far beyond repressing and marginalizing the diverse sectors of the organized Left. McCarthy and his imitators attacked not only Communists and former Communists, but anyone pushing for meaningful social change, also smear-ing liberal Democrats, liberal Republicans, and even political centrists who opposed his irresponsible tactics.[23]

"When McCarthy was stopped, finally, he was stopped because he abused his power," commented a young radical named David Horowitz. "He violated a certain propriety among elites by attacking the United States Military. But he ought to have been stopped for being a threat to the very principles on which the nation was founded ... [the] free speech and free association that the Constitution affords to the individual. ..." An older radical, Irving Howe, decrying "this age of conformity," noted that in the hands of its fearful and conservatized spokesmen, "liberalism is most skillfully and systematically advanced as a strategy for adapting to the American status quo." Horowitz lamented: "We watched our national leaders abdicate their responsibility to their own ideals of freedom, equality and self-determination of people; we saw the business world to be a world of self-interest, prestige-seeking and the quest for power; we had to bear witness as the leaders of our own academic com-munity retreated before the witch-hunters and made frantic efforts to cover our ties with the world of men." Howe stubbornly concluded: "All the forms of authority, the states and institutions and monster bureaucracies, that press in upon modern life — what have these shown us to warrant the surrender of independence?" Such protests were no more than a seemingly ineffectual current on margins of the political and cultural scene of the United States.[24]

Society's central heights were dominated, of course, by "the political directorate, the corporate rich, and the ascendant military [who] have come together as the power elite," observed sociologist C. Wright Mills. This was a leadership composed neither of "representative men whose conduct and character constitute models for American imitation and aspiration," nor of leaders whose "high position is ... a result of moral virtue [or] ... meritorious ability." Rather, Mills suggested, "they have succeeded within the American system of organized irresponsibility."[25]

Reference to conformist intellectuals, opportunistic politicians, or power elites, however, is not sufficient for explaining the seeming conservative triumph of this period. Reflecting on "the process or moral apathy and cultural decay" represented by the dominant trends of the 1950s in U.S. society, cultural historian Marty Jezer — employing concepts advanced by sociologist David Riesman and economist John Kenneth Galbraith — describes a pattern in which residents of the post-World War II "affluent society" seek "to change with the times so that they will always fit in with the most current style." Willingly choosing "the comfortable niche," the mass of conforming consumers want to "avoid risks and ... seek security rather than adventure or individualized self-achievement," and are generally inclined to "respect authority and fit readily into hierarchical corporate structures." Of course, a majority of Americans were able to find spaces — at best — only on the lowest rungs of such corporate structures (including in certain high-wage blue-collar occupations), despite their ability to own cars, sometimes homes, invariably the treasured television set. "I'll tell you what's wrong. We're lonesome," argued the idiosyncratic novelist Kurt Vonnegut, Jr. "We're being kept apart from our neighbors. Why? Because the rich people can go on taking our power away. They want us huddled in our houses, with just our wives and kids, watching television, because they can manipulate us then. They can make us buy anything, they can make us vote any way they want."[26]

In the conformist and conservative climate of the United States in the prosperous 1950s and early 1960s, the notion of radicalism as an integral element in our political life would have seemed bizarre — except to a handful of social critics on its left fringe, among whom could be found C. L. R. James and Harry Braverman.

Everyday Life

A recurrent theme of the present volume is that apparent contradictions between theory and reality can sometimes best be dealt with not by abandoning the "disappointing" theory (particularly if it represents a tradition as rich as Marxism) but instead by stepping outside of "orthodox" ways of understanding that theory, and stretching it (that is, developing it) to gain deeper insights into the unexpected reality.

Given the exhilarating left-wing expectations of the Red Decade, and particularly given the Marxist notion that a radicalizing working class in the most advanced capitalist country in the world seemed to be on the verge of moving forward to replace capitalism with socialism, imagine the shock for the substantial minority of radicalized Americans over capitalist prosperity, a ballooning consumer economy, and a deradicalized labor movement as the 1950s unfolded.

In this atmosphere the working-class majority was drawn into a middle-class self-identification (neither rich nor poor, but somewhere in the middle), and the trend among disappointed radical intellectuals clinging to their radicalism was to dismiss workers as being "brainwashed" by the allure of the American Dream. By the 1960s, many still drawn to Marxist notions were asserting that there must be another "agency" of social change — the impoverished masses of the "third world," perhaps, along with disaffected students and racial minorities in the more advanced capitalist countries.

But the notion of workers brainwashed by capitalist "mass culture" was sharply challenged as "a conception totally unhistorical" by the black Marxist historian and cultural critic C. L. R. James. "To believe that the great masses of the people are merely passive recipients of what the purveyors of popular art have given to them is in reality to see people as dumb slaves," James pointed out. He went on to emphasize the need "to examine more closely the conditions in which these new arts, the film, and with it the comic strip, the radio and jazz have arisen, in order to see exactly why they become an expression of mass response to society, crises, and *the nature and limitations of that response.*" Writing in the United States of the early 1950s, he stressed that "the mass is not merely passive. It decides what it will see. It will pay to see that." This means that in important ways it is not capitalist "culture moguls" who manipulate the working class, but the tastes and desires of the masses that shape popular culture: "The makers of movies, the publishers of comic books are in violent competition with each other for the mass to approve what they produce. Any success tends to be repeated and squeezed dry, for these people are engaged primarily in making money. *Huge and consistent successes are an indication of mass demand.*"[27]

This dovetails with the 1956 perceptions of Harry Braverman, like James trained intellectually and educated politically in the Trotskyist movement during the 1930s, and like James now trying to stretch beyond "traditional" theory to comprehend new realities. He identified positive shifts in popular consciousness regarding "a certain body of elementary ideas about race, politics, cooperation, sex and women's rights, our heritage of freedom and independence, civil liberties, art, culture, humanism, and the promise of the future." Since the 1920s, the new sensibilities had "seeped through the land — unevenly, vaguely, and in still limited doses, but noticeably." There were multiple sources: "The unions, the New Dealers, the last generation of radicals all had a lot to do with it. But even the regulation instruments of information and culture — the newspapers with their reports of strange new events around the world, the flood of paperback books, some motion pictures, increased secondary and higher education especially for veterans, and so forth — had a hand in the gradual change." In Braverman's opinion, "the result has been a considerable and growing body of humanism, toleration, sophistication, cosmopolitanism, and a general spread of a more mature mood and approach."[28]

Braverman connected such observations on popular culture with an argument that the allegedly "middle class" transformation of the U.S. working class — while having an element of truth — was greatly overstated, and that in some ways "the workers have achieved a greater consciousness of class than ever before." He elaborated:

> The worker has been conservatized by his higher standard of living, but it is a surface change which can be sloughed off with great rapidity when he realizes his income is threatened. Moreover, the worker by and large has not too much real confidence in this prosperity as a permanent affair — not because he is an economist but because the conditions of the factory, with layoffs and rumors of layoffs even in the best years and the basic insecurities of a proletarian life constantly refresh his recollections.... The worker ... knows he is an interchangeable part in mass industry, and nothing else. His car and house don't change that in his mind, and in that respect his illusions are modified.[29]

In Braverman's opinion, the realities he was pointing to demonstrated that "it is wrong to get too exclusively preoccupied with the problems and harassments of the moment, to the point where the big and slow-moving changes are forgotten." He added: "Future crises will be met by a generation unlike any that came before, better prepared in many ways, and able to move forward to great progress in short periods of time."[30]

James and Braverman also focused their attention on other "big and slow-moving changes" in daily life — at the point of production, the workplaces where the workers actually spent so much of their lives, and which were the primary source of wealth for capitalist society. They each perceived remarkable and yet commonly ignored aspects of intensifying class struggle there — especially, as Braverman demonstrated in his classic *Labor and Monopoly Capital*, through capitalists introducing technologies and changes in the labor process that increased employer control, increased productivity and profits, and at the same time de-skilled and increased the alienating qualities of workers' labor (and drove down their pay).[31]

This heightened appreciation of "everyday life," and the perception of radical elements in seemingly non-radical situations, are more common among social analysts now than was the case when James and Braverman were developing their understanding of 1950s realities. In fact, extrapolating from this understanding, some radical theorists (indeed, sometimes James himself) have suggested that — in contrast to the traditional Leninist perspective — radical consciousness was now reflected in "the resistance of everyday life" to capitalist oppression, a resistance of "infrapolitics" consisting of "daily confrontations, evasive actions, and stifled thoughts." Yet the critique advanced by political scientist Adolph Reed, Jr., is worth considering:

> Sure, there's infrapolitics — there always is, and there always will be; wherever there's oppression, there's resistance. That's one of the oldest slogans on the left. But it's also a simple fact of life. People don't like being oppressed or exploited, and they respond in ways that reflect that fact. That and a buck fifty will get you a ride on the subway. "Daily confrontations" are to political movements as carbon, water, and oxygen are to life on this planet. They are the raw material for movements of political change, and expressions of dissatisfaction that reflect the need for change, but their presence says nothing more about the potential for such a movement to exist, much less its actuality.
>
> At best, those who romanticize "everyday resistance" or "cultural politics" read the evolution of political movements teleologically; they presume that those conditions necessarily, or even typically, lead to political action. They don't. Not any more than the presence of carbon and water necessarily leads to the evolution of Homo sapiens. Think about it: infrapolitics is ubiquitous, developed political movements are rare.[32]

Reed's point seems consistent with realities that we have explored earlier in this book. If the point is accepted, this hardly throws into doubt the validity of the insights offered by James and Braverman. Rather, the question is posed: Can the organically radical elements in the consciousness and culture of America's working-class majority — elements that during the 1930s were so powerfully influenced by political and ideological forces associated with Marx and Lenin — cohere into an effective force for social change in the future?

1960s

The prosperous and relatively quiescent 1950s period that provided the context, in the United States, within which James and Braverman developed their analyses, were followed by the radical explosions of the 1960s. There is a cornucopia of rich experience related to the issues with which we have been grappling — insights, illusions, inspiring gains, and disastrous setbacks from which we can learn. Drawing from the various themes encountered in previous pages, perhaps we can better comprehend the amazing and contradictory tornado of events that made up this incredible decade.

The radicalization of the 1960s had its roots in the ideological and organizational elements of the American Left that had existed, more or less, on a fragmented and subterranean level through the 1950s. A variety of socialist, Communist, and Trotskyist currents, as well as libertarian, anarchist, left-liberal, and pacifist influences, swirled through and around and within the mushrooming protests of the decade. "What is explicitly new about the New Left is its ecumenical mixture of political traditions that were once murderous rivals in Russia, Spain, France, and the United States," journalist Jack Newfield commented in 1966. "It contains within it, and often within individuals, elements of anarchism, socialism, pacifism, existentialism, humanism, transcendentalism, bohemianism, Populism, mysticism, and black nationalism."[33]

The 1962 *Port Huron Statement* of Students for a Democratic Socialist (SDS) expressed a mood prevalent among a growing layer of student activists: "We are people of this generation, bred in at least modest comfort, housed now in universities, looking uncomfortably to the world we inherit." Emphasizing "the permeating and victimizing fact of human degradation, symbolized by the Southern struggle against racial bigotry," as well as "the enclosing fact of the Cold War, symbolized by the presence of the [Atomic] Bomb," the document's authors and supporters expressed "a yearning to believe there is an alternative to the present, that something can be done to change circumstances in the school, the workplaces, the bureaucracies, the government." There was an insistence that people "have unrealized potential for self-cultivation, self-direction, self-understanding, and creativity," and that there was a need to "replace power rooted in possession, privilege, or circumstance by power and uniqueness rooted in love, reflectiveness, reason, and creativity." This was envisioned as a "participatory democracy" in which all people could meaningfully participate in the decisions affecting their own lives — on a political level "collectively creating an acceptable pattern of social relations," and also recognizing that "the economy itself, its major resources and means of production, should be open to democratic participation and subject to democratic social regulation."[34]

The central importance of the civil rights movement reflected in the *Port Huron Statement* cannot be over-emphasized. The viciousness of the Jim Crow system in the South, in the wake of slavery and the betrayed promises of Reconstruction, had consigned black Americans to second-class citizenship, social oppression, and a reduced quality of life for three generations. A massive and highly organized movement, beginning in the early 1950s and surging forward until the late 1960s, through immense courage and sacrifices, mobilized many hundreds of thousands of people — black and white — in innumerable nonviolent protests, boycotts, marches, rallies, sit-ins, voter registration campaigns, educational efforts, community organizing projects, and other activities that brought an end to Jim Crow in the South and sharply began to address the *de facto* racism that permeated Northern society. While Martin Luther King, Jr. came to play a central leadership role and has rightly been a symbol of this struggle, he arose out of an ideological and organizational context — in which the black church blended with Social Gospel, pacifist, and socialist influences (with the ideas of Marx and Lenin as decidedly present as they were consciously understated) — and his efforts were reflected through an organizational context that involved not only his own Southern Christian Leadership Conference (operating through a network of Southern black churches), but in conjunction with a variety of other organizations, from the long-existing and moderate National Association for the Advancement of Colored People (NAACP) to the recently formed and radical Student Non-Violent Coordinating Committee (SNCC).[35]

"Civil rights activists came together in SNCC to form a community within a social struggle," comments the group's foremost historian, Clayborne Carson, who has elaborated:

SNCC workers sought to create a rationale for activism by eclectically adopting ideas from the Gandhian independence movement [of India] and from the American traditions of pacifism and Christian idealism as formulated by the Congress on Racial Equality (CORE), Fellowship of Reconciliation (FOR), and Southern Christian Leadership Conference (SCLC). SNCC, however, was typically less willing than other civil rights groups to impose its ideas on local black leaders or to restrain southern black militancy. Viewed as the "shock troops" of the civil rights movement, SNCC activists established projects in areas such as rural Mississippi considered too dangerous by other organizations. As the thrust of SNCC's activities shifted from desegregation to political rights, its philosophical commitment to nonviolent direct action gave way to a secular, humanistic radicalism influenced by Marx, Camus, Malcolm X, and most of all by the SNCC organizers' own experiences in southern black communities. In the summer of 1964 SNCC's singular qualities came to national attention when it played a leading role in bringing hundreds of northern students to Mississippi for a decisive battle over voter registration in the main bastion of southern segregation.[36]

One of the most profound contributions of the civil rights movement of this period was its demonstration of the dramatic power of nonviolent resistance. Not all civil rights activists were sold on the philosophy of Mohandas Gandhi embraced by Martin Luther King, Jr., but many accepted the notion that "tactical non-violence" was the most effective approach for dealing with Southern realities — or as Anne Braden put it, "a weapon of action, which people picked up and with which they moved against the status quo." She elaborated:

Such resistance by one individual may or may not be effective in changing a community. Sometimes it can be (the case of Rosa Parks is the prototype), but at the very least, in the thinking of advocates of nonviolence, it regenerates the individual. He becomes a resister instead of a submissive victim, gains new inner dignity, and becomes a whole human being.

But when such tactics of resistance are used by great numbers of people at the same time they take on an additional dimension. They become a very conscious weapon of social struggle, of defying tyranny and taking the offensive against it. They are a form of attack on unjust conditions, in which the attackers use every means at their disposal — their voices, their feet, their bodies, and the mass weight of their very numbers — every means except physical violence, to destroy the system they oppose.

The positive alternative to replace this destroyed system was what many called "the beloved community," a notion of an interracial (or multiracial) community with liberty and justice for all. The vision could be profoundly radical. "I don't want to be like the white man, because what he got he stole from me," said Mrs. Fannie Lou Hamer, Mississippi Delta leader associated with SNCC. "What I want is a world where what I got there won't be nobody have to steal from me because there'll be enough for everybody."[37]

What was the reaction of those who had been disillusioned by Communism to this amazing alternative vision of bringing the kingdom of God to earth? For those who ended up on the right end of the political spectrum, it was mixed. Conservative *National Review* editor Frank Meyer, struggling with cancer toward the end of his life, "became obsessed with 'barbarians' destroying 'our' civilization," comments his younger friend Garry Wills. "Elsie [his wife] could no longer argue and laugh him out of his anti-black outbursts." On the other hand, Louis Budenz "was happy to witness the passing of the Civil Rights Act of 1963, and he followed the events that abolished the 'separate but equal' policies," records his wife. "He argued with friends who belonged to the John Birch Society, whose program he rejected vehemently. He mourned the murder of Martin Luther King .... We never turned our backs on the need for social reforms aimed at abolishing discrimination based on race, nationality, or religion from American society...."[38] But there were others, further to the left, who responded even more positively and more actively. Irving Howe's critical description captures much of the reality:

> The American Communist Party was broken first by McCarthyite and government persecution, and second by an inner crisis following Khrushchev's revelations and the Hungarian revolution. Those who left out of disillusionment were heartsick people, their convictions and sometimes their lives shattered. But those who left the party or its supporting organizations because they feared government attack were often people who kept, semi-privately, their earlier convictions. Many of them had a good deal of political experience; some remained significantly placed in the network of what might be called conscience-organizations.

Naturally enough, they continued to keep in touch with one another, forming a kind of reserve apparatus based on common opinions, feelings, memories. As soon as some ferment began in the civil rights movement and the peace groups, these people were present, ready and eager; they needed no directives from the Communist Party to which, in any case, they no longer (or may never have) belonged; they were quite capable of working on their own as if they were working together, through a variety of groups and periodicals like the *National Guardian*. Organizational Stalinism declined, but a good part of its heritage remained: people who could offer political advice, raise money, write leaflets, sit patiently at meetings, put up in a pleasant New York apartment visitors from a distant state who, by chance, had been recommended by an old friend.[39]

While Howe's references are to those who had fallen away from the Communist Party, what he writes is true of the slightly faded "Reds" of other organizations as well. More than this, many of the children of these Red Decade veterans — the so-called "red diaper babies" — responded with enthusiasm to this inspiring struggle and became civil rights activists, some of them going South to work for SNCC or the Congress for Racial Equality (CORE). But it is hardly the case that all Northern youth responding to this amazing crusade against racism came from such backgrounds. The overwhelming majority were young people who had grown up dissatisfied with the somewhat stultifying political conformism and consumer culture of the 1950s, while continuing to believe deeply in the democratic values that were being constantly emphasized by politicians, by the mass media, and in the schools. Michael Harrington perceptively commented that they were drawn to activism "from a sense of the immediate contradiction between democratic posturing and the undemocratic reality," and that "this intense, even painful, consciousness of American hypocrisy has led the young radicals to people who will not, or cannot, play the national rhetorical game: the left-outs, the outcasts."[40]

Northern students influenced by the civil rights struggles began to challenge the political, social, and cultural conservatism that permeated most campuses throughout the country. At the Berkeley campus of the University of California in 1964, protesting against heavy-handed measures by the university administration to maintain restrictions on civil liberties, students formed the Free Speech Movement (FSM) that closed the institution down with a student strike and sit-ins, compelling the acceptance of First Amendment rights when the university reopened. FSM leader Mario Savio (one of those who had gone to Mississippi), commented during the struggle: "In Mississippi an autocratic and powerful minority rules, through organized violence, to suppress the vast, virtually powerless, majority. In California, the privileged minority manipulates the University bureaucracy to suppress the students' political expression. That 'respectable' bureaucracy masks the financial plutocrats; that impersonal bureaucracy is the efficient enemy in a 'Brave New World.'" He gave voice to the growing mood:

> There is a time when the operation of the machine becomes so odious, makes you so sick at heart that you can't take part; you can't even tacitly take part, and you've got to put your bodies upon the levers, upon all the apparatus, and you've got to make it stop. And you've got to indicate to the people who run it, to the people who own it, that unless you're free, the machine will be prevented from working at all.[41]

"It is, of course, true that it was contact with the Negro people that inspired the Berkeley revolt," commented Raya Dunayevskaya at the time. "It is, however, also true that the Berkeley revolt, followed by [anti-war] teach-ins, in turn, changed the climate for free speech on the pivotal question of war and peace for the whole country." A seasoned militant with decades of experience by 1965, she blended a heady philosophical mix from Marx and Hegel, emphasizing freedom and self-activity (what she termed Marxism-Humanism) while remaining vibrantly sensitive to the dynamic interpenetrations of issues and struggles both manifest and immanent:

> Apparent is the necessity for a philosophy of freedom that can meet the challenge from below, from the actual struggles for freedom, be they for civil rights in the South, or free speech in the North; be they the fight of labor with automation or the struggles of the submerged fifth of the nation that is engulfed in unemployment and in poverty in a country bulging with unprecedented profits and brazen profiteers, situated in a world of Big Powers, each fighting for domination over the whole.... This freedom philosophy is in the events of the day. When concretized for our day, Marxism-Humanism puts into words what every activist knows is true when he battles the power structure which stands in the way of freedom. It becomes imperative therefore to work out a new unity of thought and action which can release the vast untapped energies of mankind, their innate talents, so that a new human dimension, inherent in the old society, can finally emerge and make freedom a reality.[42]

While most never embraced Dunayevskaya's distinctive Marxism-Humanism, she certainly identified a radicalizing outlook that was animating increasing numbers of young people in the 1960s.

This outlook flowed naturally into a questioning of and deepening opposition to the U.S. war in Vietnam. Fred Halstead, a key antiwar organizer, noted that "the antiwar movement had to be constituted here after a prolonged period of reaction in a politically backward country without deep-rooted Marxist traditions or any mass socialist, communist, or labor parties." In fact, the old Marxist assumptions about the revolutionary role of labor appeared to be undermined by the fact that the antiwar movement "could not count on support from the conservatized union movement, except for maverick officials and some sympathy from the ranks that grew over time." Yet, as Halstead observed, "the antiwar movement began with people who were already radicalized: pacifists, socialists, communists, rebellious students, and a scattering of morally outraged individuals. At the start these were a small minority, convinced of the justness of their cause and ready to face unpopularity for their stand." Halstead adds that "the energy, resoluteness, and fortitude of this vanguard brought the movement into being and remained its prime mover." And yet within several years this became a mass movement with majority support among the American people:

> The mass antiwar movement was first of all a generational phenomenon, since the youth were being drafted and doing the fighting and dying. This was its most urgent aspect. The movement competed with the establishment for the allegiance of the American youth. The government had to conscript them or force their enlistment under the hot breath of the draft. The movement gained their voluntary participation and backing by appealing to their sense of self-preservation, consciences, and deep convictions. It won this contest hands down, and as more and more youth entered the armed forces they carried with them the ferment of antiwar ideas.[43]

More and more antiwar activists, attempting to make sense of why the U.S. government was engaged in a war in Vietnam, came to an understanding that it was designed to protect the global interests of U.S. business corporations that defined "the American way of life." As SDS spokesman Carl Oglesby explained: "All of us are born to the colossus of history, our American corporate system — in many ways an awesome organism. There is one fact that describes it: with about 5 percent of the world's people, we consume about half the world's goods."[44] Activist-poet Marge Piercy captured the horrified perception and angry reaction of a growing number of youthful radicals:

> The mouth of empire
> Eats onward through the apple of all.
> Armies of brown men
> Are roasted into coffee beans,
> Are melted into chocolate.
> Their blood is refined into oil,
> Black river oozing rainbows
> Of affluence.[45]

This naturally led to the organization of new coalitions and organizations that reflected an anti-imperialist commitment, and drew increasing numbers to some variation of Marxist and Leninist ideas. Yet the radicalization of significant layers of youth overflowed the boundaries that had been marked by the struggles of the 1930s.

The resurgence of feminism took place within this context, nourished from "old left" as well as "new left" currents — encountering fierce resistance not only in the larger society, but also within "the Movement" itself. And yet essential elements of the struggle for women's liberation would transform people on the Left as well as in the larger society in complex, profound, and multifaceted ways.[46]

In these struggles there was often a joyousness, a youthful exuberance captured by Julius Lester: "The Movement. It was a special time, a time when idealism was as palpable and delicious as a gentle rain, a time when freedom and love and justice seemed as immediate and seemed as ripe as oranges shining seductively from a tree in one's backyard. It was a time when we believed that the ideals of democracy would, at long last, gleam like endless amber waving fields of grain from the hearts and souls of every American."[47]

All of this was accompanied and increasingly interpenetrated by a complex youth-oriented "counter-culture" that blended a quest for freedom and diversity, personal authenticity, naïve utopianism, often also a pretentiousness and superficiality that lent itself to exploitation by the larger consumer culture (which had little difficulty, for example, in catering to the call for "sex, drugs, rock and roll"), and sometimes an incredible destructiveness. For many young activists — engaged in personally difficult cultural transformations that were inseparable from their radical political commitments — there was a sense that through the living of their lives they were helping to bring humanity to a new and hopefully better place. Included in this were searching, experimental, and often incredibly painful efforts to refashion the way they related to each other as friends, as comrades, as men and women, and as lovers. The aspirations and difficulties of growing into this new kind of person are suggested in a poem by Marge Piercy:

> We are trying to live
> As if we were an experiment
> Conducted by the future,
>
> Blasting cell walls
> That no protective seal or inhibition has evolved to replace.
>
> I am conducting a slow vivisection
> On my own tissues, carried out
> Under the barking muzzle of guns.
>
> Those who speak of good and simple
> In the same sandwich of mouth and teeth
> Inhabit some other universe.

Good draws blood from my scalp and files my nerves.
Good runs the yard engine of the night over my bed.
Good pickles me in the brown vinegar of guilt.
Good robs the easy words as they rattle off my teeth,
Leaving me naked as an egg.

Remember that pregnancy is beautiful only
At a distance from the distended belly.
A new idea rarely is born like Venus attended by the graces.
More commonly it's modeled of baling wire and acne.
More commonly it wheezes and tips over.

Most mutants die: only
A minority refract the race
Through the prisms of their genes.

Those slimy fish with air sacs were ugly
As they hauled up on the mud flats
Heaving and gasping. How clumsy we are
In this new air we reach with such effort
And cannot yet breathe.[48]

Just as the effort to be "good" was personally difficult for the most serious of the young activists, so did many of the qualities among the radicalized youth generate problematical developments. A moralistic commitment to use one's life and body to stop the killing in Vietnam sometimes caused young activists — not necessarily committed to the pacifism of an A. J. Muste or Dave Dellinger — to turn away from mobilizing mass protests and toward violent confrontations pitting radicalized youth against "the power structure." "Such impatient and reckless militancy was inescapable and certainly had to find room within the totality of the movement," Halstead writes. "Moreover, it was beneficial for Dellinger and his fellow radical pacifists to win youth in this mood to their nonviolent tactics, which gave a moral weight to their small confrontations and greatly reduced the level of victimization."[49]

Yet the massive killing in Vietnam continued despite all the protests. Despite gains in eliminating the Jim Crow system in the South, racism was as palpable as ever — efforts by Martin Luther King and others to overcome the economic roots of racism (through the *Freedom Budget*, the Poor People's Campaign, and other efforts) were blocked and defeated. King himself was cut down while aiding a sanitation workers strike in Memphis — an assassination that, on top of the accumulation of frustration over disappointed hopes, generated an incredible wave of urban riots. The intensifying political and cultural pressures of the late 1960s caused groups like SDS to explode into fragments, the most dramatic of which vowed to "bring the war home to Amerika" with "fighting street actions." A cult of destructive confrontation and violence began to infect sectors of the Movement. Those who rejected this path were often denounced as being "counter-revolutionary."[50]

A number of young African-American radicals were drawn to the new urban-based Black Panther Party's call for "armed self-defense" of the black community, blending such diverse elements as Mao, Malcolm X, Marx, and Bakunin in an unstable ideological mix. Some of the Black Panthers' more thoughtful members sought to build a revolutionary black nationalist alternative that would learn from and move beyond previous efforts for black liberation and revolutionary change. This inspired an enthusiastic response among many of the young radicals throughout the country. But as the experienced radical black lawyer Conrad Lynn later commented, the Panthers' "foolhardy courage" resulted in provocative statements and actions that made it seem "almost as if they were prepared to commit suicide." More than suicide was involved, however. Reacting with horror to the torture and murder by some of his comrades of one Black Panther Party member accused of disloyalty, black militant Julius Lester wrote that this was "the logical culmination of the politics we have been espousing, of violence-for-the-sake-of-violence, a politics which too quickly and too neatly divides people into categories of 'revolutionary' and 'counter-revolutionary.'" The glorification of violence and descent into destructive internal dynamics also opened the group up to victimization by the authorities and a disintegration of morale, which soon destroyed it.[51]

These and related problems that developed among many young radicals of the "new left" have been identified by some who were deeply involved and later deeply disillusioned. "While we wanted a revolution, we didn't have a plan," comment Peter Collier and David Horowitz. Horowitz writes autobiographically of "the displacement of real emotions into political fantasies; the rejection of present communities for a future illusion; the denial of flesh-and-blood human beings for an Idea of humanity that is more important than humanity itself." Without any clear notion on how to bring about revolutionary change in their own country, some succumbed to playing "the role of sympathizer of revolutions in other countries" (as the old Trotskyist James P. Cannon had put it), romanticizing what was being done by seemingly "real" revolutionaries in Asia, Africa, and Latin America. For many, this led to a cheerleading mentality that rationalized oppressive policies carried out by "third world" revolutionaries who had taken power — involving what another disillusioned "new leftist," Barry Rubin, called "a growing willingness to distort truth in the service of ideology, and a whopping double standard applied internationally. Although periodically one would hear statements about a native American radicalism, the movement was incapable of avoiding apologetics for foreign dictatorships. I thought of this last-mentioned problem as 'flunkyism' or becoming a 'Third World groupie.'" In the opinion of David Horowitz, "my dedication to the progressive cause had made me self-righteous and arrogant and blind."[52]

In fact, the 1960s decade, spilling over into the early 1970s, was far more complex, interesting, and positive than the disillusioned ex-radicals are inclined to admit. There was an explosion of mass action and creative smaller-group efforts (through what were often called "collectives") around a variety of issues and ideas. Latter-day negativism and cynicism cannot erase the inspiring, exhilarating commitment to transforming society — a massive upsurge of youthful idealism and action for civil rights of oppressed races and nationalities, against the threat of nuclear war, for civil liberties, against poverty, for campus reform, and academic freedom, against the Vietnam war, for women's liberation, against anti-gay prejudice, for cultural freedom and revitalization, against the destruction of the earth's ecology, for the elementary and revolutionary democratic demand to "let the people decide." Increasing numbers of people decided to speak truth to power, question authority, move from protest to resistance, finally to be realistic by demanding the "impossible." The radicalization process helped to show that, through collective action, people can more effectively deal with their common problems, that if enough people commit themselves to struggles that make sense, it is possible to transform the political climate, change minorities into majorities, and win meaningful victories. Some also learned that electoralism and reformist politics are traps, that ultra-leftism is a dead end, and that society will not be fundamentally transformed unless the working class (society's majority) becomes conscious of the need for this to be so.

In 1968, many became especially aware of the power of workers, thanks to the May–June events in France. That year also illustrated that the struggle for liberation is global, with the shock of the Tet offensive in Vietnam, the resistance to bureaucratic rule and Soviet invasion in Czechoslovakia, the worker-student upsurge throughout Western and Southern Europe, the brutally repressed student demonstrations in Mexico, the intensified battles for peace and justice in our own land.[53]

Even among those who had been drawn into counter-cultural and violent confrontations that alienated a majority of the American people, there was a reevaluation and reorientation reflected in a futuristic novel by Marge Piercy. In *Dance the Eagle to Sleep* a central character leads a youth rebellion that begins as cultural protest but becomes increasingly violent. "He had only thought of getting the kids out of the system," we are told. "The system was such a nightmare to him that he had not tried to decipher its machinations, but only to make people feel the weight that pressed on them." Refusing to compromise, and veering toward "apocalyptic revolution," and "the model of warfare, without the firepower to wage it, had seduced their imaginations." But those involved became "an isolated minority," and "for the passive others, the angry others, there were only the horror-story caricatures of the mass media to shape their responses." The young would-be revolutionaries turned to "secrecy" and "paramilitary measures" to ward off police infiltration, which "finally made them vulnerable to raids."

This character and others are killed in violent confrontations, but there are survivors. Piercy describes their self-critical reflections: "We thought guns made us real, but it was people, and we didn't have them. Move the people, and the system really is a paper tiger," says one. "People would always naturally be more comfy going to meetings with their brothers and sisters and arguing their itsy-bitsy doctrinaire song-and-dance routines, than going out in the streets to talk to the people. We couldn't get the message out," another complains. The commitment to continue the struggle remains: "We have to start again open and slow. We have to keep at it for twenty years.... While there are people, we haven't lost. We were right and wrong, but the system is all wrong."[54]

Among the most audacious attempts to regroup "new left" efforts into a more coherent ideological and organizational orientation was the effort by some young radicals to form what came to be known as "the New Communist Movement," influenced by the example of the Chinese Revolution and the ideas of Chinese Communist leader Mao Zedong. Among the positive elements in this effort, according to participant Max Elbaum, was that while embracing the need to reach out to and help organize U.S. workers to improve their conditions, these activists "put the cutting edge questions of racism and imperialism central to political strategy," seeking to build "a multi-racial movement out of what had evolved as a racially segregated left." Anchored in "the aspirations of the world's most downtrodden and dispossessed," they called for "the unity of every oppressed person in a project of universal human emancipation." Yet, according to Elbaum, this movement's Maoist ideology did serious damage, with an authoritarian and dogmatic bent and "near-mystical qualities" that caused the activists "to look on Marxism-Leninism more as a religion than a science" (a religion of the more dogmatic-fundamentalist variety). This contributed to fragmentation and in-fighting, and hampered the activists' ability to deal with the complex realities that faced them.[55]

Other efforts (by old-line Communists, Trotskyists, and moderate Socialists) to draw elements emerging from the "new radicalism" into a force capable of bringing socialism to America can hardly be said to have been much more successful. There were impressive spurts of youthful resurgence and some fairly good political work reflected in the W. E. B. DuBois Clubs and the Che-Lumumba Club of the Communist Party, in the tremendous vitality among "mainstream" Trotskyists of the Young Socialist Alliance and the Socialist Workers Party, in the impressive trade union work of the Trotskyist-influenced International Socialists, and in the merger of the "new left" New American Movement with the fragment of the Socialist Party associated with Michael Harrington to create the sometimes influential Democratic Socialists of America. Yet the perspective animating each of these efforts — that of assuming leadership in a deepening and expanding left-wing shift in U.S. politics — was in each case destined to be frustrated, leading to demoralization, fragmentation, and decline.[56]

The failure and decline of such efforts, however, hardly meant an end to the radicalism that had been so vibrant a force in the 1960s. The 1970s, 1980s, and 1990s saw a wide and deep proliferation of the ideas, values, and sensibilities that were common among 1960s radicals — which constitutes an element of truth in the anxious (sometimes paranoid) warnings of present-day conservatives about the evil effects of "new left" ideological and cultural "subversion." The 1950s insights of C. L. R. James and Harry Braverman concerning radical elements in the popular culture and consciousness of U.S. society are, in some ways, more relevant than ever. But with triumphant Reaganism, the pathetic disappointments of the Clinton years, and the ominous realities represented by the Bush administration in the early years of the 21st century (not to mention the overarching realities of globalization), and the persistent problems and the highly problematical situation evolving after the 2004 elections, we are brought back to Adolph Reed's challenge. Unless there is an effective, conscious, organizationally serious political movement — drawing important lessons from previous decades of struggle — to mobilize masses of people in the struggle for a better world, the future is bleak for most of us.

We should be careful about the lure of an earlier era's reassuring dogmas. "A great deal can be learned from previous left experience, and identification with the history of the revolutionary movement can be a great source of strength," Max Elbaum has noted. "The ideas of Marx and Lenin still shed light on the workings of capitalism and the process of social change. They stand out for their breadth of vision and insistence on linking theory, practical work, and organization-building in an internationalist project." But he warns that "it is an unwarranted leap from there to belief in a single and true Marxist-Leninist doctrine with an unbroken revolutionary pedigree from 1848 to the present."[57]

This suggests the value of critically and creatively reflecting on key ideas associated with Marx and Lenin: the centrality of the working class in bringing about meaningful change, and the centrality of organization in the struggles of the working-class majority.

Working Class

In the late 1960s, revolutionary Marxist theorist George Breitman was emphasizing a point missed by many at the time — that a significant working-class component was integral to the mass protest movements opposing racism, the Vietnam war, etc. "It is idiotic and insulting to think that the worker responds only to economic issues," Breitman stressed, with a blend of sensibilities consistent with those of Lenin, Trotsky, Cannon, James, and Braverman. "He can be radicalized in various ways, over various issues, and he is." Breitman developed this point at length:

> The radicalization of the worker can begin off the job as well as on. It can begin from the fact that the worker is a woman as well as a man; that the worker is Black or Chicano or a member of some other oppressed minority as well as white; that the worker is a father or mother whose son can be drafted; that the worker is young as well as middle-aged or about to retire. If we grasp the fact that the working class is stratified and divided in many ways — the capitalists prefer it that way — then we will be better able to understand how the radicalization will develop among workers and how to intervene more effectively. Those who haven't already learned important lessons from the radicalization of oppressed minorities, youth and women had better hurry up and learn them, because most of the people involved in these radicalizations are workers or come from working-class families.[58]

In the same period, both Herbert Marcuse and Henri Lefebvre — left-wing thinkers popular among "new left" activists of the 1960s — were reaching to theorize the same reality. Lefebvre noted that "an immense proletarianization," beyond just the traditional working-class layers, had been impacting on the bulk of the world's people, encompassing "the middle classes, white collar workers, landless peasants, youth and intellectuals, blacks and immigrant workers...." Marcuse was utilizing somewhat similar notions when he argued for modifying "the original concept of class" that had involved "the sharp contrast between the blue collar laboring class and other sectors of the working population." Instead, there was a need for rallying "not 'wage labor' versus capital, but rather all dependent classes against capital."[59]

Contrary to the assertions of many critics and enthusiasts, the perspectives of Marcuse and Lefebvre do not require an abandonment of Marxist fundamentals. The traditional Marxist notion of the *working class* (as we noted in Chapter 1) centers on having no means for making a living except the exchange of the ability to work (labor-power) for an income. In one way or another, this has long been the condition of the great majority of people in our society. As Marcuse and Lefebvre would have insisted, of course, today's working class is hardly the same as that of the 1880s, the 1930s, or the 1960s. While nothing is constant but change, however, the fundamental dynamics of capitalism have not passed out of existence.

Given the nature of capitalism, the working class and its vanguard layers — like various sectors of the economy — often experience processes of decomposition and recomposition. While the material basis for the fundamental Leninist political and organizational orientation undergoes transformation, therefore, it has yet to be obliterated. It is interesting to consider the strategic and organizational perspectives urged by Marcuse and Lefebvre as they anticipated the renewal of mass insurgencies that might effectively challenge the capitalist order.

Organization

Marcuse urged the crystallization of "minoritarian groups" or "nests" of activists within various workplaces, institutions, communities that would focus on non-electoral activism ("all radical opposition becomes extra-parliamentary opposition"), helping to facilitate spontaneous challenges to the status quo, and working to facilitate power shifts from the capitalists to the workers and to other oppressed groups. "Such a development would recapture a seminal achievement of the revolutionary tradition, namely, the 'councils' ('soviets'...) as organizations for self-determination, self-government (or rather preparation for self-government) in local popular assemblies." He stressed that "direct democracy, the subjection of all delegation of authority to effective control 'from below,' is an essential demand of Leftist strategy." While rejecting both the traditional Leninist vanguard party and the model of bureaucratic mass parties, Marcuse urged "not anarchy but a self-imposed discipline and authority — an authority which can only emerge in the struggle itself, recognized by those who wage the struggle."[60]

Lefebvre sketched something more elaborate which, more than 25 years later, brings to mind recent international protests against the "globalization" process imposed by the multinational corporations, International Monetary Fund, World Bank, World Trade Organization, etc.:

(1) A strategy which would join up the peripheral elements [i.e., insurgent forces in "third world" regions of Asia, Africa, and Latin America] with elements from the disturbed centers, i.e., with those elements from the working class [in more economically developed areas] who can free themselves from the ideology of growth.

(2) An orientation of [economic] growth towards specifically social needs and no longer towards individual needs. This orientation would imply the progressive limitation of growth and would avoid either breaking with it crudely or prolonging it indefinitely....

(3) A complete and detailed project for the organization of life and space, with the largest possible role for self-management but at the same time with an awareness that self-management poses as many problems as it solves.

This kind of global project, which is a route rather than a program, plan, or model, bears on collective life and can only be a collective effort which is simultaneously practical and theoretical. It can depend neither on a party nor on a political bloc; it can only be linked to a diversified, qualitative ensemble of movements, demands, and actions.[61]

While recognizing the value of "spontaneous" activity on the part of the proletariat and other oppressed sectors, Lefebvre added: "But remember Lenin's formula: spontaneity collapses spontaneously." While approaching the notion of the Leninist party with extreme caution, he nonetheless makes Lenin's thinking a touchstone for serious activism. Attributing to Lenin the notion of "such a thing as 'revolutionary spontaneity,'" he comments that "the spontaneity of the working class does not stop short of the political level .... The working class spontaneously reaches a high level of consciousness which includes political consciousness; but the collapse, too, can be extremely rapid if there is no political thought." Lefebvre stresses "Lenin's view was that the working class needed political thought, an 'appropriate initiative.' There must be an objective, a strategy: nothing can replace political thought, or a cultivated spontaneity." He suggests that "what is left to us of Leninism" is a notion of "the *conjunctural* (non-structural) revolutionary capacity" of the working class, the notion that "the working class only plays its revolutionary role when there is a particular balance of forces and where there is an initiative, a political thought orienting it."[62]

The question arises, of course, as to what forms of organization and activity are required to develop, sustain, and disseminate such political thought that can orient broad layers of the working class. Serious answers to that question can be formulated only in close connection to political activity and social struggles of the 21st century.

In his thoughtful study *The Long Detour: The History and Future of the American Left*, a seasoned and influential radical scholar and activist named James Weinstein has argued that "to be significant, an American left needs principles and programs that point in the developmental direction of our society and resonate with the historical possibilities and social concerns already on the public's mind." He adds that "such a left will require an engagement strategy in harmony with our evolving democratic traditions and political institutions."[63]

For Weinstein, however, the central thrust of such a strategy involves activists immersing themselves in local, statewide, and national election campaigns of the Democratic Party. This was, he notes, the orientation of the U.S. Communist Party from the late 1930s through the mid-1940s (when he himself was a member). It continues to be a guide, in his view, for serious activists of today and tomorrow: "Building a sustained national movement requires a commitment to continuous electoral activity, year-in and year-out."[64] And yet, piece by piece, the Democratic Party has lost the trust of many of the American people since its glory days of the 1930s. Even in those glory days, the Democratic Party was never committed to "rule by the people" over the economy. Instead, it balanced its base in the working-class majority with a loyalty to the interests of the wealthy. All too often, throughout much of the 20th century, the energies and resources of many sincere activists were drawn into electoral defeats that could be traced to this contradiction. And it was the same contradiction that betrayed those hopes when electoral victories were won.

There is more to politics, however, than simply *electoral* politics (let alone continuous electoral work on behalf of liberal pro-capitalist parties). There are certainly other ways to connect with what Weinstein refers to as "the historical possibilities and social concerns already on the public's mind" and to engage with "our evolving democratic traditions and political institutions."

The late Raymond Williams, Britain's outstanding left-wing cultural critic, insisted that electoral action (by itself) would never be capable of transforming society. He explained the need for those in the labor and socialist movements must recognize "that this transformation of society has an enemy ... hostile and organized ... which is actively trying to defeat and destroy you," and that the recognition of this has revolutionary implications. But he went beyond this to emphasize that the capitalist order is maintained not simply through power and property. "It is maintained also and inevitably by a lived culture: that saturation of habit, of experience, of outlook, from a very early age and continually renewed at so many stages of life, under definite pressures and within definite limits, so that what people come to think and feel is in large measure a reproduction of the deeply based social order which they may even in some respects think they oppose and indeed actually oppose." Williams stressed the need to confront and defeat such oppressive cultural elements in ourselves and in our communities — which meant, for him, going far beyond winning a parliamentary majority for the British Labour Party. Such a majority could have no transformative effect unless it was created in interaction with "activity [that] involves the most active elements of community politics, local campaigning, specialized interest campaigning" reminiscent of "new left" social movements of the 1960s, and also intensive and extensive cultural activism. "I believe that the system of meanings and values which a capitalist society has generated has to be defeated in general and in detail by the most sustained kinds of intellectual and educational work," he asserted. "This is a cultural process which I called 'the long revolution' and in calling it 'the long revolution' I meant that it was a genuine struggle which was part of the necessary battles of democracy and of economic victory for the organized working class."[65]

Perspectives such as these blend well with those advanced by others examined in this chapter, seeming to provide sources of hope and strategic guidelines for activists of the new millennium. Their elements have become evident in social struggles of the early 21st century.

The Global Justice Movement

The dawn of the new century has been stirred by a new global movement, challenging the multinational corporations and their financial and governmental appendages dominating our globe and seeking to shape our future in the interests of profit maximization. Since its dramatic appearance in the late 1990s, there were fluctuations in the activities and energies of this movement, particularly after the terrorist assaults of September 11, 2001 and — even more — the U.S. invasion and occupation of Iraq, which coincided with the drawing back of some of the less radical elements and the focus of others on opposition to war. Given the persistence of the policies, developments, and crises that generated the global justice protests, however, it seems likely that the movement will persist. The incredibly varied protestors have been against many things: against the exploitation of workers in all countries, against racist and sexist oppression, against militarism and war, against the domination of peoples and destruction of communities — and also against "the mad sacrifice of forests for the sake of 'profit,'" as the German working-class Marxist party-builder August Bebel once put it, against the destruction of the myriad "monuments of nature," to use Lenin's phrase. It is a movement, in conception and potential, of incredible variety, whose banners are first of all vibrantly green, and — for many — an uncompromising black in opposition to authoritarianism, with the flaming crimson of laboring humanity, and other hues as richly multicolored as the peoples of the earth.

Among the thoughtful activists in this movement is Canadian radical journalist Naomi Klein, who sees greater parallels between the radical activism of 2000 and that of the 1930s, far more than that of the 1960s — because of "how incredibly cross-generational" it is. She also notes that "local control and self-determination and sustainability are key principles for a truly international movement," elaborating: "We can reclaim internationalism and localism, and zero in on key principles of internationalism that protect self-determination. The most important principle in a labor context is the right to form unions .... All the energy and outrage around sweatshops should be concentrated on the right to self-determination and free association for workers around the world." She suggested the evolution of "what was a consumer movement into a genuine labor movement .... empowering local communities and local struggles, to enable people once again to control their own environments and workplaces.[66]

At the same time, Klein challenges traditional Marxist groups to be open to learning from the swelling ranks of youthful activists who are animated by "the longing to be whole, the longing for joy and creativity and uncommodified space. ... What I'd say to Marxists is, meet them half way. I don't see that happening. I see some groups cooperating with some of the street-level activists, but they're still waiting for them to see the light, and that's just co-optation, not cooperation." She challenges her anti-authoritarian sister and brother activists: "Everybody in the movement who is rejecting traditional hierarchical structures needs to take responsibility for what this means. If this is a movement with no followers but only leaders, then everyone has to be a leader, and that means not being afraid to say what you believe and participate in this intellectual and outreach process in a constructive way."[67]

But how is this all to be coordinated and sustained? How will it be possible to move from networking to challenging the system, and that in a manner capable, ultimately, of enabling the earth's peoples to take power from the multinational corporations? "A structure has to develop that has roots in many movements, and genuine diversity within it," Klein says. "It's not about converging into one unified movement or political party structure, but that doesn't mean that there can't be cooperation and coordinated action, a process of developing and articulating shared beliefs and principles."[68]

It may be that Lenin's revolutionary organizational perspectives will not be superseded in any practical sense. To determine to what extent that is true, it will be necessary — as Klein suggests — for there to be considerable thought, searching discussion, comradely debate, all grounded in and tested by experience. This is true not only for the movement converging around "globalization," but also for the various struggles opposing the many forms of oppression of our time — the struggles of the working class most of all. Serious socialists will need to find creative ways of utilizing the perspectives of the Leninist tradition that are in harmony with a grasp of the realities unfolding in the 21st century.

It's worth following Klein's thoughtful reflections further. In her country, there is on the one hand a reformist and socialist-influenced labor party — the New Democratic Party — that, late in the last century, excited great hopes and then, unprepared for its electoral victories, resulted in great disappointments. As this party has declined, there has also been the rise of a number of protest movements focused on a variety of issues. The party and movements are not connected. This adds up to "a weakened and ineffective" political party and "an endless series of street protests," which she sees as "a recipe for fighting like crazy to make things not quite as bad as they would be otherwise. Which is still really bad." She argues for the need for "a national party of the left" with a vision "founded on local democracy and sustainable economic development." It would be a party that struggles to bring power and resources to people on the local level to enable them "to control their own destinies, to use their expertise, to build diverse economies that are genuinely sustainable." Such "localization" should not be seen as "a dire threat to national unity" but instead as "building blocks for a unified — and diverse — culture." To Klein's way of thinking, this commitment to "self-determination, grassroots democracy, and ecological sustainability are the pieces of a new political vision" capable of involving many "who have never been represented by the so-called left," and also capable of providing a powerful alternative to the status quo.[69]

Writing from Prague, she comments: "Many of the young Czechs I met this week say that their direct experience with communism [of the Stalinist variety] and capitalism has taught them that the two systems have something in common: they both centralize power in the hands of a few, and they both treat people as if they are less than fully human." Writing from Mexico, she says:

"What sets the Zapatistas apart from your average Marxist guerrilla insurgents is that their goal is not to win control but to seize and build autonomous spaces where 'democracy, liberty, and justice' can thrive." She adds that this involves "a global call to revolution that tells you not to wait for the revolution, only to start where you stand, to fight with your own weapon," which could be a video camera, words, ideas, hope. At the same time, Klein reflects on the World Social Forum, "the coalition of forces that is often placed under the banner of anti-globalization" but has begun "collectively to recast itself as a pro-democracy movement." Challenging the power of multinational corporations and such institutions that serve them as the World Trade Organization, World Bank, and International Monetary Fund, insisting that *a better world is possible*, this movement defends the right of local communities to plan and manage their own affairs, with "the abstractions of global economics becoming day-to-day issues of homelessness, water contamination, exploding prisons and cash-starved schools." The World Social Forum, in her opinion, is hardly "a movement for a single global government but a vision for an increasingly connected international network of very local initiatives, each built on direct democracy." And yet, she pays attention to criticisms about allowing "the mushy language of democracy to avoid a more divisive discussion of class," and to dissident voices insisting that "another world is not possible unless you smash capitalism and bring in socialism!" (Also worth pondering is Tariq Ali's more recent suggestion that the World Social Forum extend its multifaceted agenda and assume a function as "a global Anti-Imperialist League.")[70]

In seeking to move forward on the basis of such insights, it may be necessary to risk the dotting of "i"s and the crossing of "t"s:

- *Activist groups.* What Marcuse called "nests of activists" (not to be confused with left-wing discussion groups) are an essential yeast in helping to bring about and sustain the movement we need. Single-issue groups have value, but simply addressing one problem is not enough, and there are too many issues for one person to be involved in, so it is logical that groups concerned with an array of issues should evolve. It may make sense for some groups, particularly those wishing to develop a division of labor necessary for addressing *multiple issues,* to use some organizational concepts from the Bolshevik experience to make themselves more durable, more effective, more capable of evolving as serious activist organizations in which there is a serious collective decision-making process that is matched by a seriousness in carrying out decisions. This would include the development of a far-reaching *program* that connects the issues and shows how they are rooted in the problems of capitalism, at the same time suggesting real alternatives; in addition to identifying the grim problems of today and envisioning a vibrant socialist participatory-democracy, such a program must indicate a flexible strategic orientation on how to get from the one to the other. Such groups also need to develop a mode of functioning that enables them to be coherent, cohesive, collective — that is, democratic: something like the original variant of *democratic centralism* before it was turned into a bureaucratic-authoritarian monstrosity. A genuinely *democratic* centralism will enable the members to test ideas, strategies, tactics, and to refine and develop (and, if need be, to change) these things based on practical experience.

- *Multi-organizational approach.* It is essential to understand that no single group is "the revolutionary vanguard." Such a vanguard, certainly in our time, is much broader and is multi-organizational. The making of the Russian Revolution — not only in February/March but also in October/November of 1917 — was by no means the exclusive domain of Lenin and the Bolsheviks. In both cases there was a fluid and multi-organizational mass movement characterized by alliances and coalitions. The revolution could not have happened, and probably cannot happen in our context, without involving that essential quality.

- *Leadership.* It is vitally important that each political and social activist assume a sense of leadership responsibility to develop her or his ideas on "what is to be done." Genuine revolutions are never made by everyone "following the leader" — in fact, that's how revolutions are killed. At the same time, history shows that not all ideas and not all strategic orientations are equally valid, fruitful, and capable of bringing about desired changes. People and groups that are able to develop fruitful ideas and orientations — and able to communicate those persuasively to broader layers — do play a very much needed leadership role. Leadership involves not only thinking and communicating, of course, but also hard work, working with others, developing skills, and helping to teach these to others.

- *Openness.* It is not preordained which individuals and groups will advance the ideas and orientations capable of leading to one or another partial victory — or to some "ultimate" revolutionary victory. It is a safe assumption that none will have a monopoly on the truth. It is likely that certain people and groups showing special leadership qualities will lead the way in developing useful ideas and orientations. Such genuine leadership qualities will emerge organically from the struggle. The point is not to obsess over who should be "the leader" — but instead for all to do good work to build struggles, organizations, movements that can be effective, that can involve more and more people, that can be developed by and tempered through (1) democratic process, and (2) experience in the struggle.

- *Unifying Campaigns.* Just as specific campaigns in the struggle for civil rights and against the Vietnam War united millions in the 1960s (and highly focused labor struggles and anti-fascist efforts united millions in the 1930s), so can unifying campaigns be developed as a focal point for future movement-building. The campaigns could be designed to resonate among large numbers of people and allow many diverse elements in society to join together in a common effort that makes sense to all. Also, a high degree of political independence of the campaign is required to (a) attract the most diverse support, (b) prevent the campaign from becoming simply the ornament or marketing device of a particular political party, and (c) put maximum popular pressure on all political figures and institutions for the realization of the campaign's goal.

Opposition to the U.S. invasion and occupation of Iraq is a powerful recent example of such a focus.

More ambitious would be a revival of A. Philip Randolph's *"Freedom Budget" for All Americans* to create full employment and eliminate poverty in the United States within a ten-year period (discussed in Chapter 1). If it could win mass support and be connected to a politically independent strategy — in contrast to the fatal failure to do this in the 1960s — it would certainly have powerful impact.

Another possibility is the United Nations Millennium Development Goals campaign, initiated in 2000 and endorsed by 191 governments. It establishes detailed proposals and projections for achieving, by 2015, eight over-arching goals: (1) eradicate extreme poverty and hunger; (2) achieve universal primary education; (3) promote gender equality and empower women; (4) reduce child mortality; (5) improve maternal health; (6) combat HIV/AIDS, malaria and other diseases; (7) ensure environmental sustainability; and (8) develop a Global Partnership for Development.[71]

Can such a campaign be successful in a global context dominated by multinational corporations and their institutional appendages (World Bank, International Monetary Fund, etc.)? To the extent that millions of supporters of the Millennium Development Goals confront that question (particularly if the campaign's goals are not met by 2015), to that extent will a powerful popular force have been mobilized to challenge the structures of power that generate intolerable conditions.

Such campaigns, if carried out successfully, necessarily alter the political–social balance of power, opening the possibility of improving the quality of life for many millions of people and transforming culture and consciousness in ways that facilitate further struggles against problematical aspects of the status quo.

• *Centrality of Class.* Those continuing to embrace the revolutionary socialist orientation developed by Marx and Lenin believe that the fundamental class relationships arising from the structure of the economy — the basis for human subsistence — do not obliterate but instead permeate and connect all other forms of identity and oppression that exist in capitalist society.

The interpenetration of the various dimensions of human identity and relationships must be grasped to achieve a more complete understanding of social dynamics. An understanding of the distinct dynamics of sexual oppression, of gender oppression, of racial oppression, are essential for grasping social reality. But this must be combined with an understanding of class oppression if we want to illuminate the realities of race, sexuality, and gender.

"The class dimension *is* privileged, if only circumstantially and politically (not analytically)," notes Marxist ethnographer Roger Lancaster, "and by this index: class exploitation necessarily produces an exploiting minority and an exploited majority. The same cannot be said for any other dimensions of oppression. Whether one is seeking to reform or overthrow *any* system of exploitation, the dynamics of class and class resistance remain, in Marx's sense, strategic and paramount."[72]

What does all of this add up to?

The global justice movement that arose at the dawn of the 21st century — it seems to me, from the vantage point of this particular moment, as a scholarly "close observer" — could evolve into an increasingly formidable entity that is strengthened by (and that therefore gives a renewed relevance to) the elements of past revolutionary experience discussed here. At the same time, a reasonable case can be made that this is unlikely —which would mean that the revolutionary tradition may end up being of little more than historical interest, making it necessary to push our way past it.

Commenting on global justice activists "making their presence felt in various ways, notably by organizing large demonstrations to coincide with international meetings, as at the 'battle of Seattle in 1999' and the 'battle of Genoa' in 2001," sociologist James Fulcher has emphasized "that although they attract considerable support, they do not present a viable alternative to capitalism." While Fulcher insists that "the search for an alternative *to* capitalism is fruitless," he is optimistic about the possibility that some of the problems associated with capitalism can be altered by those who are sufficiently practical-minded to realize that "reform does ... require an engagement with capitalism and cannot be accomplished by movements that stand outside it and merely demonstrate against it." Noted economist Jeffrey Sachs, in his challenging study *The End of Poverty*, concurs: "The movement is too pessimistic about the possibilities of capitalism with a human face, in which the remarkable power of trade and investment can be harnessed while acknowledging and addressing limitations through compensatory collective actions."[73]

But the pragmatic optimism of Sachs and Fulchar is thrown into question by realities examined earlier in this volume. Humanity is faced with an increasingly expansive destructiveness — to people, their cultures, and their natural environments — relentlessly generated by "actually existing" global capitalism as we have known it over the past two centuries. There has been an apparent acceleration of this destructiveness in recent decades.

Perhaps the story we are considering is destined to end badly, frustrating both revolutionary and reformist hopes. No responsible scholar can draw final conclusions here. As Donald Sassoon has commented, for scholars dealing with contemporary history "there are no conclusions, only postponements."[74]

Personal Conclusions

To go beyond the limitations of scholarship would involve only personal conclusions — so here are mine. The watchwords should be: do the work, engage in struggle, speak your mind, really listen to others, learn from experience, take what you do seriously, maintain your sense of humor, don't be afraid to dream. That is fundamental to Leninism: "We should dream."[75]

"Thinking means venturing beyond," in the words of the religious atheist and utopian Leninist Ernst Bloch, and he gave special stress to the regions beyond consciousness, "the Not-Yet-Conscious," a "blossoming field of questions" nourished by desire and hope. It is worth considering his philosophy of daydreams. "Everybody's life is pervaded by daydreams: one part of this is just stale, even enervating escapism, even booty for swindlers," according to Bloch, "but another part is provocative, is not content just to accept the bad which exists, does not accept renunciation. This other part has hoping at its core, and is teachable." He speculates that we can "know" our daydreams "deeper and deeper and in this way keeping them trained unerringly, usefully, on what is right. Let the daydreams grow even fuller, since this means they are enriching themselves around the sober glance; not in the sense of clogging, but of becoming clear." The daydreams can interact not "merely [with] contemplative reason which takes things as they are and as they stand, but [also with] participating reason which takes them as they go, and therefore also as they could go better."[76]

Our dreams can help us perceive and open up to new possibilities. Often they reflect realities that are not quite there — but that could be there. When connected with a thoughtful understanding of the material realities around us, they can lead us to visions of the future that are worth striving for, and the striving can change reality, make history along more hopeful lines. Ours is a time for taking the accumulated experience of struggles of workers and oppressed groups and revolutionaries of the past and making creative and critical-minded use of that experience, applying it, testing it, refining it, adding to it. Working together, learning from each other and from those we are reaching out to, we can express our individuality and blend our lives in a way that connects freedom fighters of the past with freedom fighters of the future.

One of these past fighters was Dorothy Day of the Catholic Worker movement, who warned against becoming partners-in-progress with capitalist multinational corporations — "an obscene *agape* of luxury, shared profits, blood money from a thousand battles all over the world. No, the common good, the community must be considered." This was in 1949, when Cold War anti-Communism was dominating the U.S. political scene. "Certainly we disagree with the Communist Party," she wrote, "but so do we disagree with the other political parties, dedicated to maintaining the status quo. We don't think the present system is worth maintaining." This is a thought that today gathers strength among the world's majorities. "We and the Communists have a common idea that something else is necessary, some other vision of society must be held up and worked toward," she commented, going on to emphasize a crucial insight that has greatly concerned us in the present study: "Certainly we disagree over and over with the means chosen to reach their ends, because, as we have repeated many a time, the means become the end." And she affirmed: "We want to make 'the rich poor and the poor holy,' and that is a revolution. ... We don't want luxury. We want land, bread, work, children, and the joys of community in play and work and worship."[77] That is a dream worth struggling for.

Endnotes

Introduction

1. See, for example, Ann Coulter, *Treason: Liberal Treachery From the Cold War to the War on Terror*. (Publication details for this and other sources in the footnotes of this book can be found in the bibliography.) Ms. Coulter's terminology cannot be accepted uncritically. My own position on the political spectrum cannot be categorized as "liberal," nor do most liberals have the distorted left-wing views that she attributes to them. Such irresponsible political blurring is consistent with her glorification of McCarthyism.

2. Irving Howe, Ed., *Orwell's Nineteen Eighty-Four: Text, Sources, Criticism*, 178, 247, 279, 281.

3. Ibid., 126, 136.

4. Ibid., 279–280, 281.

5. Ibid., 127, 128.

6. Neil Smith, *The Endgame of Globalization*, 30, 208; Walden Bello, *Dilemmas of Domination: The Unmaking of the American Empire*, 5. These studies, blended with Daniel Singer's final meditation, *Whose Millennium?*, provide an analytical framework consistent with that of the present volume.

7. J. William Fulbright, *The Arrogance of Power*. Fulbright's insights make greatest sense within the interpretative framework provided in William Appleman Williams' 1959 classic *The Tragedy of American Diplomacy*. On the Iraq War, a good starting place is Micah L. Sifry and Christopher Cerf, Eds., *The Iraq War Reader*. Regarding the documented allegations of recent lies, see John Prados, *Hoodwinked: The Documents That Reveal How Bush Sold Us a War*.

8. William Pfaff, "The Question of Hegemony," 221; William Kristol and Robert Kagan, "Toward a Neo-Reaganite Foreign Policy," 23, 32; Sebastian Mallaby, "The Reluctant Imperialist: Terrorism, Failed States, and the Case for American Empire," 6. Sidney Lens, *The Forging of the American Empire* demonstrates the fact that such stuff has deep roots in U.S. history.

9. Michael Ignatieff, "The Burden," 24.

10. Ibid., 24, 25, 26.

11. Ibid., 27, 50, 54.

12. Michael Hardt and Antonio Negri, *Empire*, xv, 10, 11, 15. A flaw of this brilliantly conceived book is that the authors give such restrictive definition to imperialism that, for them, "Empire" naturally supersedes it. But a more expansive definition of imperialism — the expansion of capitalist economy and exploitation beyond the borders of nation-states — is aptly captured in Harry Magdoff's assertion: "Imperialism is not a matter of choice for capitalist society; it is the way of life of such a society" (*The Age of Imperialism: The Economics of U.S. Foreign Policy*, 26). Hardt and Negri write that Empire "constructs its own relationships of power based on exploitation that are in many respects more brutal than those it destroyed," and that "the geographical and racial lines of oppression and exploitation that were established during the era of colonialism and imperialism have in many respects not declined but instead increased exponentially" (43). What this indicates is not a replacement, but rather a dramatically new phase of imperialism, similar to the "ultra-imperialism" theorized by Karl Kautsky. Lenin himself (Kautsky's severest critic) wrote that "there is no doubt that the development [of the global capitalist system] is going in the direction of a single world trust that will swallow up all enterprises and all states without exception," but he theorized that global imperialist wars and social revolutions would destroy capitalism before this "ultra-imperialist" conclusion was reached — see his 1915 introduction to Nikolai Bukharin, *Imperialism and World Economy*, 14.

13. Michael Ignatieff, "Lesser Evils," 48, 50. A small taste of what lies "outside the confines of our cozy conservative and liberal boxes" can be found in Mark Danner's fat book, complete with photographs and documents, *Torture and Truth: America, Abu Ghraib, and the War on Terror*.

14. Michael Ignatieff, *The Lesser Evil: Political Ethics in an Age of Terror*, 82, 85. Among terrorist organizations in Ignatieff's account are the Front of National Liberation that ended French rule in Algeria, the Palestine Liberation Organization, the Irish Republican Army, and the military wing of the African National Congress during the anti-apartheid struggle in South Africa. At the same time, however, he makes a sharp distinction between revolutionary "freedom fighters" (among whom, interestingly enough, he places Che Guevara) and terrorists who do such things as targeting innocent civilians to achieve specific ends. Of course, there have been "anti-terrorist" governments (including that of the United States) that have also targeted innocent civilians to achieve specific ends.

15. Ignatieff, "Lesser Evil," 50, 94.

16. Ibid., 48, 86, 94.

17. Michael Ignatieff, *The Needs of Strangers*, 127–128.

18. Whittaker Chambers, "Foot in the Door," *National Review*, June 20, 1959, reprinted in Whittaker Chambers, *Ghosts on the Roof, Selected Essays*, 349.

19. Naomi Klein, *No Logo: Taking Aim at the Brand Bullies*, 445–446.

20. John Earl Haynes and Harvey Klehr, *In Denial: Historians, Communism, and Espionage*, 226. James P. Cannon offered a very different sense of proportion in referring to the espionage, on which the two focus such passion, as "a mere detail in a side-show tent" compared with the larger political realities, in *The First Ten Years of American Communism*, 40. Seasoned and skeptical journalist Fred J. Cook seconded this point, referring to "minor spy sensations" in *The Nightmare Decade: The Life and Times of Joseph McCarthy*, 548. A similar but more recent assessment is offered by Maurice Isserman, who comments that "Haynes and Klehr deserve the gratitude of other historians" for helping to "resolve many decades-old mysteries and controversies" regarding the growth of Soviet espionage efforts that began "from small beginnings in the '30s" and "increased exponentially during the war years." Yet Isserman points out that "of the approximately 50,000 party members in those years, 49,700 were not involved in spying, even taking the highest estimate of Communist participation in the spy network," which means that "spying and Communist Party membership were not identical categories." See Maurice Isserman, "They Led Two Lives," 34.

    This is not to argue against the existence or significance of Communist spies tied to the state apparatus of the USSR. But Haynes and Klehr flatten the story. Serious works on six spies — four seasoned professionals, one a sympathetic journalist with a more limited engagement in espionage, and yet another somewhat in-between — can be found in: Gary Kern, *A Death in Washington: Walter G. Krivitsky and the Stalin Terror*; Robert Wymart, *Stalin's Spy: Richard Sorge and the Tokyo Espionage Ring*; Elisabeth Poretsky, *Our Own People: A Memoir of 'Ignace Reiss' and His Friends*; Leopold Trepper, *The Great Game*; Ruth Price, *The Lives of Agnes Smedley*; and Shareen Blair Brysac, *Resisting Hitler: Mildred Harnack and the Red Orchestra*. Similar works could be added to this sampling. They present a more complex, believable reality than the polemics of *In Denial*.

21. Stephane Courtois, Nicolas Werth, Jean-Louis Panne, Andrzej Paczkowski, Karel Bartosek, Jean-Louis Margolin, *The Black Book of Communism: Crimes, Terror, Repression*.

22. These figures come from Alan Woods, *Marxism and the U.S.A.*, 56–57. The flaw in the *Black Book* discussion of Vietnam (on pages 4 and 565–575) becomes evident through a consultation of such sources as: *The Pentagon Papers*; Stanley Karnow, *Vietnam: A History*; Marilyn B. Young, *The Vietnam Wars, 1945–1990*; and Daniel Ellsburg, *Secrets: A Memoir of the Vietnam War and the Pentagon Papers*.

23. Hal Draper, *Socialism From Below*. Draper speaks of "the two souls of socialism," one revolutionary-democratic and the other authoritarian-elitist. While one can quibble with certain aspects of Draper's argument, his fundamental point strikes me as useful and applicable to other entities that have elements consistent, but also elements inconsistent, with human freedom and dignity.

24. Daniel Bell, *Marxian Socialism in the United States*, 5, 193. In contrast, dynamic theologian and historian N. T. Wright — noting "the familiar split of history and faith" — has gloried in "the fresh epistemological air, and the new, risky choices of a single world with multiple interlocking dimensions," insisting that he "does not want to be imprisoned again in the attic (faith divorced from history) or the dungeon (history divorced from faith)." Marcus J. Borg and N. T. Wright, *The Meaning of Jesus*, 16.

Chapter 1
Marx's Manifesto after Communism's Collapse

1. Particularly good is John Cassidy, "The Next Great Thinker: The Return of Karl Marx."
2. David Horowitz, "Marx's *Manifesto*: 150 Years of Evil," in *Left Illusions, An Intellectual Odyssey*, 299, 300 307.
3. Isaiah Berlin, *Four Essays on Liberty*, 24. In *Isaiah Berlin, A Life* (93), Michael Ignatieff comments that while Berlin "loathed Marxian ideas of historical determinism," he was nonetheless "influenced by the Marxian sense that ideas and values were historical, and that values of social groups in class struggle were incompatible. Marxism accentuated his tendency to look historically at the values that liberals of his generation took as eternal verities." Horowitz's pantheon of heroic intellectuals can be found in his *Politics of Bad Faith: The Radical Assault on America's Future*, 34. Marx's relevance for current economic developments is highlighted by the introductory essay and the apt selections in Dave Renton, Ed., *Marx on Globalization*. The most valuable popular edition in English of the key text by Marx and Engels, offering valuable information on historical context and contemporary relevance, can be found in Phil Gasper, Ed. *The Communist Manifesto: A Road Map to History's Most Important Political Document*.
4. Jervis Anderson, *A. Philip Randolph, A Biographical Portrait*, 62.
5. Karl Marx and Frederick Engels, "Manifesto of the Communist Party," in Paul Le Blanc, *From Marx to Gramsci: A Reader in Revolutionary Marxist Politics*, 130.
6. Jerry Z. Muller, *The Mind and the Market: Capitalism in Modern European Thought*, 175.
7. Marx and Engels, 130
8. Alejandro Reuss et al., Eds., *Real World Globalization*.
9. Marx and Engels., 131. While the relevance to "communism's" collapse occurred independently to me and, I'm sure, to other readers of the *Manifesto* since 1990, Ellen Meiksins Wood was perhaps the first to put the observation into print — see "The Communist Manifesto After 150 Years," in *The Communist Manifesto*, 108.
10. Marx and Engels, 129.
11. Ibid., 132.
12. Ibid., 132.
13. Ibid., 127, 133–134.
14. Ibid., 136; Juliet B. Schor, *The Overworked American, The Unexpected Decline of Leisure*. The global proletarianization process is documented and discussed in Ronaldo Munck, *Globalisation and Labour, The New "Great Transformation."*
15. Donald L. Bartlett and James B. Steele. *America: What Went Wrong?*, 2–30; Sue Kirchoff, "Economy Goes Forward But Leaves Many Behind," 1, 4.
16. Keith Bradshear, "The Few, the Rich: That's America," 1; Donald L. Bartlett and James B. Steele. *America: Who Stole the Dream?*; Jeremy Brecher and Tim Costello, *Global Village or Global Pillage: Economic Reconstruction From the Bottom Up*; and Doug Henwood, *After the New Economy.*
17. Marx and Engels, 134–137, 143–144.
18. Sheila Rowbotham, *Women, Resistance and Revolution*, 51, 54, 56. A pioneering historical survey of 1939 — blending Marxist, anarchist, and feminist sensibilities — can be found in Ethel Mannin, *Woman and Revolution*, and a good collection of scholarly essays can be found in Marilyn Boxer and Jean H. Quartaert, Eds., *Socialist Women: European Socialist Feminism in the Early Nineteenth and Twentieth Century.*
19. Marx and Engels, 141–142; Sheila Rowbotham, "Dear Dr. Marx: Letter From a Socialist Feminist," in *Threads Through Time: Writings on History and Autobiography*, 226–227.
20. See Margaret Randall, *Gathering Rage: The Failure of Twentieth Century Revolutions to Develop a Feminist Agenda*, and Nancy Holmstrom, Ed., *The Socialist Feminist Project: A Contemporary Reader in Theory and Politics.*
21. A. J. Muste, "The Workers Party is Founded," *New International*, December 1934, 129; George Breitman, Paul Le Blanc, Alan Wald, *Trotskyism in the United States, Historical Essays and Reconsiderations*, 19–20.
22. A. J. Muste, *Not By Might: Christianity, The Way to Human Decency*, 213.
23. Ibid., 51; Karl Marx, "Toward the Critique of Hegel's Philosophy of Law: Introduction," *Writings of the Young Marx on Philosophy and Society*, Loyd Easton and Kurt Guddat, Eds., 257–258.

24. Muste, *Not By Might*, 51–52.
25. Nicolas Berdyaev, *The Russian Revolution*, 80.
26. Jack London, *The Iron Heel*, 64–65.
27. Ibid., 220–221.
28. Ibid., 2, 204, , 238–239.
29. Michael Harrington, *Socialism*, 54.
30. Marx and Engels, 135; August H. Nimtz, Jr., *Marx and Engels: Their Contribution to the Democratic Breakthrough*, 59. Verification that Marx and Engels, and movements they inspired, contributed significantly to advances in democracy can be found in: Michael Löwy, *The Theory of Revolution in the Young Marx*; Richard N. Hunt, *The Political Ideas of Marx and Engels*, 2 vols.; Dietrich Rueschemeyer, Evelyne Huber Stephens and John D. Stephens, *Capitalist Development and Democracy*; Geoff Eley, *Forging Democracy: The History of the Left in Europe, 1850–2000*.
31. Muste, *Not By Might*, 44.
32. Paul Tillich, *A Complete History of Christian Thought*, II, 180, 187. Relevant to Tillich's assertion of Marx as theologian is Alasdair MacIntyre, *Marxism and Christianity*.
33. Tillich, 191.
34. Karl Marx, "Contribution to the Critique of Hegel's Philosophy of Law," in Karl Marx and Frederick Engels, *Collected Works*, vol. 3, 182. In many of Marx's 1840s works we find the community/freedom/labor configuration as essential to humanity — see Loyd D. Easton and Kurt H. Guddat, Eds., *Writings of the Young Marx*, 275, 293, 303, 394–395, 457.
35. Howe, Ed., 134, 135, 175,
36. Milovan Djilas, *The New Class, An Analysis of the Communist System*, 44, 46; Ernest Mandel, *Power and Money: A Marxist Theory of Bureaucracy*, 72–73; David J. Dallin, *The Real Soviet Russia*, 121. The inequalities inherent in this system are also explored in the probing conservative critique by David R. Henderson, Robert M. McNab, and Tamas Rossas, "The Hidden Inequality of Socialism," 389–412 — whose fundamental flaw involves the dogmatic equation of socialism with bureaucratic tyranny.
37. For a survey of the complex Yugoslav experience, see: Louis Adamic, *The Eagle and the Roots*; Vladimir Dedijer, *Tito*; Milovan Djilas, *Anatomy of a Moral*; Milojko Drulovic, *Self-Management on Trial*; Bruce McFarlane, *Yugoslavia: Politics, Economics and Society*; Misha Glenny, *The Fall of Yugoslavia*; Catherine Samary, *Yugoslavia Dismembered*.
38. Freda Utley, *The Dream We Lost: Soviet Russia Then and Now*, 126.
39. Oskar Hippe, "… And Red Is the Colour of Our Flag: Memories of Sixty Years in the Workers' Movement*, 234; Stefan Heym, *Five Days in June*, 271–272. The rebellious worker's quotes are from Heym's interesting novel (written from the perspective of a dissident Communist still loyal to the German Democratic Republic), whose picture of the 1953 rising is consistent with material presented in nonfictional accounts: Mary Fulbrook, *The Nation Divided: A History of Germany, 1918–1990*, 188–192; David Childs, *East Germany*, 30–35; Rainer Hildebrandt, *The Explosion: The Uprising Behind the Iron Curtain*; Arnulf Baring, *Uprising in East Germany: June 17, 1953*.
40. Jürgen Rühle, *Literature and Revolution: A Critical Study of the Writer and Communism in the Twentieth Century*, 254. By the time that the restrictions imposed by USSR domination finally lifted in the late 1980s, and some dissident elements struggled for a genuine socialism, the decades of "actually-existing socialism" made for a rapid erosion and non-violent collapse of East Germany and the triumphal reabsorption into a larger capitalist Germany. Aspects of the story can be found in Peter Marcuse, *Missing Marx: A Personal and Political Journal of a Year in East Germany, 1989–1990*, and Dirk Philipsen, *We Were the People: Voices From East Germany's Revolutionary Autumn of 1989*.
41. Isaac Deutscher, "The Tragic Life of a Polrugarian Minister," in *Russia in Transition*, 245; Mandel, *Power and Money*, 74. Brutal interviews with real-life versions of Deutscher's composite can be found in Teresa Toranska, *"Them": Stalin's Polish Puppets*.
42. Imre Nagy, *On Communism*, 50.
43. Ibid., 49, 58, 59. The rich literature on the Hungarian uprising includes: Tamás Aczel and Tibor Meray, *The Revolt of the Mind, A Case History of Intellectual Resistance Behind the Iron Curtain*; Peter Fryer, *Hungarian Tragedy*; François Fejtö, *Behind the Rape of Hungary*; Terry Cox, Ed., *Hungary 1956 — Forty Years On*. Also see: François Fejtö, *History of the People's Democracies: Eastern Europe Since Stalin*; Zbigniew K. Brzezinski, *The Soviet Bloc: Unity and Conflict*; Chris Harman, *Bureaucracy and Revolution in Eastern*

Europe. Nagy had been a trusted Stalinist in the 1930s and 1940s, with ties to the Soviet secret police — making his left-wing critique of Stalinism, embrace of the 1956 uprising, and eventual martyrdom all the more remarkable. See Johanna Granville, "Imre Nagy, Hesitant Revolutionary," and "Imre Nagy, aka 'Volodya' — A Dent in the Martyr's Halo?" While revealing Nagy's contradictions and shadowy past, Granville characterizes his later evolution as "courageous" and "uncompromising" (28, 35).

44. Jacek Kuron and Karol Modzelewski, "An Open Letter to the Party," in Julius Jacobson, Ed., *Soviet Communism and the Socialist Vision*, 263.

45. Oliver MacDonald, Ed. *The Polish August: Documents from the Beginnings of the Polish Workers' Rebellion, Gdansk — August 1980*, 67, 126, 156.

46. Roy Medvedev, *On Socialist Democracy*, 39.

47. Ernest Mandel, *Revolutionary Marxism Today*, 150; Ernest Mandel, *Beyond Perestroika: The Future of Gorbachev's USSR*, 193–195.

48. Mandel, *Revolutionary Marxism Today*, 140.

49. Prabhat Patnaik, "The Past and Future of the Socialist Project," in *The Retreat to Unfreedom: Essays on the Emerging World Order*, 271; Vladimir Glebov (son of the old Bolshevik Lev Kamenev), quoted in Adam Hochschild, *The Unquiet Ghost: Russians Remember Stalin*, 89. A valuable overview can be found in Daniel Singer, *Whose Millennium?*, 12–43, 72–103.

50. Leszek Kolakowski, *Main Currents of Marxism*, vol. 3, 465. This point is emphasized by Moshe Lewin in *Russia, USSR, Russia* (146–147) — "the likes of Suslov and Brezhnev," key representatives of Soviet Communist "orthodoxy" in the 1970s, far from "championing the doctrine of *The Communist Manifesto*," were "dedicated to a status quo that still used some of the terminology of the 'founding fathers' but took good care to geld — actually, destroy — the very essence and content of the original." While during the 1920s and early 1930s, "in the heyday of revolutionary ideology, many propaganda themes were willingly and enthusiastically promoted by politicians, educators, and artists, and in popular festivities, paintings, films, and theatrical productions," by the 1970s "official lectures on 'scientific communism' bored everyone to death," so distant was this official ideology from "the reality of everyday life."

51. David Mandel, "'Why Is There No Revolt?' The Russian Working Class and the Labour Movement," in Leo Panitch and Colin Leys, Eds., *Working Classes, Global Realities: Socialist Register 2001*, 175. Essential works on realities in the late USSR and post-USSR are: David Mandel, *Perestroika and the Soviet People*; David Mandel, *Rabotyagi: Perestroika and After Viewed From Below, Interviews with Workers in the Former Soviet Union*; Archie Brown, *The Gorbachev Factor*; Boris Kagarlitsky, *Square Wheels: How Russian Democracy Got Derailed*; Alexander Buzgalin and Andrei Kolganov, *Bloody October in Moscow: Political Repression in the Name of Reform*; Bertram Silverman and Murray Yanowitch, *New Rich, New Poor, New Russia: Winners and Losers on the Russian Road to Capitalism.*

52. Boris Kagarlitsky, *Russia Under Yeltsin and Putin: Neo-Liberal Autocracy*, 99, 100; Cohen, 158.

53. Quoted in Stephen Cohen, *Failed Crusade: America and the Tragedy of Post-Communist Russia*, 4.

54. Roy Medvedev, *Post-Soviet Russia: A Journey Through the Yeltsin Era*, 84, 162; Stephen Kotkin, *Armageddon Averted: The Soviet Collapse 1970–2000*, 115–116; also see David Kotz and Fred Weir, *Revolution from Above: The Demise of the Soviet System.*

55. Medvedev, *Post-Soviet Russia*, 182, 183; Kotkin, 141; David Mandel, "Why Is There No Revolt?," 176–177.

56. Alexander N. Dourin, "Ten Years Later: Society, 'Civil Society,' and the Russian State," 204–207, 210–211.

57. Timothy Garton Ash, *The Polish Revolution: Solidarity*, 378, 379, 380. Also see Singer, *Whose Millennium?*, 104–128.

58. Carl Bernstein and Marco Politi, *His Holiness: John Paul II*, 497.

59. Still well worth wrestling with are Marx's transformative analysis *Capital*, volume one, and Rosa Luxemburg's critical-minded update of 1913 that describes imperialism, *The Accumulation of Capital*. A critical-minded discussion of these and other works, and of capitalism itself, can be found in Paul M. Sweezy's lucid classic *The Theory of Capitalist Development.*

60. Ralph Nader, "Introduction," *The Big Business Reader: Essays on Corporate America*, Mark Green and Robert Massie, Jr., Eds. 1.

61. Chuck Collins and Felice Yeskel, *Economic Apartheid in America, A Primer on Economic Inequality and Insecurity*, 75, 63, 61; Michael Yates, *Naming the System: Inequality and Work in the Global Economy*, 57.

62. Among sources dealing with such issues, see Tom Bottomore and Robert J. Brym, Eds., *The Capitalist Class, An International Study*.

63. Charles M. Kelly, *Class War in America: How Economic and Political Conservatives Are Exploiting Low- and Middle-Income Americans*, 42, 56, 57, 50; Kevin Phillips, *Boiling Point: Democrats, Republicans and the Decline of Middle Class Prosperity*, xxiv.

64. Eric Toussaint and Denise Comanne, "Globalization and Debt," *IMF/World Bank/WTO: The Free Market Fiasco*, Eric Toussaint and Peter Drucker, Eds., 14; Robert Went, *Globalization: Neoliberal Challenge, Radical Responses*, 21.

65. Went, 16.

66. Prabhat Patnaik, "Globalization and the Theory of Imperialism," in *The Retreat to Unfreedom*, 19, 20, 21; Ronaldo Munck, *Globalisation and Labour*, 8, 10, 11, 82.

67. Toussaint and Comanne, 8; Went, 17.

68. Went, 35.

69. Jerry Kloby, *Inequality, Power, and Development, The Task of Political Sociology*, 164.

70. Joel Kovel, *The Enemy of Nature: The End of Capitalism or the End of the World?*, 4.

71. Paul Kennedy, *Preparing for the Twenty-First Century*, 97, 105, 121.

72. Carl Marzani, *The Wounded Earth, An Environmental Survey*, 7, 39.

73. Kovel, 131; James O'Connor, *Natural Causes: Essays in Ecological Marxism*, 182.

74. John Bellamy Foster, *The Vulnerable Planet: A Short Economic History of the Environment*, 142; Marzani, 197, 199, 215, 216.

75. Shankar Vedantam, "Glacier Could Signal Faster Rise in Ocean Levels," A1; Joverl, 206–212; O'Connor, 182.

76. Quoted in John Bellamy Foster, *Marx's Ecology, Materialism and Nature*, 78–79.

77. Bertram D. Wolfe, *Marxism: One Hundred Years in the Life of a Doctrine*, 207. For a survey of theorizing about why socialism has failed to develop as an effective movement in the U.S., and discussion of the kind of "open Marxism" needed to comprehend this reality, see Paul Le Blanc, "The Absence of Socialism in the United States: Contextualizing Kautsky's 'American Worker,'" 125–170.

78. Tillich, 189.

79. Ibid., 86, 88, 89, 91.

80. Marx and Engels, 128.

81. Kim Moody, *Workers in a Lean World*.

82. Martin Luther King, Jr., *A Testament of Hope, The Essential Writings and Speeches of Martin Luther King, Jr.*, 602.

83. A. Philip Randolph Institute, *A "Freedom Budget" for All Americans*; Anderson, *A. Philip Randolph*, 344–345. For discussion plus excerpts of the Freedom Budget, see Paul Le Blanc, Ed., *Black Liberation and the American Dream: The Struggle for Racial and Economic Justice*, 65–68, 72–73, 79–82, 192–193, 237–242. Also see the comments of one Freedom Budget author on the fragmentation — thanks to the Vietnam War — of the potential alliance needed to bring the Freedom Budget into being, in Michael Harrington, *Fragments of the Century, A Social Autobiography*, 127–128. For a brief critique that dismisses the Freedom Budget (and which, in my view, misses what might have been opportunities for radical activists), see Peter Drucker, *Max Shachtman and His Left*, 293–294.

84. See Leon Trotsky et al., *The Transitional Program for Socialist Revolution*.

85. Leonardo Boff, *The Path to Hope: Fragments from a Theologian's Journey*, 56, 121.

86. Joel Kovel, *History and Spirit: An Inquiry into the Philosophy of Liberation*, 2, 3, 8–9, 12, 13.

87. Marx and Engels, 143–144.

88. Tad Szulc, *Pope John II, The Biography*, 445; Jonathan Kwitney, *The Man of the Century: The Life and Times of John Paul II*, 650; John Cort, *Christian Socialism*, 333. This far-reaching critique of capitalism by the late pontiff is generally ignored by conservative admirers, who prefer his more restrictive views on gender and sexuality, his reigning-in of social radicals, and his limited tolerance of modernist theological currents. Dissident theologian Hans Küng has tartly commented on a tendency since Pope Leo XIII's groundbreaking *Rerum Novarum* (1891) to engage in "skillful combination of absolutism within

the Church with simultaneous social (and sometimes populist) initiatives" (Küng, *The Catholic Church*, 172). There can be no doubt, however, over the sincerity or the profundity of John Paul's critique of capitalism — nor about its correspondence to the critical understanding of such matters by many insightful individuals adhering to a broad range of belief systems.

89. Martin Luther King, Jr., "Where Do We Go From Here?" in *A Testament of Hope, The Essential Writings and Speeches of Martin Luther King, Jr.*, 250, 251, 252.

Chapter 2

The Kingdom of God

1. See Nicolas Berdyaev, *The Russian Revolution*, and Richard Crossman, Ed., *The God That Failed*.
2. Howard Selsam and Harry Martel, *Reader in Marxist Philosophy, From the Writings of Marx, Engels, and Lenin*, 234–235. Also see Karl Marx and Frederick Engels, *Marx and Engels on Religion*, with an introduction by Reinhold Niebuhr.
3. Paul Siegel, *The Meek and the Militant, Religion and Power Across the World*, 37.
4. Bertrand Russell, *Why I Am Not a Christian*, 20.
5. Ibid., 204.
6. Simone Weil, *Waiting for God*, 82.
7. Albert Einstein, *Ideas and Opinions*, 46, 47.
8. Ibid., 49–50, 55, 46–47.
9. Ibid., 56–57, 48–49.
10. Ibid., 50, 47–48, 57–58.
11. Ibid., 53, 48, 49. It should be noted that Einstein's male-biased vocabulary — a product of his (and our) patriarchal culture that often refers to "men" instead of to "men and women" or "people" — obscures the often crucial role of women in the development of religion, particularly of the "heretical" currents to which he attributes such importance.
12. Erich Fromm, *Psychoanalysis and Religion*, 52–53, 63.
13. Dorothee Soelle, *Theology for Skeptics, Reflections on God*, 12, 15. Similar points are made in Walter Rauschenbusch, *A Theology for the Social Gospel*, 167–187.
14. Thomas Paine, *The Age of Reason, Being an Investigation of True and Fabulous Theology*, 33, 45, 47, 49.
15. Ibid., 50, 54, 76.
16. Joel Kovel, *History and Spirit: An Inquiry into the Philosophy of Liberation*, 178, 180, 181, 192, 195. An *asymptote* is a straight line constantly approaching a curve but not touching it.
17. Ibid., 3; Soelle, *Theology for Skeptics*, 22, 40, 100, 112. In the same spirit, theologian Uta Rank-Heineman comments that "Jesus' voice is as much a living voice as ever," but adds that "this Jesus lies buried not only in Jerusalem, but also beneath a mountain of kitsch, tall tales, and Church phraseology" (3), a point she documents while challenging what she sees as myths obscuring the actual teachings of Jesus, in *Putting Away Childish Things*. There appear to be similarities here with early forms of Christianity. Scholar Bart D. Ehrman, for example, tells us of an influential 2nd-century Christian in Rome, "Theodotus, a cobbler by trade, but evidently an inordinately thoughtful and learned one." He maintained that "Jesus was 'a mere man,' born of the sexual union of Joseph and Mary, but chosen by God at his baptism to be the savior of the world." According to Ehrman, Theodotus "may well have proclaimed a Christological view similar to that of Jesus' early followers" (*Lost Christianities*, 152–153, 253). Such observations should not be confused with entertainments offered in Dan Brown's best-selling novel *The Da Vinci Code*, which are deflated in Ehrman's *Truth and Fiction in The Da Vinci Code: A Historian Reveals What We Really Know About Jesus, Mary Magdalene, and Constantine.*
18. Will Herberg, *Faith Enacted As History: Essays in Biblical Theology*, 86, 87, 92–93.
19. Hans Meyerhoff, "Contra Simone Weil," and Jacob Taubes, "The Issue between Judaism and Christianity, Facing Up the the Unresolvable Difference," in Arthur A. Cohen, Ed., *Arguments and Doctrines: A Reader of Jewish Thinking in the Aftermath of the Holocaust*, 73, 81, 418.
20. Homer W. Smith, *Man and His Gods*, 109; Abraham J. Heschel, *The Prophets*, vol. I, 7, and *The Prophets*, vol. II, 264; Megan McKenna, *Prophets: Words of Fire*, 4–5.

21. Seyyed Hossein Nasr, "God: The Reality to Serve, Love, and Know," in Marcus Borg and Ross MacKenzie, Eds., *God at 2000*, 103; Thich Nhat Hanh, *Living Buddha, Living Christ*, 35–36, 55–56. Broader application of this is suggested in Karen Armstrong, *A History of God: The 4000-Year Quest of Judaism, Christianity and Islam*, and some similarity is evident to me in the even more broadly framed meditation Walter Kaufmann, *Religions in Four Dimensions*.

22. Eduardo Hoornaert, *The Memory of the Christian People*, 262, 262, 263.

23. Ibid., 17.

24. Sidney Hook, "The Atheism of Paul Tillich," *Religious Experience and Truth, A Symposium*, 62.

25. Ibid., 63. See Sara Diamond, *Spiritual Warfare: The Politics of the Christian Right*; R. Laurence Moore, *Selling God: American Religion in the Marketplace of Culture*; Bruce Bawer, *Stealing Jesus: How Fundamentalism Betrays Christianity*; Linda Kintz, *Between Jesus and the Market: The Emotions that Matter in Right-Wing America*; and Kimberly Blaker, Ed., *The Fundamentals of Extremism: The Christian Right in America*. Erich Fromm's point — in his stimulating study *You Shall Be As Gods: A Radical Interpretation of the Old Testament and its Tradition*, 179 — is apt: "Such believers have made God into an idol, an omniscient, omnipotent power allied with those who have power on this earth."

26. Leonardo Boff, *Jesus Christ Liberator, A Critical Christology for Our Time*, 52, 53, 72.

27. Pope John XXIII, "Pacem in Terris," in George W. Forell, Ed., *Christian Social Teachings: A Reader in Christian Social Ethics from the Bible to the Present*, 467–471. Quite valuable, with a useful overview of Church history, is Thomas Cahill, *Pope John XXIII*.

28. Albert Schweitzer, *The Quest of the Historical Jesus*, 398, 401.

29. Boff, *Jesus Christ Liberator*, 10; John Dominic Crossan, *The Birth of Christianity: Discovering What Happened in the Years Immediately After the Execution of Jesus*, 40. Two good but divergent summaries drawing from recent research are E.P. Sanders, *The Historical Figure of Jesus*, and John Dominic Crossan, *Jesus: A Revolutionary Biography*. Surveys dealing with recent debates include: Gerd Theissen and Annette Merz, *The Historical Jesus, A Comprehensive Guide*; Russell Shorto, *Gospel Truth: The New Image of Jesus Emerging from Science and History, and Why It Matters*; and Mark Allan Powell, *Jesus as a Figure in History: How Modern Historians View the Man from Galilee*. An impressive overview blending archeology and sociology can be found in Richard A. Horsley and Neil Ascher Silberman, *The Message and the Kingdom: How Jesus and Paul Ignited a Revolution and Transformed the Ancient World*. New material is presented in John Dominic Crossan and Jonathan L. Reed, *Excavating Jesus: Beneath the Stones, Behind the Texts*. Even so sharp and conservative a critic of Crossan and Horsley as Ben Witherington agrees that essential elements in the teachings of Jesus included a radical egalitarianism, a sharp challenge to existing power structures, and a commitment to radical social and political change that would involve the creation of a divinely blessed human community permeated by peace and justice (*The Jesus Quest*, 142–143, 151, 159).

30. Abraham Joshua Heschel, "The God of Israel and Christian Renewal," in *Moral Grandeur and Spiritual Audacity*, Susannah Heschel, Ed., 273, 274; Geza Vermes, *Jesus and the World of Judaism*, 35; Irving M. Zeitlin, *Jesus and the Judaism of His Time*, 119, 120, 121. Also see John Dominic Crossan, "Jesus and the Kingdom: Itinerants and Householders in Earliest Christianity," in Marcus J. Borg, Ed., *Jesus at 2000*, 21–53.

31. Alan F. Sigal, "Jesus and First Century Judaism," in Borg, Ed., *Jesus at 2000*, 59, 61, 69; Howard Thurman, *Jesus and the Disinherited*, 29. Thurman's book first appeared in 1949.

32. Richard M. Rubenstein, *My Brother Paul*, 129.

33. Walter Rauschenbusch, *Christianity and the Social Crisis*, 47, 85–91.

34. James H. Cone, *A Black Theology of Liberation*, 11.

35. Karl Kautsky, *Foundations of Christianity*, 272, 278, 280.

36. Wayne A. Meeks, *The First Urban Christians: The Social World of the Apostle Paul*; Robert H. Smith, "Were the Early Christians Middle Class? A Sociological Analysis of the New Testament," in Norman K. Gottwald, Ed., *The Bible and Liberation, Political and Social Hermeneutics*, 447, 453. See a thoughtful exposition and critique of Kautsky in David McLellan, *Marxism and Religion: A Description and Assessment of the Marxist Critique of Christianity*, 66–72. A more recent and less "reductionist" Marxist account of early Christianity is Archibald Robertson, *The Origins of Christianity*, which explicitly denies that

the early Christians were exclusively proletarian. Another interesting "non-reductionist" work can be found in Milan Machoveč, *A Marxist Looks at Jesus.*

37. Hans Küng, *Christianity: Essence, History, and Future,* 66–67.
38. Crossan, *The Birth of Christianity,* 154–155, 445, 472. Also see Gerhard E. Lenski, *Power and Privilege: A Theory of Social Stratification,* 189–296, and John H. Kautsky, *The Politics of Aristocratic Empires,* 269–292.
39. John Dominic Crossan, *The Historical Jesus: The Life of a Mediterranean Jewish Peasant,* xi, xii.
40. 1 Corinthians 1:26–29, quoted in Hoornaert, 44.
41. Hoornaert, 27, 32, 36–37, 39, 40, 42, 45.
42. Elisabeth Schlusser Fiorenza, *In Memory of Her: A Feminist Theological Reconstruction of Christian Origins,* 152, 153. Also see Elizabeth A. Johnson, *Consider Jesus: Waves of Renewal in Christology,* 97–113, and Karen Jo Torjesen, *When Women Were Priests: Women's Leadership in the Early Church and the Scandal of Their Subordination in the Rise of Christianity.*
43. Hoornaert., 34–35.
44. Kenneth Scott Latrouette, *A History of Christianity,* 94, 105, 106, 108.
45. Kautsky, 321, 323, 374, 380, 381. John Dominic Crossan presents substantial information on the impressive organizing efforts of the early Jesus movement, corroborating Kautsky's point, in *The Birth of Christianity,* 291–476.
46. Hoornaert, 15, 18, 50, 121, 218–232.
47. Kautsky, 384, 386.
48. Ibid., 387, 388, 389.
49. Latrouette, 108; Fiorenza, 334.
50. Hoornaert, 13, 16,
51. Thomas Bokenkotter, *A Concise History of the Catholic Church,* 39, 58, 89, 111.
52. Smith, *Man and His Gods,* 254–257. Malcolm Barber, *The Cathars: Dualist Heretics in Languedoc in the High Middle Ages,* 213. Also see Hans Küng, *The Catholic Church: A Short History,* 95–97.
53. Barber, 1, 107–140; Latrouette, 453–456.
54. Latrouette, 456; Smith, *Man and His Gods,* 257. Also see Helen Ellerbe, *The Dark Side of Christian History;* Hugh Trevor-Roper, *The Rise of Christian Europe;* A.G. Dickens, *Reformation and Society in Sixteenth-Century Europe;* David Christie-Murray, *A History of Heresy.*
55. V.F. Calverton, "Marxism and Religion," 718; Reinhold Niebuhr, "Religion and Marxism," 712, 713; Sidney Hook, "Marxism and Religion," 29, 34. In David McLellan's valuable survey, ample evidence suggests that the Hook/Calverton approach is most consistent with that of Lenin, although "Lenin's extreme views on religion are rendered entirely intelligible by the … appalling mixture of other-worldly spirituality and this worldly subordination to Tsarist autocracy that characterized the Russian Orthodox Church of his time" — McLellan, *Marxism and Religion,* 6, 95–105.
56. Harry Magdoff and Paul M. Sweezy, "Marxism and Religion," in *Churches in Struggle: Liberation Theologies and Social Change in North America,* William K. Tabb, Ed., 194–195. This dovetails with the insightful discussion in Hans Küng, *Does God Exist? An Answer for Today,* 217–261. A valuable Christian exposition of Marxism which thoughtfully explores connections between the two can be found in Arthur J. McGovern, S.J., *Marxism: An American Christian Perspective.* Interconnections traced among significant elements within Latin American Catholicism are discussed in Michael Löwy's *The War of Gods: Religion and Politics in Latin America.*
57. Maxim Gorky, *Mother,* 344, 345.
58. Bertram D. Wolfe, *Three Who Made a Revolution,* 506–507; Dan Levin, *Stormy Petrel: The Life and Work of Maxim Gorky,* 143–156; Robert C. Williams, *The Other Bolsheviks: Lenin and His Critics, 1904–1914,* 146–149; Siegel, *The Meek and the Militant,* 195–198; McLellan, *Marxism and Religion,* 98–103. Interesting statements on religion by Lenin, Trotsky, and two other early Communist figures, Lunacharsky and Yaroslavsky, can be found with statements from a number of figures in the labor and socialist movements in Jerome Davis, Ed., *Labor Speaks for Itself on Religion: A Symposium of Labor Leaders Throughout the World;* also see Arno J. Mayer, *The Furies: Violence and Terror in the French and Russian Revolutions,* 449–482.
59. Julius F. Hecker, *Religion Under the Soviets,* 198–199. Hecker was a victim of the purges in the late 1930s.

60. Quoted by Bertram D. Wolfe, "The Catholic Communist," in *Strange Communists I Have Known*, 55. On another occasion Larkin declared: "I belong to the Catholic Church. I stand by the Cross and the *Bible* and I stand by Marx and his *Manifesto*. I believe in the creed of the Church, apostolic, Catholic, and Roman. I believe in its saints and its martyrs, their struggles and the sufferings of my people…. We do not let the Church stand in the way of our struggle, but neither do we let our struggle stand in the way of the Church" (57–58).
61. John Spargo, *Marxian Socialism and Religion*, 88, 133, 178.
62. *James Connolly: Selected Writings*, 117.
63. Selsam and Martel, Eds., *Reader in Marxist Philosophy*, 90, 152, 272, 273, 274.
64. Reinhold Niebuhr, *The Nature and Destiny of Man, Volume II: Human Destiny*, 87.
65. Joseph Hansen et al., *Leon Trotsky, The Man and His Work*, 124.
66. Dan Levin, 147, 148.
67. Rauschenbusch, *A Theology for the Social Gospel*, 46–47; Reinhold Niebuhr, *An Interpretation of Christian Ethics*, 15, 134, 135; Reinhold Niebuhr, *The Nature and Destiny of Man, Volume I: Human Nature*, 17, 188; Abraham J. Heschel, "A Hebrew Evaluation of Reinhold Niebuhr," in Charles W. Kegley and Robert W. Bretall, Eds., *Reinhold Niebuhr, His Religious, Social, and Political Thought*, 399.

    It is hardly the case that this problem occurs primarily among secular radicals. In *Mere Christianity* (111), C. S. Lewis asks: "How is it that people who are quite obviously eaten up with Pride can say they believe in God and appear to themselves as very religious?" His answer is that "they are worshipping an imaginary God" who "approves of them and thinks them far better than ordinary people."

    This is related to the observation of Father Leo Booth in *When God Becomes a Drug: Breaking the Chains of Religious Addiction* that, for many religious believers, "their only means of gaining self-respect or self-control is to lock themselves into rigid, intolerant perfectionism, harshly judgmental of others who don't follow their rules." He defines religious addiction as "using God, a church, or a belief system as an escape from reality, in an attempt to find or elevate a sense of self-worth or self-being" (16, 38).
68. Niebuhr, *The Nature and Destiny of Man*, Volume I, 178–179.
69. A.J. Muste, "Pacifism and Perfectionism," in Nat Hentoff, Ed., *The Essays of A.J. Muste*, 313, 316–317.
70. Niehbuhr, *Interpretation of Christian Ethics*, 20.
71. Karl Rahner, *Foundations of Christian Faith: An Introduction to the Idea of Christianity*, 110–111. The italicized words appear in a personal communication to the author from Sister Christine Morkovsky, CDP, who identifies this as something Roman Catholics in the Eucharist (thanksgiving as worshipers share bread and wine) "refer to … [as] 'the sin of the world' from which they ask deliverance."
72. Ernesto Cardenal, *The Gospel of Solentiname*, vol. 4, 1–2, 6.

Chapter 3

Lenin — Who Cares?

1. Alfred G. Meyer, *Leninism*, 275.
2. It has often been pointed out that the literal meaning of the Greek word *utopia* is "no where" or "no place." On the other hand, there is another Greek word that is quite similar, *eutopia*, which means "good place" — described, theologically, by John Dominic Crossan as a place "in which God puts an end to this world of injustice and unrighteousness, here below, and replaces it with a world of justice and righteousness, here below," in John Dominic Crossan and Jonathan L. Reed, *Excavating Jesus: Beneath the Stones, Behind the Texts*, 74. Some Christian thinkers believe that God's will can accomplish such ends only through manifesting itself in human thought and action — which, in a sense, is the meaning of Jesus as Christ: the coming together of God and humanity for the purpose of challenging the earthly powers-that-be and creating a society permeated by the spirit of God (the Golden Rule). Of course, such a way of putting things has been embraced by neither Lenin nor his secular critics.
3. Andrei Codrescu, *The Hole in the Flag, A Romanian Exile's Story of Return and Revolution*, 145–146. Commenting on the touching and comic film from Germany, "Goodbye Lenin," dealing with the collapse of Communist East Germany, Celia Hart (daughter of

two key personalities of the Cuban Revolution, Armando Hart and Haydee Santamaria) — who had spent uneasy years in the German Democratic Republic not long before the Berlin Wall and Lenin statues came down — recently added: "You cannot say goodbye to Lenin if he was never welcomed. They did nothing but import his image, marginalize him, turn him into a clown subordinated to the Stalinist bureaucracy. ... Their statues were empty of content and, I think, also of form" (Celia Hart, "Welcome ... Trotsky," *International Viewpoint*, November 2005).

4. Stefan T. Possony, *Lenin: The Compulsive Revolutionary*, vii, 392; Robert Payne, *The Life and Death of Lenin*, 662. Actually, Possony and a co-thinker, Nathaniel Weyl, are themselves closer to intellectual currents that influenced Hitler — with a focus on the importance of races and genetics. One year before Possony's biography of Lenin appeared, they warned against "dysgenic developments" (i.e., downgrading the genetic pool of a population), which can take place when "a mentally inferior race, ethnic subgroup, class, caste, or other division of the social structure subjugates and proceeds to exterminate its betters" — emphasizing that "when we reach the Bolshevik Revolution of 1917, ... a new chapter in the history of internal dysgenic catastrophe opens." They specify that superior intellect "came from the nobility and, to a lesser proportion, from the middle classes [by which they mean businessmen and professionals]," so that "the degree to which the Russian people must have been genetically downgraded can be readily imagined."

   Possony and Weyl characterized Bolshevism as part of a larger trend that sought "rule by the underdog, whether he be such by reason of class or race." Their classically conservative judgment: "What it [i.e., the "underdog" class] may lack in intelligence, knowledge and ability, it makes up for in resentment, envy, the desire to destroy, the urge toward revenge, the wish to soil what is clean and to dwarf whatever towers above it." Denouncing "doctrines of equality, both within and among nations," they argued that those who are superior should not be debilitated by "guilt feelings toward those groups which are poor, ignorant, and shiftless." They insisted that it is folly "to legislate equality among nations, classes, and races, and to impose democracy upon all mankind," and warned that "mental capacity tends to be adequate among peoples and races [such as Northern Europeans] adjusted to cold and temperate climates, but inadequate among those adjusted to hot climates," that it would be a mistake for those who are superior to be "downgraded" by "reproduction patterns" predicated on notions of racial and class equality, and that "the accretion of lethal power in the hands of nation-states dominated by populations incapable of rational thought could be a harbinger of total disaster." See Nathaniel Weyl and Stefan Possony, *The Geography of Intellect*, 144, 147, 266, 267, 268, 271, 288, 289. Obviously, from this standpoint, Lenin — committed to overturning the present social order to create a new and radically democratic society of the free and the equal — is a monster.

5. Marion D. Frankfurter and Gardner Jackson, Eds., *The Letters of Sacco and Vanzetti*, 116–117; also see Paul Avrich, *The Russian Anarchists*. On Vanzetti, his anarchist comrade Nicola Sacco, and their famous case, see: Louis Joughin and Edmund M. Morgan, *The Legacy of Sacco and Vanzetti*; William Young and David Kaiser, *Postmortem: New Evidence in the Case of Sacco and Vanzetti*; and Paul Avrich, *Sacco and Vanzetti, the Anarchist Background*.

6. William J. Duiker, *Ho Chi Minh, A Life*, 97.

7. Poems by Langston Hughes ("Lenin") and Pablo Neruda ("Lines to Lenin") are from Gregory Zlobin et al., Eds., *Lenin in Profile, World Writers and Artists on Lenin*, 265, 295–296.

8. Rex A. Wade, *The Russian Revolution, 1917*, 283.

9. Ibid., 89, 91–97.

10. Ibid., 76.

11. Ibid., 207–209.

12. Raphael R. Abramovitch, *The Soviet Revolution 1917–1939*, 74, 98. In his valuable collection of original sources, *Voices of Revolution, 1917*, editor Mark D. Steinberg concludes that "when the Bolsheviks came to power ... in October 1917, they could draw considerable support from popular opinion — from deeply felt notions about class differences, from wide popular disappointment with the failures of the moderate socialists who had compromised with and even joined the 'bourgeois' government, in the belief in the need for strong state authority" (35). The same story is detailed in Trotsky's classic *The History*

of the Russian Revolution and Alexander Rabinowitch's scholarly *The Bolsheviks Come to Power.*

13. Louise Bryant, *Six Red Months in Russia*, 137; also see Virginia Gardner, *Friend and Lover: The Life of Louise Bryant*, 118–121.

14. "Nadezhda Krupskaya, "Answers to questions put by the Brain Institute in 1935," in *Lenin in Profile*, 410, 411, 414.

15. Orlando Figes, *A People's Tragedy: A History of the Russian Revolution*, 388–389. "The conflict within the group was nerve-wracking business," Krupskaya recalled of the dispute with Bogdanov, adding that Lenin, coming home after one political argument, "looked awful, and even his tongue seemed to have turned grey" — see Nadezhda Krupskaya, *Reminiscences of Lenin*, 193.

16. Robert Service, *Lenin, A Biography*, 493; Figes, 390. Service's phrase "the lovely Inessa" is in reference to the termination of an alleged affair with Inessa Armand — on whom see R.C. Elwood, *Inessa Armand: Revolutionary and Feminist*; far less scholarly but with new information is Michael Pearson, *Lenin's Mistress: The Life of Inessa Armand*. On chess, Lenin's brother Dmitry Ulyanov tells us, "after the Revolution Vladimir Ilyich practically stopped playing chess altogether, saying that it was very tiring; instead he preferred to spend his leisure playing gorodki, taking walks, and shooting," *Reminiscences of Lenin by His Relatives*, 121.

17. Isaac Don Levine, *The Man Lenin*, 13, 36, 157, 160, 176; L. Fotieva, *Pages From Lenin's Life*, 12–13; *Reminiscences of Lenin by His Relatives*, 127, 145, 148, 149; Ronald W. Clark, *Lenin, A Biography*, 48.

18. Levine, 179, 192, 193.

19. Bessie Beatty, *The Red Heart of Russia*, 431–434.

20. In Rex A. Wade's *The Russian Revolution, 1917*, 282, we are told that "the dispersal of the Constituent Assembly effectively marked the end of the revolution. By this action the Bolsheviks announced that they would not be voted from power…. Civil war was inevitable and would now determine the future of Russia and its peoples." This seems wrong for three reasons: (1) it was not simply a Bolshevik decision to disperse the Constituent Assembly — the Left Socialist-Revolutionaries and anarchists concurred, because to do otherwise would mean replacing tsarism only with a new capitalist order; (2) the revolutionary process, regardless of complexities and distortions, certainly continued through 1918 and beyond — into the 1920s; (3) more grimly decisive than the dispersal of the Constituent Assembly for "the future of Russia and its peoples" were international factors — foreign military intervention and economic blockade, and the failure of socialist revolution elsewhere, leaving revolutionary Russia isolated in its backwardness. This matter of the lack of viability of the Constituent Assembly receives intelligent analysis in Moshe Lewin, *The Soviet Century*, 282–289.

21. Albert Rhys Williams, *Through the Russian Revolution*, 276–277, 278.

22. John Reed, *Ten Days That Shook the World*, 129.

23. Granville Hicks, *John Reed, The Making of a Revolutionary*, 397; "Platform and Program, Communist Labor Party," in *Communism in America, A History in Documents*, Ed. by Albert Fried, 31. Warren Beatty's film epic "Reds" (1981) conveys something of Reed's spirit. Also see Max Eastman's loving portrait in *Heroes I Have Known.*

24. Max Eastman, *Marxism — Is It Science?*, 234; these points repeat material that Eastman originally presented in his 1926 (left-wing socialist) work *Marx, Lenin, and the Science of Revolution*, 159–160

25. Max Eastman, *Love and Revolution: My Journey Through an Epoch*, 344.

26. Max Eastman, *Since Lenin Died*, 19, 129, 130. By 1926, however, Zinoviev and Kamenev, along with others (including Lenin's widow Krupskaya), joined in an ill-fated bloc with Trotsky to resist the crystallization of Stalin's bureaucratic tyranny around the conception of "building socialism in one country."

27. Max Eastman, *The End of Socialism in Russia*, 4, 10, 19, 22.

28. Max Eastman, *Stalin's Russia and the Crisis of Socialism*, 104–105.

29. Max Eastman, *Reflections on the Failure of Socialism*, 111, 112–113.

30. Ibid., 30, 32–33; William L. O'Neill, *The Last Romantic, A Life of Max Eastman*, 238–240.

31. Freda Utley, *Odyssey of a Liberal, Memoirs*, 290, 304, 305; O'Neill, 244.

32. Eastman, *Reflections on the Failure of Socialism*, 32–33.

33. Ibid., 45, 52.
34. David Horowitz, *The Politics of Bad Faith, The Radical Assault on America's Future*, 24. Horowitz employs a scattering of impressive yet misleading statistics to make his case — but it is worth perusing a revealing exposé of "How Conservatives Lie With Statistics" in Charles M. Kelly, *Class War in America: How Economic and Political Conservatives Are Exploiting Low- and Middle-Income Americans*, 117–126. Also revealing a significant stratum of right-wing intellectuals as "masters of deceit" is David Brock's *Blinded by the Right: The Conscience of an Ex-Conservative*.

Whether Horowitz is *consciously* trying to deceive is an entirely different question. David Brock has described how his own sincere right-wing journalism ("I believed every word of my reporting was solid and true") was held in "the grip of a partisan tunnel vision that was by now such a part of my nature that it distorted my work, disabling me from finding the truth, without even knowing it" (108). Brock comments that "Horowitz renounced the extremist doctrines and violent tactics of the 1960s radicals he once practiced," adding: "The tragedy of Horowitz was that thirty years later, he was the same violent person, working in behalf of another extreme ideology" (188).

Actually, the reality is more complex. Horowitz distinguished himself in the 1960s by arguing *against* violent tactics. "No revolution was ever built on a negative vision," Horowitz had argued in 1969 against the violent "Weatherman" faction that had arisen inside the new left with which he deeply identified. "Moreover there is no reason even to attempt to build the American revolution as a negative act, a program of social demolition" ("Hand-Me-Down Marxism in the New Left," in Harold Jacobs, Ed., *Weatherman*, 103).

The tragedy may be that a thoughtful left-wing intellectual — in the grip of a dogmatic tunnel vision that would not allow for the existence of Evil on the left-end of the political spectrum — was so deeply shocked by terrible life experiences that, tunnel vision intact, he now saw the left-wing as the essence of Evil, and became locked in mortal combat with his younger self. Horowitz experienced terrible personal and political traumas (particularly unbearable pain over his own indirect responsibility for the murder of a friend by, in his view, certain members of the Black Panther Party, a group that he had supported). This helped push him from left to right. See his thoughtful reflection in David Horowitz, "Roads Not Taken," *Left Illusions, An Intellectual Odyssey*, 441–443.
35. Doug Henwood, *After the New Economy*, 79–143; G. William Domhoff, *Who Rules America? Power and Politics*; David M. Gordon, *Fat and Mean: The Corporate Squeeze of Working Americans and the Myth of Managerial "Downsizing"*; Michael Meeropol, *Surrender: How the Clinton Administration Completed the Reagan Revolution*.
36. Harry Braverman, *Labor and Monopoly Capital: The Degradation of Work in the Twentieth Century*; Harley Shaiken, *Work Transformed: Automation and Labor in the Computer Age*; Kevin Phillips, *Boiling Point: Democrats, Republicans, and the Decline of Middle Class Prosperity*; John Hinshaw and Paul Le Blanc, Eds., *U.S. Labor in the Twentieth Century*.
37. See Ronald H. Chilcote, Ed., *Imperialism: Theoretical Directions* and Wayne Ellwood, *The No-Nonsense Guide to Globalization*, but also Henwood, 145–186.
38. See Paul Kennedy, *Preparing for the Twenty-First Century* and Brian Halweil et al., *State of the World 2004*.
39. Service, *Lenin, A Biography*, 493.
40. See, for example: E. P. Thompson, *The Making of the English Working Class*, and *Customs in Common: Studies in Traditional Popular Culture*; Herbert Gutman, *Work, Culture, and Society in Industrializing America: Essays in American Working-Class and Social History*, and *Power and Culture: Essays on the American Working Class*; Vernon Lidtke, *The Alternative Culture: Socialist Labor in Imperial Germany*; Geoff Eley, *Forging Democracy: The History of the Left in Europe 1850–2000*.
41. Horowitz, *The Politics of Bad Faith*, 52. Horowitz's rather mechanistic and uni-linear conception of "progress" seems blind to ways in which aspects of earlier cultures can and do blend with more "modern" developments, and to the possibility that something which has receded under the impact (of onslaught) of "progress" may have sufficient value for us to retrieve it. Among works addressing such questions are: Frederick Engels, *The Origin of the Family, Private Property and the State*; Eleanor Leacock, *Myths of Male Dominance, Collected Articles on Women Cross-Culturally*; Ruth Benedict, "Human Nature is Not a

Trap"; Carol McAllister, "Uneven and Combined Development: Dynamics of Change and Women's Everyday Forms of Resistance in Negeri Sembilan, Malaysia," 57–98; Michael Löwy, *On Changing the World: Essays in Political Philosophy, from Karl Marx to Walter Benjamin*; Chris Harman, *A People's History of the World*; Howard Zinn, *A People's History of the United States*. Also see Chapter 2 of the present volume.

42. Quoted in Ernst Fischer and Franz Marek, *The Essential Lenin*, 73. This is from a key passage in Lenin's *The State and Revolution*, on which — along with other works by Lenin — Fischer and Marek offer a useful and relatively straightforward explication.

43. Richard Rorty, "The People's Flag Is Deepest Red," *Audacious Democracy: Labor, Intellectuals, and the Social Reconstruction of America*, Ed. by Steven Fraser and Joshua B. Freeman, 59, 60, 63. Rorty rejects Marxism explicitly and with a flourish, yet, as these remarks suggest, his writing is permeated by Marxist influences, sensibilities, and assumptions. He diverges significantly enough to merit Markar Melkonian's full-scale Marxist critique *Richard Rorty's Politics: Liberalism at the End of the American Century*, but anyone caring about the contemporary relevance of Marxism to U.S. realities should read Rorty's challenging polemic *Achieving Our Country: Leftist Thought in Twentieth-Century America*.

44. William Tabb, "Turtles, Teamsters, and Capital's Designs," 45.

45. Michael Yates, "'Workers of All Countries, Unite': Will This Include the U.S. Labor Movement?", 47.

46. C.L. R. James, "Lenin and the Vanguard Party," *The C. L. R. James Reader*, 327.

47. "Communist Manifesto" in Paul Le Blanc, *From Marx to Gramsci: A Reader in Revolutionary Marxist Politics*, 137; Rosa Luxemburg, "The Mass Strike, Political Party and Trade Unions" and "Organizational Questions of Russian Social Democracy," in Waters, Ed., *Rosa Luxemburg Speaks*, 119, 200. Also see Paul Le Blanc, "Luxemburg and Lenin on Revolutionary Organization,"41–56.

48. V. I. Lenin, "One Step Forward, Two Steps Back," in *Selected Works*, vol. 1, 306; Lenin, "The Reorganization of the Party," and "An Appeal to the Party by Delegates to the Unity Congress Who Belonged to the Faction of 'Bolsheviks,'" *Collected Works*, vol. 10, 32, 33, 314. As noted in Chapter 1, Lenin and his co-thinkers, calling themselves Socialists or Social-Democrats up through 1917, later adopted the Communist label. Also see Lars T. Lih, *Lenin Rediscovered: 'What Is to be Done?' in Context*, an incredibly rich work of scholarship that blends wide-ranging and critical connection of texts to historical contexts, cutting through polemical and academic distortions in a manner that sheds considerable light on Lenin's political throught as he helped to forge Russian Bolshevism.

49. Krupskaya, *Reminiscences of Lenin*, 167. Also see Paul Le Blanc, *Lenin and the Revolutionary Party*, and Ernest Mandel, "The Leninist Theory of Organization, in *Revolutionary Marxism and Social Reality in the 20th Century, Selected Essays of Ernest Mandel*, 77–127.

50. Figes, 736, 823–824. There are ample working-class biographies and autobiographies that collide with Figes's vodka-and-vaudeville stereotype: August Bebel from Germany, "Big Bill" Haywood from the United States, Alexander Shlyapnikov from Russia, and countless more from these and many other lands.

51. Antonio Gramsci, *Selections From the Prison Notebooks*, 144. On Gramsci, see Giuseppe Fiori, *Antonio Gramsci, Life of a Revolutionary*. Valuable discussions of his political thought can be found in Dante Germano, *Antonio Gramsci: Architect of a New Politics*, and Anne Shostock Sassoon, *Gramsci's Politics*.

52. Gramsci, 16, 199, 204–205, 332–333, 340.

Chapter 4

From Lenin to Stalin — and Back

1. Stephen Eric Bronner, "Rosa Redux: A Reply to David Camfield and Alan Johnson," 156. Actually, George Lichtheim once made a similar point in *Imperialism*: "Marxism is too important to be left to the post-Leninist sects — tiny ferocious creatures devouring each other in a drop of water" (11).

2. Stephen Eric Bronner, "Moving On: New Replies to New Critics," 226.

3. Ibid., 233.

4. See T. J. Nossiter, *Marxist State Governments in India: Politics, Economics, and Society*, and also Bogdan Szajkowski, Ed., *Marxist Local Governments in Western Europe and Japan Politics*.
5. Bronner, "Moving On," 227.
6. Rosa Luxemburg, *The Accumulation of Capital*.
7. Quoted by Richard Hyman, "Marxism and the Sociology of Trade Unionism," *Trade Unions Under Capitalism*, Tom Clarke and Laurie Clements, Eds., 389. In her 1913 classic *The Accumulation of Capital*, Luxemburg's anthropological sensitivity to the impact of capitalist expansion on the rich variety of the world's peoples and cultures is a quality one cannot find in the other key Marxists works of the early 20th century. The range of Luxemburg's thought, and key aspects of her biography and personality, are elaborated in Paul Le Blanc, Ed., *Rosa Luxemburg, Reflections and Writings*. An indispensable new collection is Peter Hudis and Kevin B. Anderson, Eds., *The Rosa Luxemburg Reader*. Also see Paul Frölich, *Rosa Luxemburg: Her Life and Work*.
8. Rosa Luxemburg, "Organizational Question of Social Democracy," *Rosa Luxemburg Speaks*, 128–129.
9. Carl Schorske, *German Social Democracy, 1905–1917*.
10. "The Russian Revolution," in Hudis and Anderson, 302.
11. "The Revolutionary Proletariat and the Right of Nations to Self-Determination," in Le Blanc, *From Marx to Gramsci*, 206.
12. Moshe Lewin, *The Making of the Soviet System: Essays in the Social History of Interwar Russia*, 22, 23.
13. Orlando Figes, *A People's Tragedy: A History of the Russian Revolution*, 391, 392; Stephen F. Cohen, *Bukharin and the Bolshevik Revolution: A Political Biography, 1888–1938*, 22–25, 34–42, 47–49, 62–69; Voline, *The Unknown Revolution*, 244; on Lunacharsky, Bogadanov, and others in their faction, see Robert C. Williams, *The Other Bolsheviks: Lenin and his Critics, 1904–1914*.
14. Figes, 392–393.
15. Lewin, *The Making of the Soviet System*, 23. Other work that seems not to exist in Bronner's universe includes not only the writings of knowledgeable participants (N. K. Krupskaya, Leon Trotsky, Victor Serge, and others), but also research of an impressive array of historians (E. H. Carr, Isaac Deutscher, Pierre Broué, Marcel Liebman, Alexander Rabinowitch, Stephen Cohen, Leopold Haimson, Roy Medvedev, Ronald Suny, Dianne Koenker, David Mandel, and many more). In *Lenin and the Revolutionary Party* I utilize and cite much of the primary and secondary literature. Anti-Lenin clichés that turn up in Bronner are also challenged by material in André Liebich's fine and sympathetic study of the Mensheviks, *From the Other Shore: Russian Social Democracy After 1921*, 29–95.
16. Lloyd C. Gardner, Walter F. LeFeber, and Thomas J. McCormick, Eds., *Creation of the American Empire*, vol. 2, 336. The interpretation offered here obviously owes much to William Appleman Williams, *The Tragedy of American Diplomacy*.
17. David R. Francis, *Russia From the American Embassy*, 332–334.
18. Ibid, 335.
19. George F. Kennan, *Russia and the West Under Lenin and Stalin*, 50–51; Walter Isaacson, "The World According to Mr. X," 16. Also see Joel Kovel, "George Kennan: Anticommunism From the Mountaintop," in *Red Hunting in the Promised Land: Anticommunism and the Making of America*.
20. Clemenceau quoted in Marc Ferro, *The Great War 1914–1918*, 212–213; Churchill quoted in William H. Chamberlin, *The Russian Revolution, vol. II, 1918–1921: From the Civil War to the Consolidation of Power*, 152.
21. Chamberlin, 168.
22. Ibid., 171. On the impact of civil war and foreign intervention, see Evan Mawdsley, "The Civil War," David S. Fogelsong, "Foreign Intervention," and William G. Rosenberg, "Problems of Social Welfare and Everyday Life," in Edward Acton, Vladimir Iu. Cherniaev, William G. Rosenberg, Eds., *Critical Companion to the Russian Revolution, 1914–1921*, 93–105, 106–114, 633–644, and Moshe Lewin, *Russia, USSR, Russia*, 42–71. On right-wing triumphs over the revolutionary left in this period, see Wolfgang Abendroth, *A Short History of the European Working Class*, 74–78.
23. Hans Kohn, *Living in a World Revolution: My Encounters with History*, 107–108.
24. Ibid., 108, 109.

25. Richard Rorty, *Philosophy and Social Hope*, 17–18.
26. Carr's comment on Wolfe, made in his presence at a scholarly conference, can be found in Richard Pipes, Ed., *Revolutionary Russia: A Symposium*, 384.
27. For biographical essentials, see Bertram D. Wolfe, *A Life in Two Centuries: An Autobiography*, and Robert Hessen, Ed., *Breaking With Communism: The Intellectual Odyssey of Bertram D. Wolfe*, with useful contextual material provided by Robert J. Alexander, *The Right Opposition: The Lovestoneites and the International Communist Opposition of the 1930s*, Ted Morgan, *A Covert Life: Jay Lovestone, Communist, Anti-Communist, and Spymaster*, and Richard Gid Powers, *Not Without Honor, The History of American Anticommunism*.
28. "Lenin and the Uses of Power," *Lenin and the Twentieth Century: A Bertram D. Wolfe Retrospective*, Ed. by Lennard D. Gerson, 179. This is consistent with Wolfe's volume *Three Who Made a Revolution* — which was aptly characterized at the time by Max Shachtman: "There is not a single other work in the world that gives such an extensive and detailed survey of the pre-1914 Russian revolutionary movement.... The immensity of the research into original sources is matched by the carefulness with which the important material is presented." But Shachtman was critical of flaws in methodology that were reflected in Wolfe's style — "the polite mockery, the faint air of condescension, the misplaced irony, the elderly skepticism toward the Russian Revolution and its leaders which is so fashionable nowadays." Max Shachtman, *The Bureaucratic Revolution: The Rise of the Stalinist State*, 172, 173.
29. Hessen, 75–76.
30. Ibid., 76. Richard N. Hunt argues, after meticulous research and analysis, that Wolfe is very much mistaken about the younger Marx's alleged "authoritarian" streak. See Richard N. Hunt, *The Political Ideas of Marx and Engels*, vol. I and *The Political Ideas of Marx and Engels*, vol. II.
31. Hessen, 157, 273–274, 279–282.
32. Arno J. Mayer, *The Furies: Violence and Terror in the French and Russian Revolutions*, 17. In the last portion of this comment, Mayer is quoting an early historian of the French Revolution, Edgar Quinet.
33. Wolfe, "The Influence of Lenin on the History of Our Times: The Question of Totalitarianism," in Gerson, 190, 199, 200, 203, 206. Richard Pipes, *The Russian Revolution* and *Russia Under the Bolshevik Regime, 1918–1924*. For additional context regarding Pipes, see Gary Dorrien, *The Neoconservative Mind: Politics, Culture, and the War of Ideology*. Pipes' two volumes ignore a considerable body of scholarship summarized in: Daniel H. Kaiser, Ed., *The Workers' Revolution in Russia 1917: The View From Below*; Harold Shukman, Ed., *The Blackwell Encyclopedia of the Russian Revolution*; Ronald Suny and Arthur Adams, Eds., *The Russian Revolution and Bolshevik Victory*.

    In the highly publicized and widely circulated volume Richard Pipes, Ed., *The Unknown Lenin: From the Secret Archive* we find interesting documents (at least in one instance offered in "a careless and sloppy" manner) but little that was actually "unknown" by readers of George Leggett's *The Cheka: Lenin's Political Police*, not to mention even earlier (and morally superior) accounts in, for example, Bertrand Russell, *The Practice and Theory of Bolshevism*, Alexander Berkman, *The Bolshevik Myth*, and Isaac Steinberg, *In the Workshop of the Revolution*. The criticism of Pipes is in R.C. Elwood, "Lenin's Testimony to the Extraordinary Investigating Commission," 268–269. Also see a more extensive critique in Peter Kenez, "The Prosecution of Soviet History: A Critique of Richard Pipes' *The Russian Revolution*," 345–352. An interesting survey of currents and countercurrents in historiography on the Russian Revolution after Communism's collapse can be found in Mike Haynes, "The Debate on Popular Violence and the Popular Movement in the Russian Revolution."
34. Samuel Farber, *Before Stalinism: The Rise and Fall of Soviet Democracy*; Neil Harding, *Leninism*; Robert Service, *Lenin, a Political Life*, 3 vols. On the other hand, if one compares Service's 2000 *Lenin, A Biography* with Ronald W. Clark's *Lenin, A Biography* — both having roughly 500 pages — the result is disappointing. Clark's older work is more balanced and reliable.
35. The case for *The State and Revolution*'s "totalitarian" nature is made in A. J. Polan, *Lenin and the End of Politics*. In contrast, see Hannah Arendt, *The Origins of Totalitarianism*, 318–319.

36. For discussion of Lenin's work, see Ralph Miliband, "Lenin's *The State and Revolution*," in *Class Power and State Power, Political Essays*, 154–166, and Jules Townshend, "Lenin's *The State and Revolution*: An Innocent Reading.*" On the Marxist idealization of Athenian democracy, see Richard N. Hunt, *The Political Ideas of Marx and Engels*, vol. I, 82–84, and *The Political Ideas of Marx and Engels*, vol. II, 253–256, and also C. L. R. James, *Any Cook Can Govern*.

37. Ralph Miliband, *Marxism and Politics*, 141.

38. Mayer, *The Furies*, 231. Among the sources which discuss such realities are those provided by a partisan of the Bolshevik regime, Victor Serge — in his *Memoirs of a Revolutionary* and his novel *Conquered City*.

39. Robert C. Tucker, *Stalin as Revolutionary: 1879–1929*, 208.

40. Lenin, "All Out for the Fight Against Denikin!" *Selected Works*, vol. 3, 240.

41. Leon Trotsky, *Terrorism and Communism*, 58, 59, 63,

42. Isaac Deutscher, *Marxism In Our Time*, 85–86. For contemporary Bolshevik explanations of what they were doing, see Al Richmond, Ed., *In Defence of the Russian Revolution, A Selection of Bolshevik Writings 1917–1923*. A worthwhile latter-day debate on such issues, including capable defense of the Bolsheviks, can be found in John Rees et al., *In Defence of October: A Debate on the Russian Revolution*.

43. Gorky quoted in Jürgen Rühle, *Literature and Revolution: A Critical Study of the Writer and Communism in the Twentieth Century*, 29; also see Maxim Gorky, *Untimely Thoughts: Essays on Revolution, Culture, and the Bolsheviks, 1917–1918*. On the theoretical issue, see Hal Draper, *The "Dictatorship of the Proletariat" From Marx to Lenin*.

44. Trotsky, *Terrorism and Communism*, 169–170. It should be added, however, that Trotsky was among the early and most consistent critics of the crystallization of bureaucratic dictatorship in the Soviet republic — see *The Challenge of the Left Opposition*, 3 vols., and Isaac Deutscher's trilogy on Trotsky's life: *The Prophet Armed, The Prophet Unarmed*, and *The Prophet Outcast*. A classic survey of dissident Communism is offered in Robert V. Daniels, *The Conscience of the Revolution: Communist Opposition in Soviet Russia*.

45. Victor Serge, *Year One of the Russian Revolution*, 353. Also see: Diane Koenker, William G. Rosenberg, and Ronald Grigor Suny, Eds., *Party, State, and Society in the Russian Civil War*; Paul Avrich, *Kronstadt 1921*; Roy Medvedev, *The October Revolution*, Alec Nove, *An Economic History of the USSR*; E. H. Carr, *The Bolshevik Revolution*, vol. II.

46. Quoted in Tony Cliff, *Lenin, vol. 3: The Revolution Besieged*, 141, 142.

47. Mayer, *The Furies*, 230.

48. Boris Souvarine, *Stalin: A Critical Survey of Bolshevism*, 253–254. One could challenge this generalization with the modifiers that the extent of revolutionary and counter-revolutionary violence, and also the extent to which the revolution is accompanied by a civil war, will determine the extent to which there is "barbarism." Of course, both the French and Russian revolutions were violent and accompanied by horrific civil wars, which is true of most revolutions — including the American (as documented in Ray Raphael's *A People's History of the American Revolution*).

49. Max Shachtman, "The 'Mistakes' of the Bolsheviks," in *The Fate of the Russian Revolution*, Sean Matagamna, Ed., 173.

50. Arendt, *The Origins of Totalitarianism*, 318–319. This perspective is substantially supported by Moshe Lewin's analysis in his recent *The Soviet Century*, 15–31, 295–300, at the conclusion of which he argues that "the conflict between Lenin and Stalin over the making of the USSR ... involved a clash between two political camps: between what was still 'Bolshevism' — a radical branch of Russian and European Social-Democracy — and a new current that emerged from the Bolshevik Party and which would become known by the name of 'Stalinism.'"

51. Vladimir Brovkin, *Russia After Lenin: Politics, Culture and Society 1921–1929*, 222. Brovkin's volume provides a valuable survey of 1920s realities, although he all too often seriously oversimplifies (sometimes to the point of caricature) complexities and contradictions in Lenin and the Bolsheviks to buttress the "Leninism-leads-to-Stalinism" thesis. Also he asserts (222): "The alternative to Stalinism would have been a multiparty system and a market economy." Arendt, I think, is closer to the mark by suggesting more than one alternative to Stalinism; also, a more likely possibility than the triumph of capitalism under Bolshevik rule would have been a particular form of *mixed economy* (which could have moved forward to socialism as working-class revolutions triumphed in more

countries). This issue has been explored in Paul Le Blanc, *Workers and Revolution: A Comparative Study of Bolshevik Russia and Sandinist Nicaragua*. For a valuable journalistic account of post-civil war developments, see Anna Louise Strong, *For the First Time in History: Two Years of Russia's New Life (August 1921 to December 1923)*, with a preface by Leon Trotsky. Qualitative shifts from the time of Lenin to that of Stalin are recorded in serious accounts by two U.S. journalists, William H. Chamberlin and Eugene Lyons, both initially very sympathetic to the Bolshevik cause. Chamberlin shows a hopeful revolution and a brutalizing civil war in *The Russian Revolution, 1917–1921*, 2 vols., the upward recovery of the 1920s in *Soviet Russia, A Living Record and a History*, and the downward descent in *Russia's Iron Age*. Lyons surveys the transition to Stalinism from the late 1920s to the mid-1930s in his devastating classic *Assignment in Utopia*. E. H. Carr, *The Bolshevik Revolution: 1917–23*, 3 vols., and *The Interregnum: 1923–24* are indispensable. For more recent scholarly work, see Lewis Siegelbaum, *Soviet State and Society Between Revolutions, 1918–1929*, plus Sheila Fitzpatrick, Alexander Rabinowitch, and Richard Stites, Eds., *Russia in the Era of NEP: Explorations in Soviet Society and Culture*, and Moshe Lewin, *Russia, USSR, Russia*.

52. Robert C. Tucker, *Stalin in Power: The Revolution From Above, 1928–1941*, 3, 8–9.

53. Ibid., 8, 65. A useful brief survey is offered in E. H. Carr, *The Russian Revolution: From Lenin to Stalin*. An essential account is offered in Roy Medvedev, *Let History Judge: The Origins and Consequences of Stalinism* — but this in no way supersedes the two classics of 1937, Leon Trotsky's *The Revolution Betrayed* and Victor Serge's *Russia Twenty Years After*.

54. The concluding eight chapters of Marx's *Capital* deal with primitive accumulation, with Marx noting that capital comes into the world "dripping from head to foot, from every pore, with blood and dirt" (*Capital*, volume I, 760).

55. The concept was developed by a one-time opponent of Stalin and ally of Trotsky, Eugen Preobrazhensky, but was given a particularly brutal reinterpretation and murderous thrust by the Stalin regime. See: Isaac Deutscher, *The Prophet Unarmed, Trotsky: 1921–1929*, 234–238, 415–418, 441–442, 454–456, and Nove, *An Economic History of the U.S.S.R.*, 125–126, 207–208, 221–223.

56. Mikhail Baitalsky, *Notebooks for the Grandchildren: Recollections of a Trotskyist Who Survived the Stalin Terror*, 324, 348, 349.

57. Ibid., 37, 38.

58. Aleksandr I. Solzhenitsyn, *The Gulag Archipelago Two*, 10; Steven Merritt Miner, "The Other Killing Machine," 11. We have noted that the word "gulag" is derived from an acronym referring to the Central Administration of Camps. Nicolaevsky and Dallin, noting the 1930 date for the formal organization of the vast network of labor camps, comment that in the Lenin era "forced labor in prisons, the Soviet leadership insisted and Soviet penologists reiterated, is slavery" — that is, something to be rejected — see David J. Dallin and Boris I. Nicolaevsky, *Forced Labor in Soviet Russia*, 153, 208, 211. This is corroborated in Oleg V. Khlevniuk, *The History of the Gulag: From Collectivization to the Great Terror*.
    Critical evaluations of Solzhenitsyn's argument can be found in Ernest Mandel, "Solzhenitsyn's Assault on Stalinism ... and on the October Revolution," in *Revolutionary Marxism and Social Reality in the 20th Century*, 19–31; Roy Medvedev, "Solzhenitsyn's Gulag Archipelago: Part II," in *Twenty-Five Years of Dissent: An American Tradition*, Irving Howe, Ed., 326–340; Daniel Singer, *The Road to Gdansk*, 19–60; and Paul N. Siegel, *The Great Reversal: Politics and Art in Solzhenitsyn*.

59. Dallin and Nicolaevsky, 154, 155–156, 299–300, 302–303.

60. Ibid., 191; Robert Conquest, *The Great Terror, A Reassessment*, 311. Ronald G. Suny, *The Soviet Experiment*, 264–265, 266; Lewin, *Russia, USSR, Russia*, 331–354; Sheila Fitzpatrick, *The Russian Revolution*, 166; Lewin, *The Soviet Century*, 397–400; Khlevniuk, *History of the Gulag*, 304–306. Champions of Conquest, John Earl Haynes and Harvey Klehr, comment that new data indicates his earlier guess of 20 million deaths during the Great Purge needs to be revised downward "to ten or as low as five million" (*In Denial*, 254). Such matters have been fiercely contested terrain among historians.

61. Dallin and Nicolaevsky, 40, 168–190, 191, 258; Joseph Berger, *Shipwreck of a Generation*, 209. Berger's memoir is especially valuable for its first-hand survey and detailed recounting of the many different varieties of "political" camp victims. Ironically, Vyshinsky — the vicious chief prosecutor during the showcase purge trials of the late 1930s that destroyed

so many of the leading old Bolsheviks — was sometimes a voice of moderation! In a letter to the secret police, he complained that many of the arrests of the period were of innocent people who might be loyal to Stalin and the regime but had engaged in "everyday babbling, grumbling, dissatisfaction with the poor work of individual persons or organizations ... and also for singing popular ditties and songs with anti-Soviet contents." See Robert W. Thurston, *Life and Terror in Stalin's Russia*, 9.

62. Elinor Lipper, *Eleven Years in Soviet Prison Camps*, 105–106.
63. Conquest, 320, 338, 339.
64. Conquest, 251.
65. Mayer, *The Furies*, 310.
66. Ibid., 658.
67. Elisabeth Young-Bruehl, *Hannah Arendt: For Love of the World*, 411; Whittaker Chambers, "The End of a Dark Age Ushers in New Dangers," *Life*, April 30, 1956, reprinted in *Ghosts on the Roof*, 280; Medvedev, *Let History Judge*, 588, 642. Some commentators, in contrast to Medvedev, argue that Stalin was a close and valued collaborator of Lenin in the pre-1917 underground — but the documented reality is closer to Medvedev's assertion, as is clear, for example, in Robert C. Tucker, *Stalin as Revolutionary*, 142–180. The same volume also indicates divergences between the two from 1917 onward. Also see Lewin, *The Soviet Century*, 14–18, and Lewin, *Russia, USSR, Russia*, 145–170, 251–254.
68. William Z. Foster, *The Russian Revolution*, 40–42, 43.
69. William Z. Foster, *Toward Soviet America*, 140–142.
70. "Memoirs of Aleksandra Chumakova," in *Samizdat: Voices of the Soviet Opposition*, George Saunders, Ed., 190, 192.
71. Anna Louise Strong, *I Change Worlds*, 394–397. Strong — a passionate supporter of the Russian Revolution and the Soviet regime — concluded that the privileges were simply a stage in the long-term abolition of inequality. See Tracy B. Strong and Helene Keyssar, *Right in Her Soul: The Life of Anna Louise Strong*.
72. Berger, 89–90.
73. Ibid., 90; Michel Reiman, *The Birth of Stalinism: The USSR on the Eve of the "Second Revolution,"* 118, 119.
74. Kevin Murphy, *Revolution and Counterrevolution: Class Struggle in a Moscow Metal Factory*, 202–217; Fred Beal, *Proletarian Journey: New England, Gastonia, Moscow*, 254.
75. Ibid., 353; Leopold Trepper, *The Great Game*, 47.
76. Sheila Fitzpatrick, *Everyday Stalinism: Ordinary Life in Extraordinary Times, Soviet Russia in the 1930s*, 8–11.
77. Ibid., 9, 10.
78. Ibid., 10, 11.
79. Mark D. Steinberg, "Introduction," Maxim Gorky, *Untimely Thoughts: Essays on Revolution, Culture, and the Bolsheviks, 1917–1918*, xxiii–xxv.
80. Wendy Goldman, "Stalinist Terror and Democracy: The 1937 Union Campaign," 1449, 1452; Lewin, *Russia, USSR, Russia*, 187, 188, 226; Lewin, *The Soviet Century*, 98. Peter Calvocoressi, Guy Wint, and John Pritchard, *The Penguin History of the Second World War*, 480, 481, 484–485.
81. Fitzpatrick, 224–225.
82. Ibid., 8–9, 14–15.
83. Alan Adler, Alix Holt, and Barbara Holland, Eds., *Theses, Resolutions, and Manifestos of the First Four Congresses of the Third International*, 235.
84. Joseph Stalin, "Interview With the First American Labor Delegation in Russia," in *What is Leninism?*, 46.
85. Quoted in Le Blanc, *Lenin and the Revolutionary Party*, 5; see V. Sorin, "Lenin's Teachings About the Party," *The Party Organizer*, May, June, and July 1931.
86. Brovkin, 46, 54, 55, 123, 209.
87. Quoted in Ruhle, 17.
88. Leon Trotsky, "What Next?" in *The Struggle Against Fascism in Germany*, 213; Brovkin, 209.
89. Thurston, 16. Riutin was arrested in 1932, and a small group of his co-thinkers (or, in some cases, people who had simply seen his document without reporting him to the authorities) were expelled from the Communist Party. While Stalin demanded Riutin's death, a majority of the central leadership (seemingly loyal Stalinists, but most of whom

would themselves be dead in a few years) disagreed. Riutin died in the gulag several years later. Also see J. Arch Getty and Oleg V. Naumov, Eds., *The Road to Terror: Stalin and the Self-Destruction of the Bolsheviks, 1932–1939*, 52–61. As the Riutin documents suggest, it is misleading to speak of the Bolsheviks' "self-destruction," as opposed to their destruction by the bureaucratic dictatorship led by Stalin. This is corroborated in V. P. Danilov, "The Historical Significance of Alternatives to Stalinism," 53–69.

90. On Lenin's struggle against Stalin, see Moshe Lewin, *Lenin's Last Struggle*. On the imposition of Stalin's brand of "Leninism" on the Communist International, see: Leon Trotsky, *The Third International After Lenin*; Helmut Gruber, Ed., *Soviet Russia Masters the Comintern: International Communism in the Era of Stalin's Ascendancy*; Fernando Claudin, *The Communist Movement, From Comintern to Cominform*, 2 vols.; Paolo Spriano, *Stalin and the European Communists*. On Stalin's "revolution from above," see Robert V. Daniels, Ed., *The Stalin Revolution*; also essays by Robert C. Tucker, Roy Medvedev, Moshe Lewin, Alexander Erlich, and Stephen Cohen in Robert C. Tucker, Ed., *Stalinism: Essays in Historical Interpretation*.

91. Medvedev, *Let History Judge*, 652; Vittorio Vidali, *Diary of the Twentieth Congress of the Communist Party of the Soviet Union*, 55.

92. Thurston, 16–18, 26, 31, 35, 38.

93. Vidali, 133, 134–135. Grim data on the purges' impact on the Communist International is provided in William J. Chase, *Enemies Within the Gates? The Comintern and the Stalinist Repression, 1934–1939*.

94. Burnett Bolloten, *The Spanish Civil War: Revolution and Counter-Revolution*, 284.

95. Vidali, 48, 62, 63. While in the Soviet Union in the pivotal year 1927, Vidali was not inclined to distinguish Stalinism from Communism. He proudly mentions his dismissing "some small, brief disillusionments" in a letter to a friend; he goes on to assert: "A Marxist has got to be a cold rationalizer, a Leninist must aim straight to his own goal," and a Communist Party member must work "to deserve the love of the comrades" — a passionate orientation that he maintained for many years. During the Spanish Civil War, as a buoyantly idealistic Italian volunteer and experienced Comintern operative, Vidali — under the name Carlos Contreras — organized the legendary Fifth Regiment. He "combined almost superhuman driving power with an unbreakable gaiety," according to Claud Cockburn. "Ruthless, but able, dedicated and imaginative" was how Carl Marzani has described his friend, who played such a key role in the defense of Madrid. See Dorothy Gallagher, *All the Right Enemies: The Life and Murder of Carlo Tresca*, 141; Bolloten, 266–271; and Carl Marzani, *The Education of a Reluctant Radical: Spain, Munich, and Dying Empires*, Book 3, 30–32. Another vital connection of Vidali's involved his relationship with the vibrant and remarkable Italian-American-Mexican photographer and activist Tina Modotti — see Mildred Constantine, *Tina Modotti: A Fragile Life*, and Patricia Albers, *Shadows, Fire, Snow: The Life of Tina Modotti*.

96. Vidali, 155.

97. Georg Lukács, *The Process of Democratization*, 128–129.

98. Vidali, 154.

99. Eugenia Semyonovna Ginzburg, *Journey Into the Whirlwind*, 176, 177.

100. Vidali, 48, 55. In fact, as he commented on his 80th birthday, Vittorio Vidali had been an enthusiastic Stalinist "for thirty or forty years," and "I must struggle against the remnants of Stalinism in myself." Some years before, he had been implicated in the 1937 murder of the Trotskyist-influenced POUM leader Andres Nin in Spain, in the 1940 conspiracy to murder Leon Trotsky in Mexico, and (perhaps less plausibly) in the 1942 murder of Italian-American anarchist Carlo Tresca. Vidali had protested that "I don't believe in killing opponents of the Soviet Union through my own actions," yet there is evidence (Gallagher, 150–162, 246–247, 263–266, and Bolloten, 506–507) that he was not free from all guilt. Trotsky himself seems to have viewed such Stalinists as Vidali as "a legitimate part of the workers' movement .... They are still inspired by October. They are a selection of revolutionary elements, abused by Moscow but honest .... They are a contradictory phenomenon. They began with October as the base, they have become deformed, but they have great courage .... Even the assailants on Trotsky's house had great courage." See "Discussions With Trotsky, June 12–25, 1940," *Writings of Leon Trotsky, 1939–40*, 282.

101. Leon Trotsky, "Stalinism and Bolshevism." *Writings of Leon Trotsky, 1936–37*, 419, 420–421.

102. See "The Crisis Has Matured," 371; "The Impending Catastrophe and How to Combat It," 248; "Can the Bolsheviks Retain State Power?" 418; "Report on the Review of the Programme and on Changing the Name of the Party," 604–605, 607 — all in V. I. Lenin, *Selected Works*, vol. 2. David Dallin and Boris Nicolaevsky comment that "doubts were alien to Lenin and his party," adding that "freedom from doubt was a prerequisite of their great dynamism" (*Forced Labor in Russia*, 150).

103. Lenin, "Political Report of the Central Committee, Seventh Congress of the R.C.P. (B.)," *Selected Works*, vol. 2, 580; Lenin, "Letter to American Workers," *Selected Works*, vol. 3, 27, 28.

105. Evelyn Anderson, *Hammer or Anvil: The Story of the German Working-Class Movement*, and Pierre Broué, *The German Revolution 1917–1923*.

106. Informative accounts from knowledgeable participant-observers — partisan and a critic alike — can be found in Victor Serge, *Year One of the Russian Revolution* plus *Russia Twenty Years After*, and Raphael R. Abramovitch, *The Soviet Revolution 1917–1939*.

107. Howard K. Beale, *Theodore Roosevelt and the Rise of America to World Power*; N. Gordon Levin, Jr., *Woodrow Wilson and World Politics: America's Response to War and Revolution*; V. G. Kiernan, *The Lords of Human Kind: Black Man, Yellow Man, and White Man in an Age of Empire*; Clive Ponting, *Churchill*.

108. Smedley Butler, "'In Time of Peace': The Army," 8. This article was part of a series run in the October, November, and December issues of the magazine *Common Sense* during 1935. Also see Scott Nearing and Joseph Freeman, *Dollar Diplomacy: A Study in American Imperialism*.

109. Lloyd C. Gardner, *Architects of Illusion, Men and Ideas in American Foreign Policy, 1941–1949*; Walter Isaacson and Evan Thomas, *The Wise Men: Six Friends and the World They Made*; William Appleman Williams, *The Tragedy of American Diplomacy*; John Dean, *Blind Ambition: The White House Years*; Walter Isaacson, *Kissinger, A Biography*.

110. Quoted from two different sources — James Burnham, *The Struggle for the World*, 55, and James Burnham, "Joys and Sorrows of Empire," 749; also see Paul Le Blanc, "From Revolutionary Intellectual to Conservative Master-Thinker: The Anti-Democratic Odyssey of James Burnham." Aspects of Burnham's (and our) context can be found in Lloyd C. Gardner, *Imperial America: American Foreign Policy Since 1898*; Harry Magdoff, *Imperialism: From the Colonial Age to the Present*; William Blum, *Killing Hope: U.S. Military and CIA Intervention Since World War II*.

111. Nathaniel Weyl and Stefan Possony, *The Geography of Intellect*, 270, 271. That the Weyl/Possony approach is scientifically dubious is indicated by more recent works, for example, Stephen Jay Gould, *The Mismeasure of Man*, and Dean Keith Simonton, *Origins of Genius: Darwinian Perspectives on Creativity*. The existence of relatively egalitarian classless societies, in contrast to Weyl's and Possony's claims, is documented in Chapter 2 of the present volume.

112. Antonio Gramsci, *Selections From the Prison Notebooks of Antonio Gramsci*, 144.

113. A. J. Muste, *Not By Might: Christianity, The Way to Human Decency*, 59; Dorothy Day, *The Long Loneliness, An Autobiography*, 86.

114. Georg Lukács, *Lenin: A Study on the Unity of His Thought*), 9–13; James P. Cannon, *The First Ten Years of American Communism, Report of a Participant*, 271, 304.

115. On continuity in Marx, Engels, Luxemburg, Trotsky, Gramsci, see Paul Le Blanc, *From Marx to Gramsci*. The discussion of Leninist thought presented here is largely based on material presented in that work and in Paul Le Blanc, *Lenin and the Revolutionary Party*. Substantial elaboration and documentation of these ten components can be found in those volumes. To place Lenin's thought on many questions discussed here within the larger framework of analyses developed by Marxists, see Jules Townshend, *The Politics of Marxism, The Critical Debates*.

116. Le Blanc, *Lenin and the Revolutionary Party*, 17–18.

117. Ibid., 44–46.

118. Ibid., 95–96.

119. Ibid., 66–67.

120. Ibid., 203–204.

121. Le Blanc, *From Marx to Gramsci*, 59; Le Blanc, *Lenin and the Revolutionary Party*, 341–342.

122. Le Blanc, *From Marx to Gramsci*, 206.

123. Le Blanc, *Lenin and the Revolutionary Party*, 104.
124. Le Blanc, *From Marx to Gramsci*, 69–70.
125. Material from Lenin presented here is drawn largely from Lenin's *Imperialism, The Highest Stage of Capitalism*, summarized in Paul Le Blanc, "Imperialism With a Human Face," 13–14; Le Blanc, *Lenin and the Revolutionary Party*, 214–217, 250–253; and Le Blanc, *From Marx to Gramsci*, 33–35. Kevin Anderson's points are in *Lenin, Hegel, and Western Marxism, A Critical Study*, 135, 141.
126. V. I. Lenin, "Letter to American Workers," *Selected Works*, vol. 3, 27; Le Blanc, *Lenin and the Revolutionary Party*, 253, 311. In the documents of the Communist International from 1919 through 1924 one finds an incredibly rich pooling of experience, analyses, and insights — almost breathtaking in their historical and geographical sweep, and impressive in their great attention to detail, as can be seen in Adler, Holt, Holland, Eds., *Theses, Resolutions and Manifestos of the First Four Congresses of the Third International*. Also see the thoughtful account of the early Communist International and its context by participant-observer Alfred Rosmer, *Moscow Under Lenin*.
127. Service, *Lenin, a Political Life*, vol. 3, 323. For an eloquent account of the "long-ago" degeneration and corruption that helps us understand the more recent collapse, see C. L. R. James, *World Revolution 1917–1936*.
128. C. Wright Mills, *The Marxists*, 35; Jean-Paul Sartre, *Search for a Method*, xxxiv, 6–8.
129. Sartre, 116. On reality's dialectical "trickiness," see Paul Le Blanc, "The Philosophy and Politics of Freedom," and John Rees, *The Algebra of Revolution: The Dialectic and the Classical Marxist Tradition*.

Chapter 5

The Red Decade

1. Eugene Lyons, *The Red Decade: The Stalinist Penetration of America*, 5–17. A solid study that challenges oversimplifications in Lyons' account without dismissing it altogether can be found in Frank A. Warren, *Liberals and Communism: The "Red Decade" Revisited*.
2. Muste also played a central role in Brookwood Labor College, which during the 1920s and early '30s helped to transform the U.S. trade union movement during the turbulent 1930s. It also helped prepare such civil rights activists of the future as Ella Baker and Pauli Murray. See: Paul Le Blanc, "Brookwood Labor College," in *Encyclopedia of American Social Movements*, volume two, Immanuel Ness, Ed., 596–603; Joanne Ooiman Robinson, *Abraham Went Out: A Biography of A. J. Muste*; Richard J. Altenbaugh, *Education for Struggle: The American Labor Colleges of the 1920s and 1930s*; Charles F. Howlett, *Brookwood Labor College and the Struggle for Peace and Social Justice in America*; Barbara Ransby, *Ella Baker and the Black Freedom Movement, A Radical Democratic Vision*, 73–74.
3. Granville Hicks, *Where We Came Out*, 68–69.
4. Studies that indicate what is argued here include Charles Rumford Walker, *American City, A Rank and File History*; Louis Adamic, *My America, 1928–1938*; Gary Gerstle, *Working-Class Americanism: The Politics of Labor in a Textile City, 1914–1960*; and Lizabeth Cohen, *Making a New Deal: Industrial Workers in Chicago, 1919–1939*.
5. Robert S. McElvaine, *The Great Depression, America, 1929–1941*, 221–223.
6. Bertram D. Wolfe, *Diego Rivera, His Life and Times*, 358–359.
7. Ibid., 359–360, 363.
8. Ibid., 368.
9. Paul Le Blanc, "Strikes of 1934," *Encyclopedia of American Social Movements*, volume two, 593–595.
10. Albert Fried, Ed., *Communism in America: A History in Documents*, 7, 281.
11. Harry Fisher, *Comrades: Tales of a Brigadista in the Spanish Civil War*, 15, 16.
12. Peter N. Carroll, *The Odyssey of the Abraham Lincoln Brigade: Americans in the Spanish Civil War*, 204. There were dissonant notes — particularly as the Communists following the USSR's dictator Joseph Stalin mobilized, brutally and lethally, against Spanish anarchists, and especially revolutionary socialists associated with the Workers Party of Marxist Unity (the POUM), who had wanted to move in a revolutionary direction. Earl Browder — enthusing over "the crushing of the reptile 'fifth column'" in Spain— asserted that "if there should arise in America anything similar to the situation in Spain where the democratic republic, while repulsing the fascist invasion, was stabbed in the back by the

'uncontrollable extremists' (a minority of the Anarchists and the Trotskyite P.O.U.M.) then we, like our brothers of the Spanish Communist Party, would be in the forefront to suppress such 'extremists' who are really agents of fascism, and render them harmless" (Earl Browder and Bill Lawrence, *Next Steps to Win the War in Spain*, 7, 11).

The perspective of the Spanish Communists — shaped by Stalin and supported by the International Brigades — would give some of the U.S. volunteers second thoughts. "Because of the soft-pedalling of its revolutionary aims, its failure to call for the expropriation of the capitalists and the distribution of land, its own followers were getting dissatisfied," reflected Sandor Voros, in regard to many workers and peasants in Spain, "while the nonparty majority was beginning to resent more and more the party's ruthless drive for absolute control" (Sandor Voros, *American Commissar*, 453). Another ex-Communist, William Herrick, went further: "We had betrayed the revolution, we were the most counter-revolutionary party in Spain" (William Herrick, *Jumping the Line: The Adventures and Misadventures of an American Radical*, 187). A majority of those in the Lincoln Battalion (and of later Lincoln vets) were inclined to embrace Browder's viewpoint. "There was a mood that said whoever isn't with us is against us," Steve Nelson would later recall. "To an extent the Stalinist influence, which led to criminal actions in the Soviet Union, also operated in Spain" (Steve Nelson, with James R. Barrett and Rob Ruck, *Steve Nelson, American Radical*, 237). But as Peter Carroll notes, "this denunciation of Trotskyists, anarchists, and left-wing Socialists, besides serving sectarian purposes, reflected a larger commitment to the Popular Front strategy" (130). That strategy is discussed later in this chapter.

13. Langston Hughes, "Tomorrow's Seed," Alvah Bessie and Albert Prago, Eds., *Our Fight: Writings by Veterans of the Abraham Lincoln Brigade, Spain 1936–1939*, 22.
14. Michael Denning, *The Cultural Front: The Laboring of American Culture in the Twentieth Century*, xvi; Alfred Kazin, *Starting Out in the Thirties*, 50.
15. Kazin, *Starting Out in the Thirties*, 12–13.
16. Annette Rubinstein, *American Literature, Root and Flower: Significant Poets, Novelists and Dramatists, 1775–1955*, two volumes in one, 769; Wendy Smith, *Real Life Drama: The Group Theatre and America, 1931–1940*, 159.
17. Kazin, *Starting Out in the Thirties*, 82; Smith, 198.
18. Marc Blitzstein, "The Cradle Will Rock," in *The Best Short Plays of the Social Theatre*, William Kozlenko, Ed., 158–159.
19. Ibid., 166–167.
20. Quoted in Tim Robbins, *Cradle Will Rock, The Movie and the Moment*, 119. This lavishly illustrated volume, and the video of Robbins' film, are well worth spending time with.
21. Max Gordon, "The Communist Party of the Nineteen-Thirties and the New Left," 18–19.
22. Fraser M. Ottanelli, *The Communist Party of the United States: From the Depression to World War II*, 143, 146, 152–153, 154. More detailed and critical is Harvey Klehr's *The Heyday of American Communism: The Depression Decade*.
23. Saul Alinsky, *John L. Lewis, An Unauthorized Biography*, 388–389; Joseph C. Goulden, *Meany: The Unchallenged Strong Man of American Labor*, 182; Bert Cochran, *Labor and Communism*, 98.
24. Ottanelli, 153, 154; Robert H. Zieger, *The CIO 1935–1955*, 255.
25. Anne Braden, "The Southern Freedom Movement in Perspective," 11–12. Also see John Egerton, *Speak Now Against the Day: The Generation Before the Civil Rights Movement in the South*. Braden's own activist contributions of five decades are chronicled in Catherine Fosl, *Subversive Southerner: Anne Braden and the Struggle for Racial Justice in the Cold War South*.
26. The breadth of radical involvement is indicated in Paul Le Blanc, *A Short History of the U.S. Working Class*, 79–92. For an account of the centrality of Socialist Party and Trotskyist contributions to the creation of the United Auto Workers, see Sol Dollinger and Genora Johnson Dollinger, *Not Automatic: Women and the Left in the Forging of the Auto Workers Union*.
27. Len De Caux, *Labor Radical: From the Wobblies to the CIO, A Personal History*, 242–243.
28. Claude McKay, *A Long Way From Home, An Autobiography*, 167–168, 171.
29. Harry Haywood, *Black Bolshevik, Autobiography of an Afro-American Communist*, 143–144.

30. Richard B. Moore, *Richard B. Moore, Caribbean Militant in Harlem: Collected Writings 1920–1972*, W. Burghardt Turner and Joyce Moore Turner, Eds., 219; Mark Naison, *Communists in Harlem During the Depression*, 12.
31. Claude McKay, *The Passion of Claude McKay: Selected Poetry and Prose, 1912–1948*, Wayne F. Cooper, Ed., 84; McKay, *A Long Way From Home*, 157, 158.
32. Claude McKay, *The Negroes in America*, xi, 77, 90.
33. McKay, *The Passion of Claude McKay*, 98.
34. Naison, *Communists in Harlem*, 12.
35. Robin D.G. Kelley, *Hammer and Hoe: Alabama Communists During the Great Depression*, 93.
36. Ibid., 107–108.
37. Robin D. G. Kelley, "Afric's Sons With Banner Red: African-American Communists and the Politics of Culture, 1919–1934," in *Race Rebels: Culture, Politics, and the Black Working Class*, 115.
38. Richard Wright, *American Hunger*, 37–38, 120.
39. McKay, *The Passion of Claude McKay*, 226, 227, 230–231, 252. Others used words differently. Dissident Communists insisted that a "workers' dictatorship" simply meant *political rule by the working class* and could not exist without being a genuine workers' democracy (which was cause for being critical of Stalinism).
40. C. L. R. James, *World Revolution 1917–1936, The Rise and Fall of the Communist International*, 292, 295–296, 298–299, 303, 304, 363.
41. William L. Patterson, *The Man Who Cried Genocide*, 98–99.
42. Haywood, *Black Bolshevik*, 146; Mark Solomon, *The Cry Was Unity: Communists and African Americans, 1917–1936*, 56–58; Harvey Klehr, John Earl Haynes, Kyrill M. Anderson, *The Soviet World of American Communism*, 218–223.
43. Robeson quoted in John Henrik Clarke, "Paul Robeson: The Artist as Activist and Social Thinker," in *Paul Robeson: The Great Forerunner*, Ed. by editors of *Freedomways*, 191, 194; Paul Robeson, *I Take My Stand*, 39.
44. Philip S. Foner, Ed. *Paul Robeson Speaks: Writings, Speeches, Interviews 1918–1974*, 94.
45. Gustav Regler, *The Owl of Minerva*, 260.
46. Paul Robeson, Jr., *The Undiscovered Paul Robeson: An Artist's Journey, 1898–1939*, 290, 306.
47. Philip S. Foner, Ed. *Paul Robeson Speaks*, 108; Martin Bauml Duberman, *Paul Robeson, A Biography*, 352–354.
48. Arno J. Mayer, *The Furies: Violence and Terror in the French and Russian Revolutions*, 662–663, 674; Roy Medvedev, *Let History Judge: The Origins and Consequences of Stalinism*, 629.
49. Medvedev, *Let History Judge*, 869. Moshe Lewin, in *Russia, USSR, Russia* (94–128) elaborates on "the disappearance of planning" generated by irrational "super-planning" and the fatal flaws embedded in the Stalinist policies of rapid industrialization, with a "command economy" yielding significant short-term gains but undermining the long-term viability of Soviet economic development.
50. John Earl Haynes and Harvey Klehr, *Venona: Decoding Soviet Espionage in America*, 7; Harvey Klehr and John Earl Haynes, *The American Communist Movement, Storming Heaven Itself*, 182. The Communist Party's self-conception is aptly presented in William Z. Foster, *History of the Communist Party of the United States*, and Philip Bart, Theodore Bassett, William W. Weinstein, and Arthur Zipser, Eds., *Highlights of a Fighting History: Sixty Years of the Communist Party, USA*.
51. A reasonably balanced general introduction can be found in Fried, Ed., *Communism in America*. Elements of the Communist impact on the labor movement can be found in Cochran, *Labor and Communism*; Steve Rosswurm, Ed., *The CIO's Left-Led Unions*; and Judith Stepan-Norris and Maurice Zeitlin, *Left Out: Reds and America's Industrial Unions*. Aspects of the impact on intellectual and cultural life can be found in Daniel Aaron, *Writers on the Left: Episodes in American Literary Communism*, Michael Denning, *The Cultural Front*, and Alan Wald, *Exiles from a Future Time: The Forging of the Mid-Twentieth-Century Literary Left*. On African-American struggles, see: Gerald Horne, "The Red and the Black: The Communist Party and African Americans in Historical Perspective," in Michael E. Brown, Ed., *New Studies in the Politics and Culture of U.S. Communism*, 199–237; Solomon, *The Cry Was Unity*; Gerald Horne, *Black Liberation/*

Red Scare: Ben Davis and the Communist Party. On Communist involvement in women's struggles, see: Rosalyn Baxandall, "The Question Seldom Asked: Women and the CPUSA," in Michael Brown, Ed., *New Studies*, 141–161; Annelise Orleck, *Common Sense and a Little Fire: Women and Working-Class Politics in the United States, 1900–1965*, 215–249, 267–276, 306–309, 313–315; Kate Weigand, *Red Feminism: American Communism and the Making of Women's Liberation*; and Daniel Horowitz, *Betty Friedan and the Making of the Feminine Mystique: The American Left, the Cold War, and Modern Feminism*, 124–131.

52. An essential "feel" for life in the Communist Party, encompassing both the experiences and accomplishments of some of its members, can be found in such memoirs as the following: John J. Abt, with Michael Myerson, *Activist and Advocate: Memoirs of an American Communist*; Bill Bailey, *The Kid From Hoboken, An Autobiography*; Howard Fast, *Being Red*; Joseph Freeman, *An American Testament, A Narrative of Rebels and Romantics*; John Gates, *The Story of an American Communist*; Dorothy Healey and Maurice Isserman, *California Red: Dorothy Healey Remembers*; Judith Kaplan and Linn Shapiro, Eds., *Red Diapers: Growing Up in the Communist Left*; Claude M. Lightfoot, *Chicago Slums to World Politics: Autobiography of Claude M. Lightfoot*; Beatrice Lumpkin, *"Always Bring a Crowd!" The Story of Frank Lumpkin, Steelworker*; Jessica Mitford, *A Fine Old Conflict*; Steve Nelson, with James R. Barrett and Rob Ruck, *Steve Nelson, American Radical*; Nell Irwin Painter, *The Narrative of Hosea Hudson, His Life as a Negro Communist in the South*.

53. The unsurpassed account remains Theodore Draper, *The Roots of American Communism*.

54. See William Z. Foster, *From Bryan to Stalin*; James R. Barrett, *William Z. Foster and the Tragedy of American Radicalism*; Emily Turnbull and James Robertson, Eds., *James P. Cannon and the Early Years of American Communism: Early Writings and Speeches, 1920–1928*; Bryan Palmer, *James P. Cannon and the Origins of the American Revolutionary Left*.

55. Whittaker Chambers, *Witness*, 192; Frank S. Meyer, *The Moulding of Communists: The Training of Communist Cadre*, 90–91.

56. Chambers, 204–205. Chambers is, characteristically, taking poetic license here, the Irish potato famine being something that took place in the 1840s. Other "Chambersian" literary distortions are enumerated in Irving Howe, "God, Man, and Stalin," *Selected Writings 1950–1990*, 21.

57. Chambers, *Witness*, 214–216.

58. Voros, *American Commissar*, 149–152.

59. Wright, *American Hunger*, 63–64, 118, 119.

60. Margaret Budenz, *Streets*, 172–174.

61. Louis Budenz, *Red Baiting: Enemy of Labor*, 9–10, 22, 23.

62. Margaret Budenz, 191–192. Some years later — when Childs temporarily ran afoul of the American Communist leadership — he secretly defected to the FBI, and for many years functioned as an agent in the upper levels of the Communist Party leadership, particularly close to Gus Hall, involved in the CPUSA's relations with the USSR, and also "fingering" two aides of Martin Luther King, Jr., Stanley Levison and Jack O'Dell, as having Communist ties. See David J. Garrow, *The FBI and Martin Luther King, Jr.*, John Barron, *Operation Solo: The FBI's Man in the Kremlin*, and John J. Abt, *Advocate and Activist*, 213–216.

63. James P. Cannon, *The First Ten Years of American Communism, Report of a Participant*, 36. A bitterly disillusioned "insider's" account is Ben Gitlow, *I Confess: The Truth About American Communism*; an invaluable detailed history is Theodore Draper, *American Communism and Soviet Russia*.

64. Draper, *American Communism and Soviet Russia*, 163–171.

65. Jay Lovestone, "Testimony of Jay Lovestone, Secretary, Independent Labor League of America," *Investigation of Un-American Propaganda Activities in the United States: Hearings Before a Special Committee on Un-American Activities (Dies Committee), House of Representatives, 75th–76th Congresses*, 7103.

66. James P. Cannon, *The History of American Trotskyism, Report of a Participant*, 14–15; Bertram D. Wolfe, *A Life in Two Centuries*, 229.

67. Lovestone, 7103, 7159.

68. Cannon, *The First Ten Years of American Communism*, 180; Max Eastman, *Love and Revolution, My Journey Through an Epoch*, 347.

69. Cannon, *The First Ten Years of American Communism*, 138, 152.

70. Ted Morgan, *A Covert Life: Jay Lovestone, Communist, Anti-Communist, and Spymaster*, 62; Cannon, *History of American Trotskyism*, 40–79; Draper, *American Communism and Soviet Russia*, 357–376.

71. Draper, *American Communism and Soviet Russia*, 405–441; Robert J. Alexander, *The Right Opposition: The Lovestoneites and the International Communist Opposition of the 1930s*, 13–41.

72. Peggy Dennis, *The Autobiography of an American Communist*, 70.

73. See Robert J. Alexander, *International Trotskyism, 1929–1985, a Documented Analysis of the Movement*; George Breitman, Paul Le Blanc, Alan Wald, *Trotskyism in the United States: Historical Essays and Reconsiderations*; Alan Wald, *The New York Intellectuals: The Rise and Fall of the Anti-Stalinist Left from the 1930s to the 1980s*; Fred Stanton, Ed., *Fighting Racism in World War II: C. L. R. James, George Breitman, Edgar Keemer, and Others*.

74. Diego Rivera and Bertram D. Wolfe, *Portrait of America*; Yvette Richards, *Maida Springer, Pan-Africanist and International Labor Leader*, 37–47; Barbara Ransby, *Ella Baker and the Black Freedom Movement*, 72, 93–98; Alexander, *The Right Opposition*, 38, 40, 42–62.

75. Alexander, *The Right Opposition*, 42–62, 113–134; Richard Gid Powers, *Not Without Honor: The History of American Anticommunism*, 178–180, 279; Mike Newburry, *The Yahoos*, 189.

76. Controversies continue to rage among scholars over the extent to which such contact involved simply exchanging ideas or opinions and the extent to which espionage was carried out — and there certainly was some of this. In addition to the previously cited volume by Haynes and Klehr, sources worth consulting on this complex and contentious issue include David J. Dallin, *Soviet Espionage*, Allen Weinstein and Alexander Vassiliev, *The Haunted Wood: Soviet Espionage in America — The Stalin Era*, Athan Theoharis, *Chasing Spies: How the FBI Failed in Counterintelligence But Promoted the Politics of McCarthyism in the Cold War Years*, and Herbert L. Packer, *Ex-Communist Witnesses: Four Studies in Fact Finding*. On Chambers see Whittaker Chambers, *Witness*, Sam Tanenhaus, *Whittaker Chambers, A Biography*, and Elinor Langer, "The Great Pumpkin." On Bentley, see Elizabeth Bentley, *Out of Bondage*, and Kathryn S. Olmsted, *Red Spy Queen: A Biography of Elizabeth Bentley*.

77. The Budenz story is perhaps best told in his wife's memoir — Margaret Budenz, *Streets*, but also see Louis Francis Budenz, *This is My Story*. A problem with the ex-Communist's conversion, Hannah Arendt once noted in her oddly titled "The Eggs Speak Up," is that the reality of a truly good and "more or less intact democratic society" to which they now swear allegiance was not "actually true. ... This is still the same world against whose complacency, injustice, and hypocrisy these same men once raised a radical protest" (*Essays in Understanding*, 281). A strength of Margaret Budenz's memoir is that she seems to have found her way back to what she knew as a radical protestor — perhaps in part because of her deep engagement with Christianity. Relevant to this is Arendt's insightful essay, "Christianity and Revolution," in the above-cited volume, 151–155.

78. George Blake Charney, *A Long Journey*, 23.

79. J. Edgar Hoover, *Masters of Deceit*, 5.

80. Georgi Dimitroff, *The United Front*, 110. For an excellent discussion of the background, see E. H. Carr, *Twilight of the Comintern, 1930–1935*. Also see Ivo Banic, Ed., *The Diary of Georgi Dimitrov, 1933–1949*, 9–112.

81. James Wechsler, *The Age of Suspicion*, 89.

82. Earl Browder, *The People's Front*, 13; also see James G. Ryan, *Earl Browder: The Failure of American Communism*.

83. Earl Browder, "The American Communist Party in the Thirties," in *As We Saw the Thirties*, Rita Simon, Ed., 237; Leo Huberman, *We the People: The Drama of America*, 346; James McGregor Burns, *Roosevelt: The Lion and the Fox, 1882–1940*, 373; David Brody, *Workers in Industrial America, Essays on the 20th Century Struggle*, 144; David Milton, *The Politics of U.S. Labor, From the Great Depression to the New Deal*, 136.

84. Brody, *Workers in Industrial America*, 142; David Brody, *In Labor's Cause*, 69; Abt, *Advocate and Activist*, 79–127; Maurice Isserman, *Which Side Were You On? The American Communist Party During the Second World War*, 208–213; Steven Fraser, *Labor Will Rule: Sidney Hillman and the Rise of American Labor*, 352–372, 495–538; Joseph Gaer, *The First Round: The Story of the CIO Political Action Committee*. Also see Arthur Schlesinger, Jr.,

A Life in the 20th Century: Innocent Beginnings, 1917–1950, 396: "If it hadn't been for us," Browder told Schlesinger, "Roosevelt would never have been elected in 1944. Our little band of 80,000 got in there and worked as hard as they could. They provided the leaven which held the whole Roosevelt coalition together." A distressed Democratic politician complained that the Political Action Committee was "inspired by internal Communists, revolutionary Socialists, Syndicalists, and an assorted variety of social reform crackpots, fellow travelers, brave-new-world, starry-eyed dreamers, dangerous un-American alien radicals, and other diverse subversive elements." The Republican vice-presidential candidate John W. Bricker charged that "the great Democratic Party has become the Hillman-Browder communistic party with Franklin Roosevelt at its front." See John Lewis Gaddis, *The United States and the Origins of the Cold War, 1941–1947*, 58–59.

85. Brody, *Workers in Industrial America*, 142, 143.
86. Irving Howe, *Socialism and America*, 93, 96, 98, 99, 101. Browder's continued loyalty to Stalin's regime, after his expulsion, resulted in his employment as the U.S. representative of a State Publishing House of the USSR, seeking to get translations of books and articles published in the United States. While becoming critical of certain policies of the Soviet government in the early 1950s, his loyalty to and defense of Stalin continued at least until 1956. See Philip Jaffe, *The Rise and Fall of American Communism*, 38–42, 161–163.
87. Cannon, *The First Ten Years of American Communism*, 39–40. For a full discussion of this problem, which includes a substantial survey of relevant literature, see: Paul Le Blanc, "Revolutionary Vanguards in the United States During the 1930s," in *U.S. Labor in the Twentieth Century, Studies in Working-Class Struggles and Insurgency*, John Hinshaw and Paul Le Blanc, Eds., 131–164.
88. Isserman, *Which Side Were You On?*, 9; Milton, *The Politics of U.S. Labor*, 136–138.
89. Earl Browder, *Victory — And After*, 80, 81, 252, 255; Isserman, *Which Side Were You On?*, 189.
90. Browder, *Victory — And After*, 30.
91. Earl Browder, *Teheran: Our Path in War and Peace*, 15, 23, 28, 47, 48, 51, 53–54, 55, 62, 63.
92. The Fifty Years Is Enough Network, Ed., *Empty Promises: The IMF, the World Bank, and the Planned Failures of Global Capitalism*, 13; Michael Yates, *Naming the System: Inequality and Work in the Global Economy*, 44.
93. Fred L. Block, *The Origins of International Economic Disorder: A Study of United States International Monetary Policy from World War II to the Present*, 39–40; Earl Latham, *The Communist Controversy in Washington From the New Deal to McCarthy*, 175–179; Ted Morgan, *Reds: McCarthyism in Twentieth-Century America*, 255–263; I. F. Stone, *The Truman Era*, 48. Right-wing allegations that I. F. Stone too was engaged in Soviet espionage and in his journalistic writing was a covertly-paid publicist for the USSR — first raised in the early 1990s and recycled, for example, in Herbert Romerstein and Eric Breindel, *The Venona Secrets: Exposing Soviet Espionage* — poses most sharply questions about the dividing line between scholarly analysis and stilted ideological polemic. See Cassandra Tate, "Who's Out to Lunch Here? I. F. Stone and the KGB," and Victor Navasky, "I. F. Stone." Additional information of interest on Harry Dexter White can be found on the website of the International Monetary Fund, which he helped to found, (www.imf.org/external/pubs/ft/fandd/1998/09/boughton.htm), and in R. Bruce Craig, *Treasonable Doubt, The Harry Dexter White Spy Case*.
94. Block, 43. Also see Lloyd C. Gardner, *Economic Aspects of New Deal Diplomacy*, 285–291. Gardner notes that White and Keynes were concerned that U.S. domination of the IMF would be utilized to "exact severe censorship over the monetary policies of its members." White expressed the worry that U.S. policy-makers would be tempted to engage in "the operation of power politics rather than of international cooperation" — fears that Gardner notes were "soon confirmed with the onset of the Cold War."
95. John Cabot Smith, *Alger Hiss, The True Story*, 72–74, 120–134; Allen Weinstein, *Perjury: The Hiss-Chambers Case*, 352–356; Alger Hiss, *Recollections of a Life*, 127–137, 150; Steven J. Bucklin, *Realism and American Foreign Policy: Wilsonians and the Kennan-Morgenthau Thesis*, 93, 94, 96. Also see Stephen C. Schlesinger, *Act of Creation: The Founding of the United Nations*, which offers considerable information and interesting judgments on various matters dealt with here.

The fact that capable and idealistic men with left-wing sympathies were placed in high positions that enabled them to help shape such key postwar institutions as the United Nations and the International Monetary Fund has been utilized by right-wing demagogues to charge "subversion" — but it seems clear that what was being subverted were the men themselves. That is, their energies and idealism were being deployed by powerful institutions and forces in U.S. society (the structure and dynamics of the government, rooted in and shaped by the needs and drives of a powerful capitalist economy) leading to results not consistent with their ideals. Another example, also a target of right-wing anti-Communists, was the brilliant physicist J. Robert Oppenheimer, who helped develop the atomic bomb and then served on the Atomic Energy Commission, and whose seduction away from his left-wing beliefs is discussed in Haakon Chevalier's bitter memoir, *Oppenheimer: The Story of a Friendship*, and — with the utilization of FBI and other records — in Ted Morgan, *Reds*, 234–239, 264–267.

96. Richard J. Walton, *Henry Wallace, Harry Truman, and the Cold War*, 67–68.

97. Elizabeth Hawes, *Hurry Up Please, It's Time*, 245. See Bettina Berch, *Radical By Design, the Life and Style of Elizabeth Hawes, Fashion Designer, Union Organizer, Best-Selling Author.*

98. Healey and Isserman, *California Red*, 110, 111; George Lipsitz, *Rainbow at Midnight: Labor and Culture in the 1940s*, 199. A sympathetic and informative volume dealing with Wallace and the Progressive Party is Norman D. Markowitz, *The Rise and Fall of the People's Century: Henry A. Wallace and American Liberalism, 1941–1948*. Also see Joseph R. Starobin, *American Communism in Crisis, 1943–1957*.

99. Godfrey Hodgson, *America in Our Time*, 77, 88. Relevant to such shifts is Elizabeth A. Fones-Wolf, *Selling Free Enterprise: The Business Assault on Labor and Liberalism, 1945–1960*, Larry Ceplair and Steven Englund, *The Inquisition in Hollywood: Politics in the Film Community, 1930–1960*, and Stephen J. Whitfield, *The Culture of the Cold War*.

100. Divergent accounts can be found in: Powers, *Not Without Honor*, 191–272; Cedric Belfrage, *The American Inquisition 1945–1960: A Profile of the "McCarthy Era"*; David Caute, *The Great Fear: The Anti-Communist Purge Under Truman and Eisenhower*; John E. Haynes, *Red Scare or Red Menace? American Communism and Anticommunism in the Cold War Era*; Ellen Schrecker, *Many Are the Crimes: McCarthyism in America*; Ronald Filipelli and Mark D. McColloch, *Cold War in the Working Class: The Rise and Decline of the United Electrical Workers*; Bud Schultz and Ruth Schultz, *It Did Happen Here: Recollections of Political Repression in America*.

101. Charles McCollester, Ed., *Fighter with a Heart: Writings of Charles Owen Rice*, 24, 31, 32, 43–46; Patrick McGeever, *Rev. Charles Owen Rice*, 62, 93, 94; Hans Kung, *The Catholic Church*, 175-180; Fred Halstead, *Out Now*, 250-251 (citing a taped interview with Msgr. Charles Owen Rich conducted by Paul Le Blanc in Pittsburgh, October 27, 1975). I. F. Stone, *The Haunted Fifties* provides an insightful survey of the political scene. Trilling quoted in Eric Bentley, *The Brecht Memoir*, 115–116. For an account of much of the context (and in the spirit) of Trilling's remarks, see William L. O'Neill, *A Better World, The Great Schism: Stalinism and The American Intellectuals*. Arthur Schlesinger, Jr. later observed that in this milieu more than one person (an example being Sidney Hook) "permitted anticommunism to consume his life to the point that his obsession ... swallowed up nearly everything else" (Schlesinger, *A Life in the Twentieth Century*, 508).

102. Steve Nelson, James R. Barrett, Rob Ruck, *Steve Nelson, American Radical*, 386–387.

103. Howard Fast, *Naked God: The Writer and the Communist Party*, 35.

104. Maurice Isserman, *If I Had a Hammer: The Death of the Old Left and the Birth of the New Left*, 3–34; Walter Bernstein, *Inside Out: A Memoir of the Blacklist*, 255. I.F.

105. The following draws from a portion of my essay "Leninism in the United States and the Decline of American Trotskyism," in Breitman, Le Blanc, and Wald, *Trotskyism in the United States*, 186–190. Also relevant to these issues is the fine novel by K. B. Gilden, *Between the Hills and the Sea*.

106. Nelson et al., *Steve Nelson, American Radical*, 284–285.

107. Frank Lovell, "The Socialist Purpose: To Educate the Working Class," in Paul Le Blanc and Thomas Barrett, Eds., *Revolutionary Labor Socialist: The Life, Ideas, and Comrades of Frank Lovell*, 133.

108. James P. Cannon, *Speeches to the Party*, 57, 58.

109. John C. Leggett, *Class, Race and Labor: Working-Class Consciousness in Detroit,* 52, 53; James Boggs, "The American Revolution: Pages from a Negro Worker's Notebook," 15, 16.

110. Stanley Aronowitz, *False Promises: The Shaping of Working Class Consciousness,* 95; Donald Clark Hodges, "Cynicism in the Labor Movement," in Maurice Zeitlin, Ed., *American Society, Inc.,* 446.

111. Hodgson, 89–90. Further discussion of conservative shifts in the U.S. labor movement can be found in Paul Le Blanc, "AFL, CIO Merge" and "Meany and Reuther Lead AFL, CIO," in *St. James Encyclopedia of Labor History Worldwide: Major Events in Labor History and Their Impact,* vol. 1, Neil Schlager, Ed., 19–23, 598–602. On intellectuals, see Richard H. Pells, *The Liberal Mind in a Conservative Age: American Intellectuals in the 1940s and 1950s.*

Chapter 6

The Anarchist Challenge

1. Henry David Thoreau, "Civil Disobedience," in George Woodcock, Ed., *The Anarchists,* 197.

2. Crane Brinton, *The Shaping of Modern Thought,* 174.

3. Emma Goldman, "My Further Disillusionment with Russia," excerpted in Alix Kates Shulman, Ed., *Red Emma Speaks: An Emma Goldman Reader,* 398–399.

4. David Graeber, "The Globalization Movement and the New New Left," in *Implicating Empire: Globalization and Resistance in the 21st Century World Order,* Stanley Aronowitz and Heather Gautney, Eds., 325–326.

5. Alex Callinicos, "The Anti-Capitalist Movement After Genoa and New York," in *Implicating Empire,* 135; Graeber, 326; David McNally, *Another World is Possible: Globalization and Anti-Capitalism,* 247, 248.

6. George Woodcock, *Anarchism: A History of Libertarian Ideas and Movements,* 9, 21; Paul Goodman, *Drawing the Line, Political Essays,* 17; Daniel Guerin, *Anarchism,* 15, 16, 27.

7. Essential information can be found in classic accounts from the 1930s — E. H. Carr, *Michael Bakunin,* and Boris Nicolaievsky and Otto Maenchen-Helfen, *Karl Marx: Man and Fighter.*

8. William L. O'Neill, Ed., *Echoes of Revolt: The Masses, 1911 to 1917,* 47, 49.

9. George Plechanoff, *Anarchism and Socialism,* 13–14; Lenin, *The State and Revolution,* excerpted in *Marx, Engels, Lenin: Anarchism and Anarcho-Syndicalism,* 282.

10. Hal Draper, *Socialism From Below,* 11, 12; a well-documented examination of Proudhon's and Bakunin's elitism and authoritarianism is provided in Hal Draper, *Karl Marx's Theory of Revolution, Volume IV: Critique of Other Socialisms,* 107–175, 270–304; Avrich's comments are in his preface to Sam Dolgoff, Ed., *Bakunin on Anarchy,* xxiv.

11. Draper, *Socialism From Below,* 12–13.

12. Emma Goldman, *Anarchism and Other Essays,* 78.

13. For an anarchist such as Emile Henry, appropriate acts of protest included blowing up in 1882 a French music hall (denounced as a "den" that attracted, "especially after midnight, the fine flower of the bourgeoisie and of commerce"), or planting a bomb in 1894, as historian James Joll recounts, "in the Café Terminus near the Gare Saint-Lazare at a time when a large crowd of modest Paris shopkeepers, clerks, and even workers were quietly drinking and listening to the band." Henry planted the bomb to protest "the revolting spectacle of society where all is base, all is cowardly, where everything is a barrier to the development of human passions, to the generous tendencies of the heart, to the free flight of thought." In 1912, Benito Mussolini — then a left-wing socialist seeking to give a new edge to his militancy in a manner consistent with what Goldman was saying — hailed the individualist-anarchist Max Stirner. "Let the way be opened for the elemental forces of the individual, for no other human reality exists except the individual," he declared. "We shall support all that exalts, amplifies the individual, that gives him greater freedom, greater well-being, greater latitude of life; we shall fight all that depresses, mortifies the individual." As Joll notes, the "extreme solipsism and violent self-expression" of some anarchist currents — nourished by "the writings of Nietzsche and Stirner ... could produce a self-made superman like Mussolini" who would soon project his followers (including some former anarchists) as the creative elite, and himself as the Leader, worthy of repudiating stupid majorities and rising above the dreary mass to lead Italy to a new age

of glory — a fascist order, it must be said, that was the repulsive antithesis of what Emma Goldman believed in. James Joll, *The Anarchists*, 130, 137, 172.

14. Gene Fellner, Ed., *Life of an Anarchist: The Alexander Berkman Reader*, 285, 328, 329, 330.

15. To do justice to anarchism in all its contradictory variety, one must examine both doctrines and lives. For a sampling of the former, see Daniel Guerin, Ed., *No Gods, No Masters: An Anthology of Anarchism*, 2 vols., and for a sampling of the latter, see two volumes by Paul Avrich — *Anarchist Portraits* and *Anarchist Voices, An Oral History of Anarchism in America*.

16. Peter Kropotkin, *Mutual Aid*; Peter Kropotkin, *The Conquest of Bread*; Prince Kropotkin, *Ethics*; *Kropotkin's Revolutionary Pamphlets: A Collection of Writings* edited by Roger N. Baldwin, 44; Max Eastman, *Marx, Lenin, and the Science of Revolution*, 130; Murray Bookchin, *Post-Scarcity Anarchism*, 240. And yet there are streams in the Marxist tradition that embrace utopian thinking — see the work of Ernst Bloch, and Michael Löwy's fine essay, "Marxism and the Utopian Vision," *On Changing the World: Essays in Political Philosophy, From Karl Marx to Walter Benjamin*, 16–22. There is also the magnificent writer, artist, designer, poet, and revolutionary William Morris, a socialist close to Marxism and sharply critical toward many anarchists of his day — see especially *"News From Nowhere"* in *Three Works by William Morris*, and E. P. Thompson, *William Morris: Romantic to Revolutionary*.

17. Noam Chomsky, "Introduction" to Guerin, *Anarchism*, viii.

18. Goodman, *Drawing the Line*, 176.

19. Paul Goodman, "Getting Into Power," in *Seeds of Liberation*, 443.

20. Lenin, in *Marx, Engels, Lenin: Anarchism and Anarcho-Syndicalism*, 273.

21. This is discussed in different ways by Paul Avrich, *The Russian Anarchists*; Michael Löwy, *Redemption and Utopia: Jewish Libertarian Thought in Central Europe*; Alfred Rosmer, *Moscow Under Lenin*, 46–49, 60–61, 97–102; and Victor Serge, *Memoirs of a Revolutionary*, 75–78, 93–94, 103–104 — though some of today's anarchist "hards" peevishly denounce Serge as "the Bolsheviks' pet anarchist."

22. See Friedrich A. Sorge, *Labor Movement in the United States, A History of the American Working Class from Colonial Times to 1890*, 210–212. Also see Paul Avrich, *The Haymarket Tragedy*; Bruce C. Nelson, *Beyond the Martyrs: A Social History of Chicago's Anarchists, 1870–1900*; and Dave Roediger and Franklin Rosemont, *Haymarket Scrapbook*.

23. The point is made by Michael Albert, *What Is To Be Undone*, 189.

24. *After Winter Must Come Spring: A Self-Critical Evaluation of the Love and Rage Revolutionary Anarchist Federation*, 23, 25.

25. Ibid., 23.

26. Marion D. Frankfurter and Gardner Jackson, Eds., *The Letters of Sacco and Vanzetti*, 308–309.

27. Avrich, *The Russian Anarchists*, 243; Anthony D'Agostino, *Marxism and the Russian Anarchists*, 217, 219; Voline, *The Unknown Revolution*.

28. Nestor Makhno, *The Struggle Against the State and Other Essays*, 64, 66, 67–68, 110.

29. Arno J. Mayer, *The Furies: Violence and Terror in the French and Russian Revolutions*, 389; Paul Avrich, *The Russian Anarchists*, 219.

30. Avrich, *The Russian Anarchists*, 239.

31. D'Agostino, 248.

32. See Gabriel Jackson, *The Spanish Republic and the Civil War, 1931–1939*, and E H. Carr, *The Comintern and the Spanish Civil War*.

33. Gerald Brenan, *The Spanish Labyrinth*, 195–196.

34. Murray Bookchin, *The Spanish Anarchists: The Heroic Years 1868–1936*, 290–291, 294, 295; Brenan, 202.

35. Bookchin, *The Spanish Anarchists*, 284; Burnett Bolloten, *The Spanish Civil War: Revolution and Counterrevolution*, 210, 211.

36. Leon Trotsky, *The Spanish Revolution, 1931–39*, 314–315.

37. In addition to previously cited works by Carr and Bolloten, see Pierre Broué and Emile Temime, *Revolution and Civil War in Spain*, and Ronald Radosh, Mary R. Habeck, Grigory Sevostianov, Eds., *Spain Betrayed: The Soviet Union in the Spanish Civil War*.

38. See Lawrence Blum and Victor J. Seidler, *A Truer Liberty: Simone Weil and Marxism*.

39. Simone Weil, "Letter to Georges Bernanos," in *Simone Weil Reader*, 74.

40. Simone Weil, "Untitled Fragment on Spain," in *Formative Writings 1921–1941*, 255; "Letter to Bernanos," in *Simone Weil Reader*, 75–77.
41. Serge, *Memoirs of a Revolutionary*, 74, 77.
42. Simone Weil, "Reflections That No One Is Going to Like," *Formative Writings*, 256.
43. A .J. Muste, "Return to Pacifism" (1936) in *The Essays of A. J. Muste*, 197, 199.
44. Ibid., 198.
45. Muste, "Getting Rid of War" (1959) in *Essays of A. J. Muste*, 387, 391.
46. Weil, "Last Thoughts," *Simone Weil Reader*, 113, 114. Weil feared that Gaullism would become a right-wing nationalist movement, opposed its tendency to demonize the German people, and was deeply troubled by its commitment to French colonialism. See Simone Petrément, *Simone Weil, A Life*, 492, 503, 506, 533. It should be added that Weil's critique of Marxism (aptly summarized in Petrément, 320–322, 502) not only forms the basis for her own rejection of it, but, more fruitfully, poses an agenda for further Marxist theoretical work: the nature and role of war in human history, the fact that oppressed people can at the same time be oppressors (a question actually confronted by "post-Weil" anti-racist and feminist theorists operating within a Marxist framework), how Marx's account of past revolutions can be reconciled with the truly emancipatory character of the projected socialist revolution, and how the oppressiveness of industrial work and the machinery of state can be overcome after such a revolution. As David McLellan comments, "her vertigo of the absolute" made it difficult for Weil "to keep her balance on the ground," but this should not "obscure the fragmentary brilliance of her writings which illuminate so many areas of the human condition" (McLellan, *Utopian Pessimist: The Life and Thought of Simone Weil*, 272).
47. Quoted in Muste, "Of Holy Disobedience" (1952) in *Essays of A. J. Muste*, 355.
48. Ibid, 356, 374; Weil, "Last Thoughts," *Simone Weil Reader*, 112–113.
49. Muste, *Non-Violence in an Aggressive World*, 34–35. God is as much Mother as Father: Carol P. Christ and Judith Plaskow, Eds., *Womanspirit Rising: A Feminist Reader in Religion*; Marcus J. Borg, *The God We Never Knew*, 57–83.
50. Muste, "The Civil Rights Movement and the American Establishment" (1965) in *Essays of A. J. Muste*, 457.
51. Ibid., 458.
52. Muste, "Getting Rid of War," and "The Fall of Man" (1964) in *Essays of A. J. Muste*, 391–392, 448–449.
53. Muste, *Non-Violence in an Aggressive World*, 87.
54. These comments can be found in Woodcock, Ed., *The Anarchist Reader*: Paul Goodman, "Normal Politics and the Psychology of Power" (96–97); Alex Comfort, "Revolution and Social Reality" (184); Nicolas Walter, "Anarchist Action" (171).

Chapter 7

Tree of Life

1. Isaiah Berlin, *Karl Marx*, 207–208.
2. Mari Jo Buhle, Paul Buhle, and Dan Georgakas, Eds., *Encyclopedia of the American*; Alan Wald, *The New York Intellectuals: The Rise and Fall of the Anti-Stalinist Left from the 1930s to the 1980s*; George H. Nash, *The Conservative Intellectual Movement in the United States*. Marxist residue certainly comes through in Whittaker Chambers, *Cold Friday*, 124–132, 141–144, 236–238, as well as in his correspondence in *Odyssey of a Friend: Whittaker Chambers' Letters to William F. Buckley, Jr. 1954–1961*, and *Notes From the Underground: The Whittaker Chambers–Ralph de Toledano Letters, 1949–1960*. Will Herberg, long after he had joined conservative ranks, commented that Karl Marx and right-wing icon Edmund Burke "shared a certain basic common ground of realistic understanding that makes both of them relevant to our times and its perplexities and problems" (comments on back cover of Ruth A. Bevan, *Marx and Burke, A Revisionist View*). Hannah Arendt commented on Chambers and some of his co-thinkers that they "are not former Communists, they are Communists 'turned upside down'" in her essay "The Ex-Communists" (*Essays in Understanding*, 393).
3. Paul M. Sweezy and Harry Magdoff, "Foreword," 7; Leo Huberman, *Man's Worldly Goods: The Story of the Wealth of Nations*, 285.

4. Hewlitt Johnson, *The Soviet Power*, 314, 315; Reinhold Niebuhr, *Reflections on the End of an Era*, 131, 148. For Johnson's views, some intellectual context is provided by John Lewis, Karl Polyani, Donald K. Kitchin, Eds. *Christianity and the Social Revolution*; also see David Caute, *The Fellow-Travellers: Intellectual Friends of Communism*, 256–263. In Niebuhr's still-influential *Moral Man and Immoral Society* one finds Leninist traces on pages 146–151, 182–192, 194–197. His context is partly suggested by a fine biography, Richard Fox, *Reinhold Niebuhr, A Biography*. Also see: Donald Meyer, *The Protestant Search for Political Realism 1919–1941*; Ralph Lord Roy, *Communism and the Churches*; James Bentley, *Between Marx and Christ, The Dialogue in German-Speaking Europe 1870–1970*; John Marsden, *Marxian and Christian Utopianism: Towards a Socialist Political Theology*; Arthur F. McGovern, *Marxism: An American Christian Perspective*.

5. Harry F. Ward, *Democracy and Social Change*, 218–219; also see Eugene P. Link, *Labor-Religion Prophet: The Times and Life of Harry F. Ward*.

6. Cedric Belfrage *South of God*, 138, 192; Sherwood Eddy, *Revolutionary Christianity*, 121, 137. More information on Williams, who was involved in the Southern Tenant Farmers Union and in the left-wing labor school, Commonwealth College, can be found in H.L. Mitchell, *Mean Things Happening in This Land: The Life and Times of H.L. Mitchell, Cofounder of the Southern Tenant Farmers Union*, 87–89, 153–163; Richard J. Altenbaugh, *Education for Struggle: The American Labor Colleges of the 1920s and 1930s*, 236–240.

7. Kirby Page, *Kirby Page, Social Evangelist: The Autobiography of a 20th Century Prophet for Peace*, 79; Kirby Page, *Individualism and Socialism: An Ethical Survey of Economic and Political Forces*, 302, 311, 312; Eddy, *Revolutionary Christianity*, 133–134; Sherwood Eddy, *Russia Today: What Can We Learn From It?*, 199–200.

8. A .J. Muste, *Non-Violence in an Aggressive World*, 57, 63–64, 181, 182, 186. Also see Jo Ann Ooiman Robinson, *Abraham Went Out: A Biography of A. J. Muste*.

9. Aldon D. Morris, *The Origins of the Civil Rights Movement: Black Communities Organizing for Change*, 141–157; John M. Glen, *Highlander, No Ordinary School*, 25, 27, 28. Also see Frank T. Adams, *James A. Dombrowski: An American Heretic, 1897–1983*. Dombrowski, whose 1936 study *Early Days of Christian Socialism in America* remains a minor classic, was a protégé of Rev. Harry F. Ward, furthest to the left of the faculty at Union Theological Seminary (eventually gravitating too close to the Communist Party to be tolerated by most of his seminarian colleagues). West, a Christian minister, went on to become Georgia state organizer for the Communist Party.

10. Myles Horton, with Judith Kohl and Hebert Kohl, *The Long Haul, An Autobiography*, 43–44. Also see Eliot Wigginton, Ed. *Refuse to Stand Silently By: An Oral History of Grass Roots Activism in America, 1921–1964*.

11. Glen, 37–38.

12. Ibid., 155–206; Anthony P. Dunbar, *Against the Grain: Southern Radicals and Prophets, 1929–1959*, 250. Horton's perspective was influenced by Lenin's view that blacks in America "should be classed as an oppressed nation, for the equality won in the Civil War of 1861–65 and guaranteed by the Constitution of the republic was in many respects increasingly curtailed in the chief Negro areas (the South) in connection with the transition from the progressive, pre-monopoly capitalism of 1860–70 to the reactionary, monopoly capitalism (imperialism) of the new era ..." (Lenin, "Statistics and Sociology," *Collected Works*, vol. 23, 275–276). The Leninist orientation, favoring "self-determination of oppressed nations," was therefore especially sensitive to the need for blacks' furnishing "their own leadership" in their own struggles. Discussions of how Lenin's perspectives impacted on American Communists (who then shared them with others) can be found in Philip S. Foner and James S. Allen, Eds., *American Communism and Black Americans: A Documentary History, 1919–1929*, Harry Haywood, *Black Bolshevik: Autobiography of an Afro-American Communist*, and Mark Solomon, *The Cry Was Unity: Communists and African Americans, 1917–1936*. Among those associated with Highlander's work during the "civil rights era" were Septima Clark, Andrew Young, Fred Shuttlesworth, Ella Baker, E. D. Nixon, Rosa Parks, and Martin Luther King, Jr. — none of whom were Leninists (though white racists used their association with the so-called "Communist training school" to red-bait them). The point here is that elements of the Leninist perspective had been absorbed into the larger political culture in ways that had positive historical consequences.

13. See F. O. Matthiessen, *American Renaissance: Art and Expression in the Age of Emerson and Whitman*. The quote evaluating themes in that book is from Henry Nash Smith, cited in Giles Gunn, *F.O. Matthiessen: The Critical Achievement*, 105.

14. Matthiessen was hardly a naïve fellow traveler of Stalinism, as some would have it. He commented on how the USSR had been "disfigured" by the "grim pressures of dictatorship." This is not surprising, given the fact that — as a passionate Christian — he seems to have had a greater sense of the possibility of evil, including in the USSR under Stalin, than was the case with the "Red Dean" of Canterbury and Harry F. Ward, with sensibilities closer to those of Niebuhr and Muste. He found something of value in Arthur Koestler's anti-Communist novel of 1941, *Darkness at Noon* (though he was shocked by the ex-Communist novelist's "bright facile negativism" as Koestler enlisted in the Cold War anti-Communist crusade). For Matthiessen, "the most thoughtful man among the labor leaders I have met," and "the nearest that America had come to producing a Marxist leader in the selfless tradition of Lenin," was the Trotskyist leader of the 1934 Minneapolis general strike, Vincent Raymond Dunne. See Paul M. Sweezy and Leo Huberman, Eds. *F.O. Matthiessen, A Collective Portrait*, 11–13, 16–17, and Frederick C. Stern, *F.O. Matthiessen, Christian Socialist as Critic*.

15. Wayne Cooper, Ed., *The Passion of Claude McKay: Selected Prose and Poetry, 1912–1948*, 305, 306, 307, 308, 311, 312, 313, 314.

16. Quoted in Bernard Crick, *George Orwell, A Life*, 523.

17. Garry Wills, *Confessions of a Conservative*, 153, 168.

18. Ibid., 114, 162.

19. Ibid., 148, 156.

20. Ibid., 164–165.

21. This is drawn from Paul Le Blanc, *A Short History of the U.S. Working Class, From Colonial Times to the Twenty-First Century*, 104–105.

22. Particularly informative and readable introductory texts well worth consulting are Jeremy Isaacs and Taylor Downing, *Cold War, 1945–1991: Companion to the CNN TV Series*, and Walter LaFeber, *America, Russia, and the Cold War, 1945–2002*. Additional insights can be gained from John Lewis Gaddis, *The United States and the Origins of the Cold War, 1941–1947*; Bert Cochran, *Harry Truman and the Crisis Presidency*; Caroline Kennedy-Pipe, *Stalin's Cold War: Soviet Strategies in Europe, 1943 to 1956*; Vladisov Zubok and Constantine Pleshakov, *Inside the Kremlin's Cold War, From Stalin to Khrushchev*; Fernando Claudin, *The Communist Movement, From Comintern to Cominform*; Walter Isaacson and Evan Thomas, *The Wise Men, Six Friends and the World They Made: Acheson, Bohlen, Harriman, Kennan, Lovett, McCloy*; and Michael J. Hogan, Ed., *The End of the Cold War, Its Meaning and Implications*.

23. Richard M. Freeland, *The Truman Doctrine and the Origins of McCarthyism: Foreign Policy, Domestic Politics, and Internal Security, 1946–1948*; David Caute, *The Great Fear: The Anti-Communist Purge Under Truman and Eisenhower*; Ellen Schrecker, *Many Are the Crimes: McCarthyism in America*.

24. David Horowitz, *Student*, 10, 16; Irving Howe, "This Age of Conformity," *Selected Writings 1950–1990*, 36, 48. An absorbing memoir of the period is Nora Sayre, *Previous Convictions: A Journey Through the 1950s*. Also see David Halberstam, *The Fifties*. Recent scholarship of interest on the corruption of significant left-liberal currents in the Cold War can be found in Frances Stoner Saunders, *Who Paid the Piper? The CIA and the Cultural Cold War*, and Volker Berghahn, *America and the Intellectual Cold War in Europe*.

25. C. Wright Mills, *The Power Elite*, 296, 360, 361.

26. Marty Jezer, *The Dark Ages: Life in the United States 1945–1960*, 107, 111, 114.

27. C. L. R. James, *American Civilization*, 122, 123.

28. Harry Braverman, "The New America," 11. This can be linked to important left-wing cultural influences discussed in Michael Denning's valuable study *The Cultural Front: The Laboring of American Culture in the Twentieth Century*, although Denning's overly broad conceptualization of the "popular front" distorts his material — as demonstrated in Frank A. Warren, "A Flawed History of the Popular Front," 112–125. Also relevant to Braverman's comments is George Lipsitz's *Rainbow at Midnight: Labor and Culture in the 1940s*.

29. Braverman, "The New America," 10. Also see Harvey Swados' classic 1957 essay, "The Myth of the Happy Worker," reprinted in Harvey Swados, *A Radical's America*, 111–120.

30. Braverman, "The New America," 11.
31. Harry Braverman, *Labor and Monopoly Capital: The Degradation of Work in the Twentieth Century*.
32. Adolph Reed, Jr., *Class Notes: Posing as Politics and Other Thoughts on the American Scene*, 3–4.
33. Jack Newfield, *A Prophetic Minority*, 16. These diverse left-wing ideological and organizational influences are documented in a number of sources, including: Maurice Isserman, *If I Had a Hammer ...: The Death of the Old Left and the Birth of the New Left*; Andrew Jamison and Ron Eyerman, *Seeds of the Sixties*; Judith Kaplan and Linn Shapiro, Eds., *Red Diapers: Growing Up in the Communist Left*; Tim Wohlforth, *The Prophet's Children: Travels on the American Left*, 4–122; and Paul Goodman, Ed. *Seeds of Liberation*. For an intriguing and quite informative counterposition of "red-diaper" reminiscences, see Ronald Radosh's sad memoir *Commies: A Journey Through the Old Left, the New Left and the Leftover Left*, and — to my mind — the less sad memoir of Robert Meeropol, *An Execution in the Family: One Son's Journey*.
34. "Appendix: The Port Huron Statement," James Miller, *"Democracy is in the Streets": From Port Huron to the Siege of Chicago*, 329, 331, 332, 333. The outstanding history of Students for a Democratic Society remains Kirkpatrick Sale, *SDS*.
35. On King's relationship to the socialist movement, see Paul Le Blanc, "Martin Luther King: Christian Core, Socialist Bedrock." For a rich account of the broader context, see Taylor Branch's trilogy — *Parting the Waters: America in the King Years 1954–63*, *Pillar of Fire: America in the King Years 1963–65*, and *At Canaan's Edge: America in the King Years 1965–1968*.
36. Clayborne Carson, *In Struggle: SNCC and the Black Awakening of the 1960s*, 2–3. In addition to writings of Marx and Marxists — often encountered in the volume composed and edited by radical sociologist C. Wright Mills, *The Marxists* — many young radicals were reading Albert Camus' existentialist classics *The Plague* and *The Rebel*, as well as *The Autobiography of Malcolm X*, and *Malcolm X Speaks*.
37. Anne Braden, "The Southern Freedom Movement in Perspective," 77, 78–79, 80. See Catherine Fosl, *Subversive Southerner: Anne Braden and the Struggle for Racial Justice in the Cold War South*.
38. Garry Wills, *Confessions of a Conservative*, 48; Margaret Budenz, *Streets*, 447–448.
39. Irving Howe, "New Styles in 'Leftism,'" in *Steady Work: Essays in the Politics of Democratic Radicalism 1953–1966*, 48. A valuable book on the left-wing newsweekly *The National Guardian* by its editors is Cedric Belfrage and James Aronson, *Something to Guard: The Stormy Life of the National Guardian 1948–1967*.
40. Michael Harrington, "The Mystical Militants" in the *New Republic*, Eds., *Thoughts of the Young Radicals*, 67.
41. Hal Draper, *Berkeley: The New Student Revolt*, 179; Newfield, 19.
42. Raya Dunayevskaya, *The Free Speech Movement and the Negro Revolution*, 42, 43.
43. Fred Halstead, *Out Now: A Participant's Account of the American Movement Against the Vietnam War*, 711, 717, 723. Also see Nancy Zaroulis and Gerald Sullivan, *Who Spoke Up? American Protest Against the War in Vietnam, 1963–1975*.
44. Carl Oglesby, "Liberalism and the Corporate State" in Paul Jacobs and Saul Landau, *The New Radicals: A Report With Documents*, 263–264.
45. Marge Piercy, from "The Consumer," *Living in the Open*, 77.
46. For the essential left-wing elements in this new wave of feminism, see: Daniel Horowitz, *Betty Friedan and the Making of the Feminine Mystique: The American Left, the Cold War, and Modern Feminism*; Sara Evans, *Personal Politics: The Roots of the Women's Liberation in the Civil Rights Movement and the New Left*; Paula Giddings, *When and Where I Enter: The Impact of Black Women on Race and Sex in America*.
47. Julius Lester, "Beyond Ideology," in Peter Collier and David Horowitz, Eds., *Second Thoughts: Former Radicals Look Back at the Sixties*, 211.
48. Piercy, "Rough Times," *Living in the Open*, 35–36.
49. Halstead, 723.
50. See Harold Jacobs, Ed., *Weatherman*.
51. Conrad Lynn, *There is a Fountain: The Autobiography of a Civil Rights Lawyer*, 209; Lester, "Beyond Ideology," 223. The three indispensable books on the Panthers are: Philip S. Foner, Ed., *The Black Panthers Speak*; Hugh Pearson, *The Shadow of the Panther: Huey*

Newton and the Price of Black Power in America, and Kathleen Cleaver and George Katsiaficas, Eds., *Liberation, Imagination, and the Black Panther Party*.

52. James P. Cannon, *The First Ten Years of American Communism, Report of a Participant*, 38; Peter Collier and David Horowitz, *Destructive Generation: Second Thoughts About the Sixties*, 15, 332; Barry Rubin, "Learning From Experience," and David Horowitz, "Why I Am No Longer a Leftist," in Collier and Horowitz, Eds., *Second Thoughts*, 50, 56. One might add that a "self-righteous and arrogant" tone can certainly be discerned in the now right-wing David Horowitz. In part, this seems to be a conscious rhetorical device (which Horowitz himself later described as "outraged, aggressive, morally certain") for assaulting leftists and liberals. See Horowitz, *Radical Son*, 358.

53. Tariq Ali and Susan Watkins, *1968: Marching in the Streets*; David Caute, *The Year of the Barricades: A Journey Through 1968*; Robert V. Daniels, *Year of the Heroic Guerrilla: World Revolution and Counterrevolution in 1968*; Ronald Fraser, *1968: Student Generation, Student Revolt*; Chris Harman, *The Fire Last Time: 1968 and After*.

54. Marge Piercy, *Dance the Eagle to Sleep*, 213, 214, 219, 220, 222.

55. Max Elbaum, *Revolution in the Air: Sixties Radicals Turn to Lenin, Mao and Che*, 319–323.

56. On the DuBois Clubs and Che-Lumumba Club, see: Jacobs and Landau, *The New Radicals*, 48–53, Michael Myerson, *These Are the Good Old Days: Coming of Age As a Radical in America's Late, Late Years*, 110–128, Angela Davis, *Angela Davis, An Autobiography*, 187–192, Dorothy Healey and Maurice Isserman, *California Red: A Life in the American Communist Party*, 208–209, 215, 217. On Trotskyists, see: Robert J. Alexander, *International Trotskyism, 1929–1985: A Documented Analysis of the Movement*, 850–910, George Breitman, Paul Le Blanc, and Alan Wald, *Trotskyism in the United States, Historical Essays and Reconsiderations*, 34–71, Barry Sheppard, *The Party: The Socialist Workers Party 1960–1988, A Political Memoir, Volume 1: The Sixties*, and Dan LaBotz, *Rank and File Rebellion: Teamsters for a Democratic Union*. On the New American Movement and Democratic Socialists of America, see Michael Harrington, *The Long-Distance Runner, An Autobiography*, 57–66 and Maurice Isserman, *The Other American: The Life of Michael Harrington*, 303–363.

57. Elbaum, 323–324.

58. Quoted in Breitman, Le Blanc, and Wald, *Trotskyism in the United States*, 54. A valuable collection of Breitman's illuminating writings, edited by Anthony Marcus, is available in *Malcolm X and the Third American Revolution: The Writings of George Breitman*.

59. Henri Lefebvre, *The Survival of Capitalism*, 97, 99; Herbert Marcuse, *Counterrevolution and Revolt*, 39. What Marcuse terms the "original concept of class" is actually a narrow, historically specific conception (roughly, that only factory workers are "real" workers) superimposed by many on the left over Marx's broader conception of what makes someone part of the working class.

60. Marcuse, *Counterrevolution and Revolt*, 41–45.

61. Lefebvre, 119. To compare this with more recent developments among activists dealing with globalization, see: Jeremy Brecher and Tim Costello, *Global Village or Global Pillage: Economic Reconstruction from the Bottom Up* and Kevin Danaher and Roger Burbach, Eds., *Globalize This! The Battle Against the World Trade Organization and Corporate Rule*.

62. Lefebvre, 94, 100–101.

63. James Weinstein, *The Long Detour: The History and Future of the American Left*, 249.

64. Ibid., 256–259, 262.

65. Bebel and Lenin quoted in John Bellamy Foster, *Marx's Ecology: Materialism and Nature*, 238, 243. Raymond Williams, "You're a Marxist Aren't You?" in *Resources of Hope*, 71, 74–76.

66. Naomi Klein, "Reclaiming Our Lives," 12, 13.

67. Ibid., 12.

68. Ibid., 13.

69. Naomi Klein, *Fences and Windows: Dispatches from the Front Lines of the Globalization Debate*, 228–233.

70. Ibid., 35, 220–221, 193–207; Tariq Ali, "Recolonizing Iraq." Also see: José Corrêa Leite, *The World Social Forum: Strategies of Resistance*; William F. Fisher and Thomas Ponniah, Eds., *Another World Is Possible: Popular Alternatives to Globalization at the World Social*

Forum; and Jai Sen, Anita Anand, Arturo Escobar, and Peter Waterman, Eds., *World Social Forum: Challenging Empires*. Also see: http://www.forumsocialmundial.org.br/home.asp. A valuable and coherent analytical framework for future activism is available in Walden Bello, *Dilemmas of Domination: The Unmaking of the American Empire*.

71. *Why Do the Millennium Development Goals Matter? From the Secretary-General's 2003 Report on Implementation of the United Nations Millennium Declaration*; for the full report, see: www.un.org/millenniumgoals. Informative essays can be found in Fantu Cheru and Colin Bradford, Eds., *The Millennium Development Goals: Raising the Resources to Tackle World Poverty*. For a sharp challenge, see Samir Amin, "The Millennium Development Goals, A Critique from the South," which makes excellent points but, in my view, misses certain opportunities for radical activists.

72. Roger Lancaster, *Life Is Hard: Machismo, Danger, and the Intimacy of Power in Nicaragua*, 282.

73. James Fulcher, *A Very Short Introduction to Capitalism*, 126, 127; Jeffrey D. Sachs, *The End of Poverty: Economic Possibilities for Our Time*, 357.

74. Donald Sassoon, *One Hundred Years of Socialism: The West European Left in the Twentieth Century*, 755.

75. V. I. Lenin, *What Is To Be Done?*, in *Selected Works*, vol. 1, 239. According to Ernst Bloch, before Marx's "forward dreaming, as Lenin says, was not reflected on, was only touched on sporadically, did not attain the concept appropriate to it" (*The Principle of Hope*, volume one, 6). Also see Richard Stites' challenging study *Revolutionary Dreams: Utopian Vision and the Experimental Life in the Russian Revolution*, 41–46.

76. Bloch, *The Principle of Hope*, volume one, 3–4, 5–6.

77. Dorothy Day, "Our Brothers, the Communists," *Dorothy Day, Selected Writings*, 271–272.

Bibliography

A. Philip Randolph Institute. *A "Freedom Budget" for All Americans*. New York: A. Philip Randolph Institute, 1966.

Aaron, Daniel. *Writers on the Left: Episodes in American Literary Communism*. New York: Harcourt Brace and World, 1961.

Abendroth,Wolfgang. *A Short History of the European Working Class*. New York: Monthly Review Press, 1973.

Abramovitch, Raphael R. *The Soviet Revolution 1917–1939*. New York: International Universities Press, 1962.

Abt, John J. with Michael Myerson. *Activist and Advocate: Memoirs of an American Communist Lawyer*. Urbana: University of Illinois Press, 1993.

Acton, Edward, Vladimir Iu. Charniaev, and William G. Rosenberg, Eds. *Critical Companion to the Russian Revolution, 1914–1921*. Bloomington: University of Indiana Press, 1997.

Aczel, Tamas and Tibor Meray. *The Revolt of the Mind: A Case History of Intellectual Resistance Behind the Iron Curtain*. New York: Frederick A. Praeger, 1959.

Adamic, Louis. *The Eagle and the Roots*. Garden City, NY: Doubleday, 1952.

———. *My America, 1928–1938*. New York: Harper and Brothers, 1938.

Adams, Frank T. *James A. Dombrowski: An American Heretic, 1897–1983*. Knoxville: University of Tennessee Press, 1992.

Adler, Alan, Alix Holt, and Barbara Holland, Eds. *Theses, Resolutions, and Manifestos of the First Four Congresses of the Third International*. London: Ink Links, 1980.

Albers, Patricia. *Shadows, Fire, Snow: The Life of Tina Modotti*. New York: Clarkson Potter, 1999.

Albert, Michael. *What Is To Be Undone*. Boston: Porter Sargent, 1974.

Alexander, Robert J. *The Right Opposition: The Lovestoneites and the International Communist Opposition of the 1930s*. Westport, CT: Greenwood Press, 1981.

Ali, Tariq. "Recolonizing Iraq," *New Left Review* #21, May-June 2003.

Ali, Tariq and Susan Watkins. *1968: Marching in the Streets*. New York: The Free Press, 1998.

Alinsky, Saul. *John L. Lewis, An Unauthorized Biography*. New York: Vintage Books, 1970.

Altenbaugh, Richard J. *Education for Struggle: The American Labor Colleges of the 1920s and 1930s*. Philadelphia: Temple University Press, 1990.

Amin, Samir. "The Millennium Deveopment Goals: A Critique from the South," *Monthly Review*, March 2006.

Anderson, Evelyn. *Hammer or Anvil: The Story of the German Working-Class Movement*. London: Victor Gollancz, 1945.

Anderson, Jervis. *A. Philip Randolph: A Biographical Portrait*. New York: Harcourt, Brace, Jovanovich, 1973.

Anderson, Kevin. *Lenin, Hegel, and Western Marxism, A Critical Study*. Urbana: University of Illinois Press, 1995.

Arendt, Hannah. *Essays in Understanding, 1930–1954*, Jerome Koen, Ed. New York: Harcourt, Brace and World.

———. *The Origins of Totalitarianism*. New York: Meridian Books, 1958.

Armstrong, Karen. *A History of God: The 4000–Year Quest of Judaism, Christianity and Islam*. New York: Alfred A. Knopf, 1993.

Aronowitz, Stanley. *False Promises: The Shaping of Working Class Consciousness*. New York: McGraw-Hill, 1973.

Aronowitz, Stanley and Heather Gautney, Eds. *Implicating Empire: Globalization and Resistance in the 21st Century World Order*. New York: Basic Books, 2003.

Ash, Timothy Garton. *The Polish Revolution: Solidarity*, third edition. New Haven, CT: Yale University Press, 2002.

Avrich, Paul. *Anarchist Portraits*. Princeton, NJ: Princeton University Press, 1988.

———. *Anarchist Voices, An Oral History of Anarchism in America*. Princeton, NJ: Princeton University Press, 1995.

———. *The Haymarket Tragedy.* Princeton, NJ: Princeton University Press, 1984.

———. *Kronstadt 1921.* New York: W. W. Norton, 1974.

———. *The Russian Anarchists.* New York: W. W. Norton, 1978.

———. *Sacco and Vanzetti, The Anarchist Background.* Princeton, NJ: Princeton University Press, 1991.

Bailey, Bill. *The Kid From Hoboken, An Autobiography.* San Francisco: Circus Lithographic Prepress/Union City, NJ: Smyrna Press, 1993.

Baitalsky, Mikhail. *Notebooks for the Grandchildren: Recollections of a Trotskyist Who Survived the Stalin Terror,* Marilyn Vogt-Downey, Ed. Atlantic Highlands, NJ: Humanities Press, 1995.

Bakunin, Mikhail. *Bakunin on Anarchy,* Sam Dolgoff, Ed. New York: Vintage Books, 1972.

Banic, Ivo, Ed. *The Diary of Georgi Dimitrov, 1933–1949.* New Haven, CT: Yale University Press, 2003.

Barber, Malcolm. *The Cathars: Dualist Heretics in Languedoc in the High Middle Ages.* Essex, UK: Longman, 2000.

Baring, Arnulf. *Uprising in East Germany: June 17, 1953.* New York: Cornell University Press, 1973.

Barrett, James R. *William Z. Foster and the Tragedy of American Radicalism.* Urbana: University of Illinois Press, 1999.

Barron, John. *Operation Solo: The FBI's Man in the Kremlin.* Washington, DC: Regnery, 1996.

Bart, Philip, Theodore Bassett, William W. Weinstein, and Arthur Zipser, Eds. *Highlights of a Fighting History: Sixty Years of the Communist Party, USA.* New York: International Publishers, 1979.

Bartlett, Donald L. and James B. Steele. *America: What Went Wrong?* Kansas City, MO: Andrews and McNeal, 1992.

———. *America: Who Stole the Dream?* Kansas City, MO: Andrews and McNeal, 1996.

Bawer, Bruce. *Stealing Jesus: How Fundamentalism Betrays Christianity.* New York: Three Rivers Press, 1997.

Beal, Fred. *Proletarian Journey: New England, Gastonia, Moscow.* New York: Hillman-Curl, 1937.

Beale, Howard K. *Theodore Roosevelt and the Rise of America to World Power.* Baltimore: Johns Hopkins University Press, 1984.

Beatty, Bessie. *The Red Heart of Russia.* New York: The Century Co., 1918.

Belfrage, Cedric. *The American Inquisition 1945–1960: A Profile of the "McCarthy Era."* New York: Thunders Mouth Press, 1989.

———. *South of God.* New York: Modern Age Books, 1941.

Belfrage, Cedric and James Aronson. *Something to Guard: The Stormy Life of the National Guardian 1948–1967.* New York: Columbia University Press, 1978.

Bell, Daniel. *Marxian Socialism in the United States.* Princeton, NJ: Princeton University Press, 1967.

Bello, Walden. *Dilemmas of Domination: The Unmaking of the American Empire.* New York: Henry Holt, 2005.

Benedict, Ruth. "Human Nature Is Not a Trap," *Partisan Review,* March-April 1943.

Bentley, Elizabeth. *Out of Bondage.* New York: Devin-Adair, 1951.

Bentley, Eric, *The Brecht Memoir.* Evanston, IL: Northwestern University Press, 1989.

Bentley, James. *Between Marx and Christ, The Dialogue in German-Speaking Europe 1870–1970.* London: Verso, 1982.

Berch, Bettina. *Radical By Design: The Life and Style of Elizabeth Hawes, Fashion Designer, Union Organizer, Best-Selling Author.* New York: E. P. Dutton, 1988.

Berdyaev, Nicolas. *The Russian Revolution.* Ann Arbor: University of Michigan Press, 1966.

Berger, Joseph. *Shipwreck of a Generation.* London: Havrill Press, 1971.

Berghahn, Volker. *America and the Intellectual Cold War in Europe.* Princeton, NJ: Princeton University Press, 2001.

Berkman, Alexander. *The Bolshevik Myth.* New York: Boni and Liveright, 1925.

———. *The Life of an Anarchist: The Alexander Berkman Reader,* Gene Fellner, Ed. New York: Four Walls Eight Windows, 1992.

Berlin, Isaiah. *Four Essays on Liberty.* London: Oxford University Press, 1971.

———. *Karl Marx,* fourth edition. London: Oxford University Press, 1978.

Bernstein, Carl and Marco Politi. *His Holiness: John Paul II.* New York: Doubleday, 1996.

Bernstein, Walter. *Inside Out: A Memoir of the Blacklist.* New York: Alfred A. Knopf, 1996.

Bessie, Alvah and Albert Prago, Eds. *Our Fight: Writings by Veterans of the Abraham Lincoln Brigade, Spain 1936–1939.* New York: Monthly Review Press, 1987.

Bevan, Ruth A. *Marx and Burke, A Revisionist View.* LaSalle, IL: Open Court Publishing Co., 1973.

Blaker, Kimberly, Ed. *The Fundamentals of Extremism: The Christian Right in America.* New Boston, MI: New Boston Books, 2003.

Bloch, Ernst. *The Principle of Hope,* 3 vols. Cambridge, MA: Harvard University Press, 1986.

Block, Fred L. *The Origins of International Economic Disorder: A Study of United States International Monetary Policy from World War II to the Present.* Berkeley: University of California Press, 1977.

Blum, Lawrence and Victor J. Seidler. *A Truer Liberty: Simone Weil and Marxism.* New York: Routledge, 1989.

Blum, William. *Killing Hope: U.S. Military and CIA Intervention Since World War II.* Monroe, ME: Common Courage Press, 1995.

Boff, Leonardo. *Jesus Christ, Liberator: A Critical Christology For Our Time.* Maryknoll, NY: Orbis Books, 1984.

———. *The Path to Hope: Fragments from a Theologian's Journey.* Maryknoll, NY: Orbis Books, 1993.

Boggs, James. "The American Revolution: Pages From a Negro Worker's Notebook," *Monthly Review,* July-August, 1963.

Bokkenkotter, Thomas. *A Concise History of the Catholic Church,* revised and expanded edition. New York: Image/Doubleday, 1990.

Bolloten, Burnett. *The Spanish Civil War: Revolution and Counterrevolution.* Chapel Hill: University of North Carolina Press, 1991.

Bookchin, Murray. *Post-Scarcity Anarchism.* San Francisco: Ramparts Press, 1971.

———. *The Spanish Anarchists: The Heroic Years 1868-1936.* Harper and Row, 1977.

Booth, Father Leo. *When God Becomes a Drug: Breaking the Chains of Religious Addiction.* New York: Tarcher/Putnam, 1991.

Borg Marcus J. *The God We Never Knew.* San Francisco: HarperCollins, 1997.

———, Ed. *Jesus at 2000.* Boulder, CO: Westview Press, 1998.

Borg, Marcus and Ross Mackenzie, Eds. *God at 2000.* Harrisburg, PA: Morehouse Publishing Co. 2000.

Borg, Marcus J. and N. T. Wright. *The Meaning of Jesus: Two Visions.* San Francisco: HarperCollins, 2000.

Bottomore, Tom and Robert J. Brym, Eds. *The Capitalist Class, An International Study.* New York: New York University Press, 1989.

Boxer, Marilyn and Jean H. Quartaert, Eds. *Socialist Women: European Socialist Feminism in the Early Nineteenth and Twentieth Century.* New York: Elsevier, 1978.

Braden, Anne. "The Southern Freedom Movement in Perspective," *Monthly Review,* July-August 1965.

Bradshear, Keith. "The Few, the Rich: That's America," *Pittsburgh Post Gazette,* April 17, 1996.

Branch, Taylor. *At Canaan's Edge: America in the King Years 1965-1968.* New York: Simon and Schuster, 2006.

———. *Parting the Waters: America in the King Years 1954-63.* New York: Simon and Schuster, 1989.

———. *Pillar of Fire: America in the King Years 1963-65.* New York: Simon and Schuster, 1998.

Braverman, Harry. *Labor and Monopoly Capital: The Degradation of Work in the Twentieth Century.* New York: Monthly Review Press, 1976.

———. "The New America," *American Socialist,* July 1956.

Brecher, Jeremy and Tim Costello. *Global Village or Global Pillage: Economic Reconstruction From the Bottom Up.* Boston: South End Press, 1994.

Breitman, George. *Malcolm X and the Third American Revolution: The Writings of George Breitman,* Anthony Marcus, Ed. Amherst, NY: Humanity Books, 2005.

Breitman, George, Paul Le Blanc, and Alan Wald. *Trotskyism in the United States, Historical Essays and Reconsiderations.* Atlantic Highlands, NJ: Humanities Press, 1996.

Brenan, Gerald. *The Spanish Labyrinth.* Cambridge, UK: Cambridge University Press, 1964.

Brett, Edward T. *The U.S. Catholic Press on Central Ameria, From Cold War Anticommunism to Social Justice.* Notre Dame, IN: University of Notre Dame Press, 2003.

Brinton, Crane. *The Shaping of Modern Thought.* Englewood Cliffs, NJ: Prentice Hall, 1963.

Brock, David. *Blinded by the Right: The Conscience of an Ex-Conservative.* New York: Three Rivers Press, 2002.

Brody, David. *In Labor's Cause*. New York: Oxford University Pres, 1993.

———. *Workers in Industrial America, Essays on the 20th Century Struggle*. New York: Oxford University Press, 1980.

Bronner, Stephen Eric. "Moving On: New Replies to Critics," *New Politics*, no. 33, Summer 2002.

———. "Rosa Redux: A Reply to David Camfield and Alan Johnson," *New Politics*, no. 32, Winter 2002.

Broué, Pierre. *The German Revolution 1917-1923*. Leiden, The Netherlands: Brill, 2004.

Broué, Pierre and Emile Temime. *Revolution and Civil War in Spain*. Cambridge, MA: MIT Press, 1970.

Brovkin, Vladimir. *Russia After Lenin: Politics, Culture, and Society 1921-1929*. London: Routledge, 1998.

Browder, Earl. *The People's Front*. New York: International Publishers, 1938.

———. *Teheran: Our Path in War and Peace*. New York: International Publishers, 1944.

———. *Victory — And After*. New York: International Publishers, 1943

Browder, Earl and Bill Lawrence. *Next Steps to Win the War in Spain*, New York: Friends of the Abraham Lincoln Brigade, 1938.

Brown, Archie. *The Gorbachev Factor*. New York: Oxford University Press, 1997.

Brown, Michael, Ed. *New Studies in the Politics and Culture of U.S. Communism*. New York: Monthly Review Press, 1993.

Bryant, Louise. *Six Red Months in Russia*. London: Journeyman Press, 1982.

Brysac, Shareen Blair. *Resisting Hitler: Mildred Harnack and the Red Orchestra*. Oxford: Oxford University Press, 2000.

Brzezinski, Zbigniew K. *The Soviet Bloc: Unity and Conflict*, revised edition. New York: Frederick A. Praeger, 1961.

Bucklin, Steven J. *Realism and American Foreign Policy: Wilsonians and the Kennan-Morganthau Thesis*. Westport, CT: Praeger, 2001.

Budenz, Louis. *Red Baiting: Enemy of Labor*. New York: Workers Library Publishers, 1937.

———. *This Is My Story*. New York: McGraw-Hill, 1947.

Budenz, Margaret. *Streets*. Huntington, IN: Our Sunday Visitor, 1979.

Buhle, Mari Jo, Paul Buhle, and Dan Georgakas, Eds., *Encyclopedia of the American Left*. New York: Oxford University Press, 1998.

Bukharin, Nikolai. *Imperialism and World Economy*. London: Merlin Press, 1972.

Burnham, James. "Joys and Sorrows of Empire," *National Review*, July 13, 1971.

———. *The Struggle for the World*. New York: John Day Co., 1947.

Burns, James McGregor. *Roosevelt: The Lion and the Fox, 1882-1940*. New York: Harcourt Brace and World, 1956.

Butler, Smedley. "'In Time of Peace': The Army," *Common Sense*, November 1935.

Buzgalin, Alexander and Andrei Kolganov. *Bloody October in Moscow: Political Repression in the Name of Reform*. New York: Monthly Review Press, 1994.

Cahill, Thomas. *Pope John XXIII*. New York: Viking, 2002.

Calverton, V. F. "Marxism and Religion," *Modern Monthly*, February 1935.

Calvocoressi, Peter, Guy Wint, and John Pritchard. *The Penguin History of the Second World War*. London: Penguin Books, 1999.

Camus, Albert. *The Plague*. New York: Random House, 1949.

———. *The Rebel*. New York: Vintage Books, 1960.

Cannon, James P. *The First Ten Years of American Communism, Report of a Participant*. New York: Lyle Stuart, 1961.

———. *The First Ten Years of American Trotskyism, Report of a Participant*. New York: Pathfinder Press, 1972.

———. *James P. Cannon and the Early Years of American Communism: Early Writings and Speeches, 1920-1928*, Emily Turnbull and James Robertson, Eds. New York: Prometheus Research Library, 1992.

———. *Speeches to the Party*. New York: Pathfinder Press, 1973.

Cardenal, Ernesto. *The Gospel of Solentiname*, 4 vols. Maryknoll, NY: Orbis Books, 1982.

Carr, E. H. *The Bolshevik Revolution, 1917-1923*, 3 vols. Baltimore: Penguin Books, 1966.

———. *The Comintern and the Spanish Civil War*. New York: Pantheon Books, 1984.

———. *The Interregnum: 1923-24*. Baltimore: Penguin Books, 1969.

———. *Michael Bakunin*. New York: Vintage Books, 1961.

———. *The Russian Revolution: From Lenin to Stalin*. New York: The Free Press, 1979.

————. *Twilight of the Comintern, 1930-1935*. New York: Pantheon Books, 1982.

Carroll, Peter N. *The Odyssey of the Abraham Lincoln Brigade: Americans in the Spanish Civil War*. Stanford, CA: Stanford University Press, 1994.

Carson, Clayborne. In *Struggle: SNCC and the Black Awakening of the 1960s*. Cambridge, MA: Harvard University Press, 1981.

Cassidy, John. "The Next Great Thinker: The Return of Karl Marx," *The New Yorker*, October 20-27, 1998.

Caute, David. *The Great Fear: The Anti-Communist Purge Under Truman and Eisenhower*. New York: Simon and Schuster, 1978.

————. *The Fellow-Travellers: Intellectual Friends of Communism*, revised. New Haven, CT: Yale University Press, 1988.

————. *The Year of the Barricades: A Journey Through 1968*. New York: HarperCollins, 1990.

Ceplair, Larry, and Steven Englund. *The Inquisition in Hollywood: Politics in the Film Community, 1930-1960*. Urbana: University of Illinois Press, 2003.

Chamberlin, William H. *The Russian Revolution, 1917-1921*, 2 vols. New York: Grosset and Dunlap, 1965.

————. *Soviet Russia, A Living Record and a History*. Boston: Little, Brown and Co., 1930.

————. *Russia's Iron Age*. Boston: Little, Brown, and Co., 1934.

Chambers, Whittaker. *Cold Friday*, Duncan Taylor-Norton, Ed. New York: Random House, 1964.

————. *Ghosts on the Roof, Selected Essays*, Terry Teachout, Ed. New Brunswick, NJ: Transaction Publishers, 1996.

————. *Notes From the Underground: The Whittaker Chambers-Ralph de Toledano Letters, 1949-1960*, Ralph de Toledano, Ed. Washington, DC: Regnery Publishing, 1997.

————. *Odyssey of a Friend: Whittaker Chambers' Letters to William F. Buckley, Jr. 1954-1961*, William F. Buckley, Ed. Printed privately by *National Review*, 1969.

————. *Witness*. New York: Random House, 1951.

Charney, George Blake. *A Long Journey*. Chicago: Quadrangle Books, 1968.

Chase, William J. *Enemies Within the Gates? The Comintern and the Stalinist Repression, 1934-1939*. New Haven, CT: Yale University Press, 2001.

Cheru, Fantu, and Colin Bradford, Eds. *The Millennium Development Goals: Raising Resources to Tackle Poverty*. London: Zed Books, 2005.

Chevalier, Haakon. *Oppenheimer: The Story of a Friendship*. New York: George Brazziller, 1965.

Chilcote, Ronald H., Ed. *Imperialism: Theoretical Directions*. Amherst, NY: Humanity Books, 2000.

Childs, David. *East Germany*. London: Ernest Benn, 1969.

Christ, Carol P. and Judith Plaskow, Eds., *Womanspirit Rising: A Feminist Reader in Religion*. San Fransciso: Harper and Row, 1979.

Christie-Murray, David. *A History of Heresy*. New York: Oxford University Press, 1976.

Clark, Ronald W. *Lenin, A Biography*. New York: Harper and Row, 1988.

Clarke, Tom and Laurie Clements. Eds. *Trade Unions Under Capitalism*. Glasgow: Fontana, 1977.

Claudin, Fernando. *The Communist Movement From Comintern to Cominform*, 2 vols. New York: Monthly Review Press, 1975.

Cleaver, Kathleen and George Katsiaficas, Eds. *Liberation, Imagination, and the Black Panther Party*. New York: Routledge, 2001.

Cliff, Tony. *Lenin*, 4 vols. London: Pluto Press, 1975-1979.

Cochran, Bert. *Harry Truman and the Crisis Presidency*. New York: Funk and Wagnalls, 1973.

————. *Labor and Communism: The Conflict That Shaped American Unions*. Princeton, NJ: Princeton University Press, 1977.

Codrescu, Andrei. *The Hole in the Flag, A Romanian Exile's Story of Return and Revolution*. New York: William Morrow and Co., 1991.

Cohen, Arthur, Ed. *Arguments and Doctrines: A Reader of Jewish Thinking in the Aftermath of the Holocaust*. New York: Harper and Row, 1970.

Cohen, Lizabeth. *Making a New Deal: Industrial Workers in Chicago, 1919-1939*. New York: Cambridge: Cambridge University Press, 1990.

Cohen, Stephen. *Bukharin and the Bolshevik Revolution: A Political Biography, 1888-1938*. New York: Vintage Books, 1975.

————. *The Failed Crusade: America and the Tragedy of Post-Communist Russia*, updated edition. New York: W. W. Norton, 2001.

Collier, Peter and David Horowitz, Eds. *Destructive Generation: Second Thoughts About the Sixties*. New York: Summit Books, 1990.

———, Eds. *Second Thoughts: Former Radicals Look Back at the Sixties*. Lanham, MD: Madison Books, 1989

Collins, Chuck and Felice Yeskel. *Economic Apartheid in America, A Primer on Economic Inequality and Insecurity*. New York: The New Press, 2000.

Conquest, Robert. *The Great Terror, A Reassessment*. New York: Oxford University Press, 1990.

Cone, James H. *A Black Theology of Liberation*. Philadelphia: J.P. Lippincott Co., 1970.

Connolly, James. *James Connolly: Selected Writings*, P. Berresford Ellis, Ed. New York: Grove Press, 1973.

Constantine, Mildred. *Tina Modotti: A Fragile Life*. San Francisco: Chronicle Books, 1993.

Cook, Fred J. *The Nightmare Decade: The Life and Times of Joseph McCarthy*. New York: Random House, 1971.

Corrêa Leite, José. *The World Social Forum: Strategies of Resistance*. Chicago: Haymarket Books, 2005.

Cort, John C. *Christian Socialism*. Maryknoll, NY: Orbis Books, 1988.

Coulter, Ann. *Treason: Liberal Treachery From the Cold War to the War on Terror*. New York: Crown Forum, 2003.

Courtois, Stephane, Nicolas Werth, Jean-Louis Panne, Andrezej Paczkowski, Karel Bartosek, and Jean-Louis Margolin. *The Black Book of Communism: Crimes, Terror, Repression*. Cambridge, MA: Harvard University Press, 1999.

Cox, Terry, Ed. *Hungary 1956 — Forty Years On*. London: Frank Cass, 1997.

Craig, R. Bruce. *Treasonable Doubt: The Harry Dexter White Spy Case*. Lawrence: University Press of Kansas, 2004.

Crick, Bernard. *George Orwell, A Life*. Harmondsworth, UK: Penguin Books, 1980.

Crossan, John Dominic. *The Birth of Christianity: Discovering What Happened in the Years Immediately After the Execution of Jesus*. San Francisco: HarperCollins, 1998.

———. *The Historical Jesus: The Life of a Mediterranean Jewish Peasant*. San Francisco: HarperCollins, 1992.

———. *Jesus: A Revolutionary Biography*. San Francisco: HarperCollins, 1994.

Crossan, John Dominic and Jonathan L. Reed. *Excavating Jesus: Beneath the Stones, Behind the Texts*. San Francisco: HarperCollins, 2002.

Crossman, Richard, Ed. *The God That Failed*. New York: Columbia University Press, 2001.

D'Agostino, Anthony. *Marxism and the Russian Anarchists*. San Francisco: Germinal Press, 1977.

Dallin, David J. *The Real Soviet Russia*, second edition. New Haven, CT: Yale University Press, 1947.

———. *Soviet Espionage*. New Haven, CT: Yale University Press, 1955.

Dallin, David J. and Boris I. Nicolaevsky. *Forced Labor in Soviet Russia*. New Haven, CT: Yale University Press, 1947.

Danaher, Kevin and Roger Burbach, Eds., *Globalize This! The Battle Against the World Trade Organization and Corporate Rule*. Monroeville. ME: Common Courage Press, 2000.

Daniels, Robert V. *The Conscience of the Revolution: Communist Opposition in Soviet Russia*. New York: Simon and Schuster, 1969.

———, Ed. *The Stalin Revolution*. Boston: Houghton Mifflin Co., 1997.

———. *Year of the Heroic Guerrilla: World Revolution and Counterrevolution in 1968*. Cambridge, MA: Harvard University Press, 1989.

Danilov, V. P. "The Historical Significance of Alternatives to Stalinism," *Russian Studies in History*, vol. 42, no. 4, Spring 2004.

Danner, Mark. *Torture and Truth: America, Abu Ghraib, and the War on Terror*. London: Granta Books, 2005.

Davis, Angela. *Angela Davis, An Autobiography*. New York: Random House, 1974.

Davis, Jerome, Ed. *Labor Speaks for Itself on Religion: A Symposium of Labor Leaders Throughout the World*. New York: Macmillan Co., 1929.

Day, Dorothy. *Dorothy Day, Selected Writings*, Robert Ellsberg, Ed. Maryknoll, NY: Orbis Books, 2003.

———. *The Long Loneliness, An Autobiography*. San Francisco: HarperCollins, 1981.

Dean, John. *Blind Ambition: The White House Years*. New York: Simon and Schuster, 1976.

De Caux, Len. *Labor Radical: From the Wobblies to the CIO, A Personal History*. Boston: Beacon Press, 1970.

Dedijer, Vladimir. *Tito*. New York: Simon and Schuster, 1953.

Denning, Michael. *The Cultural Front: The Laboring of American Culture in the Twentieth Century*. London: Verso, 1998.

Dennis, Peggy. *The Autobiography of an American Communist*. Westport, CT: Lawrence Hill, 1977.

Deutscher, Isaac. *Marxism in Our Time*. San Francisco: Ramparts Press, 1971.

———. *The Prophet Armed, Trotsky: 1879–1921*. London: Oxford University Press, 1954.

———. *The Prophet Outcast, Trotsky: 1929–1940*. London: Oxford University Press, 1963.

———. *The Prophet Unarmed, Trotsky: 1921–1929*. London: Oxford University Press, 1959.

———. *Russia in Transition*, revised edition. New York: Grove Press, 1960.

Diamond, Sara. *Spiritual Warfare: The Politics of the Christian Right*. Boston: South End Press, 1989.

Dickens, A. G. *Reformation and Society in Sixteenth-Century Europe*. New York: Harcourt, Brace and World, 1966.

Dimitroff, Georgi. *The United Front*. New York: International Publishers, 1938.

Djilas, Milovan. *Anatomy of a Moral*. New York: Frederick A. Praeger, 1959.

———. *The New Class: An Analysis of the Communist System*. New York: Frederick A. Praeger, 1957.

Dollinger, Sol and Genora Johnson Dollinger. *Not Automatic: Women and the Left in the Forging of the Auto Workers Union*. New York: Monthly Review Press, 2000.

Domhoff, G. William. *Who Rules America? Power and Politics*, fourth edition. New York: McGraw-Hill, 2001.

Dorrien, Gary. *The Neoconservative Mind: Politics, Culture, and the War of Ideology*. Philadelphia: Temple University Press, 1993.

Dourin, Alexander N. "Ten Years Later: Society, 'Civil Society,' and the Russian State," *The Russian Review*, vol. 46, no. 2, April 2003.

Draper, Hal. *Berkeley: The New Student Revolt*. New York: Grove Press, 1965.

———. *The "Dictatorship of the Proletariat" from Marx to Lenin*. New York: Monthly Review Press, 1986.

———. *Karl Marx's Theory of Revolution, Vol. IV: Critique of Other Socialisms*. New York: Monthly Review Press, 1990.

———. *Socialism From Below*, E. Haberkern, Ed. Atlantic Highlands, NJ: Humanities Press, 1992.

Draper, Theodore. *American Communism and Soviet Russia*. New York: Viking Press, 1960.

———. *The Roots of American Communism*. New York: Viking Press, 1957.

Drolovic, Milojko. *Self-Management on Trial*. London: Spokesman Books, 1978.

Drucker, Peter. *Max Shachtman and His Left, A Socialist's Odyssey Through the "American Century."* Atlantic Highlands, NJ: Humanities Press, 1994.

Duberman, Martin Dauml. *Paul Robeson, A Biography*. New York: Ballantine Books, 1989.

Duiker, William J. *Ho Chi Minh, A Life*. New York: Hyperion, 2000.

Dunayevskaya, Raya. *The Free Speech Movement and the Negro Revolution*. Detroit: News and Letters, 1965.

Dunbar, Anthony P. *Against the Grain: Southern Radicals and Prophets, 1929–1959*. Charlottesville: University Press of Virginia, 1981.

Eastman, Max. *The End of Socialism in Russia*. Boston: Little, Brown and Co., 1937.

———. *Heroes I Have Known*. New York: Simon and Schuster, 1942.

———. *Love and Revolution: My Journey Through an Epoch*. New York: Random House, 1964.

———. *Marxism — Is It Science?* London: George Allen and Unwin, 1940.

———. *Marx, Lenin and the Science of Revolution*. London: George Allen and Unwin, 1926.

———. *Reflections on the Failure of Socialism*. New York: Devin-Adair Co., 1955.

———. *Since Lenin Died*. New York: Boni and Liveright, 1925.

———. *Stalin's Russia and the Crisis of Socialism*. New York: W. W. Norton, 1940.

Eddy, Sherwood. *Revolutionary Christianity*. Chicago: Willett, Clark and Co., 1939.

———. *Russia Today: What Can We Learn From It?* New York: Farrar and Rinehart, 1934.

Editors of *Freedomways*, Ed. *Paul Robeson: The Great Forerunner*. New York: International Publishers, 1985.

Editors of the *New Republic*, Eds., *Thoughts of the Young Radicals*. New Jersey: Harrison Blaine and the New Republic, 1966.

Egerton, John. *Speak Now Against the Day: The Generation Before the Civil Rights Movement in the South*. Chapel Hill: University of North Carolina Press, 1994.

Ehrman, Bart D. *Lost Christianities: The Battles for Scripture and the Faiths We Never Knew*. New York: Oxford University Press, 2003.

———. *Truth and Fiction in the Da Vinci Code: A Historian Reveals What We Really Know About Jesus, Mary Magdalene, and Constantine.* New York: Oxford University Press, 2004.

Einstein, Albert. *Ideas and Opinions.* New York: Dell, 1979.

Elbaum, Max. *Revolution in the Air: Sixties Radicals Turn to Lenin, Mao and Che.* London: Verso, 2002.

Eley, Geoff. *Forging Democracy: The History of the Left in Europe, 1850–2000.* New York: Oxford University Press, 2002.

Ellerbe, Helen. *The Dark Side of Christian History.* San Rafael, CA: Morningside Books, 1995.

Ellsberg, Daniel. *Secrets: A Memoir of Vietnam and the Pentagon Papers.* New York: Viking, 2002.

Ellwood, Wayne. *The No-Nonsense Guide to Globalization.* London: Verso, 2003.

Elwood, R. C. *Inessa Armand: Revolutionary and Feminist.* Cambridge: Cambridge University Press, 1992.

———. "Lenin's Testimony to the Extraordinary Investigating Commission," *Canadian Slavonic Papers,* vol. XLI, nos. 3–4, September-December, 1999.

Engels, Frederick. *The Origin of the Family, Private Property, and the State.* New York: International Publishers, 1972.

Evans, Sara. *Personal Politics: The Roots of the Women's Liberation in the Civil Rights Movement and the New Left.* New York: Vintage Books, 1979.

Farber, Samuel. *Before Stalinism: The Rise and Fall of Soviet Democracy.* London: Verso, 1990.

Fast, Howard. *Being Red, A Memoir.* Boston: Houghton Mifflin, 1994.

———. *Naked God: The Writer and the Communist Party.* New York: Frederick A. Praeger, 1957.

Fejto, Francois. *Behind the Rape of Hungary.* New York: David McKay, 1957.

———. *History of the People's Democracies: Eastern Europe Since Stalin.* Harmondsworth, UK: Penguin Books, 1977.

Ferro, Marc. *The Great War 1914–1918.* London: Routledge and Kegan Paul, 1973.

The Fifty Years Is Enough Network, Ed. *Empty Promises: The IMF, the World Bank, and the Planned Failures of Capitalism.* Washington, DC: Fifty Years Is Enough, 2003.

Figes, Orlando. *A People's Tragedy: A History of the Russian Revolution.* New York: Viking, 1996.

Filippelli, Ronald L., and Mark D. McColloch. *Cold War in the Working Class: The Rise and Decline of the United Electrical Workers.* Albany: State University of New York Press, 1995.

Fiorenza, Elisabeth Schlusser. *In Memory of Her: A Feminist Theological Reconstruction of Christian Origins.* New York: Crossroad, 1994.

Fiori, Giuseppe. *Antonio Gramsci, Life of a Revolutionary.* New York: Schocken, 1973.

Fischer, Ernst and Franz Marek. *The Essential Lenin.* New York: Seabury Press, 1972.

Fisher, Harry. *Comrades: Tales of a Brigadista in the Spanish Civil War.* Lincoln: University of Nebraska Press, 1998.

Fisher, William F. and Thomas Ponniah, Eds. *Another World Is Possible: Popular Alternatives to Globalization at the World Social Forum.* London: Zed Press, 2003.

Fitzpatrick, Sheila. *Everyday Stalinism: Ordinary Life in Extraordinary Times, Soviet Russia in the 1930s.* New York: Oxford University Press, 2000.

———. *The Russian Revolution,* second edition. New York: Oxford University Press, 1994.

Fitzpatrick, Sheila, Alexander Rabinowitch, and Richard Stites, Eds. *Russia in the Era of NEP: Explorations in Soviet Society and Culture.* Bloomington: Indiana University Press, 1991.

Foner, Philip S., Ed. *The Black Panthers Speak.* New York: DeCapo Press, 1995.

Foner, Philip S. and James S. Allen, Eds. *American Communism and Black Americans: A Documentary History, 1919–1929.* Philadelphia: Temple University Press, 1987.

Fones-Wolf, Elizabeth A. *Selling Free Enterprise: The Business Assault on Labor and Liberalism, 1945–1960.* Urbana: University of Illinois Press, 1994.

Forrell, George W., Ed. *Christian Social Teachings: A Reader in Christian Social Ethics from the Bible to the Present.* Garden City, NY: Anchor Books, 1966.

Fosl, Catherine. *Subvesive Southerner: Anne Braden and the Struggle for Racial Justice in the Cold War South.* New York: Palgrave Macmillan, 2002.

Foster, John Bellamy. *Marx's Ecology: Materialism and Nature.* New York: Monthly Review Press, 2000.

———. *The Vulnerable Planet: A Short Economic History of the Environment.* New York: Monthly Review Press, 1994.

Foster, William Z. *From Bryan to Stalin.* New York: International Publishers, 1937.

———. *History of the Communist Party of the United States.* New York: International Publishers, 1952.

———. *The Russian Revolution.* Chicago: Trade Union Educational League, 1921.

———. *Toward Soviet America.* New York: International Publishers, 1932.

Fotieva, L. *Pages From Lenin's Life.* Moscow: Foreign Languages Publishing House, 1956.

Fox, Richard. *Reinhold Niebuhr, A Biography.* San Francisco: Harper and Row, 1985.

Francis, David R. *Russia From the American Embassy.* New York: Charles Scribners Sons. 1921.

Frankfurter, Marion D. and Gardner Jackson, Eds. *The Letters of Sacco and Vanzetti.* New York: E. P. Dutton and Co., 1960.

Fraser, Ronald. *1968: Student Generation, Student Revolt.* New York: Pantheon, 1988.

Fraser, Steve. *Labor Will Rule: Sidney Hillman and the Rise of American Labor.* New York: The Free Press, 1991.

Fraser, Steven and Joshua B. Freeman, Eds., *Audacious Democracy: Labor, Intellectuals, and the Social Reconstruction of America.* Boston: Houghton Mifflin, 1997.

Freeland, Richard M. *The Truman Doctrine and the Origins of McCarthyism: Foreign Policy, Domestic Politics, and Internal Security, 1946–1948.* New York: Alfred A. Knopf, 1972.

Freeman, Joseph. *An American Testament, A Narrative of Rebels and Romantics.* New York: Farrar and Rinehart, 1936.

Fried, Albert, Ed. *Communism in America: A History in Documents.* New York: Columbia University, 1997.

———. *Socialism in America: From the Shakers to the Third International, A Documentary History.* Garden City, NY: Anchor Books, 1970.

Frolich, Paul. *Rosa Luxemburg: Her Life and Work.* New York: Monthly Review Press, 1972.

Fromm, Erich. *Psychoanalysis and Religion.* New Haven, CT: Yale University Press, 1950.

———. *You Shall Be As Gods: A Radical Interpretation of the Old Testament and Its Tradition.* Greenwich, CT: Fawcett, 1966.

Fryer, Peter. *Hungarian Tragedy.* London: Dobson Books, 1956 (reprinted, London: New Park Publications, 1986).

Fulbright, J. William. *The Arrogance of Power.* New York: Vintage, 1966.

Fulbrook, Mary. *The Nation Divided: A History of Germany, 1918–1990.* New York: Oxford University Press, 1992.

Fulcher, James. *A Very Short Introduction to Capitalism.* Oxford: Oxford University Press, 2004.

Gaddis, John Lewis. *The United States and the Origins of the Cold War, 1941–1947.* New York: Columbia University Press, 1972.

Gaer, Joseph, Ed. *The First Round: The Story of the CIO Political Action Committee.* New York: Duel, Sloan and Pearce, 1944.

Gallagher, Dorothy. *All the Right Enemies: The Life and Murder of Carlo Tresca.* New York: Penguin Books, 1989.

Gardner, Lloyd C. *Architects of Illusion: Men and Ideas in American Foreign Policy, 1941–1949.* Chicago: Quadrangle Books, 1972.

———. *Economic Aspects of New Deal Diplomacy.* Madison: University of Wisconsin Press, 1964.

———. *Imperial America: American Foreign Policy Since 1898.* New York: Harcourt Brace Jovanovich, 1976.

Gardner, Lloyd C., Walter F. LeFeber, and Thomas J. McCormick, Eds. *Creation of the American Empire,* 2 vols. Chicago: Rand McNally, 1976.

Gardner, Virginia. *Friend and Lover: The Life of Louise Bryant.* New York: Horizon Press, 1982.

Garrow, David J. *The FBI and Martin Luther King, Jr.* New York: Penguin Books, 1983.

Gasper, Phil, Ed. *The Communist Manifesto: A Road Map to History's Most Important Political Document.* Chicago: Haymarket Books, 2005.

Gates, John. *The Story of an American Communist.* New York: Thomas Nelson and Sons, 1958.

Germano, Dante. *Antonio Gramsci: Architect of a New Politics.* Baton Rouge: Louisiana University Press, 1990.

Gerstle, Gary. *Working-Class Americanism: The Politics of Labor in a Textile City, 1914–1960.* New York: Cambridge: Cambridge University Press, 1989.

Getty, J. Arch, and Oleg V. Naumov. *The Road to Terror: Stalin and the Self-Destruction of the Bolsheviks, 1932–1939.* New Haven, CT: Yale University Press, 1999.

Giddings, Paula. *When and Where I Enter: The Impact of Black Women on Race and Sex in America*. New York: William Morrow, 1984.

Gilden, K. B. *Between the Hills and the Sea*. Ithaca, NY: ILR Press/Cornell University Press, 1989.

Ginzburg, Eugenia Semyonovna. *Journey Into the Whirlwind*. Harmondsworth, UK: Penguin Books, 1968.

Glen, John M. *Highlander, No Ordinary School*, second edition. Knoxville: University of Tennessee Press, 1996.

Glenny, Misha. *The Fall of Yugoslavia*. New York: Penguin, 1993.

Goldman, Emma. *Anarchism and Other Essays*. New York: Dover Books, 1969.

———. *Red Emma Speaks: An Emma Goldman Reader*, Ed. by Alix Kates Shulman. New York: Schocken Books, 1983.

Goldman, Wendy. "Stalinist Terror and Democracy: The 1937 Union Campaign," *The American Historical Review*, vol. 110, no. 5, December 2005.

Goodman, Paul. *Drawing the Line, Political Essays*. New York: Free Life Editions, 1977.

———, Ed. *Seeds of Liberation*. New York: George Braziller, 1964.

Gordon, David M. *Fat and Mean: The Corporate Squeeze of Working Americans and the Myth of Managerial "Downsizing."* New York: Free Press, 1996.

Gordon, Max, "The Communist Party of the Nineteen-Thirties and the New Left," *Socialist Revolution*, January-February 1976.

Gorky, Maxim. *Mother*. New York: Collier Books, 1962.

———. *Untimely Thoughts: Essays on Revolution, Culture, and the Bolsheviks, 1917–1918*. New Haven, CT: Yale University Press, 1995.

Gottwald, Norman K., Ed. *The Bible and Liberation, Political and Social Hermeneutics*. Maryknoll, NY: Orbis Books, 1984.

Gould, Stephen Jay. *The Mismeasure of Man*. New York: W. W. Norton, 1981.

Goulden, Joseph C. *Meany: The Unchallenged Strong Man of American Labor*. New York: Atheneum, 1972.

Gramsci, Antonio. *Selections From the Prison Notebooks*, Quinton Hoare and Geoffroy Nowell Smith, Eds. New York: International Publishers, 1973.

Granville, Johanna. "Imre Nagy, Hesitant Revolutionary," and "Imre Nagy, aka 'Volodya' — A Dent in the Martyr's Halo?," *Cold War International History Project Bulletin*, no. 5, Spring 1995.

Green, Mark and Robert Massie, Jr. *The Big Business Reader: Essays on Corporate America*. New York: Pilgrim Press, 1980.

Gruber, Helmut, Ed. *Soviet Russia Masters the Comintern: International Communism in the Era of Stalin's Ascendancy*. Garden City, NY: Anchor Books, 1974.

Guerin, Daniel. *Anarchism*. New York: Monthly Review Press, 1970.

———, Ed. *No Gods, No Masters: An Anthology of Anarchism*, 2 vols. San Francisco: AK Press, 1998.

Gunn, Giles. *F.O. Matthiessen: The Critical Achievement*. Seattle: University of Washington Press, 1975.

Gutman, Herbert. *Power and Culture: Essays on the American Working Class*. New York: Pantheon, 1987.

———. *Work, Culture, and Society in Industrializing America: Essays in American Working-Class and Social History*. New York: Random House, 1977.

Halberstam, David. *The Fifties*. New York: Ballantine Books, 1994.

Halstead, Fred. *Out Now: A Participant's Account of the American Movement Against the Vietnam War*. New York: Monad/Pathfinder Press, 1978.

Brian Halweil, Lisa Mastny, Erik Assadourian, Christopher Flavin, Hilary French, Gary Gardner, Danielle Nierenberg, Sandra Postel, Michael Renner, Radhika Sarin, Janet Sawin, Amy Vickers, Linda Starke. *State of the World 2004*. New York: W. W. Norton, 2004.

Hansen, Joseph, et al. *Leon Trotsky, The Man and His Work*. New York: Merit Publishers, 1969.

Harding, Neil. *Leninism*. Durham, NC: Duke University Press, 1996.

Hardt, Michael and Antonio Negri. *Empire*. Cambridge, MA: Harvard University Press, 2001.

Harman, Chris. *Bureaucracy and Revolution in Eastern Europe*. London: Pluto Press, 1974.

———. *The Fire Last Time: 1968 and After*. London: Bookmarks, 1988.

———. *A People's History of the World*. London: Bookmarks, 1999.

Harrington, Michael. *Fragments of a Century, A Social Autobiography.* New York: Saturday Review Press, 1973.

———. *The Long-Distance Runner, An Autobiography.* New York: Henry Holt and Co., 1988.

———. *Socialism.* New York: Bantam Books, 1973.

Hart, Celia. "Welcome . . . Trotsky," *International Viewpoint,* November 2005 (http://www.internationalviewpoint.org/).

Hawes, Elizabeth. *Hurry Up Please, It's Time.* New York: Reynal and Hitchcock, 1946.

Haynes, John Earl. *Red Scare or Red Menace? American Communism and Anticommunism in the Cold War Era.* Chicago: Ivan R. Dee, 1996.

Haynes, John Earl and Harvey Klehr. *The American Communist Movement, Storming Heaven Itself.* New York: Twayne Publishers, 1992.

———. *In Denial: Historians, Communism, and Espionage.* San Francisco: Encounter Books, 2003.

———. *Venona: Decoding Soviet Espionage in America.* New Haven, CT: Yale University Press, 1999.

Haynes, Mike. "The Debate on Popular Violence and the Russian Revolution," *Historical Materialism,* vol. 1, no. 2 (1998).

Haywood, Harry. *Black Bolshevik, Autobiography of an Afro-American Communist.* Chicago: Liberator Press, 1978.

Healey, Dorothy and Maurice Isserman. *California Red: Dorothy Healey Remembers.* New York: Oxford University Press, 1990.

Hecker, Julius F. *Religion Under the Soviets.* New York: Vanguard Press, 1927.

Henderson, David R., Robert M. McNab, and Tamas Rossas. "The Hidden Inequality of Socialism," *The Independent Review,* vol. IX, no. 3, Winter 2005.

Henwood, Doug. *After the New Economy.* New York: The New Press, 2005.

Herberg, Will. *Faith Enacted As History: Essays in Biblical Theology,* Bernhard W. Anderson, Ed. Philadelphia: The Westminster Press, 1976.

Herrick, William. *Jumping the Line: The Adventures and Misadventures of an American Radical.* Oakland, CA: AK Press, 2001.

Heschel, Abraham J. *Moral Grandeur and Spiritual Audacity,* Susanna Heschel, Ed. New York: Noonday Press, 1998.

———. *The Prophets,* 2 vols. New York: Harper and Row, 1975.

Heym, Stefan. *Five Days in June.* Buffalo, NY: Prometheus Books, 1978.

Hicks, Granville. *John Reed, The Making of a Revolutionary.* New York: Macmillan Co., 1936.

———. *Where We Came Out.* New York: Viking Press, 1954.

Hildenbrandt, Rainer. *The Explosion: The Uprising Behind the Iron Curtain.* Boston: Little, Borwn and Co., 1955.

Hinshaw, John and Paul Le Blanc, Eds. *U.S. Labor in the Twentieth Century: Studies in Working-Class Struggles and Insurgency.* Amherst, NY: Humanity Books, 2000.

Hippe, Oskar. *And Red Is the Color of Our Flag: Memories of Sixty Years in the Workers' Movement.* London: Index Books, 1991.

Hiss, Alger. *Recollections of a Life.* New York: Henry Holt and Co., 1988.

Hochschild, Adam. *The Unquiet Ghost: Russians Remember Stalin.* Boston: Houghton Mifflin Co., 2003.

Hodgson, Godfrey. *America in Our Time.* Garden City, NY: Doubleday and Co., 1976.

Hogan, Michael J., Ed. *The End of the Cold War, Its Meaning and Implications.* Cambridge: Cambridge University Press, 1992.

Holmstrom, Nancy, Ed. *The Socialist Feminist Project: A Contemporary Reader in Theory and Politics.* New York: Monthly Review, 2003.

Hook, Sidney. "Marxism and Religion," *Modern Monthly,* March 1935.

———, Ed. *Religious Experience and Truth, A Symposium.* New York: New York University Press, 1961.

Hoornaert, Eduardo. *The Memory of the Christian People.* Maryknoll, NY: Orbis Books, 1988.

Hoover, J. Edgar. *Masters of Deceit.* New York: Pocket Books, 1964.

Horne, Gerald. *Black Liberation/Red Scare: Ben Davis and the Communist Party.* Newark, DE: University of Delaware Press, 1994.

Horowitz, Daniel. *Betty Friedan and the Making of the Feminine Mystique: The American Left, the Cold War, and Modern Feminism.* Amherst: University of Massachusetts Press, 1998.

Horowitz, David. *Left Illusions, An Intellectual Odyssey*, Jamie Glaszov, Ed. Dallas: Spence Publishing Co., 2003.
———. *Radical Son, A Generational Odyssey*. New York: The Free Press, 1997.
———. *The Politics of Bad Faith: The Radical Assault on America's Future*. New York: Simon and Schuster, 1998.
———. *Student*. New York: Ballantine Books, 1962.
Horsley, Richard A. and Neil Ascher Silberman. *The Message and the Kingdom: How Jesus and Paul Ignited a Revolution and Transformed the Ancient World*. New York: Grosset/Putnam, 1997.
Horton, Myles with Judith Kohl and Herbert Kohl. *The Long Haul, An Autobiography*. New York: Doubleday, 1990.
Howe, Irving, Ed. *Orwell's Nineteen Eighty-Four: Text, Sources, Criticism*, second edition. New York: Harcourt Brace Jovanovich, 1982.
———. *Selected Writings 1950–1990*. New York: Harcourt Brace Jovanovich, 1990.
———. *Socialism and America*. New York: Harcourt, Brace, Jovanovich, 1985.
———. *Steady Work: Essays in the Politics of Democratic Radicalism 1953–1966*. New York: Harcourt, Brace and World, 1966.
———, Ed. *Twenty-Five Years of Dissent: An American Tradition*. New York: Metheun, 1979.
Howlett, Charles F. *Brookwood Labor College and the Struggle for Peace and Social Justice in America*. Lewiston, NY: Edwin Mellen Press, 1993.
Huberman, Leo. *Man's Worldly Goods: The Story of the Wealth of Nations*. New York: Harper and Brothers, 1936.
———. *We the People: The Drama of America*, new and enlarged edition. New York: Harper and Brothers, 1947.
Hudis, Peter and Kevin Anderson, Eds. *The Rosa Luxemburg Reader*. New York: Monthly Review Press, 2004.
Hunt, Richard N. *The Political Ideas of Marx and Engels*, 2 vols. Pittsburgh: University of Pittsburgh Press, 1974 and 1984.
Ignatieff, Michael. "The Burden," *New York Times Magazine*, January 5, 2003.
———. *Isaiah Berlin, A Life*. New York: Henry Holt and Co., 1999.
———. "Lesser Evils," *New York Times Magazine*, May 2, 2004.
———. *The Lesser Evil: Political Ethics in an Age of Terror*. Princeton, NJ: Princeton University Press, 2004.
———. *The Needs of Strangers*. New York: Picador, 2001.
Isaacs, Jeremy and Taylor Downing. *Cold War, 1945–1991: Companion to the CNN TV Series*. Boston: Little Brown and Co., 1998.
Isaacson, Walter. *Kissinger, A Biography*. New York: Touchstone Books/Simon and Schuster, 1993.
Isaacson, Walter and Evan Thomas. *The Wise Men: Six Friends and the World They Made*. New York: Touchstone Books/Simon and Schuster, 1986.
Isserman, Maurice. *If I Had A Hammer: The Death of the Old Left and the Birth of the New Left*. New York: Basic Books, 1987.
———. "They Led Two Lives," *New York Times Book Review*, May 9, 1999.
———. *The Other American: The Life of Michael Harrington*. New York: Public Affairs, 2000.
———. *Which Side Were You On? The American Communist Party During the Second World War*. Middleton, CT: Wesleyan University Press, 1982.
Jackson, Gabriel. *The Spanish Republic and the Civil War, 1931–1939*. Princeton, NJ: Princeton University Press, 1967.
Jacobs, Harold, Ed. *Weatherman*. San Francisco: Ramparts Press, 1970.
Jacobs, Paul and Saul Landau. *The New Radicals: A Report With Documents*. New York: Vintage Books, 1966.
Jacobson, Julius, Ed. *Soviet Communism and the Socialist Vision*. New Brunswick, NJ: Transaction Books, 1972.
Jaffe, Philip. *The Rise and Fall of American Communism*. New York: Horizon Press, 1975.
James, C. L. R. *American Civilization*. Cambridge, MA: Blackwell, 1993.
———. *Any Cook Can Govern*. Detroit: Bewick, 1988.
———. *The C. L. R. James Reader*, Anna Grimshaw, Ed. Cambridge, MA: Blackwell, 1992.
———. *World Revolution 1917–1936: The Rise and Fall of the Communist International*. Atlantic Highlands, NJ: Humanities Press, 1993.

Jamison, Andrew and Ron Eyerman. *Seeds of the Sixties*. Berkeley: University of California Press, 1995.

Jezer, Marty. *The Dark Ages: Life in the United States 1945–1960*. Boston; South End Press, 1982.

Johnson, Elizabeth A. *Consider Jesus: Waves of Renewal in Christology*. New York: Crossroad, 1994.

Johnson, Hewlitt. *The Soviet Power*. New York: Modern Age Books, 1940.

Joll, James. *The Anarchists*. New York: Grosset and Dunlap, 1966.

Joughin, Louis and Edmund M. Morgan. *The Legacy of Sacco and Vanzetti*. Princeton, NJ: Princeton University Press, 1978.

Kagarlitsky, Boris. *Russia Under Yeltsin and Putin: Neo-Liberal Autocracy*. London: Pluto Press, 2002.

———. *Square Wheels: How Russian Democracy Got Derailed*. New York: Monthly Review Press, 1994.

Kaiser, Daniel H., Ed. *The Workers' Revolution in Russia 1917*. Cambridge: Cambridge University Press, 1987.

Kaplan, Judith and Linn Shapiro, Eds. *Red Diapers: Growing Up in the Communist Left*. Urbana: University of Illinois Press, 1998.

Karnow, Stanley. *Vietnam: A History*. New York: Viking, 1983.

Kaufmann, Walter. *Religions in Four Dimensions*. New York: Readers Digest Press, 1976.

Kautsky, John H. *The Politics of Aristocratic Empires*. New Brunswick, NJ: Transaction Publishers, 1997.

Kazin, Alfred. *Starting Out in the Thirties*. Ithaca, NY: Cornell University Press, 1989.

Kegley, Charles W. and Robert W. Bretail, Eds., *Reinhold Niebuhr: His Religious, Social, and Political Thought*. New York: Macmillan Co., 1956.

Kelley, Robin D. G. *Hammer and Hoe: Alabama Communists During the Great Depression*. Chapel Hill: University of North Carolina Press, 1990.

———. *Race Rebels: Culture, Politics, and the Black Working Class*. New York: The Free Press, 1996.

Kenez, Peter. "The Prosecution of Soviet History: A Critique of Richard Pipes' *The Russian Revolution*," *The Russian Review*, 50 (1991).

Kiernan, V. G. *The Lords of Human Kind: Black Man, Yellow Man, and White Man in an Age of Empire*. London: Cresset Library, 1988.

Kelly, Charles M. *Class War in America: How Economic and Political Conservatives Are Exploiting Low- and Middle-Income Americans*. Santa Barbara, CA: Fifthian Press, 2000.

Kennan, George F. *Russia and the West Under Lenin and Stalin*. Boston: Little, Brown and Co., 1961.

Kennedy, Paul. *Preparing for the Twenty-First Century*. New York: Random House, 1993.

Kennedy-Pipe, Caroline. *Stalin's Cold War: Soviet Strategies in Europe, 1943 to 1956*. Manchester, UK: Manchester University Press, 1995.

Kern, Gary. *A Death in Washington: Walter G. Krivitsky and the Stalin Terror*. New York: Enigma Books, 2003.

Khlevniuk, Oleg V. *The History of the Gulag: From Collectivization to the Great Terror*. New Haven, CT: Yale University Press, 2004.

King, Jr., Martin Luther. *A Testament of Hope: The Essential Writings and Speeches of Martin Luther King, Jr.*, James M. Washington, Ed. San Francisco: HarperCollins, 1986.

Kintz, Linda. *Between Jesus and the Market: The Emotions That Matter in Right-Wing America*. Durham, NC: Duke University Press, 1997.

Kirchoff, Sue. "Economy Goes Forward But Leaves Many Behind," *USA Today*, November 22, 2005.

Klehr, Harvey. *The Heyday of American Communism: The Depression Decade*. New York: Basic Books, 1984.

Klehr, Harvey, John Earl Haynes, and Krill M. Anderson. *The Soviet World of American Communism*. New Haven, CT: Yale University Press, 1998.

Klein, Naomi. *Fences and Windows: Dispatches from the Front Lines of the Globalization Debate*. New York: Picador, 2002.

———. *No Logo: Taking Aim at the Brand Bullies*. New York: Picador, 1999.

———. "Reclaiming Our Lives," *Workers' Liberty*, January 2001.

Kloby, Jerry. *Inequality, Power, and Development: The Task of Political Sociology*. Atlantic Highlands, NJ: Humanities Press, 1997.

Koenker, Diane, William G. Rosenberg, and Ronald Grigor Suny, Eds. *Party, State and Society in the Russian Civil War*. Bloomington: Indiana University Press, 1989.

Kohn, Hans. *Living in a World Revolution: My Encounters with History.* New York: Pocket Books, 1965.

Kolakowski, Leszek. *Main Currents of Marxism*, 3 vols. New York: Oxford University Press, 1981.

Kotkin, Stephen. *Armageddon Averted: The Soviet Collapse 1970–2000.* New York: Oxford University Press, 2001.

Kotz, David and Fred Weir. *Revolution from Above: The Demise of the Soviet System.* London: Routledge, 1997.

Kovel, Joel. *The Enemy of Nature: The End of Capitalism or the End of the World?* London: Zed Books, 2002.

————. *History and Spirit: An Inquiry into the Philosophy of Liberation.* Boston: Beacon Press, 1991.

————. *Red Hunting in the Promised Land: Anticommunism and the Making of America.* New York: Basic Books, 1994.

Kozlenko, William. *The Best Short Plays of the Social Theatre.* New York: Random House, 1939.

Kristol, William and Robert Kagan. "Toward a Neo-Reaganite Foreign Policy," *Foreign Affairs*, July/August 1996.

Kropotkin, Peter. *The Conquest of Bread.* New York: Vanguard Press, 1926.

————. *Ethics.* New York: Tudor Publishing Co., 1947.

————. *Kropotkin's Revolutionary Pamphlets: A Collection of Writings*, Roger N. Baldwin, Ed. New York: Dover, 1970.

————. *Mutual Aid.* Boston: Porter Sargent, no date.

Krupskaya, Nadezhda. *Reminiscences of Lenin.* New York: International Publishers, 1970.

Kung, Hans. *The Catholic Church: A Short History.* New York: Random House, 2003.

————. *Christianity: Essence, History, and Future.* New York: Continuum, 1996.

————. *Does God Exist? An Answer for Today.* New York: Vintage Books, 1981.

Kwitney, Jonathan. *The Man of the Century: The Life and Times of John Paul II.* New York: Henry Holt, 1997.

LaBotz, Dan. *Rank and File Rebellion: Teamsters for a Democratic Union.* London: Verso, 1990.

LaFeber, Walter. *America, Russia, and the Cold War, 1945–2002.* Boston: McGraw-Hill, 2002.

Lancaster, Roger. *Life Is Hard: Machismo, Danger, and the Intimacy of Power in Nicaragua.* Berkeley: University of California Press, 1992.

Langer, Elinor. "The Great Pumpkin," *The Nation*, February 17, 1997.

Latham, Earl. *The Communist Controversy in Washington, From the New Deal to McCarthy.* Cambridge, MA: Harvard University Press, 1966.

Latrouette, Kenneth Scott. *A History of Christianity*, revised edition, 2 vols. New York: Harper and Row, 1975.

Leacock, Eleanor. *Myths of Male Dominance, Collected Articles on Women Cross-Culturally.* New York: Monthly Review Press, 1981.

Le Blanc, Paul. "The Absence of Socialism in the United States: Contextualizing Kautsky's 'American Worker,'" *Historical Materialism*, vol. 11, no. 3 (2003).

————, Ed. *Black Liberation and the American Dream: The Struggle for Racial and Economic Justice.* Amherst, NY: Humanity Books, 2003.

————, Ed. *From Marx to Gramsci: A Reader in Revolutionary Marxist Politics.* Atlantic Highlands, NJ: Humanities Press, 1996.

————. "From Revolutionary Intellectual to Conservative Master-Thinker: The Anti-Democratic Odyssey of James Burnham," *Left History*, vol. 3, no. 1, Spring/Summer 1995.

————. *Lenin and the Revolutionary Party.* Atlantic Highlands, NJ: Humanities Press, 1993.

————. "Luxemburg and Lenin on Revolutionary Organization," *International Marxist Review*, vol. 2, no. 3, Summer 1987.

————. "Martin Luther King: Christian Core, Socialist Bedrock," *Against the Current* no. 96, January-February, 2002.

————. "The Philosophy and Politics of Freedom," *Monthly Review*, January 2003.

————, Ed. *Rosa Luxemburg: Reflections and Writings.* Amherst, NY: Humanity Books, 1999.

————. *A Short History of the U.S. Working Class, From Colonial Times to the Twenty-First Century.* Amherst, NY: Humanity Books, 1999.

————. *Workers and Revolution: A Comparative Study of Bolshevik Russia and Sandinist Nicaragua* (doctoral dissertation in history, University of Pittsburgh). Ann Arbor, MI: University Microfilms International, 1989.

Le Blanc, Paul and Thomas Barrett, Eds. *Revolutionary Labor Socialist: The Life, Ideas, and Comrades of Frank Lovell*. Union City, NJ: Smyrna Press, 2000.
Lefebvre, Henri. *The Survival of Capitalism*. New York: St. Martin's Press, 1976.
Leggett, George. *The Cheka: Lenin's Political Police*. Oxford: Oxford University Press, 1981.
Leggett, John C. *Class, Race and Labor: Working-Class Consciousness in Detroit*. New York: Oxford University Press, 1968.
Lenin, Vladimir Ilyich. *Collected Works*, 45 volumes. Moscow: Progress Publishers, 1960–1970.
———. *Selected Works*, 3 vols. New York: International Publishers, 1967.
Lens, Sidney. *The Forging of American Empire*. Chicago: Haymarket Books, 2004.
Lenski, Gerhard E. *Power and Privilege: A Theory of Social Stratification*. Chapel Hill: University of North Carolina Press, 1984.
Levin, Dan. *Stormy Petrel: The Life and Work of Maxim Gorky*. New York: Appleton-Century, 1965.
Levin, Jr., N. Gordon. *Woodrow Wilson and World Politics: America's Response to War and Revolution*. New York: Oxford University Press, 1973.
Levine, Isaac Don. *The Man Lenin*. New York: Thomas Seltzer, 1924.
Lewin, Moshe. *Lenin's Last Struggle*. New York: Vintage Books, 1970.
———. *The Making of the Soviet System: Essays on the Social History of Interwar Russia*. New York: Pantheon Books, 1985.
———. *Russia, USSR, Russia: The Drive and Drift of a Super*state. The New Press, 1995.
———. *The Soviet Century*. London: Verso, 2005.
Lewis, C. S. *Mere Christianity*. New York: Collier Books, 1960.
Lewis, John, Karl Polyani, Donald K. Kitchin, Eds. *Christianity and the Social Revolution*. London: Victor Gollancz, 1935.
Lichtheim, George. *Imperialism*. New York: Praeger Publishers, 1971.
Lidtke, Vernon. *The Alternative Culture: Socialist Labor in Imperial Germany*. New York: Oxford University Press, 1985.
Liebich, Andre. *From the Other Shore: Russian Social Democracy After 1921*. Cambridge, MA: Harvard University Press, 1997
Lightfoot, Claude. *Chicago Slums to World Politics: Autobiography of Claude M. Lightfoot*, Timothy V. Johnson, Ed. New York: International Publishers, 1985.
Lih, Lars T. *Lenin Rediscovered: 'What Is to be Done?' in Context*. Leiden, Netherlands: Brill, 2006.
Link, Eugene P. *Labor-Religion Prophet: The Times and Life of Harry F. Ward*. Boulder, CO: Westview Press, 1984.
Lipper, Elinor. *Eleven Years in Soviet Prison Camps*. Chicago: Henry Regnery Co., 1951.
Lipsitz, George. *Rainbow at Midnight: Labor and Culture in the 1940s*. Urbana: University of Illinois Press, 1994.
London, Jack. *The Iron Heel*. New York: Bantam Books, 1971.
Love and Rage. *After Winter Must Come Spring: A Self-Critical Evaluation of the Love and Rage Revolutionary Anarchist Federation*. New York: Freedom Road Socialist Organization, 2001.
Lovestone, Jay. "Testimony of Jay Lovestone, Independent Labor League," *Investigation of the Un-American Propaganda Activities in the United States: Hearings Before a Special Committee on Un-American Activities (Dies Committee), House of Representatives, 75th–76th Congresses*. Washington, DC: Government Printing Office, 1939–1940.
Löwy, Michael. *On Changing the World: Essays in Political Philosophy, from Karl Marx to Walter Benjamin*. Atlantic Highlands, NJ: Humanities Press, 1992.
———. *Redemption and Utopia: Jewish Libertarian Thought in Central Europe*. Stanford, CA: Stanford University Press, 1992.
———. *The Theory of Revolution in the Young Marx*. Chicago: Haymarket Press, 2005.
———. *The War of Gods: Religion and Politics in Latin America*. London: Verso, 1996.
Lukács, Georg. *Lenin: A Study on the Unity of His Thought*. Cambridge, MA: MIT Press, 1971.
———. *The Process of Democratization*. Albany: State University of New York Press, 1991.
Lumpkin, Beatrice. *"Always Bring a Crowd!" The Story of Frank Lumpkin, Steelworker*. New York: International Publishers, 1999.
Luxemburg, Rosa. *The Accumulation of Capital*. London: Routledge and Kegan Paul, 1951.
———. *Rosa Luxemburg Speaks*, Mary-Alice Waters, Ed. New York: Pathfinder Press, 1970.
Lynn, Conrad. *There is a Fountain: The Autobiography of a Civil Rights Lawyer*. Westport, CT: Lawrence Hill, 1979.
Lyons, Eugene. *Assignment in Utopia*. New York: Harcourt, Brace and Co., 1937.
———. *The Red Decade: The Stalinist Penetration of America*. Indianapolis: Bobs-Merrill, 1941.

Machoveč, Milan. *A Marxist Looks at Jesus*. Philadelphia: Fortress, 1976.

MacIntyre, Alasdair. *Marxism and Christianity*. Notre Dame, IN: University of Notre Dame press, 1984.

MacDonald, Oliver, Ed. *The Polish August: Documents from the Beginnings of the Polish Workers' Rebellion, Gdansk — August 1980*. San Francisco: Ztangi Press, 1981.

Magdoff, Harry. *The Age of Imperialism: The Economics of U.S. Foreign Policy*. New York: Monthly Review Press, 1968.

———. *Imperialism: From the Colonial Age to the Present*. New York: Monthly Review Press, 1978.

Makhno, Nestor. *The Struggle Against the State and Other Essays*. San Francisco: AK Press, 1996.

Malcolm X. *Malcolm X Speaks*, George Breitman, Ed. New York: Grove Press, 1966.

Malcolm X, with Alex Haley. *The Autobiography of Malcolm X*. New York: Grove Press, 1966.

Mallaby, Sebastian. "The Reluctant Imperialist: Terrorism, Failed States, and the Case for American Empire," *Foreign Affairs*, March/April 2002.

Mandel, David. *Perestroika and the Soviet People*. Montreal: Black Rose Books, 1991.

———. *Rabotyagi: Perestroika and After Viewed from Below, Interviews with Workers in the Former Soviet Union*. New York: Monthly Review Press, 1994.

Mandel, Ernest. *Beyond Perestroika: The Future of Gorbachev's USSR*. London: Verso, 1989.

———. *Power and Money: A Marxist Theory of Bureaucracy*. London: Verso, 1992.

———. *Revolutionary Marxism and Social Reality, Selected Essays*, Steve Bloom, Ed. Atlantic Highlands, NJ: Humanities Press, 1994.

———. *Revolutionary Marxism Today*. London: New Left Books, 1979.

Mannin, Ethel. *Woman and Revolution*. London: Secker and Warburg, 1938.

Marcuse, Herbert. *Counterrevolution and Revolt*. Boston: Beacon Press, 1972.

Marcuse, Peter. *Missing Marx. A Personal and Political Journal of a Year in East Germany, 1989–1990*. New York: Monthly Review Press, 1991.

Markowitz, Norman D. *The Rise and Fall of the People's Century: Henry A. Wallace and American Liberalism, 1941–1948*. New York: The Free Press, 1973.

Marsden, John. *Marxian and Christian Utopianism: Towards a Socialist Political Theology*. New York: Monthly Review Press, 1991.

Marx, Karl. *Capital, Volume One*. New York: Vintage Books, 1977.

———. *Capital*, volume I. New York: International Publishers, 1967.

———. *Writings of the Young Marx on Philosophy and Society*, Loyd Easton and Kurt Guddat, Eds. Garden City, NY: Anchor Books, 1967.

Marx, Karl and Frederick Engels, *Collected Works*, 50 vols. New York: International Publishers, 1976–2005.

———. *Marx and Engels on Religion*. New York: Schocken Books, 1964.

Marx, Engels, Lenin: Anarchism and Anarcho-Syndicalism. Moscow: Progress Publishers, 1974.

Marzani, Carl. *The Education of a Reluctant Radical: Spain, Munich, and Dying Empires, Book 3*. New York: Topical Books, 1994.

———. *The Wounded Earth: An Environmental Survey*. Reading, MA: Addison-Wellsley, 1972.

Matagamna, Sean, Ed. *The Fate of the Russian Revolution*. London: Phoenix Press, 1998.

Matthiessen, F. O. *American Renaissance: Art and Expression in the Age of Emerson and Whitman*. New York: Oxford University Press, 1941.

Mayer, Arno J. *The Furies: Violence and Terror in the French and Russian Revolutions*. Princeton, NJ: Princeton University Press, 2000.

McAllister, Carol. "Uneven and Combined Development: Dynamics of Change and Women's Everyday Forms of Resistance in Negeri Sembilan, Malaysia," *Review of Radical Political Economics*, vol. 23, nos. 3 and 4, Fall and Winter, 1991.

McCollester, Charles, Ed. *Fighter with a Heart: Writings of Charles Owen Rice, Pittsburgh Labor Priest*. Pittsburgh: University of Pittsburgh Press, 1996.

McFarlane, Bruce. *Yugoslavia: Politics, Economics, and Society*. London: Pinter Publications, 1988.

McGeever, Patrick J. *Rev. Charles Owen Rice, Apostle of Contradiction*. Pittsburgh: Duquesne University Press, 1989.

McGovern, S.J., Arthur J. *Marxism: An American Christian Perspective*. Maryknoll, NY: Orbis Books, 1984.

McElvane, Robert S. *The Great Depression, America, 1929–1941*. New York: Times Books, 1993.

McKay, Claude. *A Long Way from Home, An Autobiography*. New York: Harcourt Brace and World, 1970.

———. *Negroes in America.* Port Washington, NY: Kennikat Press, 1979.

———. *The Passion of Claude McKay: Selected Poetry and Prose, 1912-1948*, Wayne F. Cooper, Ed. New York: Schocken Books, 1973.

McKenna, Megan. *Prophets: Words of Fire.* Maryknoll, NY: Orbis Books, 2001.

McLellan, David. *Marxism and Religion: A Description and Assessment of the Marxist Critique of Christianity.* London: Macmillan Press, 1987.

———. *Utopian Pessimist: The Life and Thought of Simone Weil.* New York: Poseidon Press, 1990.

McNally, David. *Another World Is Possible: Globalization and Anti-Capitalism.* Winnipeg: Arbeiter Ringer Publishing, 2002.

Medvedev, Roy. *Let History Judge: The Origins and Consequences of Stalinism.* New York: Columbia University Press, 1989.

———. *The October Revolution.* New York: Columbia University Press, 1979.

———. *On Socialist Democracy.* New York: W. W. Norton, 1975.

———. *Post-Soviet Russia: A Journey Through the Yeltsin Era.* New York: Columbia University Press, 2000.

Melkonian, Markar. *Richard Rotry's Politics: Liberalism at the End of the American Century.* Amherst, NY: Humanity Books, 1999.

Meeks, Wayne A. *The First Urban Christians: The Social World of the Apostle Paul*, second edition. New Haven, CT: Yale University Press, 2003.

Meeropol. Michael. *Surrender: How the Clinton Administration Completed the Reagan Revolution.* Ann Arbor: University of Michigan Press, 1998.

Meeropol, Robert. *An Execution in the Family: One Son's Journey.* New York: St. Martin's Press, 2003.

Meyer, Alfred G. *Leninism.* New York: Frederick A. Praeger, 1962.

Meyer, Donald. *The Protestant Search for Political Realism 1919-1941.* Middletown, CT: Wesleyan University Press, 1988.

Meyer, Frank. *The Moulding of Communists: The Training of Communist Cadre.* New York: Harcourt Brace and Co., 1961.

Miliband, Ralph. *Class Power and State Power, Political Essays.* London: Verso, 1983.

———. *Marxism and Politics.* Oxford: Oxford University Press, 1977.

Miller, James. *"Democracy is in the Streets": From Port Huron to the Siege of Chicago.* New York: Simon and Schuster, 1987.

Mills, C. Wright. *The Marxists.* New York: Dell Publishing Co., 1961.

———. *The Power Elite.* New York: Oxford University Press, 1956.

Milton, David. *The Politics of U.S. Labor, From the Great Depression to the New Deal.* New York: Monthly Review Press, 1982.

Miner, Merritt. "The Other Killing Machine," *New York Times Book Review*, May 11, 2003.

Mitchell, H.L. *Mean Things Happening in This Land: The Life and Times of H.L. Mitchell, Cofounder of the Southern Tenant Farmers Union.* Montclair, NJ: Allanheld, Osmun, 1979.

Mitford, Jessica. *A Fine Old Conflict.* New York: Alfred A. Knopf, 1977.

Moody, Kim. *Workers in a Lean World.* London: Verso, 1997.

Moore, R. Laurence. *Selling God: American Religion in the Marketplace of Culture.* New York: Oxford University Press, 1994.

Moore, Richard B. *Richard B. Moore, Caribbean Militant in Harlem: Collected Writings 1920-1972*, W. Burghardt Turner and Joyce Moore Turner, Ed. Bloomington: Indiana University Press, 1992.

Morgan, Ted. *A Covert Life: Jay Lovestone, Communist, Anti-Communist, and Spymaster.* New York: Random House, 1999.

———. *Reds: McCarthyism in Twentieth-Century America.* New York: Random House, 2003.

Morris, Aldon D. *The Origins of the Civil Rights Movement: Black Communities Organizing for Change.* The Free Press, 1984.

Morris, William. *Three Works by William Morris.* New York: International Publishers, 1968.

Muller, Jerry Z. *The Mind and the Market: Capitalism in Modern European Thought.* New York: Alfred A. Knopf, 2002.

Munck, Ronaldo. *Globalisation and Labour, "The Great Transformation."* London: Zed Books, 2002.

Murphy, Kevin. *Revolution and Counterrevolution: Class Struggle in a Moscow Metal Factory.* New York: Berghahn Books, 2005.

Muste, A. J. *The Essays of A. J. Muste*, Nat Hentoff, Ed. New York: Simon and Schuster, 1970.

————. *Non-Violence in an Aggressive World*. New York: Harper and Brothers, 1940.

————. *Not By Might: Christianity, The Way to Human Decency*. New York: Harper and Brothers, 1947.

Myerson, Michael. *These Are the Good Old Days: Coming of Age As a Radical in America's Late, Late Years*. New York: Grossman Publishers, 1970.

Nagy, Imre. *On Communism*. New York: Frederick A. Praeger, 1957.

Naison, Mark. *Communists in Harlem During the Depression*. Urbana: University of Illinois Press, 1983.

Nash, George H. *The Conservative Intellectual Movement in the United States*. New York: Basic Books, 1976.

Navasky, Victor. "I. F. Stone," *The Nation*, July 21, 2003.

Nearing, Scott and Joseph Freeman. *Dollar Diplomacy: A Study in American Imperialism*. New York: B. W. Huebsch and Viking Press, 1926.

Nelson, Bruce C. *Beyond the Martyrs: A Social History of Chicago's Anarchists, 1870–1900*. New Brunswick, NJ: Rutgers University Press, 1988.

Nelson, Steve, with James R. Barrett and Rob Ruck. *Steve Nelson, American Radical*. Pittsburgh: University of Pittsburgh Press, 1981.

Ness, Immanuel, Ed. *Encyclopedia of American Social Movements*, 4 vols., Armonk, NY: M. E. Sharpe, 2004.

Newburry, Mike. *The Yahoos*. New York: Marzani and Munsell, 1964.

Newfield, Jack *A Prophetic Minority*. New York: Signet Books, 1967.

New York Times, Ed. *The Pentagon Papers: The Secret History of the Vietnam War*. New York: Bantam Books, 1971.

Nicolaievsky, Boris and Otto Maenchen-Helfen. *Karl Marx: Man and Fighter*. Harmondsworth, UK: Penguin Books, 1976.

Niebuhr, Reinhold. *An Interpretation of Christian Ethics*. New York: Harper and Brothers, 1935.

————. *Moral Man and Immoral Society* New York: Charles Scribner's Sons, 1932.

————. *The Nature and Destiny of Man*, 2 vols. New York: Charles Scribner's Sons, 1964.

————. *Reflections on the End of an Era*. New York: Charles Scribner's Sons, 1934.

————. "Religion and Marxism," *Modern Monthly*, February 1935.

Nimtz, Jr., August H. *Marx and Engels: Their Contribution to the Democratic Breakthrough*. Albany: State University of New York Press, 2000.

Nossitor, T. J. *Marxist State Governments in India: Politics, Economics, and Society*. London: Pinter Publishers, 1988.

Nove, Alec. *An Economic History of the USSR*. Harmondsworth, UK: Penguin Books, 1982.

O'Connor, James. *Natural Causes: Essays in Ecological Marxism*. New York: Guilford Press, 1998.

Olmstead, Kathryn S. *Red Spy Queen: A Biography of Elizabeth Bentley*. Chapel Hill: University of North Carolina Press, 2002.

O'Neill, William L. *A Better World, The Great Schism: Stalinism and the American Intellectuals*. New York: Simon and Schuster, 1982.

————. Ed. *Echoes of Revolt: The Masses, 1911 to 1917*. Chicago: Quadrangle Books, 1966.

————. *The Last Romantic: A Life of Max Eastman*. New York: Oxford University Press, 1978.

Oreleck, Annelise. *Common Sense and a Little Fire: Women and Working-Class Politics in the United States, 1900–1965*. Chapel Hill: University of North Carolina Press, 1995.

Ottanelli, Fraser M. *The Communist Party of the United States: From the Depression to World War II*. New Brunswick, NJ: Rutgers University Press, 1991.

Packer, Herbert L. *Ex-Communist Witnesses: Four Studies in Fact Finding*. Stanford, CA: Stanford University Press, 1962,

Page, Kirby. *Individualism and Socialism: An Ethical Survey of Economic and Political Forces*. New York: Farrar and Rinehart, 1933.

————. *Kirby Page, Social Evangelist: The Autobiography of a 20th Century Prophet for Peace*. Nyack, NY: Fellowship Press, 1975.

Paine, Thomas. *The Age of Reason, Being an Investigation of True and Fabulous Theology*. Mineda, NY: Dover Publications, 2004.

Painter, Nell Irwin. *The Narrative of Hosea Hudson, His Life as a Negro Communist in the South*. Cambridge, MA: Harvard University Press, 1979.

Palmer, Bryan. *James P. Cannon and the Origins of the American Revolutionary Left*. Urbana: University of Illinois Press, forthcoming 2006.

Panitch, Leo and Colin Leys, Eds. *Working Classes, Global Realities: Socialist Register 2001*. New York: Monthly Review Press, 2001.

Patniak, Prebhat. *The Retreat to Unfreedom: Essays on the Emerging World Order*. New Dehli: Tulika, 2003.

Patterson, William L. *The Man Who Cried Genocide*. New York: International Publishers, 1971.

Payne, Robert. *The Life and Death of Lenin*. New York: Avon Books, 1967.

Pearson, Hugh. *The Shadow of the Panther: Huey Newton and the Price of Black Power in America*. Reading, MA: Perseus Books, 1994.

Pearson, Michael. *Lenin's Mistress: The Life of Inessa Armand*. New York: Random House, 2001.

Pells, Richard H. *The Liberal Mind in a Conservative Age: American Intellectuals in the 1940s and 1950s*. New York: Harper and Row, 1985.

Petrement, Simone. *Simone Weil, A Life*. New York: Pantheon Books, 1976.

Pfaff, William. "The Question of Hegemony," *Foreign Affairs*, January/February 2002.

Philipson, Dirk. *We Were the People: Voices From East Germany's Revolutionary Autumn of 1989*. Durham, NC: Duke University Press, 1993.

Phillips, Kevin. *Boiling Point: Democrats, Republicans, and the Decline of Middle Class Prosperity*. New York: HarperCollins, 1993.

Piercy, Marge. *Dance the Eagle to Sleep*. Greenwich, CT: Fawcett. 1971.

———. *Living in the Open*. New York: Alfred A. Knopf, 1976.

Pipes, Richard, Ed. *Revolutionary Russia, A Symposium*. Garden City, NY: Anchor Books, 1969.

———. *The Russian Revolution*. New York: Alfred A. Knopf, 1990.

———. *Russia Under the Bolshevik Regime, 1921–1924*. New York: Alfred A. Knopf, 1994.

———. Ed. *The Unknown Lenin: From the Secret Archive*. New Haven, CT: Yale University Press, 1996.

Plechanoff, George. *Anarchism and Socialism*. Chicago: Charles H. Kerr, 1912.

Polan, A. J. *Lenin and the End of Politics*. London: Metheun, 1984.

Ponting, Clive. *Churchill*. London: Sinclair-Stevenson, 1994.

Poretsky, Elizabeth. *Our Own People: A Memoir of 'Ignace Reiss' and His Friends*. Ann Arbor: University of Michigan Press, 1969.

Possony, Stefan T. *Lenin: The Compulsive Revolutionary*. Chicago: Henry Regnery Co., 1964.

Powell, Mark Allan. *Jesus as a Figure in History: How Modern Historians View the Man From Galilee*. Louisville, KY: Westminster John Knox Press, 1998.

Powers, Richard Gid. *Not Without Honor: The History of American Anticommunism*. New York: The Free Press, 1995.

Prados, John. *Hoodwinked: The Documents That Reveal How Bush Sold Us a War*. New York: The New Press, 2004.

Price, Ruth. *The Lives of Agnes Smedley*. New York: Oxford University Press, 2005.

Rabinowitch, Alexander. *The Bolsheviks Come to Power: The Revolution of 1917 in Petrograd*. New York: W. W. Norton, 1976.

Radosh, Ronald. *Commies: A Journey Through the Old Left, the New Left and the Leftover Left*. San Francisco: Encounter Books, 2001.

Radosh, Ronald, Mary R. Habeck, and Grigory Sevostianov, Eds., *Spain Betrayed: The Soviet Union in the Spanish Civil War*. New Haven, CT: Yale University Press, 2000.

Rahner, Karl. *Foundations of Christian Faith: An Introduction to the Idea of Christianity*. New York: Crossroad, 1987.

Randall, Margaret. *Gathering Rage: The Failure of Twentieth Century Revolutions to Develop a Feminist Agenda*. New York: Monthly Review Press, 1992.

Ranke-Heineman, Uta. *Putting Away Childish Things*. San Francisco: HarperCollins, 1995.

Ransby, Barbara. *Ella Baker and the Black Freedom Movement, A Radical Democratic Vision*. Chapel Hill: University of North Carolina Press, 2003.

Raphael, Ray. *A People's History of the American Revolution: How Common People Shaped the Fight for Independence*. New York: Harper Collins, 2002.

Rauschenbusch, Walter. *Christianity and the Social Crisis*. Louisvlle, KY: Westminster/John Knox Press, 1991.

———. *A Theology for the Social Gospel*. New York: Macmillan, 1918.

Reed, John. *Ten Days That Shook the World*. New York: Signet Books, 1967.

Regler, Gustav. *The Owl of Minerva*. New York: Farrar, Strauss and Cudhay, 1960.

Reed, Jr., Adolph. *Class Notes: Posing as Politics and Other Thoughts on the American Scene*. New York: New Press, 2000.

Rees. John. *The Algebra of Revolution: The Dialectic and the Classical Marxist Tradition.* London: Routledge, 1998.

Rees, John, Samuel Farber, and Robert Service. *In Defence of October: A Debate on the Russian Revolution.* London: Bookmarks, 1997.

Reiman, Michel. *The Birth of Stalinism: The USSR on the Eve of the "Second Revolution."* Bloomington: Indiana University Press, 1987.

Reminiscences of Lenin by His Relatives. Moscow: Foreign Languages Publishing House, 1956.

Renton, Dave, Ed. *Marx on Globalization.* London: Lawrence and Wishart, 2001.

Reuss, Alejandro, T. Williamson, J. Winner, and the Dollars and Sense Collective., Ed. *Real World Globalization,* seventh edition. Boston: Dollars and Sense, 2002.

Richards, Yvette. *Maida Springer, Pan-Africanist and International Labor Leader.* Pittsburgh: University of Pittsburgh Press, 2000.

Richmond, Al, Ed. *In Defence of the Russian Revolution, A Selection of Bolshevik Writings 1917–1923.* London: Porcupine Press, 1995.

Rivera, Diego and Bertram D. Wolfe. *Portrait of America.* New York: Covici-Friede, 1934.

Robbins, Tim. *Cradle Will Rock, The Movie and the Moment.* New York: Newmarket Press, 2000.

Robertson, Archibald. *The Origins of Christianity.* New York: International Publishers, 1954.

Robeson, Paul. *I Take My Stand.* Boston: Beacon Press, 1971.

———. *Paul Robeson Speaks: Writings, Speeches, Interviews 1918–1974,* Philip S. Foner, Ed. New York: Bruner/Mazel, 1978.

Robeson, Jr., Paul. *The Undiscovered Paul Robeson: An Artist's Journey, 1898–1939.* New York: John Wiley and Sons, 2001.

Robinson, Joanne Ooiman. *Abraham Went Out: A Biography of A. J. Muste.* Philadelphia: Temple University Press, 1981.

Roediger, Dave and Franklin Rosemont, Ed. *Haymarket Scrapbook.* Chicago: Charles H. Kerr, 1986.

Romerstein, Herbert and Eric Breindel. *The Venona Secrets: Exposing Soviet Espionage.* Washington, DC: Regnery, 2000.

Rorty, Richard. *Achieving Our Country: Leftist Thought in Twentieth-Century America.* Cambridge, MA: Harvard University Press, 1999.

———. *Philosophy and Social Hope.* London: Penguin Books, 1999.

Rosmer, Alfred. *Moscow Under Lenin.* New York: Monthly Review Press, 1971.

Rosswurm, Steve, Ed. *The CIO's Left-Led Unions.* New Brunswick, NJ: Rutgers University Press, 1992.

Rowbotham, Sheila. *Threads Through Time: Writings on History and Autobiography.* London: Penguin Books, 1999.

———. *Women, Resistance and Revolution.* New York: Vintage Books, 1972.

Roy, Ralph Lord. *Communism and the Churches.* New York: Harcourt, Brace and Co., 1960.

Rubenstein, Richard M. *My Brother Paul.* New York: Harper and Row, 1972.

Rubinstein, Annette. *American Literature, Root and Flower: Significant Poets, Novelists and Dramatists, 1775–1955,* two volumes in one. Beijing: Foreign Language Teaching and Research Press, 1988.

Rueschmeyer, Dietrich, Evelyne Huber Stephens, and John D. Stephens. *Capitalist Development and Democracy.* Chicago: University of Chicago Press, 1992.

Rühle, Jürgen. *Literature and Revolution: A Critical Study of the Writer and Communism in the Twentieth Century.* New York: Frederick A. Praeger, 1969.

Russell, Bertrand. *The Practice and Theory of Bolshevism.* London: George Allen and Unwin, 1920.

———. *Why I Am Not a Christian.* New York: Simon and Schuster, 1957.

Ryan, James G. *Earl Browder: The Failure of American Communism.* Tuscaloosa: University of Alabama Press, 1997.

Sachs, Jeffrey D. *The End of Poverty: Economic Possibilities for Our Time.* New York: The Penguin Press, 2005.

Sale, Kirkpatrick. *SDS.* New York: Random House, 1973.

Samary, Catherine. *Yugoslavia Dismembered.* New York: Monthly Review Press, 1995.

Sartre, Jean-Paul. *Search for a Method.* New York: Vintage Books, 1968.

Sassoon, Anne Shostock. *Gramsci's Politics,* second edition. Minneapolis: University of Minnesota Press, 1987.

Sassoon, Donald. *One Hundred Years of Socialism: The West European Left in the Twentieth Century.* New York: The New Press, 1996.

Saunders, Frances Stoner. *Who Paid the Piper? The CIA and the Cultural Cold War*. London: Granta Books, 1999.

Saunders, George, Ed. *Samizdat: Voices of the Soviet Opposition*. New York: Monad Press, 1974.

Sayre, Nora. *Previous Convictions: A Journey Through the 1950s*. Rutgers, NJ: Rutgers University Press, 1995.

Schlager, Neil, Ed. *St. James Encyclopedia of Labor History Worldwide: Major Events in Labor History and Their Impact*, 2 vols. Detroit: St. James Press/Thomson and Gale, 2003.

Schlesinger, Jr., Arthur M. *A Life in the 20th Century: Innocent Beginnings, 1917–1950*. Boston: Houghton Mifflin, 2000.

Schlesinger, Stephen C. *Act of Creation: The Founding of the United Nations*. Cambridge, MA: Westview Press, 2003.

Schor, Juliet B. *The Overworked American: The Unexpected Decline of Leisure*. New York: Basic Books, 1991.

Schorske, Carl. *German Social Democracy, 1905–1917*. New York: John Wiley and Sons, 1955.

Schrecker, Ellen. *Many Are the Crimes: McCarthyism in America*. New York: Princeton, NJ: Princeton University Press, 1998.

Schultz, Bud and Ruth Schultz. *It Did Happen Here: Recollections of Political Repression in America*. Berkeley: University of California Press, 1989.

Schweitzer, Albert. *The Quest of the Historical Jesus*. New York: Macmillan, 1968.

Selsam, Howard and Harry Martel, Eds. *Reader in Marxist Philosophy, From the Writings of Marx, Engels, and Lenin*. New York: International Publishers, 1963.

Sen, Jai, Anita Anand, Arturo Escobar, and Peter Waterman, Eds., *World Social Forum: Challenging Empires*. New Dehli: Viveka Foundation, 2004.

Serge, Victor. *Conquered City*. London: Writers and Readers, 1978.

———. *Memoirs of a Revolutionary*. London: Writers and Reader, 1984.

———. *Russia Twenty Years After*. Atlantic Highlands: Humanities Press, 1996.

———. *Year One of the Russian Revolution*. Chicago: Holt, Rinehart and Winston, 1972.

Service, Robert. *Lenin, A Biography*. Cambridge, MA: Harvard University Press, 2000.

———. *Lenin, A Political Life*, 3 vols. Bloomington: Indiana University Press, 1985–1995.

Shachtman, Max. *The Bureaucratic Revolution: The Rise of the Stalinist State*. New York: The Donald Press, 1962.

Shaiken, Harley. *Work Transformed: Automation and Labor in the Computer Age*. New York: Holt, Rinehart and Winston, 1985.

Sheppard, Barry. *The Party: The Socialist Workers Party 1960–1988, A Political Memoir, Volume 1: The Sixties*. Melbourne, Australia: Resistance Books, 2005.

Shorto, Russell. *Gospel Truth: The New Image of Jesus Emerging from Science and History, and Why It Matters*. New York: Riverhead Books, 1997.

Shukman, Harold, Ed. *The Blackwell Encyclopedia of the Russian Revolution*. New York: Basil Blackwell, 1988.

Siegel, Paul. *The Great Reversal: Politics and Art in Solzhenitsyn*. San Francisco: Walnut Publishing Co., 1991.

———. *The Meek and the Militant: Religion and Power Across the World*. London: Zed Books, 1986.

Siegelbaum, Lewis. *Soviet State and Society Between Revolutions, 1918–1929*. Cambridge: Cambridge University Press, 1992.

Sifry, Micha L. and Christopher Cerf, Eds. *The Iraq War Reader: History, Documents, Opinions*. New York: Simon and Schuster, 2003.

Silverman, Bertram and Murray Yanowitch. *New Rich, New Poor, New Russia: Winners and Losers on the Russian Road to Capitalism*, expanded edition. Armonk, NY: M. E. Sharpe, 2000.

Simonton, Dean Keith. *Origins of Genius: Darwinian Perspectives on Creativity*. New York: Oxford University Press, 1999.

Singer, Daniel. *The Road to Gdansk*. New York: Monthly Review Press, 1982.

———. *Whose Millennium? Theirs or Ours?* New York: Monthly Review Press, 1999.

Smith, Homer W. *Man and His Gods*. New York: Grosset and Dunlap, 1952.

Smith, John Cabot. *Alger Hiss, The True Story*. Harmondsworth, UK: Penguin Books, 1977.

Smith, Neil. *The Endgame of Globalization*. New York: Routledge, 2005.

Smith, Wendy. *Real Life Drama: The Group Theatre and America, 1931–1940*. New York: Alfred A. Knopf, 1990.

Soelle, Dorothee. *Theology for Skeptics, Reflections on God*. Minneapolis: Fortress Press, 1995.

Solomon, Mark. *The Cry Was Unity: Communists and African-Americans, 1917–1936*. Jackson: University of Mississippi Press, 1998.

Solzhenitsyn, Aleksandr I. *The Gulag Archipeligo*, 3 vols. New York: Harper and Row, 1975.

Sorge, Friedrich A. *Labor Movement in the United States, A History of the American Working Class from Colonial Times to 1890*. Westport, CT: Greenwood Press, 1977.

Souvarine, Boris. *Stalin: A Critical Survey of Bolshevism*. New York: Longman, Green and Co., 1939.

Spargo, John. *Marxian Socialism and Religion*. New York: B. W. Huebsch, 1915.

Spriano, Paolo. *Stalin and the European Communists*. London: Verso, 1985.

Stanton, Fred, Ed. *Fighting Racism in World War II: C. L. R. James, George Breitman, Edgar Keemer, and Others*. New York: Monad Press, 1980.

Starobin, Joseph. *American Communism in Crisis, 1943–1957*. Berkeley: University of California Press, 1972.

Steinberg, Mark D., Ed. *Voices of Revolution, 1917*. New Haven, CT: Yale University Press, 2001.

Steinberg, Isaac. *In the Workshop of the Revolution*. London: Victor Gollancz, 1955.

Stepan-Norris, Judith and Maurice Zeitlin. *Left Out: Reds and America's Industrial Unions*. New York: Cambridge: Cambridge University Press, 2003.

Stern, Frederick C. *F. O. Matthiessen, Christian Socialist as Critic*. Chapel Hill: University of North Carolina Press, 1981.

Stites, Richard. *Revolutionary Dreams: Utopian Vision and the Experimental Life in the Russian Revolution*. New York: Oxford University Press, 1989.

Stone, I. F. *The Haunted Fifties*. New York: Vintage Books, 1969.

———. *The Truman Era*. New York: Vintage, 1972.

Strong, Anna Louise. *For the First Time in History: Two Years of Russia's New Life (August 1921–December 1923)*. New York: Boni and Liveright, 1924.

———. *I Change Worlds*. New York: Garden City Publishing Co., 1937.

Strong, Tracy B. and Helene Keyssar. *Right in Her Soul: The Life of Anna Louise Strong*. New York: Random House, 1983.

Suny, Ronald G. *The Soviet Experiment: Russia, the Soviet Union, and the Successor States*. New York: Oxford University Press, 1998.

Suny, Ronald and Arthur Adams, Eds. *The Russian Revolution and Bolshevik Victory*. Lexington, MA: D. C. Heath and Co., 1990.

Swados, Harvey. *A Radical's America*. Boston: Little, Brown and Co., 1962.

Sweezy, Paul. *The Theory of Capitalist Development*. New York: Monthly Review Press, 1968.

Sweezy, Paul M. and Leo Huberman, Eds. *F. O. Matthiessen, A Collective Portrait*. New York: Henry Schuman, 1950.

Sweezy, Paul M.and Harry Magdoff, "Foreword [to special issue on Lenin]," *Monthly Review*, April 1970.

Szajkowski, Bogdan. *Marxist Local Governments in Western Europe and Japan*. London: Francis Pinter Publishers, 1986.

Szulc, Tad. *Pope John Paul II, The Biography*. New York: Scribners, 1995.

Tabb, William K., Ed. *Churches in Struggle: Liberation Theologies and Social Change in North America*. New York: Monthly Review Press, 1986.

———. "Turtles, Teamsters, and Capital's Designs," *Monthly Review*, July-August, 2000.

Tanenhaus, Sam. *Whittaker Chambers, A Biography*. New York: Random House, 1997.

Tate, Cassandra. "Who's Out to Lunch Here? I. F. Stone and the KGB," *Columbia Journalism Review*, November/December 1992.

Theoharis, Athan. *Chasing Spies: How the FBI Failed in Counterintelligence But Promoted the Politics of McCarthyism in the Cold War Years*. Chicago: Ivan R. Dee, 2002.

Thich Nhat Hahn. *Living Buddha, Living Christ*. New York: Riverhead Books, 1997.

Thiessen, Gerd and Annette Merz. *The Historical Jesus, A Comprehensive Guide*. Minneapolis: Fortress Press, 1998.

Thompson, E. P. *Customs in Common: Studies in Traditional Popular Culture*. New York: The New Press, 1993.

———. *The Making of the English Working Class*. New York: Vintage Books, 1968.

———. *William Morris: Romantic to Revolutionary*. New York: Pantheon, 1976.

Thurman, Howard. *Jesus and the Disinherited*. Boston: Beacon Press, 1996.

Thurston, Robert W. *Life and Terror in Stalin's Russia*. New Haven, CT: Yale University Press, 1996.

Tillich, Paul. *A Complete History of Christian Thought*, two volumes in one. New York: Harper and Row, 1968.

Toranska, Teresa. *"Them": Stalin's Polish Puppets*. New York: Harper and Row, 1987.

Torjesen, Karen Jo. *When Women Were Priests: Women's Leadership in the Early Church and the Scandal of Their Subordination in the Rise of Christianity*. San Francisco: HarperCollins, 1993.

Toussaint, Eric and Peter Drucker, Eds. *IMF/World Bank/WTO: The Free Market Fiasco*. Amsterdam: International Institute for Research and Education, 1995.

Townshend, Jules. "Lenin's *The State and Revolution*: An Innocent Reading," *Science and Society*, vol. 63, no. 1, Spring 1999.

———. *The Politics of Marxism, The Critical Debates*. London: Leiscester University Press, 1996.

Trepper, Leopold. *The Great Game*. New York: McGraw-Hill, 1977.

Trevor-Roper, Hugh. *The Rise of Christian Europe*. New York: Harcourt Brace and World, 1965.

Trotsky, Leon. *The Challenge of the Left Opposition*, 3 Vols., Naomi Allen and George Saunders, Eds. New York: Pathfinder Press, 1975–81.

———. *The History of the Russian Revolution*, three volumes in one. New York: Simon and Schuster, 1936.

———. *The Revolution Betrayed*. New York: Doubleday, Doran, 1937.

———. *The Spanish Revolution, 1931–39*, Ed. by Naomi Allen and George Breitman New York: Pathfinder Press, 1973.

———. *The Struggle Against Fascism in Germany*, George Breitman and Merry Maisel, Eds. New York: Pathfinder Press, 1971.

———. *Terrorism and Communism*. Ann Arbor: University of Michigan Press, 1961.

———. *The Third International After Lenin*. New York: Pathfinder Press, 1970.

———. *The Transitional Program for Socialist Revolution*. New York: Pathfinder Press, 1977.

———. *The Writings of Leon Trotsky, 1929–1940*, 14 volumes. New York: Pathfinder Press, 1973–1979.

Tucker, Robert C. *Stalin as Revolutionary: 1879–1929*. New York: W. W. Norton, 1974.

———. *Stalin in Power: The Revolution From Above, 1928–1941*. New York: W. W. Norton, 1992.

United Nations. *Why Do the Millennium Development Goals Matter? From the Secretary-General's 2003 Report on Implementation of the United Nations Millennium Declaration*. New York: United Nations Department of Public Information, 2003.

Utley, Freda. *The Dream We Lost: Soviet Russia Then and Now*. New York: John Day Co., 1940.

———. *Odyssey of a Liberal, Memoirs*. Washington, DC: Washington National Press, 1970.

Vandantam, Shankar. "Glacier Melt Could Signal Faster Rise in Ocean Levels," *Washington Post*, February 17, 2006.

Vermes, Geza. *Jesus and the World of Judaism*. Philadelphia: Fortress Press, 1984.

Vidali, Vittorio. *Diary of the Twentieth Congress of the Communist Party of the Soviet Union*. Westport, CT: Lawrence Hill and Co., 1984.

Voline. *The Unknown Revolution*. New York: Free Life Editions, 1975.

Voros, Sandor. *American Commissar*. Philadelphia: Chilton Co., 1961.

Wade, Rex A. *The Russian Revolution, 1917*. Cambridge: Cambridge University Press, 2000.

Wald, Alan. *Exiles From a Future Time: The Forging of the Mid-Twentieth-Century Literary Left*. Chapel Hill: University of North Carolina Press, 2002.

———. *The New York Intellectuals: The Rise and Fall of the Anti-Stalinist Left from the 1930s to the 1980s*. Chapel Hill: University of North Carolina Press, 1987.

Walker, Charles Rumford. *American City, A Rank and File History*. New York: Farrar and Rinehart, 1937.

Walton, Richard J. *Henry Wallace, Harry Truman, and the Cold War*. New York: Viking Press, 1976.

Ward, Harry F. *Democracy and Social Change*. New York: Modern Age Books, 1940.

Warren, Frank A. "A Flawed History of the Popular Front," *New Politics*, Winter 1999.

———. *Liberals and Communism: The "Red Decade" Revisited*. Bloomington: Indiana University Press, 1966.

Wechsler, James. *The Age of Suspicion*. New York: Random House, 1953.

Weigand, Kate. *Red Feminism: American Communism and the Making of Women's Liberation*. Baltimore: Johns Hopkins University Press, 2002.

Weil, Simone. *Formative Writings 1921–1941*, Dorothy Tuck Mcfarland and Wilhelmina Van Ness, Eds. Amherst: University of Massachusetts Press, 1988).

———. *Simone Weil Reader,* George A. Panichas, Ed. Wakefield, RI: Moyer Bell Limited, 1977.
———. *Waiting for God.* New York: Harper and Row, 1973.
Weinstein, Allen. *Perjury: The Hiss-Chambers Case.* New York: Alfred A. Knopf, 1978.
Weinstein, Allen and Alexander Vassiliev. *The Haunted Wood: Soviet Espionage in America — The Stalin Era.* New York: Random House, 1999.
Weinstein, James. *The Long Detour: The History and Future of the American Left.* Boulder, CO: Westview, 2003.
Went, Robert. *Globalization: Neoliberal Challenge: Radical Responses.* London: Pluto Press, 2000.
Weyl, Nathaniel and Stefan Possony. *The Geography of Intellect.* Chicago: Henry Regnery Co., 1963.
What Is Leninism? New York: International Publishers, 1936.
Whitfield, Stephen J. *The Culture of the Cold War,* second edition. Baltimore: Johns Hopkins University, 1996.
Wigginton, Eliot, Ed. *Refuse to Stand Silently By: An Oral History of Grass Roots Activism in America, 1921–1964.* New York: Anchor Books, 1992.
Williams, Albert Rhys. *Through the Russian Revolution.* New York: Monthly Review Press, 1967.
Williams, Raymond. *Resources of Hope.* London: Verso, 1989.
Williams, Robert C. *The Other Bolsheviks: Lenin and His Critics, 1904–1914.* Bloomington: Indiana University Press, 1986.
Williams, William Appleman. *The Tragedy of American Diplomacy.* New York: W. W. Norton, 1988.
Wills, Garry. *Confessions of a Conservative.* New York: Penguin Books, 1980.
Witherington III, Ben. *The Jesus Quest: The Third Search for the Jew of Nazareth,* new expanded edition. Downes Grove, IL: InterVarsity Press, 1997.
Wolfe, Bertram D. *Breaking With Communism: The Intellectual Odyssey of Bertram D. Wolfe,* Robert Hessen, Ed. Stanford, CA: Hoover Institution Press, 1990.
———. *Diego Rivera, His Life and Times.* New York: Alfred A. Knopf, 1939.
———. *Lenin and the Twentieth Century: A Bertram D. Wolfe Retrospective,* Lennard D. Gerson, Ed. Stanford, CA: Hoover Institution Press, 1984.
———. *A Life in Two Centuries: An Autobiography.* New York: Stein and Day, 1981.
———. *Marxism: One Hundred Years in the Life of a Doctrine.* New York: Dell Publishing Co., 1967.
———. *Strange Communists I Have Known.* New York: Stein and Day, 1982.
———. *Three Who Made a Revolution.* New York: Dial Press, 1948.
Wohlforth, Tim. *The Prophet's Children: Travels on the American Left.* Atlantic Highlands, NJ: Humanities Press, 1994.
Woodcock, George. *Anarchism: A History of Libertarian Ideas and Movements.* New York: Meridian Books, 1969.
———. Ed. *The Anarchist Reader.* Glasgow, UK: Fontana, 1977.
Wood, Ellen Meiksins. "The Communist Manifesto After 150 Years," in *The Communist Manifesto.* New York: Monthly Review Press, 1998.
Woods, Alan. *Marxism in the U.S.A.* Fargo, ND: Wellred Books, 2005.
Wright, Richard. *American Hunger.* New York: Harper and Row, 1983.
Wymart, Robert. *Stalin's Spy: Richard Sorge and the Tokyo Espionage Ring.* New York: St. Martin's Press, 1998.
Yates, Michael. *Naming the System: Inequality and Work in the Global Economy.* New York: Monthly Review Press, 2003.
———. "'Workers of All Countries, Unite': Will This Include the U.S. Labor Movement?" *Monthly Review,* July-August, 2000.
Young, Marilyn B. *The Vietnam Wars, 1945–1990.* New York: HarperCollins, 1991.
Young, William and David Kaiser. *Postmortem: New Evidence in the Case of Sacco and Vanzetti.* Amherst: University of Massachusetts Press, 1985.
Young-Bruehl, Elisabeth. *Hannah Arendt: For Love of the World.* New Haven, CT: Yale University Press, 1982.
Zaroulis, Nancy and Gerald Sullivan. *Who Spoke Up?, American Protest Against the War in Vietnam 1963–1975.* New York: Holt, Rinehart and Winston, 1984.
Zeitlin, Irving M. *Jesus and the Judaism of His Time.* New York: Polity Press, 1988.
Zeitlin, Maurice, Ed. *American Society, Inc.* Chicago: Markham, 1970.
Zieger, Robert H. *The CIO 1935–1955.* Chapel Hill: University of North Carolina Press, 1995.
Zinn, Howard. *A People's History of the United States.* New York: HarperCollins, 2004.

Zlobin, Georgy et al., Eds. *Lenin in Profile, World Writers and Artists on Lenin.* Moscow: Progress Publishers, 1975.
Zubok, Vladisov and Constantine Pleshakov. *Inside the Kremlin's Cold War, From Stalin to Khrushchev.* Cambridge, MA: Harvard University Press, 1996.

Index